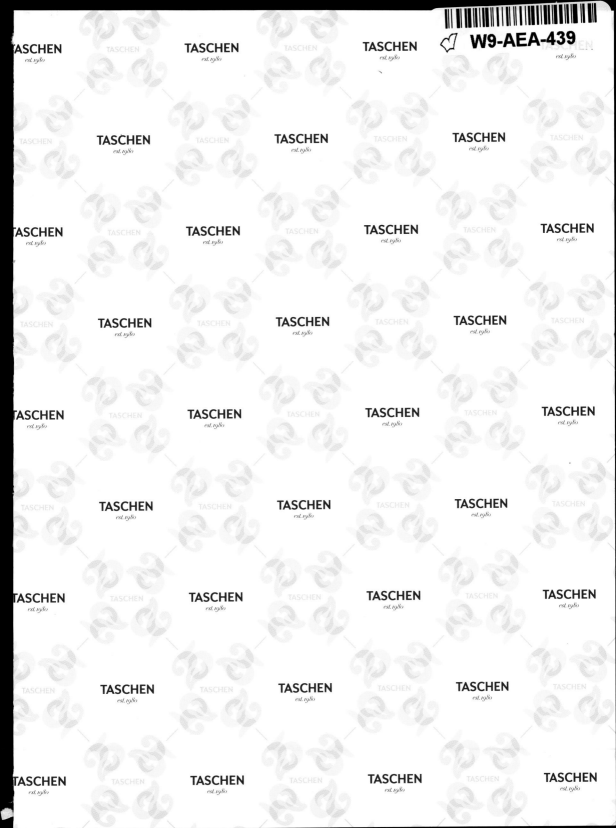

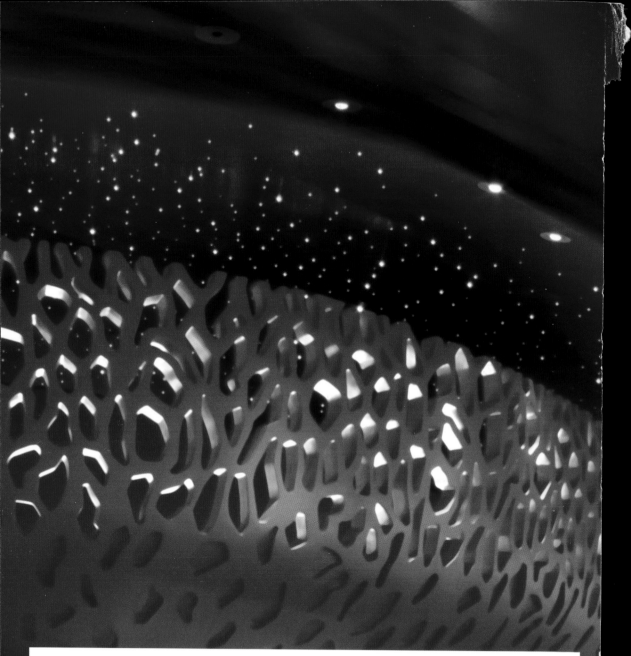

IMPRINT

PROJECT MANAGEMENT
Florian Kobler, Cologne

EDITORIAL COORDINATION
Julia Krumhauer, Cologne

PRODUCTION
Thomas Grell, Cologne

DESIGN
Sense/Net Art Direction,
Andy Disl and Birgit
Eichwede, Cologne
www.sense-net.net

GERMAN TRANSLATION
Caroline Behlen, Berlin;
pp.10-13
Christiane Court,
Frankfurt

FRENCH TRANSLATION
Jacques Bosser, Paris

© **2010 TASCHEN GMBH**
Hohenzollernring 53
D – 50672 Cologne
www.taschen.com

ORIGINAL EDITION
© 2006 TASCHEN GMBH

PRINTED IN SOUTH KOREA
ISBN: 978–3–8365–2345–5

ARCHITECTURE NOW!

Architektur heute / L'architecture d'aujourd'hui
Philip Jodidio

TASCHEN

CONTENTS

INTRODUCTION

OUT OF THE BOX

Architecture has broken out of the box, literally and figuratively. New technologies in design and construction have at last begun to utterly transform the built environment. In part because of these developments, boundaries that have separated architecture from art and design are also falling. The very idea of space and how it is manipulated has evolved through the understanding provided by a number of artists whose expression necessarily involves the third dimension. All of this curiously does not mean that Modernism is dead. It is just that there are so many new possibilities offered to architects that even minimalist forms are emerging from different points of view. The object is surely not just to reproduce what came before, but also to rethink architecture. This book is by no means an exhaustive selection of the architecture of the past three or five years, but it does represent a subjective overview of numerous building types and trends on an international basis. It is no accident that most of the architects featured in this book have not been in previous volumes of *Architecture Now*. Koolhaas or Herzog & de Meuron are here, but so are Philippe Rahm and Klein Dytham. Rahm (formerly of Décosterd & Rahm) is exploring the frontiers between physiology and architecture, while Astrid Klein and Mark Dytham are shaking up the Tokyo scene with everything from a 274-meter construction screen (Green Green Screen, Omotesando) to their SuperDeluxe space, described by them as "a place of fun and experimentation. A gallery, a bar, a kitchen, a jazz club, and a film studio. A cinema. A library, a school, a concert hall, and a theater." Set aside your preconceived ideas. This is Architecture Now!

SPACE MAKES ART

Museums have long been the object of particular attention from architects. Frank Lloyd Wright's Guggenheim in New York and many others showed that unusual or intriguing architecture can have an impact on the success of an institution, sometimes even creating a public demand even when the art collection concerned is not formidable (Guggenheim Bilbao). The adventures of Thomas Krens, the dynamic director of the Guggenheim appeared set to continue as he launched one project after another in distant parts of the globe, but Krens was abruptly replaced by his second in charge, Lisa Dennison in 2005. While it appears that Jean Nouvel's Guggenheim Rio is not about to be built, Krens helped organize a competition for a new museum in Guadalajara, Mexico in 2004–05. Won by Enrique Norten, the competition elicited other interesting proposals, such as that of Asymptote. Perching their design on the city's canyon edge, the New Yorkers let their imagination and their computers run free, creating a sculptural, almost liquid form that would have called on the same "non-standard" technologies as ONL's Flyotel. Another museum that will remain virtual is François Roche's Green Gorgon, a competition entry for Lausanne's new museum of contemporary art. Inspired by nature and protean in form, the Green Gorgon sprang from the Frenchman's insistence that architecture must tell a story, that it should be enriched by "fiction." In this instance the collaboration between Charles Perrault (1628–1703), author of the classic fairy tale book *Histoires ou contes du temps passé* (1697), and the garden designer André Le Nôtre (1613–1700) of the labyrinth at Versailles was the starting point for the proposal of R&Sie. As Roche says, Le Nôtre and Perrault did not so much create a mathematical design as they attempted to develop a place where visitors would accept to "lose themselves." "It is precisely that heterotypic dimension that conditions our proposal," concludes Roche.

BIG AND SEXY

Well-known architects often start their careers with small projects. Frank O. Gehry made himself a name with bits of chain link fence and tarmac on his kitchen floor. Big projects are another kettle of fish, as Gehry found when he designed the Disney Concert Hall in Los Angeles. Other architects write books and do drawings as Rem Koolhaas and Zaha Hadid did before they hit the big time. It just takes a while until a client with enough money will trust an innovative architect with a major building. The largest and most politically sensitive project of the brilliant Catalan architect Enric Miralles was completed only after his untimely death. But many are still not convinced by his Scottish Parliament in Edinburgh (completed by his former partner and wife Benedetta Tagliabue of EMBT and the local firm RMJM Scotland Ltd). The complexities of the project led to an official inquiry into the work, that concluded that there had been insufficient communication between EMBT and RMJM and too little control of expenses. Since expense overruns are thought to be typical of inventive architect, this example does little to shore up the reputation of the profession. Perhaps overly complicated, the Scottish Parliament was not as much the victim of an architect's hubris as it was of bureaucratic delay and indecision. In the official report on the project Lord Fraser of Carmyllie submitted to the Scottish Parliament on June 24, 2004, it is written that "Tempting as it is to lay all the blame at the door of a deceased wayward Spanish architectural genius, his stylized fashion of working and the strained relationship between his widow and RMJM in Edinburgh, the analysis of the Auditor General is unimpeachable. Costs rose because the client (first the Secretary of State and latterly the Parliament) wanted increases and changes or at least approved of them in one manifestation or another."[1]

It may be that private clients stimulate the efficiency of famous architects more than public ones. Then again, it may indeed be difficult for talented architects who are used to small projects to suddenly take on large ones. Massimiliano Fuksas is used to fairly large jobs, but none on the scale of his Fiera Milano, the new fair site of the Italian city. Essentially completed in a record time of 27 months, the complex measures no less than 1.4 million square meters in floor area and features a 1.5 kilometer-long central walkway whose artful ebb and flow seems to have been the product of a sophisticated computer program. In fact, Fuksas, based in Rome and Paris, does not actually use computers for his own designs. Naturally his office staff makes abundant use of the latest technology, but the architect prefers to draw or even to paint his buildings before turning them into digital wonders. In this case, he was inspired by storms or even tornadoes for the walkway's signature covering. Although much is made of the virtues of the computer, it is apparent in Milan that using relatively traditional means, Fuksas has been able to create a very contemporary form in an efficient and timely way. This success eluded EMBT in Edinburgh with the attenuating circumstances already described.

NATURE RULES

Though it may be that the fashion for virtual architecture is going the way of minimalism, some of the most interesting work being done currently involves sophisticated technology and the exploration of nature as a source for form and function. Whatever the future price of oil, ecologically oriented architecture has a bright future, if only for reasons of cost. The reduction of pollution is also a significant goal of what

[1] www.scottish.parliament.uk/vli/holyrood

is commonly called "sustainability." The New York architect Michael McDonough, who worked for some time with SITE, has embarked on the construction of what might be called the ultimate sustainable house. His e-House "integrates over 100 new or advanced technologies (including high performance or historical or 'alternate' technologies) and proposes to develop a new lexicon for sustainable architecture theory." Energy efficiency is a goal, but even more the idea that the house can somehow form an "organic entity," respectful of its setting, or of local traditions. McDonough's effort to integrate the use of so many forms of technology is in itself interesting. He suggests that the very future of architecture may lie with such a holistic approach, one that makes use of as much knowledge as possible above and beyond the more basic structural language. Rather than creating a functioning shell, he proposes to make a building that will almost literally live and breathe with its occupants.

Dennis Dollens takes a different approach to nature, finding architectural inspiration in growth patterns. His recent work, such as the Digitally-Grown Tower published here, makes use of a program called Xfrog. As Dollens explains, "Xfrog is software made by a company called Greenworks in Germany. It employs botanic, L-system algorithms used in computational biological simulations to grow plants and landscapes for laboratory tests. Greenworks has taken L-systems and added proprietary programming that factors in things like gravity and phototropism and they have built an icon-based desktop. The software is basically used for futuristic landscapes or very realistic modeling for landscaping. I think I am the only person using it for such experimental architectural growth." In other words, what would happen if you could actually simulate botanic growth patterns in an architectural context? The result would most probably be efficient and would look quite different from existing architecture, while having a firm base in the reality of nature. Others like Frei Otto or Buckminster Fuller have experimented at the fringe between architecture and nature, but Dennis Dollens is using very recent computer technology to take this type of idea several steps further. Aside from his own designs, Dollens has worked to alert the academic community to the potential gains to be found in a cross-disciplinary approach that would enrich design through contact with science. As he writes, "…As designers, we should incorporate research methodologies and techniques rooted in science into the design process. For example, designers might look at the spatial, material, and structural qualities of shells, plants, or bones for attributes worth exploring. Such an engagement with process and research will eventually deepen our considerations of natural properties, subsequently manifested in environmentally responsible ways, while at the same time revealing forms extrapolated from nature—not merely designs emerging from *a priori* taste. There are potential collaborations in which scientists and designers could articulate and coordinate research goals, but for that to happen, a specific new type of design education must be evolved. One of the useful, if basic, guiding premises underlying such a development is the question: *How would nature solve this design problem?* The question could be incorporated easily into current design education as an evolutionary seed without overthrowing existing design pedagogy. Plant it and it will grow."

The Swiss architect Philippe Rahm has made quite a name for himself despite having actually built very little. With his former partner Gilles Décosterd (Décosterd & Rahm), he has actively explored underlying physiological factors that are frequently ignored or obviated in contemporary architecture. What happens, he asks, when factors like humidity, light, or oxygen content in the air are willfully manipulated? Taking virtual architecture a step further into the twilight zone of science, his *Ghost Flat* imagined a space whose furnishing and functions would be different according to the part of the light spectrum used. "The bedroom appears between 400 and 500 nanometers, the living room between 600 and 800 nanometers. The bathroom is localized in the ultraviolet, between 350 and 400." More worrisome is the work *ND Cult*. Imagine a roomy glass box with piped-in gas. Oxygen is reduced to six percent and the visitor enters "a space on the borderline of death, where perception and consciousness are modified in a way probably close to that of mystical states. Under these extreme physical conditions, the space is extremely dangerous, irreversible brain damage is possible and the risk of death is real." *ND* stands for Near Death. It might be interesting to recall Bill Viola's description of the third act of *Tristan* here: "We are plunged into the agony and delirium of death and suffering, replete with visions, dreams and hallucinatory revelations that play across the surface of a dying man's mind." Philippe Rahm's work has been shown extensively in art museums and Décosterd & Rahm were in charge of the Swiss Pavilion for the 2002 Venice Architecture Biennale. Their work there, called the Hormonorium, made use of 528 florescent tubes placed in the floor of the pavilion, with a resulting stimulation of the retina, which transmits information to the pineal gland causing a decrease in melatonin secretion. By so lowering the level of this hormone in the body, this environment allows us to experience a decrease in fatigue, a probable increase in sexual desire, and regulation of our moods. The architects also lowered the oxygen level in the pavilion from the normal 21 % to 14.5 %, or that found at an altitude of about 3000 meters in the Swiss mountains. As they explained, "This oxygen-rarified space causes slight hypoxia, which may initially be manifested by clinical states such as confusion, disorientation or bizarre behavior, but also a slight euphoria due to endorphin production. After about ten minutes, there is a measurable "natural" increase in erythropoietin (EPO) and hematocrit levels, as well as a strengthening of the cardiovascular and respiratory systems. The kidneys produce erythropoietin. This protein hormone reaches the bone marrow, where it stimulates the production of red blood cells, thus increasing the supply of oxygen to the muscles. Decreasing the oxygen level will therefore have a stimulating effect that may improve the body's physical capabilities by up to 10%."

Many significant figures of contemporary architecture, from Frank O. Gehry to Santiago Calatrava, have willfully broken the barriers between architecture, art or engineering. Understanding that science has made great progress, some architects see no problem with making use of the imagery and process of other fields to innovate. Purists will say that none of this has to do with architecture, but as advances in computer technology make the "non-standard" vision of building design a reality, the question of why barriers exist between disciplines at all is raised. Whether in a more modest and comprehensible way, as when François Roche bases a project on the encounter of Charles Perrault and André Le Nôtre, or in the brave new world of Marcos Novak, there is one constant: architecture is out of the box.

Philip Jodidio, Grimentz
(This is an abridged version of the essay written for *Achitecture Now! 4*, originally published in 2006.)

EINLEITUNG

RAUS AUS DEM KASTEN

Die Architektur hat sich aus dem Kasten befreit, buchstäblich und symbolisch. Neue Bau- und Entwurfstechnologien tragen dazu bei, die gebaute Umwelt gänzlich umzuformen. Nicht zuletzt dank dieser Entwicklungen werden auch die Grenzen, die Architektur von Kunst und Design trennen, immer durchlässiger. Eine neue Vorstellung von Raum und wie mit ihm umzugehen ist bildete sich durch die Interpretation einer Reihe von Künstlern heraus, deren Ausdrucksformen zwingend die dritte Dimension einschließen. All dies bedeutet seltsamerweise nicht, dass die Moderne ausgedient hat. Es heißt nur, dass sich der Architektenschaft viele neue Möglichkeiten bieten, und dass selbst minimalistische Formen aus unterschiedlichen Überlegungen heraus zum Spektrum gehören. Das Ziel besteht gewiss nicht darin, einfach nur das Vorhergegangene zu wiederholen, sondern auch die Architektur neu zu überdenken. Dieses Buch umfasst keineswegs eine erschöpfende Auswahl der Architektur der letzten drei bis fünf Jahre, aber es gibt auf internationaler Ebene einen subjektiven Überblick über zahlreiche Bautypen und Trends. Es ist kein Zufall, dass ein Großteil der in diesem Buch behandelten Architekten in keinem der früheren Bände von *Architecture Now* enthalten ist. Zwar sind Koolhaas oder Herzog & de Meuron vertreten, aber ebenso Philippe Rahm sowie Klein Dytham. Rahm (vormals Décosterd & Rahm) lotet die Grenzgebiete zwischen Physiologie und Architektur aus, während Klein Dytham die Szene in Tokio aufmischen mit Projekten wie der Green Green Screen, Omotesando, einem 274 m langen »Bauzaun«, oder ihrem SuperDeluxe Raum, den sie als »einen Ort für Spaß und Experimentieren« bezeichnen: Galerie, Bar, Küche, Jazzklub und Filmstudio, Kino, Bibliothek, Schule, Konzerthalle und Theater. Vergessen Sie ihre überkommenen Vorstellungen. Das hier ist »Architecture Now«!

RAUM ERZEUGT KUNST

Schon seit längerem findet die Bauaufgabe Museum das besondere Interesse von Architekten. Frank Lloyd Wrights Guggenheim Museum in New York und zahlreiche weitere zeigten, dass ungewöhnliche oder interessante Architektur den Erfolg der jeweiligen Institution befördern, ja zuweilen das öffentliche Interesse wecken kann, selbst wenn die betreffende Kunstsammlung nicht gerade eindrucksvoll ist (Guggenheim Bilbao). Die Abenteuer von Thomas Krens, dem dynamischen Direktor der Guggenheim-Foundation, dauern an, während er in entfernten Weltgegenden ein Projekt nach dem anderen lanciert. Während es scheint, als solle Jean Nouvels Guggenheim Rio nicht realisiert werden, sorgte Krens für die Organisation eines Wettbewerbs für ein neues Museum in Guadalajara, Mexiko. Dieser zeitigte außer dem Entwurf des Siegers Enrique Norten weitere interessante Vorschläge wie den von Asymptote. Die New Yorker platzierten ihren Entwurf auf den Rand eines Canyons und ließen ihrer Fantasie und ihren Computern freien Lauf. So entstand eine plastische, nahezu fließende Form, für die die gleichen nicht-standardisierten Verfahren zum Einsatz kommen würden wie für das Flyotel von ONL. Ein weiteres Museum, das virtuell bleiben wird, ist François Roches Green Gorgon, ein Wettbewerbsbeitrag für Lausannes neues Museum für zeitgenössische Kunst. Das von der Natur inspirierte Green Gorgon mit seiner proteischen Form verkörpert die Überzeugung Roches, Architektur müsse eine Geschichte erzählen und solle mit »Fiktion« angereichert werden. In diesem Fall stellte die Zusammenarbeit von Charles Perrault (1628–1703), dem Autor des klassischen Märchenbuchs *Histoires ou contes du temps passé* (1697), und dem Gartenarchitekten André Le Nôtre (1613–1700) am Labyrinth von Versailles den Ausgangspunkt der Planung von R&Sie dar. Wie Roche erläutert, schufen Perrault und Le Nôtre weniger ein mathematisches Gebilde, als dass sie versuchten einen Ort zu gestalten, an dem sich die Besucher »verlieren« konnten. »Es ist genau diese heterotypische Dimension, die unseren Entwurf bedingt«, folgert Roche.

GROSS UND SEXY

Bekannte Architekten haben ihre Laufbahn häufig mit kleinen Projekten begonnen. Frank O. Gehry machte sich einen Namen mit Stücken von Maschendraht und Tarmac auf seinem Küchenboden. Wie Gehry herausfand, als er die Walt Disney Concert Hall in Los Angeles entwarf, sind große Projekte etwas ganz anderes. Andere Architekten verfassen Bücher und fertigen Zeichnungen an wie Rem Koolhaas und Zaha Hadid es taten, ehe sie erfolgreich wurden. Es dauert einfach seine Zeit, ehe ein Auftraggeber mit genügend Geld einem innovativen Architekten ein größeres Gebäude anvertraut. Das größte und politisch heikelste Projekt des brillanten Katalanen Enric Miralles wurde erst nach seinem frühen Tod fertig. Viele sind allerdings nach wie vor nicht von seinem Schottischen Parlament in Edinburgh überzeugt, das von seiner Partnerin und Ehefrau Benedetta Tagliabue von EMBT und der ortsansässigen Firma RMJM Scotland Ltd. fertig gestellt wurde. Die Komplexität des Gebäudes führte zu einer offiziellen Untersuchung des Projekts, die zu dem Schluss kam, die Kommunikation zwischen EMBT und RMJM sei unzureichend gewesen, desgleichen die Kontrolle der Ausgaben. Da überzogene Kosten für ein typisches Folgeproblem innovativer Architekten gehalten werden, trägt dieses Beispiel nicht gerade zur Verbesserung der Reputation dieses Berufsstandes bei. Das vielleicht übermäßig komplexe Parlamentsgebäude war nicht so sehr ein Opfer der Hybris des Architekten, als das bürokratischer Verzögerungen und Unentschlossenheit. In dem offiziellen Bericht zu dem Projekt, den Lord Fraser of Carmyllie dem schottischen Parlament am 24. Juni 2004 vorlegte, heißt es: »Wenn die Versuchung auch groß ist, die ganze Schuld auf ein verstorbenes, unberechenbares Architekturgenie aus Spanien, seine hypertrophe Arbeitsweise und die gespannte Beziehung zwischen seiner Witwe und RMJM in Edinburgh zu schieben, ist die Analyse des obersten Revisors doch unanfechtbar. Die Kosten stiegen, weil der Auftraggeber (zuerst der Außenminister und neuerdings das Parlament) Vergrößerungen und Änderungen wünschten oder sie zumindest in der einen oder anderen Form billigten.«[1]

Es mag sein, dass private Auftraggeber der Leistungsfähigkeit eines berühmten Architekten eher Impulse geben als öffentliche. Andererseits könnte es für begabte, an kleine Projekte gewöhnte Architekten in der Tat schwierig sein, plötzlich eine große Aufgabe zu übernehmen. Massimiliano Fuksas ist mit ziemlich großen Aufgaben vertraut, aber mit keinen vom Kaliber seiner Fiera Milano, dem neuen Messegelände der Stadt. Der in der Rekordzeit von 27 Monaten im Wesentlichen fertig gestellte Komplex umfasst nicht weniger als 1,4 Millionen m^2 Grundfläche und einen 1,5 km langen, zentralen Weg; das kunstvolle Auf und Ab der Wegüberdachung scheint das Produkt eines ausgeklügelten Computerprogramms zu sein. Der in Rom und Paris ansässige Fuksas verwendet jedoch für seine Entwurfszeichnungen keine Computer. Selbstverständlich machen seine Mitarbeiter regen Gebrauch von der neuesten Technik, aber der Architekt selbst zieht es vor, seine Gebäude zu zeichnen oder sogar zu malen, ehe sie in digitale Wunderwerke verwandelt werden. In diesem Fall regten ihn Stürme oder sogar Tornados zu der Überdachung des Gehwegs an. Es ist zwar viel von den Vorzügen des Computers die Rede, aber in Mailand ist zu sehen, dass Fuksas mit relativ traditionellen Mitteln in der Lage ist, in effizienter, termingerechter Weise eine sehr zeitgemäße Form zu erzeugen. Angesichts der oben beschriebenen, hinderlichen Begleitumstände blieb dieser Erfolg EMBT in Edinburgh versagt.

---

[1] www.scottish.parliament.uk/vli/holyrood

DIE NATUR HERRSCHT

Wenngleich es sein kann, dass der Trend zur virtuellen Architektur den Weg des Minimalismus einschlägt, hat ein Teil der interessantesten, gegenwärtig in Arbeit befindlichen Projekte, mit komplexer Technik und dem Erforschen der Natur als Quelle für Form und Funktion zu tun. Ganz gleich wie der künftige Ölpreis aussehen wird, ökologisch ausgerichtete Architektur steht vor einer glänzenden Zukunft und sei es nur aus Kostengründen. Die Reduzierung der Umweltverschmutzung ist ein weiteres, wichtiges Ziel der so genannten Nachhaltigkeit. Der eine Zeit lang bei SITE tätige New Yorker Architekt Michael McDonough hat sich daran gemacht, das möglicherweise ultimative, nachhaltige Haus zu errichten. Sein e-House, so schreibt er, »integriert über 100 neue oder ausgereifte Technologien, darunter Hochleistungstechnologien, historische und alternative Technologien. Mit dem Haus schlagen wir die Entwicklung eines neuen Wortschatzes für nachhaltige Architekturtheorie vor.« Ein Ziel ist die sparsame Nutzung von Energie, aber noch wichtiger ist die Vorstellung, das Haus könne eine »organische Einheit« bilden, die ihre Umgebung und lokale Traditionen achtet. McDonoughs Bemühen, so viele technologische Möglichkeiten in kombinierter Form zu nutzen, ist schon an sich interessant. Er äußert die Ansicht, die wahre Zukunft der Architektur könne in einem solch holistischen Ansatz liegen, der sich über die grundlegendere, konstruktive Sprache weit hinaus so viel Wissen wie möglich zunutze macht. Anstatt eine funktionierende Hülle zu schaffen, spricht er sich dafür aus, ein Gebäude herzustellen, das beinahe buchstäblich mit seinen Bewohnern lebt und atmet.

Dennis Dollens nähert sich der Natur auf andere Weise und findet architektonische Anregungen in Wachstumsmodellen. Seine neuesten Arbeiten machen sich ein Programm namens Xfrog zunutze. Dollens erläutert: »Xfrog ist Software, die von der deutschen Firma Greenworks hergestellt wird. Sie nutzt botanische L-System-Algorithmen, die in computergestützten, biologischen Simulationen verwendet werden, um für Laborzwecke Pflanzen und Landschaften entstehen zu lassen. Greenworks nimmt die L-Systeme und ergänzt eigene Programmierungen, die Faktoren wie Schwerkraft und Fototropismus einberechnen und erstellt einen mithilfe von Icons operierenden Desktop. Die Software wird für futuristische Landschaften oder sehr realistische Landschaftsgestaltungen verwendet. Ich glaube, ich bin der einzige, der sie für derart experimentelles Architekturwachstum einsetzt.« Mit anderen Worten, was geschähe, wenn man tatsächlich botanische Wachstumsmodelle in einem Architekturkontext simulieren könnte? Das Ergebnis wäre höchstwahrscheinlich sehr effizient und sähe völlig anders aus als die vorhandene Architektur, wobei es eine solide Grundlage in der realen Natur hätte. Andere Architekten wie Frei Otto oder Buckminster Fuller experimentierten bereits an der Grenze zwischen Architektur und Natur. Dennis Dollens verwendet nun die neueste Computertechnik, um diese Ideen voranzutreiben. Abgesehen von seinen eigenen Entwürfen arbeitet Dollens daran, der akademischen Gemeinschaft den potenziellen Nutzen eines fachübergreifenden Vorgehens bewusst zu machen, das das Bauen durch Kontakt mit der Wissenschaft bereichern könnte. Er schreibt: »Als Designer sollten wir wissenschaftlich fundierte Methoden und Technologien in den Entwurfsprozess einbeziehen. Beispielsweise könnten Planer auf der Suche nach erforschenswerten Merkmalen die räumlichen, materiellen oder konstruktiven Eigenschaften von Muscheln, Pflanzen oder Knochen betrachten. Diese Beschäftigung mit Prozessen und Forschung wird sich in ökologisch vertretbaren Verfahren niederschlagen, während gleichzeitig von der Natur abgeleitete Formen zutage kommen – nicht nur Entwürfe, die vorrangig von den Vorlieben des Verfassers abhängen. Es ist eine Zusammenarbeit denkbar, bei der Wissenschaftler und Designer Forschungsziele formulieren und koordinieren; ehe das geschieht, müsste allerdings ein neuer Typ von Entwurfsausbildung entwickelt werden. Eine der Leitlinien, die einer solchen Entwicklung zugrunde lägen, wäre die Frage: Wie würde die Natur diese Entwurfsfrage lösen? Die Frage ließe sich leicht als evolutionärer Samen in die gegenwärtige Entwurfsausbildung einfügen, ohne die bestehende Pädagogik zu kippen. Einmal gepflanzt, wird er wachsen.«

Obwohl der Schweizer Architekt Philippe Rahm noch nicht viel gebaut hat, genießt er einen guten Ruf. Mit seinem früheren Partner Gilles Décosterd hat er grundlegende, physiologische Faktoren erforscht, die in der zeitgenössischen Architektur häufig außer Acht gelassen werden. Er fragt, was geschieht, wenn Faktoren wie Feuchtigkeit, Licht oder der Sauerstoffgehalt der Luft vorsätzlich manipuliert werden. Die virtuelle Architektur wird von ihm einen Schritt weiter in die Grauzone der Wissenschaft geführt, indem er mit *Ghost Flat* einen Raum vorstellt, dessen Möblierung und Funktionen sich in Abhängigkeit vom genutzten Teil des Lichtspektrums verändern. »Das Schlafzimmer erscheint zwischen 400 und 500, das Wohnzimmer zwischen 600 und 800 Nanometer Wellenlänge. Das Badezimmer ist auf den ultravioletten Bereich zwischen 350 und 400 Nanometer Wellenlänge beschränkt.« Beunruhigender ist das Projekt *ND Cult*. Man stelle sich einen geräumigen Glaskasten vor, in den Gas eingeleitet wird. Der Sauerstoff wird auf sechs Prozent reduziert, und der Besucher betritt »einen Raum an der Grenze zum Tod, in dem Wahrnehmung und Bewusstsein in einer Weise modifiziert werden, die vermutlich dem mystischer Zustände ähnlich ist. Unter diesen Extrembedingungen ist der Raum äußerst gefährlich, irreversible Hirnschädigung möglich und das Todesrisiko real.« *ND* bedeutet Near Death (dem Tod nahe). In diesem Zusammenhang ist es vielleicht interessant, an Bill Violas Beschreibung vom dritten Akt des »Tristan« zu erinnern: »Wir werden in Agonie und Delirium von Tod und Leiden gestürzt, voller Visionen, Träume und halluzinatorischer Offenbarungen, wie sie durch das Bewusstsein eines Sterbenden huschen«. Décosterd & Rahm zeichneten verantwortlich für den Schweizer Pavillon auf der Architekturbiennale 2002 in Venedig. Das *Hormonorium* verwendete 528 in den Boden des Pavillons eingelassene Leuchtröhren zur Stimulierung der Netzhaut, die Informationen an die Zirbeldrüse leitet und damit eine Abnahme der Melatoninproduktion bewirkt. Durch den so im Körper abgesenkten Hormonspiegel nimmt in diesem Raum die Müdigkeit ab, mit einiger Wahrscheinlichkeit steigt das sexuelle Lustempfinden und Stimmungsschwankungen werden reguliert. Darüber hinaus senkten die Architekten im Pavillon den Sauerstoffgehalt von den normalen 21 Prozent auf 14,5 Prozent ab, und damit auf den Wert, der auf einer Höhe von 3000 m in den Schweizer Alpen herrscht. Sie erläutern: »Die in diesem Raum vorhandene, dünne Luft verursacht einen leichten Sauerstoffmangel im Blut, der sich anfangs durch klinische Zustände wie Verwirrung, Desorientierung oder seltsames Verhalten äußern kann, aufgrund der Endorphinausschüttung aber auch durch leichte Euphorie. Nach etwa zehn Minuten tritt eine messbare, natürliche Erhöhung der Pegel von Erythroproietin (EPO) und Haematokrit auf, die eine Stärkung des Herz-Kreislauf-Systems und der Atmung zur Folge haben. Das Protein Erythroproietin wird in den Nieren gebildet, gelangt dann ins Knochenmark, wo es die Bildung von roten Blutkörperchen anregt und damit die Abgabe von Sauerstoff an die Muskeln erhöht. Das Senken des Sauerstoffgehalts hat demzufolge eine belebende Wirkung, die die physischen Fähigkeiten des Körpers um bis zu zehn Prozent steigern kann.«

Zahlreiche bedeutende Vertreter der zeitgenössischen Architektur, von Frank O. Gehry bis Santiago Calatrava, haben absichtlich die Barrieren zwischen Architektur, Kunst oder Technik durchbrochen. In dem Wissen um die großen Fortschritte der Wissenschaft haben einige Architekten keine Schwierigkeiten damit, zum Zweck der Innovation von Bildsprache und Verfahren anderer Gebiete Gebrauch zu machen. Puristen werden sagen, nichts davon habe etwas mit Architektur zu tun, aber in dem Maß wie Computertechnologie den »non-standard«-Entwurf zur Realität werden lässt, stellt sich die Frage, weshalb es überhaupt Barrieren zwischen Sachgebieten gibt. Sei es François Roche, der ein Projekt auf die Begegnung von Charles Perrault und André Le Nôtre gründet, oder die schöne neue Welt von Marcos Novak: Es gibt eine Konstante – die Architektur ist aus dem Kasten heraus.

Philip Jodidio, Grimentz

(Dies ist eine gekürzte Version des Essays, der für die ursprünglich 2006 erschienene Ausgabe von *Architecture Now! 4* verfasst wurde.)

INTRODUCTION

HORS DE LA BOÎTE

Au propre comme au figuré, l'architecture a rompu avec la fameuse boîte. Les nouvelles technologies de conception et de construction commencent enfin à transformer notre façon d'aborder le bâti. Conséquence partielle de ces développements, les frontières qui séparaient l'architecture de l'art et du design s'estompent. L'idée même d'espace et la façon dont il est manipulé évoluent grâce aux nouvelles perspectives ouvertes par un certain nombre d'artistes dont la pratique fait appel aux trois dimensions. Tout ceci ne signifie pas pour autant la mort du modernisme, mais simplement que les nouvelles possibilités offertes aux architectes sont si nombreuses que l'on peut même voir des solutions minimalistes naître de points de vue très différents. L'objectif n'est certainement pas de se contenter de reproduire ce qui a été fait auparavant, mais aussi de repenser l'architecture. Ce livre n'est en aucun cas une sélection exhaustive de l'architecture des trois ou quatre dernières années, mais un survol subjectif de multiples types de bâtiments et de tendances vus sous un angle international. Ce n'est pas un hasard si la plupart des architectes présentés dans cet ouvrage ne figuraient pas dans les précédents volumes d'*Architecture Now*. Koolhaas ou Herzog & de Meuron sont là, mais aussi Philippe Rahm et Klein Dytham. Rahm (récemment encore associé de l'agence Décosterd & Rahm) explore les frontières entre physiologie et architecture, tandis qu'Astrid Klein et Mark Dytham bousculent la scène tokyoïte avec des réalisations spectaculaires comme leur écran de verdure de 274 mètres de long (Green Green Screen, Omotesando) et leur superbe espace SuperDeluxe, qu'ils décrivent comme « un lieu de plaisir et d'expérimentation. Une galerie, un bar, une cuisine, un club de jazz et un studio de cinéma. Un cinéma. Une bibliothèque, une école, une salle de concert et un théâtre ». Laissez de côté vos idées préconçues. Voici ce qu'est l'architecture d'aujourd'hui…

L'ESPACE FAIT L'ART

Les musées ont longtemps été l'objet d'une attention particulière de la part des architectes. Le Guggenheim de Frank Lloyd Wright à New York et de nombreuses autres institutions ont montré qu'une architecture inhabituelle et même provocante pouvait exercer un impact notable sur le succès d'une institution, voire créer un afflux de public supplémentaire, même lorsque les collections présentées n'étaient pas d'une importance extrême (Guggenheim Bilbao). Les aventures de Thomas Krens, le dynamique directeur du Guggenheim, se poursuivent et il continue à lancer projet après projet sur différents points du globe. Si le Guggenheim de Jean Nouvel à Rio n'est pas près d'être construit, Krens a organisé un concours pour un nouveau musée à Guadalajara au Mexique. Remporté par Enrique Norten, il a suscité d'autres propositions intéressantes, par exemple celle d'Asymptote. En perchant leur projet au bord d'un canyon, les architectes new-yorkais ont lâché la bride à leur imagination et à leurs ordinateurs et créé une forme sculpturale, quasi liquide, qui aurait fait appel aux mêmes technologies non-standard que le Flyotel d'ONL. Un autre projet restera dans les cartons, celui de François Roche pour le nouveau musée d'art contemporain de Lausanne. Protéiforme et inspirée par la nature, sa « Green Gorgon » répond à la passion de l'architecte français pour une architecture qui raconte une histoire, qui soit enrichie par une fiction. Ici, c'est la collaboration entre Charles Perrault (1628–1703) auteur des *Histoires ou contes du temps passé* (appelés aussi *Contes de ma mère l'Oye*, 1697) et le jardinier André Le Nôtre (1613–1700) pour le labyrinthe de Versailles qui ont été le point de départ de la proposition de R&Sie. Pour Roche, Le Nôtre et Perrault n'ont pas tant créé un dessin mathématique qu'imaginé un lieu dans lequel les visiteurs accepteraient « de se perdre ». « C'est précisément cette dimension hétérotypique qui conditionne notre proposition », conclut François Roche.

BIG AND SEXY

Les architectes devenus célèbres ont souvent commencé leur carrière par de petits projets. Frank O. Gehry s'est fait connaître par son utilisation de la résille métallique ou de l'asphalte sur le sol de sa cuisine, mais les grands projets sont une autre paire de manches, comme il a pu le découvrir en concevant le Walt Disney Concert Hall à Los Angeles. D'autres écrivent des livres ou dessinent avant de se retrouver en couverture des journaux, comme Rem Koolhaas ou Zaha Hadid. Il faut simplement du temps pour qu'un client assez fortuné fasse confiance à un architecte novateur et le charge d'un grand chantier. Le projet le plus important et le plus politiquement sensible du brillant architecte catalan Enric Miralles n'a été achevé qu'après sa mort prématurée. Beaucoup cependant ne sont toujours pas convaincus par cet immeuble du Parlement écossais (terminé par son associée et épouse Benedetta Tagliabue d'EMBT en collaboration avec l'agence locale RMJM Scotland Ltd.). Les complexités du projet ont conduit à la création d'une commission d'enquête qui a conclu à une insuffisance de communication entre EMBT et RMJM et à un contrôle des dépenses trop laxiste. Les dépassements budgétaires sont assez typiques des interventions des praticiens inventifs et cet exemple n'a pas contribué à relever la réputation de la profession. Peut-être parce qu'il était trop compliqué, le Parlement écossais a été la victime des retards et de l'indécision administratifs bien plus que de l'ego de l'architecte. Dans le rapport officiel remis par Lord Fraser of Carmyllie le 24 juin 2004, il est écrit : «Aussi tentant soit-il de reporter le blâme sur un génie architectural espagnol décédé, sur sa façon de travailler et sur les relations tendues entre sa veuve et RMJM à Édimbourg, l'analyse de l'auditeur général est incontestable. Les coûts se sont accrus parce que les clients (le secrétaire d'État en premier lieu, puis le Parlement) ont demandé des travaux supplémentaires et des modifications ou les ont, du moins, approuvés d'une façon ou d'une autre ».[1]

Il se peut que les clients privés stimulent davantage les grands architectes que la commande publique. Mais, là encore, il est parfois difficile pour des hommes de talent habitués à de petits projets de prendre brusquement en charge des chantiers importants. Massimiliano Fuksas est coutumier de chantiers d'assez grandes dimensions mais d'aucun à l'échelle de sa Fiera Milano, les nouvelles installations de la célèbre foire de la capitale lombarde. Achevé pour l'essentiel en un temps record de vingt-sept mois, ce complexe couvre pas moins de 1,4 millions de m^2 et se caractérise par une allée centrale de 1,5 km de long, dont le profil judicieux semble sorti d'un logiciel d'ordinateur sophistiqué. En fait, Fuksas, basé à Rome et à Paris, ne se sert pas vraiment d'ordinateurs pour ses réalisations propres. Son agence utilise bien sûr abondamment les technologies les plus récentes, mais il préfère dessiner ou même peindre ses projets avant de les confier aux miracles de la numérisation. À Milan, il s'est inspiré des tempêtes ou même des tornades pour la couverture de l'allée. Bien que l'on fasse grand cas des prouesses de l'informatique, il est clair ici qu'en faisant appel à des moyens relativement traditionnels l'architecte a su créer une forme très contemporaine, de façon efficace et en respectant les délais. Son succès ôte à Édimbourg (EMBT) les circonstances atténuantes décrites plus haut.

LES LOIS DE LA NATURE

S'il se peut que la mode de l'architecture virtuelle suive les traces de celle du minimalisme, certaines des recherches les plus intéressantes menées actuellement concernent des technologies sophistiquées et l'exploration de nature en tant que source de formes et de fonc-

[1] www.scottish.parliament.uk/vli/holyrood

tions. Quel que soit le prix futur du baril de pétrole, l'architecture de sensibilité écologique est assurée d'un brillant avenir, ne serait-ce que pour des raisons de coût. La réduction de la pollution est également un objectif important pour ce que l'on appelle aussi le « développement durable ». L'architecte new-yorkais Michael McDonough, qui a travaillé quelque temps avec SITE, s'est embarqué dans la construction de « la maison écologique absolue ». Sa e-House « intègre plus de cent technologies nouvelles ou d'avant-garde (dont des technologies hautes performances, historiques ou alternatives) et se propose de mettre au point un nouveau langage pour la théorie de l'architecture durable. » L'efficacité énergétique est un but, mais plus encore, l'idée que la maison puisse constituer d'une certaine façon une « entité organique », respectant son cadre ou les traditions locales. L'effort de l'architecte pour intégrer de si nombreuses formes de technologie est, en soi, intéressant. Il suggère que l'avenir même de l'architecture est lié à une approche aholistique ayant recours à des connaissances aussi nombreuses que possible au-delà du langage structurel de base. Plutôt que de créer une coquille qui « fonctionne », il propose une construction qui, littéralement, vivrait et respirerait à l'unisson avec ses occupants.

Dennis Dollens approche la nature de manière différente et trouve son inspiration architecturale dans les modèles de croissance. L'une de ses récentes recherches, la Digitally-Grown Tower publiée ici, utilise un logiciel appelé Xfrog. Dollens explique : « Xfrog est un logiciel allemand mis au point par la société Greenworks. Il utilise des algorithmes botaniques appelés L-systems qui sont utilisés en laboratoire pour les simulations numérisées de la pousse des plantes et de l'évolution des paysages. Greenworks a ajouté aux L-systems des capacités de programmation qui prennent en compte des éléments comme la gravité et le phototropisme et ont construit un »bureau« à base d'icônes. Ce logiciel sert essentiellement au dessin de paysages futuristes ou à la modélisation très réaliste de paysages. Je pense être le seul à l'utiliser pour l'étude expérimentale de la croissance architecturale. » En d'autres termes, qu'arriverait-il si vous pouviez réellement appliquer des modèles de croissance botanique simulée à un projet architectural ? Le résultat serait probablement riche en enseignements et prendrait des aspects assez différents de l'architecture existante, tout en reposant sur une base solide : la réalité de la nature. D'autres architectes, comme Frei Otto ou Buckminster Fuller, ont mené des expériences à la limite de l'architecture et de la nature, mais Dollens utilise les toutes dernières technologies informatiques pour pousser encore plus loin ce type de réflexion. Parallèlement à ses travaux personnels, il tente d'alerter la communauté universitaire sur les gains potentiels d'une approche transdisciplinaire susceptible d'enrichir la conception grâce aux contacts avec la science. Ainsi écrit-il : « …En tant que concepteurs, nous devrions intégrer les techniques et les méthodologies de la recherche scientifique dans notre processus de conception. Par exemple, des designers pourraient mettre à profit les qualités spatiales, matérielles et structurelles des coquillages, des plantes et des os. Un tel engagement dans la recherche et les processus pourra peut-être approfondir notre prise en compte des propriétés naturelles, qui seraient mises en œuvre, par la suite, de manière responsable à l'égard de l'environnement, tout en permettant l'émergence de formes extrapolées de celles de la nature et pas seulement de projets issus d'un goût a priori. Il existe des possibilités de collaborations entre scientifiques et créateurs. Ils pourraient articuler et coordonner leurs buts de recherche, mais pour que cela se produise, un nouveau type de formation spécifique à la conception doit apparaître. L'une des idées-forces, même si elle est très simple, qui sous-tendent un tel développement, est la question : *Comment la nature résoudrait-elle ce problème de conception ?* La question pourrait facilement être intégrée dans la formation actuelle au design et à l'architecture, comme une graine d'évolution qui ne renverserait pas forcément la pédagogie existante. Plantez-la et elle poussera. »

L'architecte suisse Philippe Rahm jouit déjà d'une certaine réputation, bien qu'il n'ait que peu construit. Avec son ancien associé, Gilles Décosterd, il a très activement exploré des facteurs physiologiques que l'architecture contemporaine ignore ou repousse le plus souvent. Que se passe-t-il, demande-t-il, lorsque des facteurs comme l'humidité, la lumière ou la quantité d'oxygène dans l'air sont volontairement manipulés? Emmenant l'architecture virtuelle un peu plus loin encore dans une zone sous-exploitée des sciences, son *Ghost Flat* (*Appartement fantôme*) imaginait un espace dont le mobilier et les fonctions se modifieraient selon la partie du spectre lumineux utilisé. «La chambre apparaît entre 400 et 500 nanomètres, le séjour entre 600 et 800. La salle de bains est localisée dans les ultraviolets, entre 350 et 400.» Plus inquiétante encore est l'œuvre intitulée *ND Cult*. Imaginez une spacieuse boîte de verre dans laquelle on injecterait du gaz à l'aide d'un tuyau. L'oxygène est réduit à 6% et le visiteur pénètre dans un «espace à la limite de la mort, où la perception et la conscience sont modifiés d'une façon probablement proche de celle d'états mystiques. Dans ces conditions physiques extrêmes, l'espace devient extrêmement dangereux, des atteintes irréversibles au cerveau peuvent se produire et le risque de mort est réel». *ND* signifie *Near Death*, la «presque mort». Il est intéressant ici de se rappeler la description du troisième acte de *Tristan et Isolde* par Bill Viola: «Nous sommes plongés dans l'agonie et le délire de la mort et de la souffrance, submergés par les visions, les rêves et les révélations hallucinées qui affleurent à l'esprit de l'homme en train de mourir.» Décosterd & Rahm ont été en charge du pavillon suisse de la Biennale d'architecture de Venise en 2002. Leur participation, appelée *Hormonorium*, fait appel à 528 tubes fluorescents répartis dans le sol du pavillon pour créer une stimulation de la rétine, laquelle transmet l'information à la glande pinéale, provoquant une diminution de la secrétion de mélatonine. «En réduisant le taux de cette hormone dans le corps, cet environnement nous permet d'expérimenter une diminution de la fatigue, un accroissement probable du désir sexuel et une régulation de l'humeur.» Les architectes avaient également abaissé le taux d'oxygène de 21% à 14,5%, c'est-à-dire celui existant à une altitude de 3000 m dans les Alpes suisses. «Ce volume d'air à oxygène raréfié provoque une légère hypoxie, qui peut dans un premier temps se manifester par des états cliniques comme la confusion, la désorientation ou un comportement bizarre, mais également une légère euphorie due à la production d'endomorphine. Au bout d'une dizaine de minutes, on constate une augmentation ‹naturelle› du taux d'érythropoïétine (EPO), de l'hématocrite, ainsi qu'une accélération des systèmes respiratoires et cardio-vasculaires. Les reins produisent de l'EPO. Cette hormone protéique atteint la moelle épinière où elle stimule la production de globules rouges et donc accroît l'apport d'oxygène aux muscles. La diminution du taux d'oxygène exerce alors un effet stimulant qui peut améliorer les capacités physiques du corps jusqu'à 10%.

Nombre de représentants importants de l'architecture contemporaine, de Frank O. Gehry à Santiago Calatrava, ont volontairement rompu les barrières entre l'architecture, l'art et l'ingénierie. Comprenant que la science a accompli d'immenses progrès, quelques architectes ne voient aucun problème dans le fait d'utiliser l'imagerie et les processus mis au point dans d'autres domaines pour innover dans le leur. Les puristes diront que tout cela n'a rien à voir avec l'architecture. Pourtant, alors que les avancées de l'informatique font que la notion non-standard de la conception architecturale est devenue une réalité, la question du pourquoi des barrières entre les disciplines est soulevée. Que ce soit d'une façon plus modeste et compréhensible, comme lorsque François Roche fait reposer un projet sur la rencontre entre Charles Perrault et André Le Nôtre, ou encore dans «le meilleur des mondes» de Marcos Novak, on ne peut que remarquer un point commun: l'architecture est sortie de la boîte.

Philip Jodidio, Grimentz
(Version abrégée de l'essai paru dans *Architecture Now! 4*, initialement publié en 2006.)

DAVID ADJAYE

Adjaye/Associates, 23–28 Penn Street, London N1 5DL, UK
Tel: +44 20 77 39 49 69, Fax: +44 20 77 39 34 84, e-mail: info@adjaye.com
Web: www.adjaye.com

DAVID ADJAYE was born in 1966 in Dar-Es-Salaam, Tanzania. He studied at the Royal College of Art (Masters in Architecture, 1993), and worked in the offices of David Chipperfield and Eduardo Souto de Moura before creating his own firm in London in 2000 (Chassay Architects, 1988–90; David Chipperfield Architects, 1991; Eduardo Souto de Moura Architects, 1991; Adjaye & Russell, 1994–2000). He has been widely recognized as one of the leading architects of his generation in the UK, in part because of the talks he has given in various locations such as the Architectural Association, the Royal College of Art and Cambridge University, as well as Harvard, Cornell or the Universidad de Luisdad in Lisbon. He was also the co-presenter of the BBC's six-part series on modern architecture "Dreamspaces." Deyan Sudjic selected his Idea Store library in East London for the exhibition highlighting 100 projects that are changing the world at the 8ᵗʰ Venice Biennale of Architecture in 2002. His offices currently employs a staff of 35, and some of his key works are: Studio/home for Chris Ofili, London (1999); Extension to house, St. John's Wood (1998); Siefert Penthouse, London (2001); Elektra House, London (2001); Studio/gallery/home for Tim Noble and Sue Webster, London (2002); and the SHADA Pavilion, London (2000, with artist Henna Nadeem. Current work includes: The Nobel Peace Center, Oslo (published here, 2002–05); Bernie Grant Performing Arts Center, Tottenham London (2001–06); Stephen Lawrence Centre, Deptford, London (2004–06); a visual arts building for the London-based organizations inIVA/Autograph, and the Museum of Contemporary Art/Denver, Denver, Colorado (2004–07).

DAVID ADJAYE, 1966 in Daressalam, Tansania, geboren, studierte am Londoner Royal College of Art, wo er 1993 die Prüfung zum Master of Architecture ablegte. Ehe er im Jahr 2000 in London sein eigenes Büro eröffnete, arbeitete er von 1988 bis 1990 bei Chassay Architects, 1991 im Büro von David Chipperfield und bei Eduardo Souto de Moura und anschließend von 1994 bis 2000 im Büro Adjaye & Russell. Er gilt weithin als einer der führenden britischen Architekten seiner Generation. Diesen Ruf verdankt er z.T. den Vorträgen, die er in verschiedenen Institutionen wie der Architectural Association, dem Royal College of Art und den Universitäten Cambridge, Harvard, Cornell sowie der Universidad de Luisdad in Lissabon hielt. Darüber hinaus fungierte er als Co-Moderator von »Dreamspaces«, einer sechsteiligen Serie der BBC über moderne Architektur. Deyan Sudjic wählte seine »Idea-Store«-Bibliothek in East London für die Ausstellung der 100 Projekte, die die Welt verändert haben, aus; sie wurde im Rahmen der VIII. Architekturbiennale in Venedig gezeigt. Zu den bedeutendsten Arbeiten seines Büros, das gegenwärtig 35 Mitarbeiter beschäftigt, gehören: ein Studio mit Wohnung für Chris Ofili, London (1999), die Erweiterung eines Hauses in St. John's Wood (1998), das Siefert Penthouse, London (2001), das Elektra House, London (2001), ein Atelier mit Galerie und Wohnung für Tim Noble und Sue Webster, London (2002), sowie der SHADA Pavillon, London (2000), in Zusammenarbeit mit der Künstlerin Henna Nadeem. Zu seinen vor kurzem fertig gestellten bzw. im Bau befindlichen Projekten zählen: das hier publizierte Nobel-Friedenszentrum, Oslo (2002–05), das Bernie Grant Performing Arts Centre in Tottenham, London (2001–06), das Stephen Lawrence Centre in Deptford, London (2004–06), ein Kunstmuseum für die in London ansässigen Organisationen inIVA/Autograph sowie das Museum für zeitgenössische Kunst in Denver, Colorado (2004–07).

DAVID ADJAYE, né en 1966 à Dar-es-Salaam (Tanzanie), étudie au Royal College of Art (Master of Architecture, 1993), puis travaille dans les agences de David Chipperfield et d'Eduardo Souto de Moura avant de créer sa propre structure à Londres en 2000 (Chassay Architects, 1988–90; David Chipperfield Architects, 1991; Eduardo Souto de Moura Architects, 1991; Adjaye & Russell, 1994–2000). Il est généralement reconnu comme l'un des plus brillants architectes de sa génération au Royaume-Uni, entre autres, grâce aux conférences qu'il a données un peu partout, notamment à l'Architectural Association, au Royal College of Art, à Cambridge University, Harvard, Cornell ou l'Universidad de Luisdad à Lisbonne. Il a été coprésentateur, à la BBC, de deux épisodes de *Dreamspaces*, une série télévisée en six parties sur l'architecture. Sa bibliothèque Idea Store, dans l'East London, a été sélectionnée par Deyan Sudjic pour la grande exposition des « 100 projets qui ont changé le monde » présentée à la 8ᵉ Biennale d'architecture de Venise en 2002. Son agence emploie actuellement trente-cinq collaborateurs. Parmi ses principales réalisations une maison-atelier pour Chris Ofili, Londres (1999); l'extension d'une maison, St. John's Wood (1998); la Siefert Penthouse, Londres (2001); la Maison Elektra, Londres (2001); l'atelier-galerie-maison de Tim Noble et Sue Webster, Londres (2002) et le Shada Pavilion, Londres (2000), en collaboration avec l'artiste Henna Nadeem. Ses chantiers actuels comprennent le Centre Nobel de la paix, Oslo (2002–05), publié ici; le Bernie Grant Arts Centre, Tottenham, Londres (2001–06); le Stephen Lawrence Centre, Deptford, Londres (2004–06), et le Museum of Contemporary Art/Denver, Denver, Colorado (2004–07).

NOBEL PEACE CENTER

Oslo, Norway, 2002–05

Floor area: 1500 m². Client: Nobel Peace Institute. Cost: € 14.1 million

The **NOBEL PEACE CENTER** was created by an act of the Norwegian Parliament in 2000. At first conceived as a museum for the Peace Prize, its function was subsequently enlarged to the explanation of conflicts and the role of the Prizewinners. As the Museum explains the selection of the architect after a competition, "The capacity for communication and dialogue through spatial manipulation was a decisive factor in commissioning architect David Adjaye and associates in London as the visual interpreter of the Center's concept. The global diversity of the Peace Prize, combined with a desire to create a Center that is dynamic and aesthetically cohesive – not merely visually pleasing, but engaging all the senses – also underpinned this decision. "Spatial manipulation" is what he calls his own work, and his projects are often the result of collaboration with artists, among them Chris Ofili, winner of the Turner Prize. Opened on June 11, 2005, the Center is located in the former Vestbanen Railway Station, an 1872 Italianate building set near the harbor and the City Hall of Oslo. A free-standing entrance portal that looks like a piece of contemporary sculpture greets visitors, its perforated skin forming a map of world-wide centers of conflict. Adjaye plays on color in the reception area (saturated red), in the Passage of Honor (gold) or in the Café de la Paix restaurant (green patterns designed by Chris Ofili). He has also collaborated for the exhibitions with the American David Small (Small Design Firm) who created video displays, working with material gathered by project historians, or an electronic "book" that recounts the life of Alfred Nobel. The cost of the building work was 14.1 million euros and the so-called Communications Project, of which the interior fittings are part, 7.4 million.

Das **NOBEL-FRIEDENSZENTRUM** wurde aufgrund eines Beschlusses des norwegischen Parlaments von 2000 gebaut. Ursprünglich sollte ein Museum für den Friedenspreis errichtet werden, dessen Funktion aber erweitert und umfasst jetzt auch die Erläuterung von Konflikten und Informationen zur Rolle der Preisträger. Die Auswahl des Architekten wurde folgendermaßen begründet: »Die Förderung von Kommunikation und Dialog durch die Gestaltung des Raums war ein wichtiger Grund, Adjaye/Associates als visuelle Interpreten des Konzeptes des Friedenszentrums zu beauftragen. Die globale Vielseitigkeit des Friedenspreises in Verbindung mit dem Wunsch, ein dynamisches und ästhetisch einheitliches Zentrum zu schaffen, das nicht nur optisch gefällt, sondern alle Sinne in Anspruch nimmt, unterstützte die Entscheidung. ›Raummanipulation‹ nennt Adjaye seine Architektur, und bei seinen Projekten arbeitet er oft mit Künstlern zusammen, unter ihnen Chris Ofili.« Das Zentrum wurde am 11. Juni 2005 eröffnet und befindet sich im ehemaligen Vestbanen-Bahnhof, einem Gebäude von 1872 im italienischen Stil in der Nähe des Hafens und des Rathauses von Oslo. Ein freistehender, einer zeitgenössischen Skulptur ähnelnder Portalbogen begrüßt den Besucher. Seine perforierte Oberfläche zeigt eine Landkarte der weltweiten Konfliktgebiete. Im Gebäude spielt Adjaye mit Farben: Der Eingangsbereich ist in sattem Rot gehalten, »Der Weg der Ehre« in Gold und das Restaurant Café de la Paix in grünen Mustern, die Ofili gestaltete. Die Ausstellungen wurden zusammen mit dem Amerikaner David Small, der die Videofilme schuf, konzipiert. Small arbeitete dabei u. a. mit Material, das Historiker sammelten, und mit einem elektronischen »Buch«, das das Leben von Alfred Nobel ausführlich darstellt. Die Kosten für das Gebäude lagen bei umgerechnet 14,1 Millionen Euro, das »Kommunikationsprojekt«, zu dem die Innenraumgestaltung gehört, belief sich auf 7,4 Millionen Euro.

Le **CENTRE NOBEL DE LA PAIX** a été créé par un acte du Parlement norvégien en 2000. Conçu pour être le musée du prix Nobel de la paix, sa fonction a été élargie à l'explication des conflits et du rôle des titulaires du prix. L'institution a justifié son choix de l'architecte : « L'aptitude à la communication et au dialogue par la manipulation spatiale a été un facteur clé dans notre décision de confier aux Londoniens Adjaye/Associates l'interprétation visuelle du concept du Centre. La diversité internationale du prix Nobel de la paix, combinée au désir de créer un Centre dynamique et esthétiquement cohérent – visuellement agréable et engageant dans tous les sens du terme – explique également cette décision ». La « manipulation spatiale » est l'une des expressions d'Adjaye pour décrire son travail, et ses projets résultent souvent d'une collaboration avec des artistes, parmi lesquels Chris Ofili, prix Turner 1998. Ouvert le 11 juin 2005, le Centre est installé dans l'ancienne gare de chemin de fer de Vestbanen, bâtiment italianisant de 1872, à proximité du port et de l'hôtel de ville d'Oslo. Un portail d'entrée indépendant, semblable à une sculpture contemporaine, accueille les visiteurs, sa peau perforée dessinant une carte des conflits dans le monde. Adjaye joue sur la couleur dans la zone d'accueil (rouge saturé), dans le passage d'honneur (or) ou dans le restaurant du Café de la Paix (motifs verts de Chris Ofili). Pour les expositions, il a collaboré avec l'Américain David Small qui a créé des installations vidéo à partir de matériaux réunis par des historiens et un « livre » électronique sur la vie d'Alfred Nobel. Le coût du bâtiment s'est élevé à 14,1 millions d'euros et le projet dit « de communication », dont faisait partie l'aménagement intérieur, à 7,4 millions d'euros.

The former Vestbanen Railway Station (1872) was refurbished and a powerful rectangular entrance canopy added opposite the main entrance of the building.

Der ehemalige Vestbanen-Bahnhof von 1872 wurde umgebaut; vor dem Haupteingang wurde ein schwerer rechteckiger Portalbogen platziert.

L'ancienne gare de Vestbanen (1872) a été restaurée et un portique rectangulaire aux formes puissantes implanté devant l'entrée du bâtiment.

The red entrance area and the spectacular Passage of Honor, with its portraits of Nobel Peace Prize laureates, set the tone of the project, using the generous spaces of the building to their maximum effect.

Der rote Eingangsbereich und der spektakuläre »Weg der Ehre« mit Porträts der Nobelpreisträger bestimmen die Atmosphäre im Gebäude und nutzen dessen großzügige Räumlichkeiten mit maximaler Wirkung.

L'entrée de couleur rouge et le spectaculaire « passage d'honneur » orné des portraits des lauréats du prix Nobel de la paix donnent le ton à ce projet qui tire le maximum d'effets des généreux volumes du bâtiment.

AUER+WEBER

Auer+Weber+Assoziierte
Haussmannstrasse 103a
70188 Stuttgart
Germany

Tel: +49 711 26 84 04 0
Fax: +49 711 26 84 04 88
e-mail: stuttgart@auer-weber.de
Web: www.auer-weber.de

ESO Hote

Fritz Auer, born in Tübingen in 1933, studied at the Technische Hochschule in Stuttgart beginning in 1953. He obtained a scholarship from the Cranbrook Academy of Arts and received his Master of Architecture degree there in 1959. He became a partner in the firm of Behnisch & Partner in 1966 and created the office **AUER+WEBER** in 1980. Carlo Weber was born in Saarbrücken in 1934 and also attended the Technische Hochschule in Stuttgart before going to the Beaux Arts in Paris. Like Auer, he became a partner at Behnisch & Partner in 1966. They have worked extensively on urban renewal, in Bonn, Stuttgart and other cities. They completed the University Library of Magdeburg in 2003; the Welle department store in Bielefeld in 2003; and are working on the Science Park of Ulm; the Alter Hof urban renewal project in Munich; retirement centers in Landau, Pforzheim-Huchenfeld and Keltern-Ellmendingen; the General Archives of Karlsruhe and the District Administration Center in Tübingen.

Fritz Auer, 1933 in Tübingen geboren, begann sein Studium 1953 an der Technischen Hochschule in Stuttgart. Er erhielt ein Stipendium von der Cranbrook Academy of Arts und schloss dort 1959 mit einem Master of Architecture ab. 1966 wurde er Partner im Büro Behnisch & Partner und gründete 1980 das Architekturbüro **AUER+WEBER**. Carlo Weber, geboren 1934 in Saarbrücken, studierte ebenfalls an der Technischen Hochschule Stuttgart, bevor er nach Paris ging, um dort die Ecole des Beaux-Arts zu besuchen. Wie Auer wurde er 1966 Partner im Büro Behnisch & Partner. Auer+Weber haben sich ausgiebig mit Stadterneuerung in Bonn, Stuttgart und anderen Städten beschäftigt. 2003 wurde die Universitätsbibliothek in Magdeburg fertig gestellt, ebenfalls 2003 das Welle-Kaufhaus in Bielefeld. Derzeit in der Planung sind der Wissenschaftspark in Ulm, das Sanierungsprojekt Alter Hof in München, Altenzentren bzw. Pflegestifte in Landau, Pforzheim-Huchenfeld und Keltern-Ellmendingen, das Generallandesarchiv in Karlsruhe und das Landratsamt in Tübingen.

Fritz Auer, né à Tübingen en 1933, a commencé ses études à la Technische Hochschule de Stuttgart en 1953. Il a été boursier de la Cranbrook Academy of Arts où il a obtenu son Master of Architecture en 1959. Devenu partenaire de l'agence Behnisch & Partner en 1966, il a créé sa propre structure, **AUER+WEBER**, en 1980. Carlo Weber, né à Sarrebruck en 1934, a également commencé ses études à la Technische Hochschule de Stuttgart, puis les a poursuivies à l'École nationale supérieure des beaux-arts de Paris. Comme Auer, il a été partenaire de Behnisch & Partner. Ils ont eu en charge de nombreux projets de rénovation urbaine, notamment à Bonn et à Stuttgart. Parmi leurs réalisations : la Bibliothèque universitaire de Magdebourg (2003) et le grand magasin Welle à Bielefeld (2003). Ils travaillent actuellement au projet de Parc des sciences d'Ulm, à celui de la rénovation urbaine de l'Alter Hof à Munich, à des maisons de retraite à Landau, Pforzheim-Huchenfeld et Keltern-Ellmendingen, des Archives générales de Karlsruhe et du Centre administratif du district de Tübingen.

ESO HOTEL

Cerro Paranal, Chile, 1998–2002

Floor area: 12 000 m². Cubic volume: 40 000 m³. Client: ESO European Southern Observatory, Munich.
Cost: €11 million

This 12 000 m², 11 million euro hotel is located at an altitude of 2400 m in the mountainous northern area of the Atacama desert in Chile. The reason for th unusual location is the proximity of the Very Large Telescope (VLT) on the Cerro Paranal. Operated by the European Southern Observatory (ESO), an organization base in Munich, the VLT is "the most powerful telescope based on earth." The **ESO HOTEL** serves the scientists and engineers who work in the facility. As the architec describe it, "For the relatively short time of their stays under extreme climatic conditions – intense sunlight, extreme dryness, high wind speeds, great fluctuations in tem perature and the danger of earthquakes – a place has been created far away from civilization where they can relax and rest between the strenuous phases of their wor Reminiscent of an oasis, it provides 120 hotel rooms, a canteen and lounge areas, as well as a swimming pool, fitness center and library." Auer+Weber have set the hote into a natural depression in the ground, allowing only a 35-meter-wide dome over the central lounge to rise above the horizon line. This obviously unusual setting seem to have inspired the architects to create a structure which is at once in harmony with the surroundings and yet provides refuge and a point from which to observe natur

Das 12 000 m² große, 11 Millionen Euro teure Hotel befindet sich auf einer Höhe von 2400 m in der bergigen Atacamawüste im Norden Chiles. Grund für die sen ungewöhnlichen Standort ist die Nähe zum Riesenteleskop auf dem Cerro Paranal, das vom European Southern Observatory (ESO), einer Organisation mit Sitz in Mür chen, betrieben wird. Das Very Large Telescope (VLT) ist »das stärkste Teleskop der Erde«. Das **ESO HOTEL** steht den Wissenschaftlern und Ingenieuren, die in der Eir richtung arbeiten, zur Verfügung. Die Architekten beschreiben es so: »Für die relativ kurze Zeit, die die Mitarbeiter unter extremen klimatischen Bedingungen – intensiv Sonneneinstrahlung, extreme Trockenheit, starke Windgeschwindigkeiten, große Temperaturunterschiede und die Gefahr von Erdbeben – hier verbringen, wurde weit we von der Zivilisation ein Ort geschaffen, an dem man sich entspannen und zwischen den anstrengenden Phasen der Arbeit ausruhen kann. Das Hotel ähnelt einer Oase es bietet 120 Hotelzimmer, eine Kantine, Loungebereiche, einen Swimmingpool, ein Fitnesszentrum und eine Bibliothek.« Auer+Weber haben das Hotel in einer natürl chen Senke angeordnet, so dass nur die flache Kuppel über der zentralen Lounge mit einem Durchmesser von 35 m über die Horizontlinie hinausragt. Die außerge wöhnliche Lage hat die Architekten dazu inspiriert, ein Gebäude zu schaffen, das einerseits mit der Umgebung harmoniert, gleichzeitig aber ein Refugium und ein Ort fü Naturbeobachtungen ist.

Cet hôtel de 12 000 m² réalisé pour un budget de 11 millions d'euros est situé à 2400 m d'altitude dans le nord du désert montagneux d'Atacama au Chili. L raison du choix de ce site étrange est la proximité du Très Grand Télescope du Cerro Paranal. Géré par l'European Southern Observatory basé à Munich, le TGT est plus puissant télescope jamais construit. L'**HÔTEL ESO** est destiné aux scientifiques et ingénieurs qui y travaillent. Les architectes présentent ainsi l'esprit de leur pro jet : « Pour la durée relativement brève de leurs séjours dans des conditions climatiques particulièrement rudes – soleil intense, sècheresse extrême, vents très forts grandes fluctuations de la température et risques sismiques – il fallait créer un lieu où l'on puisse se détendre et se reposer entre des tours de service épuisants. Rap pelant une oasis, [l'hôtel] offre 120 chambres, un restaurant, des salles de repos, une piscine, un centre de remise en forme et une bibliothèque. » Auer+Weber or implanté le bâtiment au cœur d'une dépression naturelle. Seule la coupole de 35 mètres de diamètre coiffant le salon central s'élève au-dessus de la ligne d'horizor Ce site étonnant leur a inspiré une structure qui s'harmonise à son cadre naturel, tout en offrant un refuge et un endroit d'où l'on peut observer la nature.

In this lunar landscape, the architecture takes on an ethereal presence, its repetitive façade emitting light from cutouts that alternate with more open glazed areas.

Die Architektur hat in dieser Mondlandschaft eine unwirkliche Präsenz. Die ausgestanzten Fensteröffnungen in der gleichmäßigen Fassade reflektieren das Licht; dazwischen sind verglaste Flächen angeordnet.

Dans ce paysage lunaire, l'architecture revêt une présence éthérée. La lumière émane de la façade au rythme répétitif, à travers des découpes alternant avec des plans vitrés.

Though it appears to be no more than a bar from certain angles, the hotel is carefully inserted into the dry, undulating landscape whose only other remarkable feature is the ESO telescope.

Aus bestimmten Blickwinkeln betrachtet scheint das Hotel die Form eines einfachen Riegels zu haben. Tatsächlich ist es jedoch behutsam in die trockene, bergige Umgebung eingefügt, in der ansonsten nur das ESO-Teleskop auffällt.

Bien que, sous certains angles, il fasse penser à une barre, l'hôtel est judicieusement inséré dans son paysage lunaire et désertique, à proximité de l'autre intervention humaine remarquable dans la région, le Très Grand Télescope ESO.

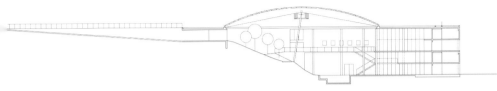

Where the earth offers a spectacle of desolation, the architects have correctly chosen to make use of light. The earth and the sky are the spectacle here and the hotel opens toward both, while protecting its residents from the surrounding harshness.

Wo die Erde nur ein »Schauspiel der Verlassenheit« bietet, haben sich die Architekten richtigerweise dafür entschieden, das Licht zu nutzen. Erde und Himmel sind hier die wesentlichen Elemente, und beiden öffnet sich das Hotel. Gleichzeitig schützt es seine Bewohner vor der unwirtlichen Umgebung.

Parce que le sol lui-même n'offre qu'un spectacle de désolation, les architectes ont décidé d'utiliser la lumière au maximum. La terre et le ciel sont le spectacle sur lequel s'ouvre cet hôtel chargé de protéger ses hôtes d'un environnement hostile.

SHIGERU BAN

Shigeru Ban Architects
5–2–4 Matsubara
Setagaya-ku, Tokyo 156-0043
Japan

Tel: +81 333 24 67 60
Fax: +81 333 24 67 89
e-mail: tokyo@shigerubanarchitects.com
Web: www.shigerubanarchitects.com

Bianimale Nomadic Mus

Born in 1957 in Tokyo, **SHIGERU BAN** studied at the Southern California Institute of Architecture (SciArc) from 1977 to 1980. He attended the Cooper Unio School of Architecture, where he studied under John Hejduk (1980–82). He worked in the office of Arata Isozaki (1982–83) before founding his own firm in Tokyo i 1985. His work includes numerous exhibition designs like the Alvar Aalto show at the Axis Gallery, Tokyo (1986). His buildings include the Odawara Pavilion, Kanagaw (1990); the Paper Gallery, Tokyo (1994); the Paper House, Lake Yamanaka (1995); and the Paper Church, Takatori, Hyogo (1995). He has also designed ephemeral struc tures such as his Paper Refugee Shelter made with plastic sheets and paper tubes for the United Nations High Commission for Refugees (UNHCR). He designed the Japan ese Pavilion at Expo 2000 in Hanover. Current work includes a small museum of Canal History in Pouilly-en-Auxois, France; the Schwartz Residence, Sharon, Connecti cut; Forest Park Pavilion – Bamboo Gridshell-02, St. Louis, Missouri; Mul(ti)houses, Mulhouse, France; Sagaponac House/Furniture House-05, Long Island, New York Hanegi Forest Annex, Setagaya, Tokyo; and the new Pompidou Center in Metz, France.

SHIGERU BAN, 1957 in Tokio geboren, studierte von 1977 bis 1980 am Southern California Institute of Architecture (SCI-Arc) und von 1980 bis 1982 bei Joh. Hejduk an der Cooper Union School of Architecture in New York. Von 1982 bis 1983 arbeitete er im Büro von Arata Isozaki und gründete 1985 seine eigene Firma i Tokio. Shigeru Ban gestaltete zahlreiche Ausstellungen, so die 1986 in der Galerie Axis in Tokio gezeigte Alvar-Aalto-Schau. Zu seinen Bauten gehören u. a. der Odawa ra Pavillon in Kanagawa (1990), die Paper Gallery in Tokio (1994), das Paper House am Yamanaka-See (1995) und die Paper Church in Takatori, Hyogo (1995). Ban ha auch Behelfsbauten entworfen wie sein für den Hohen Flüchtlingskommissar der Vereinten Nationen (UNHCR) aus Plastikfolie und Pappröhren gebauter Paper Refuge Shelter. Für die Expo 2000 in Hannover plante er den japanischen Pavillon. Zu seinen jüngsten Projekten zählen ein kleines Museum für die Geschichte des Kanalbau im französischen Pouilly-en-Auxois, das Haus Schwartz in Sharon, Connecticut, der Forest Park Pavilion – Bamboo Gridshell-02 in St. Louis, Missouri, die Mul(ti)house im französischen Mulhouse, das Haus Sagaponac/Furniture House-05 in Long Island, New York, sowie ein Gebäude in Hanegi Forest, Setagaya, Tokio, und das Centre Pompidou in Metz.

Né en 1957 à Tokyo, **SHIGERU BAN** étudie au Southern California Institute of Architecture (SCI-Arc) de 1977 à 1980, puis à la Cooper Union School of Archi tecture, où il suit l'enseignement de John Hejduk (1980–82). Il travaille pour Arata Isozaki (1982–83), avant de fonder son agence à Tokyo en 1985. Il a conçu de nom breuses expositions (notamment celle sur Alvar Aalto, Axis Gallery, Tokyo, 1986). Parmi ses réalisations architecturales : le Pavillon Odawara, Kanagawa (1990) ; la Pape Gallery, Tokyo (1997) ; la Maison de papier, Lac Yamanaka (1995) et l'Église de papier, Takatori, Hyogo (1995). Il conçoit également des structures éphémères, comm son abri pour réfugiés en feuilles de plastique et tubes de carton, pour le Haut Commissariat aux Réfugiés (HCR) des Nations Unies. Il a signé le pavillon japonais à l'Ex po 2000 de Hanovre. Parmi ses réalisations figurent le Centre d'interprétation du canal de Bourgogne (Pouilly-en-Auxois, France) et, en cours, la Schwartz Residence (Sharon, Connecticut) ; le Forest Park Pavilion – Bamboo Gridshell-02 (Saint Louis, Missouri) ; Mul(ti)houses (Mulhouse, France) ; Sagaponac House/Furniture House-05 (Long Island, New York) ; un bâtiment dans la forêt de Hanegi (Setagaya, Tokyo) et le nouveau Centre Pompidou à Metz (France).

BIANIMALE NOMADIC MUSEUM

New York, New York, USA, 2005

Floor area: 4180 m². Client: Ashes and Snow, LLC.
Cost: not disclosed

The **BIANIMALE NOMADIC MUSEUM** was a 4180 m² structure intended to house *Ashes and Snow*, an exhibition of large-scale photographs by Gregory Colbert, on view in New York from March 5 to June 6, 2005. No less than 205 meters long, the 16-meter-high rectangular building was made up essentially of steel shipping containers and paper tubes made from recycled paper, with inner and outer waterproof membranes and coated with a waterproof sealant. Located on Pier 54 of Manhattan's Lower West side, the building had a central 3.6-meter-wide wooden walkway composed of recycled scaffolding planks lined on either side with river stones. The overall impression of this structure was not unlike that of a temple, or as the architect wrote, "The simple triangular gable design of the roof structure and ceremonial, columnar interior walkway of the museum echo the atmosphere of a classical church." The first building to be made from shipping containers in New York, the Nomadic Museum is an intriguing effort to employ recyclable materials to create a large-scale structure. Despite the rather difficult access to the site and high entrance fee, many New Yorkers went to visit Ban's museum, perhaps more intrigued by its spectacular outer and interior forms than by the theatrical photographs of Colbert.

Das 4180 m² große **NOMADISCHE MUSEUM** wurde eigens für die Ausstellung »Ashes and Snow« errichtet. Die Show, vom 5. März bis zum 6. Juni 2005 in New York zu sehen, zeigte die großformatigen Fotografien von Gregory Colbert. Nicht weniger als 205 m lang, bestand die 16 m hohe rechteckige Konstruktion im Wesentlichen aus Frachtcontainern und Papprohren aus recyceltem Papier, die innen und außen mit einer wasserdichten Folie versehen und wasserundurchlässig imprägniert waren. Standort der Konstruktion war der Pier 54 auf der Lower West Side im Süden Manhattans. Ein 3,6 m breiter Weg aus recycelten Gerüstbrettern, auf beiden Seiten mit Flussbettsteinen gefasst, führte durch die Mitte des Gebäudes. Der Gesamteindruck ähnelte dem eines Tempels oder mit den Worten des Architekten: »Das dreieckige, einfache Satteldach und der zeremonielle, von Stützen gesäumte innere Weg des Museums erinnern an die Atmosphäre in einer alten Kirche.« Das Nomadische Museum war das erste Gebäude in New York, das aus Frachtcontainern gebaut wurde – ein verblüffender Versuch, recycelbares Material für eine Konstruktion in großem Maßstab zu verwenden. Trotz des hohen Eintrittgeldes und des eher schwierigen Zugangs zum Standort besuchten viele New Yorker Shigeru Bans Museum. Möglicherweise waren sie mehr an dessen spektakulären inneren und äußeren Formen als an den theatralischen Fotografien von Colbert interessiert.

Ce **MUSÉE NOMADE** était une structure éphémère de 4180 m² conçue pour l'exposition de photographies de très grand format de Gregory Colbert, « Ashes and Snow », organisée par la Bianimale Foundation que dirige l'artiste, qui s'est déroulée à New York (Hudson River at 13th Street) du 5 mars au 6 juin 2005. Cette construction rectangulaire de 205 m de long sur 16 m de haut était essentiellement composée de conteneurs d'expédition en acier et de tubes de carton recyclé, totalement imperméabilisés et gainés d'un isolant étanche. Installé sur le Pier 54 dans le quartier du Lower West Side à Manhattan, le bâtiment était traversé par une allée centrale de 3,6 m de large en planches d'échafaudage recyclées, bordées de galets des deux côtés. L'impression donnée était celle d'un temple où, comme l'a écrit l'architecte, « le dessin très simple du pignon triangulaire de la toiture et l'allée principale bordée de colonnes évoquaient l'atmosphère d'une église classique ». Premier bâtiment réalisé à New York à partir de conteneurs, le Nomadic Museum est une intéressante tentative d'utilisation à grande échelle de matériaux recyclables. Malgré l'accès assez difficile au site et le prix élevé de l'entrée, de nombreux New-Yorkais ont visité cette exposition, peut-être plus par curiosité pour cette construction spectaculaire que pour les photographies théâtrales de Colbert.

Built out of paper tubes and shipping containers, Ban's Nomadic Museum actually seemed very much at home in its dockside setting.

Bans Nomadic Museum aus Papprohren und Frachtcontainern passte in die Umgebung der Docks sehr gut hinein.

L'environnement portuaire convenait parfaitement au Nomadic Museum de Ban, construit à partir de conteneurs d'expédition en acier et de tubes en carton.

By alternating the alignments of the containers, Ban made the long building much more visually interesting than it might have been had he simply stacked the elements in solid rows.

Ban ordnete die Container auf Lücke an. Dadurch wurde das lange Gebäude optisch viel interessanter, als wenn er die Container einfach nur aufeinander gestapelt hätte.

En alternant ses alignements de conteneurs, Ban a rendu cette longue construction plus intéressante visuellement qu'avec un empilement uniforme.

Though the Nomadic Museum was extremely simple, and repetitive in its structural principles, the vast interior space with its controlled natural lighting and central wooden walkway immediately took on the appearance of a temple-like space.

Obwohl das Nomadic Museum ein extrem einfaches Gebäude mit einer repetitiven Struktur war, strahlte der riesige Innenraum mit seiner kontrolliert eingesetzten Tageslicht-lichtung und dem hölzernen Mittel-gang eine sakrale Atmosphäre aus.

De principe structurel extrêmement simple et répétitif, le Nomadic Museum n'en offre pas moins un vaste volume intérieur doté d'un éclairage naturel contrôlé et d'une allée centrale en bois qui évoque l'image d'un temple.

PAPER TEMPORARY STUDIO

6th floor terrace, Centre Georges Pompidou, Paris, France, 2004

Floor area: 115 m². Client: Shigeru Ban Architects. Cost: not disclosed

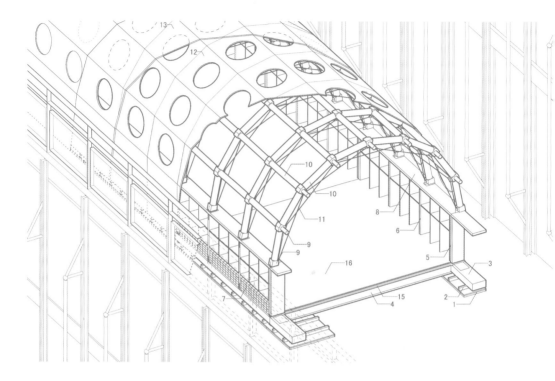

As Shigeru Ban describes this project, "After winning the competition for Centre Pompidou Metz, Centre Pompidou's new facility in the city of Metz, I suggeste half jokingly to Mr Bruno Racine, the director of the Centre Pompidou that 'The agreed design fee is not sufficient for an architectural office from a foreign country li us to rent an office in Paris. So if you could lend us space on the terrace, we can build our temporary office.' Unexpectedly, Racine agreed and Ban created a 115 n temporary arched office on top of the Piano & Rogers landmark. With the approval of Renzo Piano, Ban designed a paper tube structure with some use of timber a steel. The roof is made of titanium dioxide PTFE membrane, regular PTFE membrane, and PVC membrane. The interior is finished with tile carpet, wood deck and Vit furniture. Since one of Racine's original requirements was that the office be fully visible to Centre Pompidou visitors, Shigeru Ban concludes, 'Please come visit us wh you have chance to come to Paris. Though as we are part of the exhibit, it would require that you buy an admission ticket at the entrance.'"

Shigeru Ban beschreibt dieses Projekt so: »Nachdem ich den Wettbewerb für das Centre Pompidou Metz (eine neue Dependance des Centre Pompidou) gewo nen hatte, schlug ich dem Direktor, Bruno Racine, halb im Scherz vor: ›Das Entwurfshonorar reicht für ein Architekturbüro aus dem Ausland wie wir es sind nicht au Büroräume in Paris zu mieten. Wenn Sie uns Platz auf Ihrer Terrasse überlassen, können wir dort ein temporäres Büro bauen.‹ Wider Erwarten stimmte Racine zu, ur Ban entwarf ein 115 m² großes, halbtonnenförmiges Büro auf dem Dach des Wahrzeichens von Piano und Rogers. Mit Renzo Pianos Zustimmung entwickelte Ban ei Konstruktion aus Papprohren, die durch wenig Holz und Stahl ergänzt wird. Das Dach besteht aus einer PTFE-Folie aus Titandioxid, einer normalen PTFE-Folie und ei PVC-Folie. Der Innenraum ist mit Teppichfliesen, einem Holzdeck und Möbeln von Vitra gestaltet. Da eine der ursprünglichen Forderungen von Racine war, dass das Bü jederzeit für Besucher des Centre Pompidou zu besichtigen sei, sagt Shigeru Ban: »Bitte besuchen Sie uns, wenn Sie die Möglichkeit haben, nach Paris zu kommen. wir Teil der Ausstellung sind, müssen Sie dafür aber eine Eintrittskarte für das Museum kaufen.«

Shigeru Ban présente ainsi ce projet : « Après avoir remporté le concours du Centre Pompidou à Metz, j'ai expliqué en plaisantant à demi à Bruno Racine, dire teur du Centre, que les honoraires d'une agence étrangère comme la nôtre ne nous permettaient pas de louer des bureaux à Paris et donc, que s'il nous prêtait un pe d'espace sur sa terrasse, nous pourrions y construire des bureaux temporaires. » Surprise : Bruno Racine donna son accord et Ban créa ces bureaux en forme d'arch de 115 m² tout en haut du monument signé par Piano et Rogers. Avec l'approbation de Renzo Piano, Ban conçut une structure faite de tubes de carton et de diverse pièces de bois et d'acier. Le toit se compose de trois membranes en PTFE au dioxyde de titane, PTFE classique et PVC. Le sol est en bois recouvert de dalles de moquette et les meubles viennent de chez Vitra. Comme l'une des demandes de Bruno Racine était que les visiteurs du Centre puissent voir ces bureaux, Ban les y invite : « Ven donc nous voir si vous avez la chance de passer par Paris, mais comme nous faisons partie des pièces exposées, vous devrez acheter un billet d'entrée... »

Sitting on top of the Pompidou Center, just opposite the Georges Restaurant and the entrance to the temporary exhibition areas, Ban's studio is alien to the Piano and Rogers architecture, and yet somehow fits in comfortably.

Bans Büro auf dem Dach des Centre Georges Pompidou liegt direkt gegenüber dem Restaurant »Georges« und dem Eingang zu den Sonderausstellungen. Mit der Architektur von Piano und Rogers hat es wenig gemein, fügt sich aber trotzdem gut ein.

Tout en haut du Centre Pompidou, face au restaurant Georges et à l'entrée des expositions temporaires, l'atelier de Ban, s'il reste étranger à l'architecture de Piano et Rogers, ne s'en est pas moins confortablement installé.

A flexible, bright and open workspace allows Ban and his team to be permanently in proximity to their client for the Pompidou Center Metz project on which he is working.

Der flexibel nutzbare, helle und offene Arbeitsraum von Ban und seinem Team liegt in der Nähe des Büros seines Auftraggebers – derzeit plant Ban das Centre Pompidou Metz.

Cet espace de travail flexible, ouvert et lumineux, permet à Shigeru Ban et à son équipe de travailler à proximité de leur commanditaire pour le Centre Pompidou de Metz.

Visitors to the Pompidou Center's exhibitions can get a glimpse inside the Paper Temporary Studio after they pass through the ticketing area near the building's famous moving walkway.

Nachdem die Besucher des Centre Georges Pompidou in der Nähe der berühmten Rolltreppen ihre Eintrittskarte gekauft haben, können sie einen Blick in das Paper Temporary Studio werfen.

Les visiteurs des expositions du Centre peuvent apercevoir le Paper Temporary Studio après la billetterie, à quelques mètres seulement du fameux escalier mécanique.

BARCLAY & CROUSSE

Barclay & Crousse Architecture
7, Passage Saint Bernard
75011 Paris
France

Tel: +33 149 23 51 36
Fax: +33 148 07 88 32
e-mail: atelier@barclaycrousse.com
Web: www.barclaycrousse.com

Casa Equ

JEAN-PIERRE CROUSSE was born in 1963. He was educated at the Universidad Ricardo Palma in Lima, Peru and at Milan Polytechnic, Milan, Italy were he received a European architecture degree. **SANDRA BARCLAY** was born in 1967 and also studied at the Universidad Ricardo Palma, before getting a French architecture degree (D. P. L. G.) at the Ecole d'architecture de Paris-Belleville (1993). Their built work includes the reconstruction of the Musée Malraux, Le Havre, France (1999); an office building in Malakoff, Paris, France (2003); the M House, Cañete, Peru (2001); B House, Cañete, Peru (1999); and a renovation of the City Hall of Epinay-sur-Seine, France (2004). Projects include the H House in the Gers region of France (2005); the B&F House in the Haute Savoie region of France and welfare housing in Malakoff, Paris (2005).

JEAN-PIERRE CROUSSE, geboren 1963, studierte an der Universidad Ricardo Palma in Lima, Peru, und am Politecnico in Mailand, wo er einen europäischen Architekturabschluss erwarb. **SANDRA BARCLAY** wurde 1967 geboren und studierte ebenfalls an der Universidad Ricardo Palma, bevor sie 1993 ihren französischen Architekturabschluss (D. P. L. G.) an der Ecole d'Architecture de Paris-Belleville machte. Zu ihren realisierten Projekten gehören die Sanierung des Musée Malraux in Le Havre (1999), ein Bürogebäude in Malakoff, Paris (2003), das Haus B und das Haus M in Cañete, Peru (1999 und 2001), und die Instandsetzung des Rathauses von Epinay-sur-Seine (2004). Projektiert sind u. a. das Haus H im Departement Gers (2005), das Haus B&F in der Haute Savoie und ein sozialer Wohnungsbau in Malakoff, Paris (2005).

JEAN-PIERRE CROUSSE, né en 1963, a étudié à l'Universidad Ricardo Palma à Lima (Pérou) et à l'École Polytechnique de Milan où il a obtenu son diplôme européen d'architecte. **SANDRA BARCLAY**, née en 1967, a également fait ses études à l'Universidad Ricardo Palma, puis à l'École d'architecture de Paris-Belleville (1993). Elle est architecte D. P. L. G. Parmi leurs réalisations : la rénovation du musée Malraux, Le Havre, France (1999) ; un immeuble de bureaux, Malakoff, France (2003) ; la maison B et la maison M (1999 et 2001, Cañete, Pérou) et la rénovation de l'hôtel de ville d'Épinay-sur-Seine, France (2004). Ils ont actuellement en projet la Maison H dans le Gers (2005), la Maison B&F en Haute-Savoie et des logements sociaux à Malakoff.

CASA EQUIS

Cañete, Peru, 2003

Floor area: 174 m². Client: Juan Carlos Verme. Cost: $75 000

CASA M

CASA EQUIS

This 174 m² residence was built in the same area as the architects' B House and their earlier M House (located directly next to the Casa Equis). As the archi tects say, the project "attempts to create the intimacy or domesticity necessary in order to live in the desert where the house is located, without denying or falsifying the situation." They chose to fully occupy the site and to create "a pure prism, that landed in the dunes, but gives the impression that it was always there." Their concept was to dig the living spaces out of the "pre-existing" prism, "a little like archeologists clearing away the sand and revealing Pre-Columbian ruins." Creating a maximum amount of ambiguity between exterior and interior spaces, they attempted to relate each area of the house to the sky or the neighboring ocean. Cut into the hillside, the house has an upper level entry from the road with and social spaces (living/dining, kitchen and suspended swimming pool), and a lower level with master bedroom, chil dren's room and guest room, terraces and a beach entrance. The Casa Equis won the prize for the best work of architecture at the Fourth Ibero-American Architecture Biennale in Lima, Peru (2004).

Das 174 m² große Einfamilienhaus befindet sich in derselben Gegend wie das Haus B und das frühere Haus M der Architekten, das direkt neben der Casa Equis steht. Wie Barclay & Crousse sagen, versuchen sie mit dem Projekt »die Intimität und Häuslichkeit zu schaffen, die man braucht, um in der Wüste zu leben, wo dieses Haus steht, ohne die Situation zu leugnen oder zu verfälschen«. Sie entschieden sich dafür, das Grundstück komplett zu bebauen und »ein reines Prisma« zu schaffen »das in den Dünen gelandet ist, aber den Eindruck vermittelt, als ob es schon immer hier gewesen sei«. Die konzeptionelle Idee war, die Wohnräume aus einem gedank lich schon vorhandenen Prisma »auszugraben«, »ungefähr so, wie Archäologen Sand abtragen, um präkolumbianische Ruinen freizulegen.« Jeder Bereich des Hauses sollte in einen Bezug zum Himmel und zum nahe gelegenen Ozean gesetzt werden, wodurch ein Maximum an Doppeldeutigkeit zwischen Außen- und Innenraum erreich wurde. Das Haus ist in das hügelige Terrain eingeschnitten; auf der oberen Ebene liegen der straßenseitige Eingang und die gemeinschaftlich genutzten Räume (Wohn- und Essraum, Küche) sowie ein aufgeständerter Swimmingpool. Auf der unteren Ebene sind das Elternschlafzimmer, ein Kinder- und Gästezimmer, Terrassen sowie ein Strandeingang angeordnet. Die Casa Equis gewann den ersten Preis in der Kategorie Architektur bei der IV. Iberoamerikanischen Architekturbiennale in Lima (2004).

Cette résidence de 174 m² a été construite non loin de la Maison B et de la Maison M réalisées par les mêmes architectes. Pour ses auteurs, ce projet tente de « créer l'intimité ou les conditions de vie familiale requises pour vivre dans le désert où se trouve la maison, sans nier ni truquer la situation ». Ils ont choisi d'occuper la totalité du terrain et de créer « un prisme pur, qui aurait atterri dans les dunes, tout en donnant l'impression d'avoir toujours été là ». Leur concept était de creuser la zone de vie dans le prisme « préexistant », « un peu comme des archéologues dégagent le sable pour mettre au jour des ruines précolombiennes ». En créant le maxi mum d'ambiguïté entre les espaces intérieurs et extérieurs, ils ont voulu créer un lien entre chaque zone de la maison et le ciel ou l'océan tout proche. Découpée dans le flanc de la dune, l'entrée de la maison donnant sur la route est au niveau supérieur, qui regroupe les parties communes (séjour, salle à manger, cuisine, piscine sus pendue), tandis qu'au niveau inférieur se trouvent la chambre principale, celle des enfants, une chambre d'amis, des terrasses et l'accès à la plage. Cette maison a rem porté le prix de la meilleure œuvre à la 4ᵉ Biennale ibéro-américaine d'architecture de Lima en 2004.

The earlier Casa M by the same architects and the Casa Equis sit side-by-side on a cliff above the ocean. Variations on a theme, they both offer luxury and sophistication in a very rough natural setting.

Die Casa M und die Casa Equis – beide von Barclay & Crousse – liegen nebeneinander auf einem Felsen über dem Ozean. Als Variationen eines Themas bieten sie den Bewohnern Luxus und Kultiviertheit in einer kargen Natur.

Conçues par les mêmes architectes, la Casa M (plus ancienne) et la Casa Equis ont été édifiées côte à côte sur une falaise dominant l'océan. Variations sur un même thème, elles offrent à la fois luxe et sophistication dans un cadre naturel sauvage.

Alternating opaque and transparent surfaces, the architects use a strict, geometric vocabulary that opens toward the powerful natural setting while setting clear defensive boundaries.

Die Architekten benutzen ein streng geometrisches Vokabular aus geschlossenen und transparenten Flächen. Sie öffnen das Haus zur dominanten Umgebung, schaffen gleichzeitig aber auch klare und schützende Grenzen.

Alternant surfaces opaques et transparentes, les architectes ont utilisé un vocabulaire géométrique strict qui permet une ouverture sur un cadre naturel très présent tout en fixant clairement des limites quasi défensives.

...suspended pool, where a child ...ms to hover far above the ...shing waves, is one of the more ...usual features of the Casa Equis.

Der brückenartige Pool, in dem ein Kind hoch über der Brandung zu schweben scheint, ist eine Besonderheit der Casa Equis.

La piscine suspendue dans laquelle une enfant semble flotter au-dessus de vagues déferlantes de l'océan, est l'un des éléments les plus surprenants de la Casa Equis.

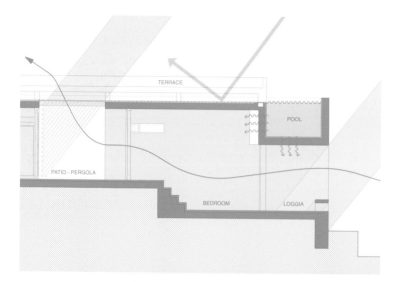

TERRACE

POOL

PATIO - PERGOLA

BEDROOM

LOGGIA

Large flat surfaces of color with ample use of light wood intentionally give a warmer aspect to the interior than to the exterior of the house. Sparsely furnished, the house is fully turned toward the spectacle of nature, while offering its residents a high level of civilized amenity.

Großzügige Farbflächen und viel helles Holz geben den Innenräumen bewusst einen wärmeren Ton als der äußeren Hülle. Das sparsam möblierte Haus ist vollständig auf das Naturschauspiel ausgerichtet und bietet seinen Bewohnern gleichzeitig ein hohes Maß an Komfort.

Ses vastes plans colorés et l'utilisation généreuse du bois clair donnent à l'intérieur un aspect plus chaleureux que celui de l'extérieur. Meublée avec parcimonie, la maison est tournée vers le spectacle de la nature, tout en offrant à ses résidents un excellent niveau de confort raffiné.

BAUMRAUM

baumraum
Andreas Wenning
Roonstrasse 49
28203 Bremen
Germany

Tel: +49 421 70 51 22
Fax: +49 421 794 63 51
e-mail: a.wenning@baumraum.de
Web: www.baumraum.de

Plendelhof Tree H...

Andreas Wenning was born in 1965. He studied as a cabinet maker in Weinheim, Germany (1982–85), and as an architect at the Technical University of Breme... where he obtained his degree in 1995. He worked in the office of Jose Garcia Negette in Sydney, Australia (2000–01) and he created his own office, **BAUMRAUM**, i... Bremen in 2003. Aside from the tree house published here, he has worked on web-like "grabnet" rope structures for trees (Lower Saxony Horticultural Show, Wolfsburg 2004) or organized seminars on "The Body Language of Trees," or "Building a Tree House without Impairing the Tree." His firm offers to build unique tree houses fo... clients. He has just finished a pavilion made of Corten steel for the Science Center of the University of Bremen.

Andreas Wenning wurde 1965 geboren. Von 1982 bis 1985 machte er eine Lehre als Möbeltischler in Weinheim. 1995 erwarb er an der Hochschule Bremen sei... Architekturdiplom. Er arbeitete im Büro von Jose Garcia Negette in Sydney (2000–01) und gründete 2003 in Bremen sein eigenes Büro **BAUMRAUM**. Neben dem hie... gezeigten Baumhaus entwarf Wenning netzartige, in Bäumen aufgehängte Seilkonstruktionen (»Fangnetze«) für die Niedersächsische Gartenschau 2004 in Wolfsburg un... hielt Seminare, z. B. »Die Körpersprache von Bäumen« oder »Baumhäuser bauen ohne Beschädigung des Baumes«. Das Büro bietet den Bau von einzigartigen Baum... häusern an. Erst kürzlich wurde ein Pavillon für das Wissenschaftszentrum der Universität Bremen aus Corten-Stahl fertig gestellt.

Andreas Wenning, né en 1965, a étudié l'ébénisterie à Weinheim, Allemagne (1982–85) et l'architecture à l'Université technique de Brême, dont il est sorti diplôm... en 1995. Il a travaillé dans l'agence Jose Garcia Negette à Sydney, Australie (2000–01) et créé la sienne, **BAUMRAUM**, à Brême en 2003. En dehors de la « maiso... dans l'arbre » publiée ici, il a élaboré des structures en cordage « grabnet » pour arbres, Exposition horticole de Basse-Saxe, Wolfsburg (2004) et organisé des séminaire... sur « Le langage corporel des arbres » ou « Construire une maison dans les arbres sans abîmer les arbres ». Son agence propose de construire des maisons dans le... arbres originales. Il vient d'achever un pavillon en acier Corten pour le Centre des sciences de l'Université de Brême.

PLENDELHOF TREE HOUSE

Gross-Henstedt, Germany, 2002–03

Floor area: 6 m² plus 4 m² terrace. Client: Andreas Wenning. Cost: €14 500

Andreas Wenning designed this tree house for two beech trees located at the Plendelhof Stables, about 30 kilometers south of Bremen, Germany. Set 8.6 meters off the ground the 950-kilo structure measures 7.5 x 2.6 meters and is two meters high. The triangular main frame is made of 100mm x 200mm larch beams. It is covered with larch boards, with 80mm of insulation between the inner and outer panels. The insulation allows the tree house to be used even in winter with a small heater inside. The total cost of the project was 14 500 euros. The house was designed to be small and yet to provide enough comfort for sleeping. Views in all directions and a sun terrace were also part of the original goals of the design. The architect opted for a "suspended structure anchored to the beeches with steel ropes." Assembled to the greatest extent possible on the ground, the house had to be easy to install without damage to the trees. Wenning also insists that the tree house does not "restrict the movement of the trees in terms of wind and growth." Although children can use this tree house, given its height off the ground it seems almost better suited to adults. Entered through a hatch, the tree house has a boat-like atmosphere inside.

Auf dem Plendelhof etwa 30 km südlich von Bremen befindet sich das von Andreas Wenning entworfene Baumhaus. Die in zwei Buchen gebaute, 950 kg schwere Konstruktion schwebt 8,6 m über dem Boden, misst 7,5 x 2,6 m und ist 2 m hoch. Der tragende, dreieckige Rahmen besteht aus Lärchenhölzern mit Querschnitten von 100 x 200 mm. Er ist mit zwei Schichten aus Lärchenholzbrettern verkleidet, zwischen denen eine 80 mm starke Dämmung angeordnet ist. Aufgrund der Dämmung und eines kleinen Heizgerätes kann das Baumhaus sogar im Winter benutzt werden. Die Gesamtkosten lagen bei 14 500 Euro. Das Haus sollte eher klein sein, aber ausreichenden Komfort bieten, um darin zu schlafen. Ziel des Entwurfs war auch, Ausblicke in alle Richtungen zu bieten und eine Sonnenterrasse vorzusehen. Der Architekt entschied sich für eine »Konstruktion, die mit Stahlseilen in den Buchen verankert ist«. Das Baumhaus wurde zum größten Teil auf der Erde zusammengefügt und sollte mit einfachen Mitteln an den Bäumen befestigt werden können, ohne diese zu beschädigen. Wenning besteht darauf, dass es »die Bewegung der Bäume, die durch Wind oder Wachstum verursacht werden, nicht behindert«. Auch wenn Kinder das Baumhaus benutzen können, ist es aufgrund seiner Höhe besser für Erwachsene geeignet. Eine Luke bildet den Eingang; in seinem Inneren herrscht eine bootsartige Atmosphäre.

Andreas Wenning a conçu cette maison à proximité des écuries de Plendelhof, à 30 km environ au sud de Brême. Calée entre deux hêtres à 8,6 m du sol, cette construction de 950 kg mesure 7,5 x 2,6 m pour 2 m de haut. L'ossature principale, triangulaire, est en poutres de mélèze de 10 x 20 cm de section. L'ensemble est habillé à l'intérieur comme à l'extérieur de planches de mélèze séparées par 80 mm de matériau isolant, ce qui permet d'utiliser la maison même en hiver, avec un petit radiateur. Le budget total du projet s'est élevé à 14 500 euros. La maison est petite, mais suffisante pour y dormir, et offre un petit solarium et des perspectives dans toutes les directions. L'architecte a opté pour une « structure suspendue accrochée aux arbres par des câbles d'acier ». Assemblée pour sa plus grande partie au sol, elle a pu être hissée sans dommage pour les arbres. Wenning insiste sur le fait que cette maison « n'entrave pas le mouvement des arbres, qu'il soit dû au vent ou à leur croissance ». Si les enfants peuvent l'utiliser, elle semble mieux adaptée à des adultes tant elle est loin du sol. À l'intérieur, où l'on pénètre par une trappe, on se sent comme dans un bateau.

The tree house obviously obeys different rules than its earthbound cousins, but Andreas Wenning has done everything necessary to protect the trees while creating a spectacular modern getaway almost nine meters off the ground.

Ein Baumhaus gehorcht zweifellos anderen Regeln als seine bodenständigen Verwandten. Andreas Wenning hat alles dafür getan, die Bäume zu schützen und einen spektakulären, modernen Rückzugsort fast 9 m über dem Erdboden zu schaffen.

La maison dans l'arbre obéit à des règles différentes de celles qui sont appliquées à ses cousines terrestres. Andreas Wenning a tout fait pour respecter les arbres, tout en créant ce spectaculaire abri moderne à près de neuf mètres du sol.

The triangular plan of the tree house is visible in these images, as is the careful placement of windows that allow visitors to take full advantage of the unexpected view.

Hier zu sehen sind der dreieckige Grundriss des Baumhauses und die überlegte Anordnung der Fenster, die dem Besucher optimale und überraschende Ausblicke bieten.

Ces images mettent en évidence le plan triangulaire de la maison et la disposition étudiée des fenêtres qui permettent de profiter pleinement de vues surprenantes.

CARAMEL

Caramel Architekten ZT GmbH
Katherl.Haller.Aspetsberger
Schottenfeldgasse 60/36
1070 Vienna
Austria

Tel: +43 15 96 34 90
Fax: +43 15 96 34 90 20
e-mail: kha@caramel.at
Web: www.caramel.at

Hou

CARAMEL was created in 2000 by Günter Katherl, born in 1965 in Vöcklabruck, Austria, Martin Haller, born in 1966 in Mittelberg, Vorarlberg, and Ulrich Aspets berger, born in 1967 in Linz. Their most recent commissions have resulted from their successful participation in international competitions. In addition to the realizatio of three large-scale projects – Wifi in Dornbirn (an advanced training center); Transfusionsmedizin LKH-Salzburg hospital institute, and the Betriebsgebäude, Ansfelde (plant facility) – the trio also devotes themselves to design studies and unconventional single-family dwelling projects. Other areas of activity include lectures, teaching and art projects, such as a remote-controlled "rain cloud" with which Caramel provided a "cool" surprise to visitors on the grounds of the Venice Architecture Biennal in 2004.

CARAMEL wurde 2000 von Günter Katherl, geboren 1965 in Vöcklabrück, Österreich, Martin Haller, geboren 1966 in Mittelberg, Vorarlberg, und Ulrich Aspets berger, geboren 1967 in Linz, gegründet. Ihre neuesten Aufträge entwickelten sich aus ihrer erfolgreichen Teilnahme an internationalen Wettbewerben. Zusätzlich zu de Realisierung von drei großen Projekten – Wifi in Dornbirn (ein modernes Trainingszentrum), ein Krankenhausinstitut für Transfusionsmedizin für das LKH Salzburg und di Betriebswerkstätte in Ansfelden – arbeitet das Trio an Entwurfsstudien und unkonventionellen Einfamilienhausprojekten. Die Architekten halten außerdem Vorträge, unter richten und beschäftigen sich mit Kunstprojekten, beispielsweise der ferngesteuerten »Regenwolke«, mit der Caramel 2004 den Besuchern der Architekturbiennale in Venedig eine »kühle« Überraschung bereitete.

L'agence **CARAMEL** a été fondée en 2000 par trois architectes autrichiens : Günter Katherl (né en 1965 à Vöcklabruck), Martin Haller (né en 1966 à Mittelberg et Ulrich Aspetsberger (né en 1967 à Linz). Leurs succès à divers concours internationaux leur ont valu récemment un certain nombre de commandes. En dehors de troi projets à grande échelle – Wifi à Dornbin (un centre de formation avancée), l'Institut médical de transfusion de l'hôpital LKH-Salzbourg et une usine à Ansfelden – le tri se consacre à des recherches de design et des projets de maisons individuelles hors des sentiers battus. Leurs activités comprennent également des conférences, l'en seignement et des projets artistiques comme le *Nuage de pluie* télécommandé avec lequel ils ont surpris les visiteurs de la 9e Biennale d'architecture de Venise en 2004

HOUSE H

Linz, Austria, 2002–04

Floor area: 249 m². Volume: 790 m³. Client: not disclosed.
Cost: € 350 000

This 245 m² residence is located on an 820 m² site overlooking the city of Linz and the Alps in the distance. Built with reinforced concrete and a fine steel struc￼ture, the house is clad in "polyurethane foil which was sprayed on a layer of oriented strand board (OSB), creating a homogenous surface that extends to the roof, wa￼and the bottom of the 13.5-meter cantilevered living room. This cantilever protects the children's play area from the rain and sun. The house is entered on the west si￼of the middle floor that contains a foyer, the kitchen, and a children's playroom. A half story up, the floating, glazed living room offers a panoramic view to the south. T￼angled overhang of the living room is clearly the defining architectural gesture of the house. Above the kitchen, the architects created a small TV lounge and an offic￼The ground floor is set into a slope that opens to the garden. A master bedroom, three children's rooms and two bathrooms, a fitness area and a wine cellar make ￼this lower level. Caramel collaborated with interior designer Friedrich Stiper for this house, as they had on another project for the same client, a conversion for the Lin￼based advertising company "Reklamebüro" completed in 2000. The garden design was the work of Doris Pühringer.

Das 245 m² große Einfamilienhaus mit Blick auf die Stadt Linz (und Fernblick auf die Alpen) steht auf einem 820 m² großen Grundstück. Es besteht aus Stah￼beton sowie einer filigranen Stahlkonstruktion und ist mit einer Schicht aus Polyurethan umhüllt, die auf OSB-Platten (Oriented Strand Board) gesprüht wurde. Die￼homogene Oberfläche findet sich auch auf dem Dach, den Wänden und der Unterseite des 13,5 m weit auskragenden Wohnraums. Die Auskragung schützt den Spie￼bereich der Kinder vor Regen und Sonne. Man betritt das Haus auf der Westseite der mittleren Ebene, wo sich der Eingangsbereich, die Küche und ein Spielraum für d￼Kinder befinden. Ein halbes Geschoss darüber bietet der fließende, verglaste Wohnraum einen Panoramablick Richtung Süden. Ganz offensichtlich definiert die archite￼tonische Geste des winkelförmig auskragenden Wohnraums das Haus. Über der Küche ordneten die Architekten eine kleine TV-Lounge und ein Büro an. Das Erdgescho￼ist in einen Hang hinein geschoben, der sich zum Garten hin öffnet. Auf dieser unteren Ebene liegen das Elternschlafzimmer, drei Kinderzimmer, zwei Badezimmer, e￼Fitnessbereich und ein Weinkeller. Wie bei einem anderen Projekt für denselben Bauherrn (einem Umbau für die in Linz ansässige Werbeagentur »Reklamebüro«, d￼2000 fertig gestellt wurde) arbeitete Caramel bei diesem Projekt mit dem Innenarchitekten Friedrich Stiper zusammen. Der Entwurf für den Garten stammt von Dor￼Pühringer.

Cette résidence de 245 m² est située sur un terrain de 820 m² dominant la ville de Linz et donnant, au loin, sur les Alpes. Elle est bâtie en béton armé sur u￼ossature en acier et habillée d'un film de polyuréthane projeté sur des panneaux d'OSB pour créer une surface homogène qui recouvre la toiture, les murs et la ba￼d'un séjour de 13,5 m de long en porte-à-faux. Ce dernier protège la zone de jeux des enfants du soleil et de la pluie. On entre par le côté ouest de l'étage interm￼diaire qui comprend le vestibule, la cuisine et la salle de jeux. Un demi-étage plus haut, le séjour vitré, comme suspendu, offre une vue panoramique plein sud. Son port￼à-faux incliné constitue le geste architectural majeur de la maison. Au-dessus de la cuisine ont été créés un petit salon de télévision et un bureau. Le rez-de-chaussé￼découpé dans la pente et ouvrant sur le jardin, est réservé à la chambre de maîtres et à trois chambres d'enfants, deux salles de bains, une salle de gymnastique et ￼cellier. Caramel a collaboré avec l'architecte d'intérieur Friedrich Stiper avec lequel l'agence avait déjà travaillé sur un autre projet pour le même client, le réaménag￼ment de l'agence de publicité Reklamebüro de Linz, achevé en 2000. Le jardin a été dessiné par Doris Pühringer.

With its spectacular cantilevered volume, House H has an unexpected sequence of strong cutaway shapes inside as well (below). Ample glazing around the cantilevered living space emphasizes an impression of lightness given by the house as seen from certain angles.

Der spektakulär auskragende Baukörper des Hauses H weist auch in seinem Inneren einige kräftige subtraktive Schnitte auf (unten). Die großzügige Verglasung des Wohnraums verstärkt den Eindruck der Leichtigkeit, den das Haus aus verschiedenen Blickwinkeln bietet.

Dans son porte-à-faux spectaculaire, la maison H présente une séquence inattendue de formes découpées aussi bien à l'intérieur qu'au-dessous. Sous certains angles, les vastes ouvertures vitrées autour du séjour renforcent l'impression de légèreté.

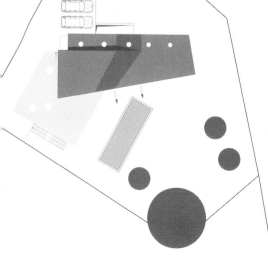

CASEY BROWN

Casey Brown Architecture
Level 1/ 63 William Street
NSW 2010 East Sydney
Australia

Tel: +61 293 60 79 77
Fax: +61 293 60 21 23
e-mail: cba@caseybrown.com.au
Web: www.caseybrown.com.au

James-Robertson H

Robert Brown received his degrees in architecture from the University of New South Wales (1976 and 1979) and from Columbia University Graduate School ⋅ Architecture in New York (1992–93). He worked with Fisher Lucas Architects in Sydney (1976), Julian Harap Architects in London (1983) and with the Heritage Counc NSW (1984–86) before creating Dawson Brown Partnership (1986–89), Dawson Brown + Ackert Architecture (1989–92) and Dawson Brown Architecture (1993–2004 In 2004, he created the firm **CASEY BROWN** with partner Caroline Casey. The James-Robertson House published here won a 2004 Residential Architecture Award from the Royal Australian Institute of Architects (NSW Chapter). Recent projects include the Sastrugi Ski Lodge, Thredbo (2000); Graigee Lee House, Palm Beach, Sydne (2001); Bungan Beach House, Bungan Beach, Sydney (2003). Current projects include: Djikul 5 Star boutique Hotel, Palm Cove, Queensland; Cliff House, Coogee, Sydne Whale Beach House, Whale Beach, Sydney.

Robert Brown studierte an der University of New South Wales Architektur (Abschlüsse 1976 und 1979) und später an der Columbia University Graduate Schoo of Architecture in New York (1992–93). 1976 arbeitete er in Sydney bei Lucas Architects, 1983 bei Julian Harap Architects in London und 1984 bis 1986 beim Herita ge Council von New South Wales. Anschließend gründete er Dawson Brown Partnership (1986–89), später Dawson Brown + Ackert Architecture (1989–92) und Dawso Brown Architecture (1993–2004). Zusammen mit Caroline Casey eröffnete Brown 2004 **CASEY BROWN**. Das hier gezeigte James-Robertson House gewann 2004 eine Preis des Royal Australian Institute of Architects (Verband New South Wales) in der Kategorie Wohnbauten. Zu seinen neueren Projekten gehören die Sastrugi Ski Lodg in Thredbo (2003), das Graigee Lee House in Palm Beach, Sydney (2001), und das Bungan Beach House in Bungan Beach, Sydney (2003). Neueste Projekte sind u. a das kleine und exklusive Djikul 5 Star Hotel in Palm Cove, Queensland, das Cliff House in Coogee, Sydney, und das Whale Beach House in Whale Beach, Sydney.

Robert Brown est diplômé en architecture de l'Université de Nouvelle-Galles du Sud (1976 et 1979) et de la Graduate School of Architecture de Columbia Un versity à New York (1992–93). Il a travaillé pour Fisher Lucas Architects à Sydney (1976), Julian Harap Architects à Londres (1983) et le Heritage Council NSW (1984–86 avant de fonder Dawson Brown Partnership (1986–89), Dawson Brown + Ackert Architecture (1989–92) et Dawson Brown Architecture (1993–2004). En 2004, il a cré l'agence **CASEY BROWN** avec sa partenaire Caroline Casey. La James-Robertson House présentée ici a remporté le prix de l'Architecture résidentielle 2004 du Roya Australian Institute of Architects (pour la Nouvelle-Galles du Sud). Parmi ses récents projets : la Sastrugi Ski Lodge, Thredbo (2000) ; la maison Graigee Lee, Palm Beach Sydney (2001) ; la maison de plage de Bungan, Bungan, Sydney (2003). Il travaille actuellement au « boutique-hôtel » 5 étoiles Djikul (Palm Cove, Queensland), et su deux maisons à Sydney, Cliff House et Whale Beach House.

JAMES-ROBERTSON HOUSE

Great Mackerel Beach, New South Wales, Australia, 2001–03

Floor area: 183 m². Client: Marcia and Dougal James-Robertson.
Cost: €1.26 million

Although Great Mackerel Beach is located relatively close to the city of Sydney, it can only be acceded to by ferry, which means that its fifty houses are very secluded. The architect Robert Brown and his family spend time there, as do Marcia and Dougal James-Robertson, his clients for this residence. The black-painted exposed steel frame pavilions are anchored in the rock and set on a massive sandstone retaining wall. Largely glazed, the sidewalls and roofs are covered in corrugated copper. They are set on a massive, irregular wall of sandstone blocks, carved by hand from the cliff-side site. The lower double pavilion contains guest bedrooms with a kitchen and dining and living area on the top floor. The upper pavilion contains the owner's private area. The interior design work was done by Robert Brown's partner Caroline Casey, and includes a silver ash dining table four meters long and 60 mm thick. The site area is 720 m² and the house has a floor area of 183 m².

Great Mackerel Beach befindet sich relativ nah bei Sydney, ist aber nur mit der Fähre zu erreichen. Die 50 Häuser, die es dort gibt, liegen daher sehr für sich. Wie die Bauherren Marcia und Dougal James-Robertson verbringen der Architekt Robert Brown und seine Familie hier oft ihre Zeit. Die Pavillons mit einer schwarz gestrichenen, sichtbaren Stahlkonstruktion sind im Felsboden verankert und stehen auf einer massiven Stützmauer aus Sandstein. Die Dächer und die seitlichen, großflächig verglasten Wände sind mit gewelltem Kupferblech verkleidet. Den Sockel der Pavillonbauten bildet eine schwere, unregelmäßige Wand aus Sandsteinblöcken; diese wurden aus der Felsküste auf dem Grundstück in Handarbeit herausgeschnitten. Im tiefer gelegenen zweigeschossigen Pavillon befinden sich auf der unteren Ebene Schlafräume für Gäste, darüber eine Küche, Ess- und Wohnraum. Der obere Pavillon ist dem Besitzer vorbehalten. Die Innenräume wurden von Robert Browns Partnerin Caroline Casey gestaltet: Dazu gehört ein 4 m langer Esstisch aus Silberesche mit einer 60 mm dicken Tischplatte. Das Grundstück ist 720 m² groß, die Gesamtfläche des Hauses beträgt 183 m².

Bien que Great Mackerel Beach soit relativement proche de Sydney, on ne peut y accéder que par un ferry, ce qui explique le calme dont jouissent ses cinquante maisons. L'architecte Robert Brown et sa famille y séjournent, ainsi que Marcia et Dougal James-Robertson, ses clients. Les pavillons à ossature en acier peint en noir, ancrés dans la roche, semblent posés sur un mur de soutènement en grès massif. Ils sont largement vitrés et leurs murs latéraux, ainsi que leurs toits, sont habillés de cuivre ondulé. Le double pavillon inférieur regroupe les chambres d'invités, une cuisine ainsi qu'une zone de repas et de séjour à l'étage. Le pavillon supérieur contient la suite du propriétaire. L'aménagement intérieur a été exécuté par l'associée de Robert Brown, Caroline Casey, et comprend une table de repas en hêtre cendré de 4 m de long et 6 cm d'épaisseur. La surface du terrain est de 720 m², celle de la maison de 183 m².

The James-Robertson House is dug into a steep site whose vegetation has been protected, accentuating the contrast between nature and the light and airy openness of the architecture.

Das James-Robertson House steht auf einem steil abfallenden Grundstück. Die Vegetation konnte erhalten werden, wodurch der Kontrast zwischen der Natur und der leichten, luftigen Offenheit der Architektur betont wird.

La maison James-Robertson est nichée dans une pente abrupte dont la végétation a été préservée, ce qui accentue le contraste entre la nature luxuriante et la légèreté aérienne de l'architecture.

The upper volume containing the owner's space is visible in the image to the far right, with the guest pavilions below. Floor-to-ceiling glazing allows unobstructed views of the remarkable natural setting.

Ganz rechts: Der obere Baukörper enthält die Räume des Bauherrn; darunter liegen die Pavillons für die Gäste. Geschosshohe Fenster gewähren unverstellte Ausblicke auf die einzigartige Umgebung.

Le volume du haut contient l'appartement du propriétaire, visible à l'extrême droite. Les pavillons des invités sont situés en dessous. Le vitrage intégral offre une vue totalement dégagée sur le remarquable cadre naturel.

The lower, double volume, with the
dining area, also seen on the right
hand page and on the previous page.
Although its lines are clean and
direct, the architecture offers an
unexpected flow of spaces from one
area to the next, and out toward the
water.

Der untere Zwillingsbaukörper mit
dem Essbereich (zu sehen ebenfalls
auf der rechten und auf der vorher-
gehenden Seite): Die Linienführung
der Architektur ist sauber und direkt
und bietet überraschend fließende
Räume zwischen den verschiedenen
Bereichen und zum Ozean.

Le double volume inférieur comprend
la zone des repas (page de droite et
page précédente). Grâce à ses lignes
nettes et directes, l'architecture crée
un étonnant flux spatial d'une zone
à l'autre, ainsi que vers l'extérieur et
l'océan.

The black, exposed steel frame of the house contrasts with the corrugated copper used for the roofs in these images. Above, a rear entrance path made of wood with natural rocks accentuates the Japanese feeling evident in some aspects of the house.

Die sichtbare schwarze Stahlkonstruktion kontrastiert mit den Dächern aus gewelltem Kupferblech. Oben: Ein hölzerner Weg führt zu einem hangseits liegenden Eingang. Das Holz in Verbindung mit dem natürlichen Felsgestein unterstreicht die japanisch anmutende Atmosphäre, die in einigen Bereichen des Hauses zu spüren ist.

L'ossature apparente en acier peint en noir contraste avec le cuivre ondulé utilisé en toiture. Ci-dessus, le cheminement en bois flanqué de rochers naturels qui conduit à l'entrée arrière accentue l'esprit japonisant évident de certains aspects de la maison.

COX RICHARDSON

Cox Richardson Architects & Planners
Level 2, 204 Clarence Street
NSW 2000 Sydney
PO Box Q193 NSW 1230
Australia

Tel: +61 292 67 95 99
Fax: +61 292 64 58 44
e-mail: sydney@cox.com.au
Web: www.cox.com.au

PHILIP COX graduated from Sydney University in architecture in 1962. He was a Royal Australian Institute of Architects (RAIA) silver medalist and was award the NSW Board of Architects Traveling Scholarship. He graduated from Sydney University with a diploma in Town & Country Planning in 1972. From 1963 to 1967, Ph Cox worked with Ian McKay. The Cox Group was created in Sydney in 1967 as Philip Cox & Partners. The firm now has offices in Sydney, Perth, Brisbane, Melbourne a Canberra as well as in Beijing and Dubai, and they currently employ 250 persons in Australia. Philip Cox has received numerous awards in recognition of his contri tion to architecture, including the RAIA Gold Medal in 1984. He is a Professor of Architecture at the University of NSW, a member of International Advisory Committee the National University of Singapore and member of the International Advisory to the Urban Redevelopment Authority of Singapore. Major projects include: Yulara Tour Resort, Central Australia (1984); Sydney Football Stadium, Moore Park, NSW (1988); National Tennis Center, Melbourne, VIC (1988); Sydney Exhibition Center, Darli Harbor, NSW (1988); Sydney International Aquatic Centre, Homebush Bay, NSW (1994); Star City, Pyrmont, Sydney, NSW (1997); Singapore Expo, Singapore (1999); a the Sydney SuperDome and Car Park, Homebush Bay, NSW (1999). Current work includes the Qingdao Beijing Olympics Sailing Facility.

PHILIP COX machte 1962 an der Sydney University seinen Architekturabschluss. Vom Royal Australian Institute of Architects (RAIA) wurde er mit einer Silb medaille ausgezeichnet, und die Architektenkammer von New South Wales verlieh ihm ein Reisestipendium. 1972 erwarb er, ebenfalls an der Sydney University, ein Abschluss in Stadt- und Regionalplanung. Von 1963 bis 1967 arbeitete Philip Cox bei Ian McKay. The Cox Group wurde 1967 unter dem Namen Philip Cox & Partners Sydney gegründet. Das Büro unterhält Zweigstellen in Sydney, Perth, Brisbane, Melbourne und Canberra, außerdem in Peking und Dubai. In Australien beschäftigt es z zeit 250 Mitarbeiter. Philip Cox' Beitrag zur Architektur wurde durch eine Vielzahl von Auszeichnungen gewürdigt, z. B. 1984 mit der RAIA Goldmedaille. Er ist Profess für Architektur an der University of New South Wales, Mitglied des Internationalen Beratergremiums der National University of Singapore und Mitglied des Internation len Beratungsgremiums des Amts für Stadterneuerung in Singapur. Zu seinen Großbauten gehören das Yulara Tourist Resort in Zentralaustralien (1984), das Sydney Fo ball Stadion in Moore Park (1988), das National Tennis Center in Melbourne (1988), das Sydney Exhibition Center in Darling Harbor (1988), das Sydney International Aqu tic Center in Homebush Bay (1994), Star City, Pyrmont, Sydney (1997), ferner die Singapore Expo in Singapur (1999) und der Sydney SuperDome and Car Park Homebush Bay (1999). Die Olympischen Sportstätten der Segler in Qingdao, Peking, sind derzeit im Bau.

PHILIP COX est diplômé en architecture (1962) urbanisme et aménagement rural (1972) de l'Université de Sydney. Il a reçu une bourse de voyage du New Sou Wales Board of Architects et la médaille d'argent du Royal Australian Institute of Architects (RAIA). De 1963 à 1967, il a travaillé avec Ian McKay, puis a créé à Sydn en 1967, Philip Cox & Partners, qui s'est développé à l'échelle nationale et internationale pour devenir ensuite le Cox Group : l'agence, qui emploie 250 personnes Australie, possède aujourd'hui des bureaux à Sydney, Perth, Brisbane, Melbourne, Canberra, comme à Pékin et Dubaï. Philip Cox a reçu de nombreuses récompens pour ses contributions à l'architecture dont la Médaille d'or du RAIA en 1984. Il est professeur d'architecture de l'Université de Nouvelle-Galles du Sud et membre Comité consultatif international pour l'Urban Redevelopment Authority de Singapour. Parmi ses réalisations majeures : Yulara Tourist Resort, Territoire-du-Nord (1984) stade de football de Sydney, Moore Park (1988) ; le Centre national du tennis, Melbourne (1988) ; le Centre d'expositions de Sydney, Darling Harbor (1988) ; le Cen aquatique international de Sydney, Homebush Bay (1994) ; Star City, Pyrmont, Sydney (1997) ; Singapore Expo, Singapour (1999), le Superdome de Sydney, Homebu Bay (1999). Il réalise actuellement les équipements pour les compétitions de voile des Jeux olympiques de Pékin.

LONGITUDE 131°

Yulara, Northern Territory, Australia, 2002

Area: 15 tents, each 40 m²; central facility: 500 m² on two floors. Client: Voyages Resorts & Hotels.
Cost: €3.15 million

The fifteen tents of the facility are
stretched in a wide arc in the vast
emptiness surrounding Ayers Rock,
visible above right.

Die 15 »Hotelzelte« sind in der riesigen
Leere, die Ayers Rock umgibt, entlang
einer geschwungenen Linie angeordnet (oben rechts).

Les quinze « tentes » de l'hôtel dessinent un arc dans le désert d'Ayers
Rock (en haut à droite).

This "self-contained boutique hotel" with fifteen rooms is located just two kilometers from the Kata Tjuta National Park and within view of Ayers Rock. It is an extension to the 200-hectare Yulara Tourist Resort, completed by Philip Cox in 1984. Located south-west of the city of Alice Springs, the Park is the heart of the Aboriginal land of Australia, and contains two world-renowned natural monuments – Ayers Rock, also known as *Uluru*, a mass of arkosic sandstone that rises 348 meters out of the desert floor, considered to be sacred ground by the Aborigines, and *Kata Tjuta*, also known as *The Olgas*, a group of thirty rounded red domes as high as 5... meters. With summer temperatures rising above 40° and dune flora and fauna to protect, the hotel is raised up on steel piles, and roofed in three layers of fabric. T... architects explain, "The rooms are a simple box plan, with sliding panels that open half the façade and fully glazed south-facing walls making the most of the expansive view. The walls diverge slightly to open the view still further."

Das »selbstständig funktionierende Boutique-Hotel« mit 15 Räumen ist nur 2 km vom Kata Tjuta National Park entfernt und liegt in Sichtweite von Ayers Rock. bildet die Erweiterung des 200 ha großen, ebenfalls von Philip Cox geplanten Yulara Tourist Resort, das 1984 fertig gestellt wurde. Der südwestlich von Alice Sprin... gelegene Park ist das Herz des von den Aborigines bewohnten Gebietes und bietet zwei weltweit bekannte Naturdenkmäler – Ayers Rock, auch *Uluru* genannt, ein m... siver Felsen aus Sandstein, der 348 m aus der ebenen Wüste emporragt und von den Ureinwohnern als heiliger Ort angesehen wird, und *Kata Tjuta*, auch bezeichnet *The Olgas*, eine Gruppe von 30 gerundeten, roten, bis zu 546 m hohen Felsen. Wegen der Temperaturen, die im Sommer auf über 40° Celsius steigen, und um die Düne... fauna und -flora zu schützen, steht das Hotel auf Stahlstützen und hat ein dreilagiges Dach aus Stoff. Die Architekten erläutern: »Die Räume haben einen einfachen Rec... eckgrundriss. Mit Schiebeelementen kann die Hälfte der Fassade geöffnet werden; die vollständig verglaste Fassade nach Süden nutzt den weiten Ausblick optimal a... Um den Ausblick noch weiter zu vergrößern, sind die Wände leicht gegeneinander verschoben.«

Ce «boutique hotel autarcique» de quinze chambres se trouve à deux kilomètres à peine du parc national d'Uluru-Kata Tjuta, en vue d'Ayers Rock. C'est u... extension du Yulara Tourist Resort de 200 hectares achevé par Cox en 1984. Au sud-ouest d'Alice Springs, le parc se trouve au cœur du pays aborigène et contient de... monuments naturels célèbres dans le monde entier, Ayers Rock, également appelé Uluru, monolithe de grès rouge dominant le désert de ses 348 m et considéré com... un territoire sacré pour les Aborigènes, et Kata Tjuta (ou les monts Olgas), groupe de trente rochers arrondis rouges dont l'altitude s'élève jusqu'à 546 m. Parce que... températures grimpent à plus de 40° en été et que la flore et la faune spécifiques des dunes doivent être protégées, l'hôtel est posé sur des pilotis d'acier et sa toi... re est constituée de trois couches de toile. L'architecte explique que «les chambres sont dessinées sur le plan d'une simple boîte, avec des panneaux coulissants... ouvrent la moitié de la façade, entièrement vitrée vers le sud pour bénéficier au maximum de la vue. Les murs s'écartent légèrement pour amplifier encore la vision pa... ramique».

The central facility of Longtitude 131 is more than ten times larger than the guest tents, and yet it assumes a similar architectural vocabulary. The whole sits lightly on the land.

Das Hauptgebäude von Longitude 131° ist mehr als zehnmal so groß wie ein Hotelzelt, zeigt jedoch ein ähnliches architektonisches Vokabular. Die gesamte Anlage wird durch Leichtigkeit gekennzeichnet.

Le bâtiment central de Longitude 131 (ci-dessous) est plus de dix fois plus grand que les pavillons des hôtes, tout en reprenant le même vocabulaire architectural. L'ensemble est délicatement posé sur le sol du désert.

With their stretched canopies offering some protection from the difficult climate, the tents are glazed and lifted above the earth. To the left, a section of the central building.

Die aufgespannten Vordächer bieten etwas Schutz vor dem Wüstenklima. Die »Zelte« sind aufgeständert und an einer Seite verglast; links ein Schnitt durch das Hauptgebäude.

Les tentes, munies d'auvents de toile tendue pour protéger de la redou-table chaleur, sont vitrées et sur pilotis. À gauche, un partie du bâtiment central.

DILLER + SCOFIDIO + RENFRO

Diller + Scofidio + Renfro, 601 West 26th Street, 1815, New York, New York 10001, USA
Tel: +1 212 260 7971, Fax: +1 212 260 7924
e-mail: disco@dsrny.com, Web: www.dsrny.com

Elizabeth Diller is Professor of Architecture at Princeton University and Ricardo Scofidio is Professor of Architecture at The Cooper Union in New York. Accordin to their own description, "**DILLER + SCOFIDIO + RENFRO** is a collaborative, interdisciplinary studio involved in architecture, the visual arts and the performing arts. Th team is primarily involved in thematically-driven experimental works that take the form of architectural commissions, temporary installations and permanent site-specif installations, multimedia theater, electronic media, and print." Charles Renfro was born in Houston, Texas, in 1964. Prior to joining Diller + Scofidio in 1997, Renfro worke with several offices in New York including Smith-Milller+Hawkinson and Ralph Appelbaum Associates. He was promoted to partner in 2004. Their work include "Slither," 100 units of social housing in Gifu, Japan, and *Moving Target*, a collaborative dance work with Charleroi/Danse Belgium. Installations by Diller + Scofidio hav been seen at the Cartier Foundation in Paris (*Master/Slave*, 1999); the Museum of Modern Art in New York and the Musée de la Mode in Paris. Recently, they comple ed The Brasserie Restaurant, Seagram Building, New York (1998-99); the Blur Building, Expo 02, Yverdon-les-Bains, Switzerland (2000-02) and were selected as arch tects for the Institute of Contemporary Art in Boston, the Eyebeam Institute in the Chelsea area of Manhattan, and Lincoln Center, New York. They recently complete *Facsimile*, a permanent media installation for the San Francisco Arts Commission at the new Moscone Convention Center West, as well as a master plan for Brookly Academy of Music Cultural District in collaboration with Rem Koolhaas. They designed the Viewing Platforms at Ground Zero in Manhattan, and they are also working o a major project to redesign the area surrounding the Tivoli Park in Copenhagen.

Elizabeth Diller ist als Professorin für Architektur an der Princeton University, Ricardo Scofidio als Professor für Architektur an der Cooper Union School of Arch tecture in New York tätig. Ihrer eigenen Beschreibung zufolge ist »**DILLER + SCOFIDIO + RENFRO** ein interdisziplinäres Gemeinschaftsprojekt, das sich mit Architektu bildender und darstellender Kunst beschäftigt. Das Team führt hauptsächlich experimentelle Arbeiten durch, die sich auf der Grundlage von Architektur, Installation, Mult mediapräsentation, elektronischen Medien und Druckgrafik mit bestimmten Themen auseinandersetzen.« Charles Renfro, geboren 1964 in Houston, Texas, arbeitete fü verschiedene New Yorker Architekturbüros – darunter Smith-Miller+Hawkinson und Ralph Appelbaum Associates – bevor er seine Tätigkeit bei Diller + Scofido aufnahn 2004 wurde er Partner. Zu ihren Projekten zählen u. a.: »Slither«, 100 Sozialwohnungen in Gifu, Japan, und *Moving Target*, eine Tanztheaterproduktion in Zusammena beit mit der Tanzformation Charleroi/Danse Belgium. Installationen von Diller + Scofidio wurden in der Fondation Cartier in Paris (*Master/Slave*, 1999), im Museum c Modern Art in New York und im Musée de la Mode in Paris gezeigt. Zu ihren neueren Architekturarbeiten gehören das Restaurant The Brasserie im Seagram Building New York (1998–99) und das Blur Building für die Expo 2002 im schweizerischen Yverdon-les-Bains (2000–02). Außerdem erhielten sie die Aufträge für das Institute c Contemporary Art in Boston, das Eyebeam Institute im Stadtteil Chelsea in Manhattan sowie das Lincoln Center in New York. Kürzlich wurde *Facsimile*, eine ständig Medieninstallation für die San Francisco Arts Commission am neuen Moscone Convention Center West fertig gestellt; ebenso – in Zusammenarbeit mit Rem Koolhaas ein Master Plan für die Brooklyn Academy of Music Cultural District. Sie haben die Aussichtsplattform für Ground Zero in Manhattan entworfen und arbeiten an eine Großprojekt zur Umgestaltung der Umgebung des Tivoli in Kopenhagen.

Elizabeth Diller est professeur associé à Princeton et Ricardo Scofidio professeur d'architecture à The Cooper Union, New York. Selon eux, «**DILLER + SCOFI DIO + RENFRO** est une agence interdisciplinaire coopérative qui se consacre à l'architecture, aux arts plastiques et à ceux du spectacle. L'équipe travaille essentielle ment sur des recherches thématiques expérimentales qui peuvent prendre la forme de commandes architecturales, d'installations temporaires, d'installations perma nentes adaptées au site, de théâtres multimédia, de médias électroniques et d'édition ». Charles Renfro est né à Houston, Texas, en 1964. Avant de rejoindre Diller Scofidio en 1997, il a travaillé pour plusieurs agences new-yorkaises dont Smith-Miller+Hawkinson et Ralph Appelbaum Associates. Il est devenu partenaire en 2004 Parmi leurs projets récents : Slither, 100 logements sociaux (Gifu, Japon), *Moving Target*, œuvre chorégraphique en collaboration avec Charleroi/Danse (Belgique). Le installations de Diller + Scofidio ont été présentées à la Fondation Cartier à Paris, *Master/Slave* (1999) au Museum of Modern Art de New York et au musée de la Mod à Paris. Plus récemment, ils ont achevé le restaurant Brasserie, Seagram Building, New York (1998–99) ; le pavillon d'exposition Blur Building, Expo 02, Yverdon-les Bains, Suisse (2002) et ont été sélectionnés pour l'Institute of Contemporary Art de Boston, l'Eyebeam Institute à Manhattan (Chelsea) et le Lincoln Center (New York Ils ont dernièrement livré *Facsimile*, une installation média permanente pour la San Francisco Arts Commission, au nouveau Moscone Convention Center West, ainsi qu le plan directeur de la Brooklyn Academy of Music Cultural District en collaboration avec Rem Koolhaas. Ils ont conçu les plates-formes d'observation de Ground Zero Manhattan et travaillent également sur un important projet de restructuration des abords immédiats du parc de Tivoli à Copenhague.

THE HIGH LINE

New York, New York, USA, 2004

Length: 2.5 km. Client: Friends of the High Line. Cost: not disclosed

The **HIGH LINE** is an unused elevated railway spur running about 2.5 kilometers from the Jacob Javits Convention Center in New York to Gansevoort Street in the meatpacking district on Manhattan's Lower West Side. The so-called West Side Improvement Project, including the High Line, built because of the number of accidents involving trains serving Manhattan's docks, was put into effect in 1929. Intended to avoid the negative effects of subway lines over crowded streets, the High Line cuts through the center of city blocks. Increasing truck traffic led to the demolition of parts of the High Line in the 1960s and a halt to train operations in 1980. Despite efforts to demolish the remaining structure to allow new construction, a good part of the High Line survived and a group called Friends of the High Line, created in 1999 eventually convinced authorities to renovate it rather than to allow its destruction. Diller + Scofidio + Renfro have participated in a collective proposal for the High Line including the landscape architects Field Operations, the artist Olafur Eliasson, the Tanya Bonakdar Gallery, the engineers Buro Happold and a number of other parties to renovate and bring new life to a disused part of the city. As they say, "Inspired by the melancholic, unruly beauty of the High Line, where nature has reclaimed a once vital piece of urban infrastructure, the team retools this industrial conveyance into a postindustrial instrument of leisure reflection about the very categories of 'nature' and 'culture' in our time. By changing the rules of engagement between plant life and pedestrians, our strategy of agri-tecture combines organic and building materials into a blend of changing proportions that accommodate the wild, the cultivated, the intimate, and the hyper-social." The United States Senate voted a credit of 18 million dollars for the project in July 2005, and the Museum of Modern Art in New York presented an exhibition of the Diller + Scofidio + Renfro scheme until October 30, 2005.

Die **HIGH LINE** ist eine 2,5 km lange, nicht mehr benutzte Hochbahntrasse, die von der Gansevoort Street im Meatpacking District auf der Lower West Side von Manhattan bis zum Jacob Javits Convention Center führt. Der Bau der High Line war Teil des so genannten West Side Improvement Project, das 1929 eingerichtet wurde, da es zu zahlreichen Unfällen mit den die Docks andienenden Zügen gekommen war. Um die negativen Auswirkungen von Stadtbahnen, die direkt über vielbefahrenen Straßen verlaufen, zu vermeiden, wurde die High Line so gelegt, dass sie die Blöcke mittig durchschneidet. Aufgrund des erhöhten LKW-Verkehrs wurden in den 1960er Jahren Teile der High Line abgebrochen; 1980 wurde der Zugverkehr ganz eingestellt. Obwohl es Versuche gab, die noch vorhandenen Abschnitte abzureißen und eine neue Konstruktion zu errichten, blieb ein größerer Teil der High Line erhalten. Die Friends of the High Line setzten sich seit 1999 gegen den Abriss und für die Sanierung ein und konnten die zuständigen Behörden überzeugen. Diller + Scofidio + Renfro haben – zusammen mit den Landschaftsarchitekturbüro Field Operations, dem Künstler Olafur Eliasson, der Tanya Bonakdar Gallery, dem Ingenieurbüro Happold und vielen anderen Beteiligten – einen Vorschlag erarbeitet, wie die Konstruktion saniert und dieser ausrangierte Teil der Stadt wiederbelebt werden kann. Sie sagen: »Die melancholische, ungestüme Schönheit der High Line und die Tatsache, dass sich die Natur hier ein früher wichtiges Element der städtischen Infrastruktur zurückerobert hat, inspirierte uns. Das Team deutet die industrielle Transporttrasse in ein postindustrielles Instrument der Reflexion über Freizeit um. Dabei geht es genau um die Kategorien ›Natur‹ und ›Kultur‹ in der heutigen Zeit. Indem wir die Regeln der gegenseitigen Verpflichtungen zwischen der Pflanzenwelt und den Fußgängern ändern, verbindet unsere Strategie der ›Agritektur‹ organische Materialien und Baumaterialien zu einer Mischung mit veränderlichen Anteilen, die das Wilde, das Kultivierte, das Persönliche und das Hypersoziale umfasst.« Im Juli 2005 stimmte der amerikanische Senat einem Kredit von umgerechnet 15 Millionen Euro zu; in einer Ausstellung bis zum 30. Oktober 2005 zeigte das Museum of Modern Art in New York das Konzept von Diller + Scofidio + Renfro.

La **HIGH LINE** est une ancienne voie ferrée aérienne serpentant sur 2,5 km, du Jacob Javits Convention Center jusqu'à Gansevoort Street, à Meatpacking District (quartier des bouchers) dans le Lower West Side à Manhattan. Le West Side Improvement Project, qui comprenait la High Line construite en surélévation en réaction aux nombreux accidents provoqués par les trains qui desservaient les docks de Manhattan, datait de 1929. Pour pallier les inconvénients de lignes de métro passant au-dessus des rues bondées, la High Line passe carrément au milieu des blocs d'immeubles. L'accroissement de la circulation des camions a conduit à la démolition partielle de cette ligne dans les années 1960 et le trafic ferroviaire y a définitivement cessé en 1980. Malgré plusieurs tentatives de démolition de l'ensemble pour permettre de nouvelles constructions, une bonne partie de la ligne subsiste et une association, les Amis de la High Line, créée en 1999, a fini par convaincre les autorités de la rénover plutôt que de la supprimer. Diller + Scofidio + Renfro ont participé à un collectif regroupant, entre autres, les architectes paysagistes Field Operations, l'artiste Olafur Eliasson, la Tanya Bonakdar Gallery, les ingénieurs Buro Happold, collectif qui se proposait de redonner vie à ce quartier abandonné. « Inspirés par la beauté anarchique et mélancolique de la High Line, où la nature a reconquis un élément d'infrastructure urbaine jadis vital, nous avons transformé cet outil industriel en un instrument postindustriel de loisirs, en une réflexion sur la signification réelle des classifications entre « nature » et « culture » de notre époque. En changeant les règles des rapports entre la vie végétale et les piétons, notre stratégie d'*agri-tecture* mélange matériaux organiques et matériaux de construction selon des proportions variables pour accueillir le sauvage et le cultivé, l'intime et l'hypersocial. » Le Sénat américain a voté, en juillet 2005, un crédit de 15 millions d'euros pour le projet de Diller Scofidio + Renfro, qui a été exposé au Museum of Modern Art de New York.

8' - 0" primary path   4' - 0" splinter path   3' - 0" splinter path

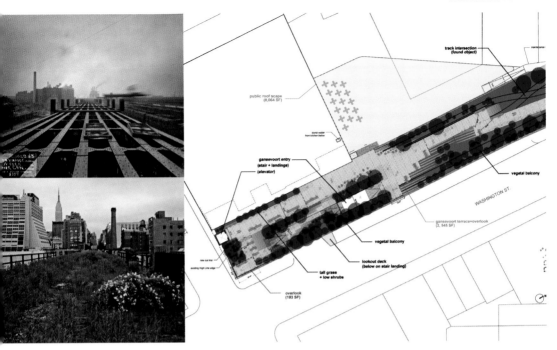

e High Line squeezes between
ildings on Manhattan's Lower West
te. Drawings above give an idea of
e variety of architectural and
tanical solutions chosen by the
chitects involved.

e High Line schlängelt sich durch
e Häuser auf Manhattans Lower
est Side. Die Zeichnungen zeigen
e vielfältigen architektonischen und
ndschaftsplanerischen Lösungen der
rschiedenen Architekten.

La High Line se faufile entre
les bâtiments du Lower West Side de
Manhattan. Les dessins ci-dessus
donnent une idée de la variété des
solutions architecturales et végé-
tales retenues par les architectes.

DENNIS DOLLENS

Dennis Dollens
40 Camino Cielo
Santa Fe, New Mexico 87 506
USA

Tel: +1 505 988 9236
Fax: +1 505 988 5820
e-mail: exodesic@mac.com
Web: www.tumbletruss.com

Digitally-Grown T

Born in Los Angeles in 1950, **DENNIS DOLLENS** has taught Design Biomimetics in the Genetic Architectures Program and in the Department of Ecology an
Architecture at the Universitat Internacional de Catalunya's School of Architecture (Barcelona) for four years. He lectures internationally on Digital-Biomimetic Architec
ture and on his work in schools of industrial design and architecture. He is currently working on a PhD at the University of Strathclyde, Glasgow. His studios are in Sant
Fe, New Mexico and Barcelona, Spain and his most recent books are *D2A: Digital to Analog* (translated into Spanish and published as *De lo digital a lo analógico*) an
DBA: Digital-Botanic Architecture. His current architectural work includes the Spiral Bridge, Pyrenées, France (with Ignasi Pérez Arnal, 2004); Digital-Computing Cente
Marfa, Texas (2005–); and a residence in Santa Fe, New Mexico (2004–).

DENNIS DOLLENS, 1950 in Los Angeles geboren, lehrte an der Architekturfakultät der Universitat Internacional de Catalunya in Barcelona im Programm Gene
tische Architektur biomimetisches Entwerfen, außerdem unterrichtete er vier Jahre lang am Fachbereich Ökologie und Architektur. An Architektur- und Designfakultäte
in zahlreichen Ländern hält er Vorträge über seine Projekte und zum Thema »Digital-biomimetische Architektur«. Derzeit promoviert er an der University of Strathclyd
Glasgow. Er hat Ateliers in Santa Fe, New Mexico, und in Barcelona. In jüngster Zeit veröffentlichte er zwei Bücher, *D2A: Digital to Analog*, das auch auf Spanisch erschie
(*De lo digital a lo analógico*), und *DBA: Digital-Botanic Architecture*. Zu seinen neuesten Projekten gehören die Spiralbrücke in den französischen Pyrenäen (mit Igna
Pérez Arnal, 2004), das Digital-Computing Center in Marfa, Texas (2005–), und ein Wohnhaus in Santa Fe, New Mexico (2004–).

Né à Los Angeles en 1950, **DENNIS DOLLENS** a enseigné la biomimétique du design dans le cadre du programme d'architectures génétiques et au départe
ment d'écologie et d'architecture de l'École d'architecture de l'Universitat Internacional de Catalunya (Barcelone) pendant quatre ans. Il donne des conférences dans d
nombreux pays sur l'architecture numérique-biomimétique et sur son œuvre dans des écoles de design industriel et d'architecture. Il prépare actuellement un PhD
l'Université de Strathclyde à Glasgow. Il a des agences à Santa Fe (Nouveau-Mexique) et Barcelone (Espagne) et a récemment publié *D2A ; Digital to Analog* et *D-B-A
Digital-Botanic Architecture*. Ses dernières réalisations architecturales comprennent le Pont en spirale, Pyrénées, France (avec Ignasi Pérez Arnal, 2004), le Digital-Com
puting Center, Marfa, Texas (2005–) et une maison à Santa Fe, Nouveau-Mexique (2004–).

DIGITALLY-GROWN TOWER

New York, New York, USA, 2005

Floor area: 22 500 m². Height: 42.5 m. Client: Lumen, Inc.
Cost: $27 million

Imagined for a site on Manhattan's Lower East Side, this tower was designed with software called Xfrog. Made by the German firm Greenworks, Xfrog cons
of "botanic, L-system algorithms used in computational biological simulations to grow plants and landscapes for laboratory tests and simulations." The work done by D
lens consists in "changing the software's growth parameters in order to direct digital growth from reproducing botanic organisms like trees or shrubs into producing arc
tectural elements like an experimental frame for a new building." Beginning with the seed pods of penstemon (*Penstemon palmeri*), Dollens proposes a design that i
a radically different appearance from almost any existing tower, and yet has a solid basis in the forms of nature. Further, digitally-driven manufacturing can be adap
to this type of concept. Dollens writes, "The unifying concept behind this project is that computational growth of architectural structures and systems can be influenc
by biomimetic observations without falling into traditional categories of 'organic architecture.' In addition, the potential of biological science, biotechnology, and dig
manufacturing, arriving at a union where architectural production and new possibilities for non-toxic architecture come together, begins to make sense."

Der Turm, geplant für die Lower East Side in Manhattan, wurde mit der Software Xfrog entworfen. Das von der deutschen Firma Greenworks entwickelte Pr
gramm besteht aus »botanischen, L-System-Algorithmen, die in ›computerbiologischen‹ Simulationen verwendet werden, um Pflanzen und Landschaften für Laborte
und -simulationen zu generieren«. Dollens »verändert die Wachstumsparameter des Programms, so dass die Reproduktion botanischer Organismen wie Bäume o
Sträucher in eine Produktion architektonischer Elemente − z. B. ein experimentelles Tragwerk für ein neues Gebäude − umgewandelt wird.« Ausgehend von den Scho
der Pflanze Penstemon palmeri schlägt Dollens einen Turm vor, der sich radikal von fast allen gebauten Türmen unterscheidet. Seine solide Basis sind jedoch Formen a
der Natur. Darüber hinaus kann eine digital gestützte Produktion aus diesem Entwurfskonzept abgeleitet werden. Dollens schreibt:»Grundgedanke des Projektes ist, d
computergeneriertes Wachstum von architektonischen Strukturen und Systemen durch biomimetische Beobachtungen beeinflusst werden kann, ohne in die bekann
Kategorien einer organischen Architektur zu verfallen. Dass die Potenziale der Biologie, Biotechnologie und der digitalen Produktion gebündelt werden, ist sinnvoll. Dara
ergeben sich neue Möglichkeiten einer schadstofffreien Architektur.«

Cette tour a été conçue à l'aide du logiciel Xfrog, pour un terrain du Lower East Side à Manhattan. Mis au point par la société allemande Greenworks, Xfr
consiste en « algorithmes botaniques dits L-systems, utilisés pour les simulations biologiques virtuelles étudiant en laboratoire la croissance des végétaux et l'évolut
des paysages ». Le travail de Dennis Dollens a consisté à « modifier les paramètres de croissance du logiciel pour réorienter la croissance numérique des organism
botaniques de reproduction − arbres et buissons −, vers la production d'éléments architecturaux comme, par exemple, une ossature expérimentale pour une nouve
construction ». Partant de graines de penstemon (*Penstemon palmeri*), il propose ainsi un plan dont l'aspect diffère de presque toutes les tours existan
à ce jour, tout en s'appuyant sur une base formelle naturelle solide. Des processus de fabrication pilotée par ordinateur peuvent être adaptés à ce type de concept. D
lens écrit : « Le concept qui sous-tend ce projet est que la croissance virtuelle des structures et systèmes architecturaux peut être influencée par des observations b
mimétiques sans tomber dans les catégories traditionnelles de l'architecture dite ‹ organique ›. De plus, la possibilité d'une collaboration de la biologie, de la biotechn
logie et de la fabrication numérisée au bénéfice d'une production architecturale et de nouvelles possibilités d'architecture non toxique commence à faire sens. »

Using a program intended to mimic plant growth, Dennis Dollens has created the basis for a different type of architecture, whose esthetics owe more to biology than to Euclidean geometry.

Dennis Dollens verwendet ein Programm, das den Wuchs von Pflanzen simuliert und schafft so die Basis für einen neuartigen Architekturtypus, dessen Ästhetik mehr mit Biologie als mit euklidischer Geometrie zu tun hat.

Grâce à un programme qui reproduit les schémas de croissance des plantes, Dennis Dollens a jeté les bases d'une architecture d'un type nouveau dont l'esthétique doit plus à la biologie qu'à la géométrie euclidienne.

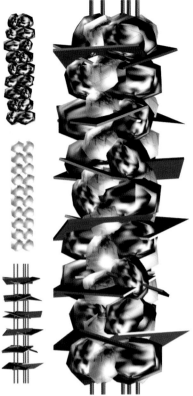

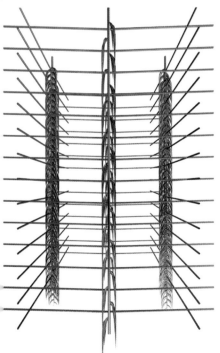

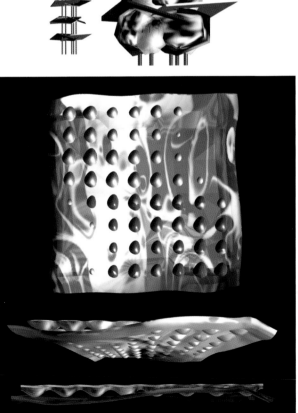

STEFAN EBERSTADT

Stefan Eberstadt
Westendstrasse 30
80339 Munich
Germany

Tel: +49 89 16 70 98
Fax: +49 89 50 09 67 56
e-mail: stefan.eberstadt@adbk.mhn.de

Rucksack

Born in 1961, the artist **STEFAN EBERSTADT** lives and works in Munich. He worked as an apprentice carpenter and studied sculpture at the Academy of Fi Arts in Munich from 1982 to 1988 under Eduardo Paolozzi. He also studied in London and Bath during the same period. He received a Fellowship from the Bavarian Aca emy of Beaux Arts in 1993, the Travel Grant to New York City from the Bavarian State in 1994 and the Project Scholarship for Fine Art from the City of Munich 2004. From 1995 to 2001 he taught at the Academy of Fine Arts in Munich. His work has been shown internationally, in particular at the Gallery Ulrich Fiedler in Colog and the Rocket Gallery in London. He was included in *Come-in. Interior as Medium of Contemporary Art in Germany*, a touring exhibition hosted by the Museum of Co temporary Art in São Paulo.

Der 1961 geborene Künstler **STEFAN EBERSTADT** lebt und arbeitet in München. Er war Auszubildender in einer Tischlerei und studierte u. a. unter Eduardo Pa lozzi von 1982 bis 1988 Bildhauerei an der Akademie der Bildenden Künste in München. In diesem Zeitraum studierte er auch in London und Bath. 1993 erhielt er v der Bayerischen Akademie der Schönen Künste ein Stipendium, 1994 vom Freistaat Bayern ein Reisestipendium nach New York und 2004 von der Stadt München e Projektstipendium. Von 1995 bis 2001 unterrichtete er an der Akademie der Bildenden Künste in München. Seine Arbeit wird international gezeigt, speziell in der Ga rie Ulrich Fiedler in Köln und der Rocket Gallery in London. Er hat außerdem an der Tourneeausstellung *Come-in. Interieur als Medium der zeitgenössischen Kunst Deutschland*, kuratiert vom Museum of Contemporary Art, São Paulo, teilgenommen.

Né en 1961, l'artiste **STEFAN EBERSTADT** vit et travaille à Munich. Il a été apprenti charpentier et a étudié la sculpture auprès d'Eduardo Paolozzi à l'Acad mie des beaux-arts de Munich de 1982 à 1988. Il a également suivi des cours à Londres et Bath au cours de la même période. Il a reçu une bourse de l'Académie bav roise des beaux-arts et la Bourse de voyage à New York du Land de Bavière en 1994 ainsi que la Bourse de projet pour les beaux-arts de la Ville de Munich en 2004. 1995 à 2001, il a enseigné à l'Académie des beaux-arts de Munich. Son œuvre a été présentée dans de nombreux pays, en particulier à la galerie Ulrich Fiedler à Colog et à la Rocket Gallery à Londres. Il figure dans *Come-in, Interior as Medium of Contemporary Art in Germany*, exposition itinérante organisée par le musée d'Art conte porain de São Paulo.

RUCKSACK HOUSE

Leipzig/Cologne, Germany, 2004–05

Floor area: 9 m². Client: Prototype by Stefan Eberstadt, Munich and courtesy Fiedler Contemporary, Cologne.
Cost: €25 000 (production cost); €50 000 (prototype)

Stefan Eberstadt had the unusual idea of simply adding space to an existing building. As he says, "New space gets slung onto an existing space by a simpl clear and understandable method. This reactivates the idea of the self-built anarchistic tree house, this time however, more prominently placed and structurally en neered. Our common perception needs to be challenged since it gets irritated when the plain façade of a building is suddenly interrupted by a box-shaped volume ed ing out into the realm of the street." Working with Thomas Beck, a structural engineer from Munich, he devised a welded steel structure with plywood cladding that w hung by steel cables from the Federkiel Stiftung/Halle 14 in Leipzig from September to November 2004 in the context of the exhibition *Xtreme Houses*. It was present again in Cologne in September 2005 during the international architectural symposium *Plan05 – Forum of Contemporary Architecture*. Measuring 250 x 360 x 250 c the **RUCKSACK HOUSE** is "an attempt to explore the boundary between architecture and art." It has been described as a "walk-in sculpture" but it clearly has an archite tural presence. Eberstadt concludes: "Today the task for art is to influence the design and the aesthetic structures of our environment. Art cannot be seen as an isolat factor, rather it should challenge and interact with other fields like architecture and design. In order to exist, art has to get involved in fields operating outside of its own

Stefan Eberstadt hatte die ungewöhnliche Idee, Raum einfach an ein bestehendes Gebäude anzufügen. Er sagt: »Neuer Raum wird auf einfache, klare und ve ständliche Weise an vorhandenen Raum ›drangeworfen‹. Damit wird die Idee des selbstgebauten, anarchistischen Baumhauses reaktiviert; hier jedoch tritt es deutlich in Erscheinung und ist baukonstruktiv durchgearbeitet. Unsere alltägliche Wahrnehmung wird dabei herausgefordert: Eine glatte Fassade, die plötzlich durch einen k tenartigen, in den Straßenraum hineinragenden Baukörper unterbrochen wird, erzeugt Irritationen.« In Zusammenarbeit mit Thomas Beck, einem Statiker aus Münche entwickelte Eberstadt eine geschweißte Stahlkonstruktion mit einer Sperrholzverkleidung, die mithilfe von Stahlseilen von der Halle 14 der Leipziger Baumwollspinne (Stiftung Federkiel) abgehängt wurde. Diese Aktion fand von September bis November 2004 im Zusammenhang mit der Ausstellung *Xtreme Houses* statt. Auf dem inte nationalen Architektursymposion *Plan05 – Forum für Zeitgenössische Architektur* wurde die Konstruktion im September 2005 in Köln noch einmal gezeigt. Das **RUC SACKHAUS** mit den Maßen 250 x 360 x 250 cm ist »der Versuch, die Grenzen zwischen Architektur und Kunst zu erforschen«. Es wurde als begehbare Skulptur bezeic net, hat aber eine deutliche architektonische Präsenz. Abschließend sagt Eberstadt: »Heute besteht die Aufgabe der Kunst darin, das Design und die ästhetisch Strukturen unserer Umwelt zu beeinflussen. Kunst kann nicht als ein isolierter Faktor gesehen werden, vielmehr sollte sie andere Bereiche – z. B. Architektur und Desi – herausfordern und mit ihnen interagieren. Um zu existieren, muss Kunst Bereiche mit einbeziehen, die sich außerhalb ihrer eigenen Sphäre befinden.«

Stefan Eberstadt a eu l'idée simple de donner du volume à un bâtiment existant. Il explique : « Le nouveau volume est greffé sur celui existant au moyen d'u méthode simple, claire et compréhensible. Ceci réactive l'idée de la maison dans l'arbre à caractère anarchique, ‹ à construire soi-même ›, mais implantée de façon pl visible et structurellement mieux étudiée. Notre perception a besoin d'être mise au défi car elle s'irrite de voir la façade neutre d'un immeuble brutalement interromp par un volume en forme de boîte se projetant vers la rue. » En collaboration avec Thomas Beck, ingénieur structurel munichois, il a conçu une structure en acier sou habillée de contreplaqué, accrochée par des câbles en acier en haut de la Halle 14 de la Federkiel Stiftung à Leipzig où se tenait, de septembre à novembre, l'expo tion *Xtreme Houses*. Le projet fut exposé à nouveau à Cologne en septembre 2005 lors du symposium international d'architecture *Plan05 – Forum of Contemporary Arc tecture*. Cette **MAISON SAC À DOS** de 2,50 x 3,60 x 2,50 m, est « une tentative d'exploration des frontières entre l'art et l'architecture ». Elle a été décrite comme u « sculpture pénétrable » mais possède à l'évidence une présence architecturale. Eberstadt conclut : « Aujourd'hui, l'art a pour rôle d'influencer le design et les structur esthétiques de notre environnement. Il ne peut être considéré comme un facteur isolé, mais doit se confronter et interagir avec d'autres secteurs comme l'architectu et le design. Pour exister, l'art doit s'impliquer dans des champs autres que le sien ».

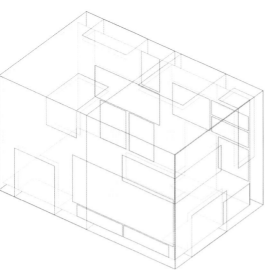

By placing windows in unexpected
locations, Stefan Eberstadt heigh-
tens the almost Surreal impression
created by the Rucksack House,
seen here hanging from a building
in Leipzig.

Indem Stefan Eberstadt die Fenster
an überraschenden Stellen positio-
niert, betont er den fast surrealen
Eindruck des Rucksackhauses;
die Abbildung zeigt es angehängt
an ein Gebäude in Leipzig.

En implantant les fenêtres à
des endroits surprenants, Stefan
Eberstadt renforce l'impression
presque surréaliste donnée par
sa « maison sac à dos », ici suspendue à un immeuble de Leipzig.

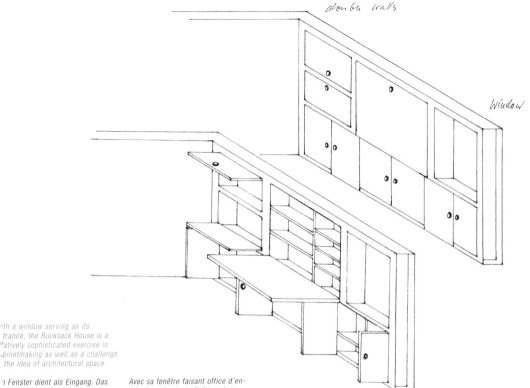

double walls

Window

*th a window serving as its
trance, the Rucksack House is a
atively sophisticated exercise in
binetmaking as well as a challenge
the idea of architectural space.

Fenster dient als Eingang. Das
cksackhaus ist eine relativ an-
ruchsvolle »Tischlerarbeit« und
ellt die Vorstellung von architek-
nischem Raum auf die Probe.

Avec sa fenêtre faisant office d'entrée, la maison sac à dos est un
exercice de menuiserie assez sophistiqué et un défi à l'idée même
d'espace architectural.

EMBT

EMBT – Enric Miralles – Benedetta Tagliabue
Passatge de la Pau, 10 Bis. Pral.
08002 Barcelona
Spain

Tel: +34 934 12 53 42
Fax: +34 934 12 37 18
e-mail: info@mirallestagliabue.com
Web: www.mirallestagliabue.com

Born in Barcelona in 1955, **ENRIC MIRALLES** received his degree from the Escuela Técnica Superior de Arquitectura in that city in 1978. He died in 2000. lectured there, at Columbia University in New York, at Harvard, and at the Architectural Association in London. He formed a partnership with Carme Pinós in 1983 won a competition for the Igualada Cemetery Park on the outskirts of Barcelona in 1985 (completed in 1992). Contrary to the minimalism of other local architects Albert Viaplana and Helio Piñón, with whom he worked from 1974 to 1984, or Estève Bonnel, Miralles was known for the exuberance of his style. While interest deconstruction as it is applied to literature, Miralles is skeptical about its application to architecture. His work includes the Olympic Archery Ranges, Barcelona (1989– the La Mina civic center, Barcelona (1987–92), the Morella Boarding School, Castelló (1986–94), and the Huesca Sports Hall (1988–94). **BENEDETTA TAGLIABUE** born in Milan and graduated from the Instituto Universitario di Architettura di Venezia in 1989. She studied and worked in New York (with Agrest & Gandelsonas) 1987 to 1989. She worked for Enric Miralles beginning in 1992, first becoming a partner, then leading the studio after the death of Miralles.

ENRIC MIRALLES (1955–2000) wurde in Barcelona geboren und studierte dort an der Escuela Técnica Superior de Arquitectura, an der er später auch le Außerdem unterrichtete er an der Columbia University in New York, in Harvard und an der Architectural Association in London. Mit Carme Pinós gründete Enric Mir 1983 ein Büro. 1985 gewann er den Wettbewerb für die Friedhofsanlage Igualada am Stadtrand von Barcelona (Fertigstellung 1992). Im Gegensatz zu anderen k lanischen Architekten wie Albert Viaplana und Helio Piñón, für die er von 1974 bis 1984 arbeitete, oder auch Estève Bonnel, ist Miralles' Architektur nicht dem Min lismus verpflichtet, sondern zeichnet sich durch eine überschwängliche Sprache aus. Er war am Dekonstruktivismus in der Literatur interessiert, stand seiner Anwen in der Architektur jedoch skeptisch gegenüber. Zu seinen Projekten gehören die olympischen Anlagen für das Bogenschießen in Barcelona (1989–91), das La-M Gemeindezentrum in Barcelona (1987–92), das Morella-Internat in Castelló (1986–94) und das Sportzentrum in Huesca (1988–94). **BENEDETTA TAGLIABUE**, geb in Mailand, machte 1989 am Instituto Universitario di Architettura di Venezia ihren Abschluss. Von 1987 bis 1989 studierte und arbeitete sie in New York (bei Agre Gandelsonas). Seit 1992 war sie für Enric Miralles tätig, wurde seine Partnerin und übernahm nach dessen Tod die Leitung des Büros.

Né à Barcelone en 1955 et mort en 2000, **ENRIC MIRALLES** était diplômé de la Escuela Tecnica Superior de Arquitectura de cette ville (1978). Il y a ense ainsi qu'à Columbia University à New York, à Harvard et à l'Architectural Association de Londres. Il s'est associé à Carme Pinós en 1973 et a remporté le concours le parc du cimetière d'Igualada, dans la banlieue de Barcelone, en 1985 (achevé en 1992). À l'opposé du minimalisme d'autres praticiens catalans, comme Albert plana et Helio Pinón avec lesquels il a travaillé de 1974 à 1984, ou encore Esteve Bonell, Miralles était connu pour l'exubérance de son style. Intéressé par le déc tructivisme en littérature, il s'est toujours montré sceptique sur ses applications à l'architecture. Son œuvre comprend le stade de tir à l'arc des Jeux olympiques de celone (1989–91); le centre municipal de La Mina, Barcelona (1987–92); le pensionnat de Morella, Castello (1986–94) et la salle de sport de Huesca (1988– **BENEDETTA TAGLIABUE**, née à Milan, est diplômée de l'Istituto universitario di architettura de Venise (1989). Elle a étudié et travaillé à New York (chez Agrest et delsonas) de 1987 à 1989 puis, à partir de 1992, avec Enric Miralles, dont elle fut la compagne. Elle a pris la direction de l'agence à sa mort.

SCOTTISH PARLIAMENT

Edinburgh, UK, 1998–2004

Floor area: 31 894 m². Client: Scottish Parliament.
Cost: €370 million

Inaugurated by Queen Elizabeth II on October 9, 2004, four years after the death of Enric Miralles, the **SCOTTISH PARLIAMENT** was from the outset a controversial project, in part because of its sensitive site at the end of the Royal Mile in Edinburgh. The project was carried out in a joint venture by Enric Miralles, Benedetta Tagliabue EMBT Arquitectes Associats and RMJM Scotland, M. A. H. Duncan, T. B. Stewart. With a site area of 18 289 m² plus 17 329 m² that was landscaped and a total floor area of 31 894 m², the building was created essentially with precast concrete, metal frames and laminated wood. As the architects wrote, "The land itself will be a material, a physical building material… the Scottish Parliament will be slotted into the land… to carve in the land the form of gathering people together." 14 000 tons of granite from Kemnay Quarry in Aberdeenshire were used as were 2000 tons of Black Belfast granite imported from South Africa for the overlaid mosaic panels. The profile of these panels is intended to evoke the outline of the *Reverend Robert Walker skating in Duddingston Loch,* a painting by Henry Raeburn conserved at the Scottish National Gallery. Winner of a 2005 RIBA Architecture Award, the Parliament building elicited this commentary: "The building is a statement of sparkling excellence. On the Memory Wall, one of the statements reads, 'Say little and say it well.' This building is definitely saying a lot rather than little, but it definitely says it well." The most distinctive exterior feature of the building, aside from its obvious complexity, is the roof inspired by upturned boats. Press sources indicate that the final cost of the project was some 635 million euros (the architects list 370 million euros as the cost), whereas the July 1998 budget had been fixed at 80 million euros. A public inquiry held at the Land Court in Edinburgh, headed by Lord Fraser of Carmyllie, concluded that the two architectural firms involved had had great difficulty communicating, and that costs had not been sufficiently controlled by all concerned. Lord Fraser issued a series of ten recommendations to avoid such difficulties for future Scottish public projects.

Vier Jahre nach Enric Miralles' Tod eröffnete Königin Elisabeth II. am 9. Oktober 2004 das neue **SCHOTTISCHE PARLAMENTSGEBÄUDE**. Von Beginn an war das Projekt umstritten, was z.T. an seinem sensiblen Standort am Ende der Royal Mile in Edinburgh liegt. Das Parlamentsgebäude ist ein Gemeinschaftsprojekt von Enric Miralles, Benedetta Tagliabue EMBT Arquitectes Associats und RMJM Scotland, M. A. H. Duncan, T. B. Stewart. Das Grundstück ist 31 894 m² groß, 17 329 m² davon wurden landschaftsplanerisch gestaltet. Betonfertigteile und ein Tragwerk aus Stahl und Brettschichtholz sind für das Gebäude charakteristisch. Die Architekten schreiben: »Das Terrain selbst wird ein Material sein, ein physisches Baumaterial … das Parlamentsgebäude wird in das Terrain ›eingenutet‹ sein … um in den Boden die Form, die sich bildet, wenn Menschen zusammenkommen, einzumeißeln.« 14 000 t Granit aus den Steinbrüchen von Kemnay in Aberdeenshire wurden verbaut, außerdem 2000 t Black Belfast-Granit aus Südafrika, die für die äußere, mosaikartige Verkleidung verwendet wurden. Das Muster soll an den Umriss eines Gemäldes von Henry Raeburn erinnern, das in der Scottish National Gallery hängt: *Reverend Robert Walker skating in Duddingston Loch.* Das Gebäude wurde mit dem 2005 RIBA Architecture Award ausgezeichnet und gab Anlass zu folgendem Kommentar: »Das Gebäude ist ein brillantes Statement. Eine Aussage auf der ›Wand der Erinnerung‹ lautet: ,Sag wenig, aber das Wenige gut‹. Dieses Gebäude sagt definitiv viel, nicht wenig, aber ganz sicher sagt es das gut.« Neben seiner offensichtlichen Komplexität sind das prägnanteste äußere Merkmal des Gebäudes die Dachkonstruktionen, die an umgedrehte Boote erinnern. Presseberichten zufolge beliefen sich die Kosten des Gebäudes auf umgerechnet 635 Millionen Euro (die Architekten geben die Kosten mit 370 Millionen Euro an). Im Juli 1998 waren die Kosten auf 80 Millionen Euro festgelegt worden. Eine öffentliche Untersuchung durch das Landgericht Edinburgh unter Vorsitz von Lord Fraser of Carmyllie kam zu dem Ergebnis, dass die beiden beteiligten Architekturbüros sehr schlecht miteinander kommunizierten und dass die Kosten von allen Beteiligten nicht ausreichend kontrolliert worden waren. Eine Liste mit zehn Empfehlungen wurde herausgegeben, um bei zukünftigen öffentlichen Bauten in Schottland ähnliche Probleme zu vermeiden.

Inauguré par la reine Elizabeth II le 9 octobre 2004, quatre ans après la disparition d'Enric Miralles, le **PARLEMENT ÉCOSSAIS** aura été dès le départ un projet controversé, en partie parce qu'il était situé dans une zone sensible à l'extrémité du Royal Mile à Édimbourg. Il a été réalisé collectivement, par Enric Miralles, Benedetta Tagliabue EMBT Arquitectes Associats et RMJM Scotland, M. A. H. Duncan, T. B. Stewart. Sur un terrain de 31 894 m² dont 17 329 m² ont été paysagés, le bâtiment à ossature de métal est essentiellement construit en béton préfabriqué et bois lamellé-collé. Comme l'écrit l'architecte, « le sol lui-même sera un matériau, un matériau physique de construction… le Parlement écossais sera inséré dans le sol… de façon à graver dans la terre l'empreinte d'un lieu fait pour réunir les gens. » 14 000 tonnes de granit de la carrière de Kemnay dans l'Aberdeenshire ont été utilisées ainsi que 2000 tonnes de granit Black Belfast importé d'Afrique du Sud pour former une mosaïque de panneaux. Le profil de ces panneaux est censé évoquer les contours d'une œuvre du peintre Henry Raeburn, *Le Révérend Robert Walker patinant sur le Loch de Duddington,* conservée à la National Gallery écossaise. Le bâtiment a remporté le prix d'architecture 2005 du RIBA, accompagné du commentaire suivant: « Cette réalisation est une brillante affirmation d'excellence. Sur le ‹ Mur de la mémoire ›, une des citations dit ‹ Parlez peu et parlez bien ›. Non seulement ce bâtiment dit beaucoup plus que ‹ peu ›, mais il le dit particulièrement bien. » L'élément extérieur le plus caractéristique, en dehors d'une évidente complexité, est le toit inspiré de coques de bateaux inversées. Des sources journalistiques ont parlé d'un coût final de quelque 635 millions d'euros (contre les 370 millions indiqués par les architectes, alors que le budget avait été fixé, en 1998, à 80 millions d'euros. Une enquête publique, menée par Lord Fraser of Carmyllie, a conclu que les deux agences d'architecture mises en cause avaient eu la plus grande difficulté à communiquer et que les coûts n'avaient pas été suffisamment contrôlés par les services concernés. Lord Fraser a publié une série de dix recommandations pour éviter que les mêmes problèmes se reproduisent pour de futurs projets publics en Écosse.

the context of Edinburgh's very ditional "Royal Mile" the new Scot- h Parliament stands out as being te different, which has of course to a good deal of criticism.

Im Kontext von Edinburghs altehrwür- diger Royal Mile fällt das neue Schot- tische Parlament besonders auf, was natürlich schon zu Kritik von vielen Seiten geführt hat.

Dans le contexte du très traditionalis- te Royal Mile d'Édimbourg, le nou- veau Parlement écossais affirme sa différence et cela a entraîné, comme l'on pouvait s'y attendre, de multiples controverses.

This image shows the rather abrupt transition from Edinburgh's stone architecture to that of the new Parliament building. Although there are other modern buildings nearby, the EMBT design brings a surprisingly complex vision of contemporary architecture to the area.

Edinburghs steinerne Architektur und das neue Parlamentsgebäude stehen recht übergangslos nebeneinander. In der näheren Umgebung gibt es auch andere moderne Gebäude, im Bau von EMBT manifestiert sich jedoch eine überraschend komplexe Vorstellung von aktueller Architektur.

On voit bien ici la transition assez brutale entre l'architecture de pierre de la capitale écossaise et celle du Parlement. Même si d'autres bâtiments modernes se trouvent à proximité, le projet d'EMBT impose sa vision très complexe de l'architecture contemporaine dans un quartier protégé.

Large glazed areas bring a good deal of the Scottish capital's limited supply of daylight into the building. This is no minimalist design, in fact it might be considered something of the opposite, a dense, almost willfully "difficult" vision.

Große Glasflächen bringen einen hohen Anteil des in der schottischen Hauptstadt nicht im Übermaß vorhandenen Lichts in das Gebäude. Das Parlament ist kein minimalistischer Bau – ganz im Gegenteil stellt es eine dichte, fast absichtlich »schwierige« Vision vor.

De vastes pans vitrés compensent la faiblesse de la lumière naturelle qui, en Écosse, dure de longs mois. Le projet du Parlement, qui est tout sauf minimaliste – et peut-être même à l'exact opposé – exprime une vision dense qui recherche presque volontairement la difficulté.

The visitor or user of the building is bombarded with a cacophony of forms that does not appear to resolve itself into an "organic" type of architecture. Highly original, the building is the result of a complex and criticized selection and control process.

Der Besucher bzw. Benutzer wird mit einer Kakofonie von Formen bombardiert, die aber nicht in eine organische Architektur münden. Das einzigartige Gebäude ist das Resultat eines komplexen und kontroversen Auswahl- und Kontrollprozesses.

Le visiteur ou l'usager de ce bâtiment est bombardé d'une cacophonie de formes ne pouvant se réduire à un vocabulaire de type organique. Très original, le Parlement est l'aboutissement d'un processus de sélection et de contrôle complexe, et critiqué.

SHUHEI ENDO

Shuhei Endo Architecture Institute
2–14–5 Tenma, Kita-ku
Osaka 530–0043
Japan

Tel: +81 663 54 74 56
Fax: +81 663 54 74 57
e-mail: endo@paramodern.com
Web: www.paramodern.com

Rooftect

Born in Shiga Prefecture in 1960, **SHUHEI ENDO** obtained his masters degree from the Kyoto City University of Art in 1986. He worked after that with the architect Osamu Ishii and established his own firm, the Shuhei Endo Architecture Institute, in 1988. His work has been widely published and he has received numerous prizes including the Andrea Palladio International Prize in Italy (1993). His recent work includes his Slowtecture S, Maihara, Shiga (2002); Growtecture S, Osaka (2002); Springtecture B, Biwa-cho, Shiga (2002); Bubbletecture M, Maihara, Shiga (2003); Rooftecture C, Taishi, Hyogo (2003); Rooftecture H, Kamigori, Hyogo (2004); and Bubbletecture O, Maruoka, Fukui (2004).

SHUHEI ENDO, 1960 in der Präfektur Shiga geboren, erwarb 1986 seinen Masterabschluss an der Kyoto City University of Art in Kioto. Danach arbeitete er bei Osamu Ishii und gründete 1988 sein eigenes Büro, das Shuhei Endo Architecture Institute. Für seine Bauten, die umfassend publiziert wurden, hat er zahlreiche Preise erhalten, darunter den italienischen Andrea Palladio International Award (1993). Zu seinen jüngsten Bauten gehören Slowtecture S in Maihara, Shiga (2002), Growtecture S in Osaka (2002), Springtecture B in Biwa-cho, Shiga (2002), Bubbletecture M in Maihara, Shiga (2003), Rooftecture C in Taishi, Hyogo (2003), Rooftecture H in Kamigori, Hyogo (2004) und Bubbletecture O in Maruoka, Fukui (2004).

Né dans la préfecture de Shiga en 1960, **SHUHEI ENDO** est Master of Architecture de l'Université d'art de Kyoto (1986). Il a ensuite travaillé auprès de l'architecte Osamu Ishii et créé son agence, Shuhei Endo Architecture Institute, en 1988. Son œuvre a été largement publiée et il a reçu de nombreux prix, dont le Prix international Andrea Palladio en Italie (1993). Parmi ses travaux récents : la Slowtecture S, Maihara, Shiga (2002) ; la Growtecture S, Osaka (2002) ; la Rooftecture C, Taishi, Hyogo (2003) ; la Rooftecture H, Kamigori, Hyogo (2004) et lka Bubbletecture O, Maruoka, Fukui (2004).

ROOFTECTURE S

Kobe, Hyogo, 2005

Floor area: 66 m². Client: Ryosuke and Yasuko Uenishi.
Cost: € 120 000

This 66 m² steel frame house occupies just 50.3 m² of the total 130 m² triangular lot. Twenty meters long, the site varies in depth between 1.5 and 4 meters. This is in part due to the steep inclination of the location, facing the Inland Sea. It is covered in galvanized steel sheet. Interior materials include galvanized steel, plywood and wood flooring. As Endo says, "The main theme of this house has been the archaic problem involving slopes and architecture… States of liberation and closure created though the interaction with the slope define this house's spatial quality." Perched on a retaining wall, the house has a wrap-around roof that undoubtedly dictated the choice of its name **ROOFTECTURE S**. Japanese houses are often quite small, given the high population density, particularly along the country's east coast. Like much of Endo's other work, this house challenges the assumptions of architecture and finds an appropriate solution for a particularly difficult and tight location.

Das 66 m² große Haus mit einer Stahlskelettkonstruktion nimmt nur 50,3 m² des dreieckigen, 130 m² großen Grundstücks ein. Dieses hat eine Länge von 20 m, seine Breite beträgt 1,5 bis 4 m. Das liegt z. T. an der steil ansteigenden Topografie des Standortes am japanischen Binnenmeer. Das Haus ist mit verzinktem Stahlblech eingedeckt. Zu den Materialien im Inneren gehören verzinkter Stahl, Sperrholz und Fußböden aus Holz. Endo erläutert: »Das Hauptthema dieses Hauses ist das grundlegende Problem, das sich aus einer Hanglage in Verbindung mit Architektur ergibt… Stadien zwischen Befreiung und Umschließung, die durch die Wechselwirkung zwischen Hang und Haus entstehen, bestimmen die räumlichen Qualitäten des Hauses.« Das Dach, das dem auf eine Stützmauer aufgesetzten Haus seinen Namen **ROOFTECTURE S** gab, wickelt sich um den Baukörper. Wohnhäuser in Japan sind oft recht klein, was an der hohen Bevölkerungsdichte speziell an der Ostküste des Landes liegt. Wie viele andere Gebäude Endos fordert Rooftecture S die gängigen Vorstellungen von Architektur heraus und findet für ein besonders schwieriges und enges Grundstück eine angemessene Lösung.

Cette maison à ossature de bois de 66 m² de surface n'occupe que 50,3 m² d'une parcelle triangulaire de 130 m². En effet, le terrain de vingt mètres de long donnant sur la mer Intérieure du Japon est très fortement incliné et ne mesure que 1,5 à 4 m de profondeur. La maison est recouverte de tôle d'acier galvanisé et utilise à l'intérieur le même acier, le contreplaqué et des planchers en bois. Pour Endo, « le thème principal de cette maison était l'éternel problème posé par les rapports entre une pente et l'architecture… Des situations de libération et de fermeture se créent par interaction avec la pente et définissent le caractère spatial de cette maison ». Juchée sur un mur de soutènement, elle a un toit enveloppant, comme drapé autour d'elle, qui lui vaut son nom de **ROOFTECTURE S**. Les maisons japonaises sont souvent assez petites du fait de la densité démographique du pays, en particulier sur la côte est. Comme beaucoup d'autres réalisations d'Endo, celle-ci remet en cause les certitudes de l'architecture et apporte une solution appropriée à un terrain particulièrement étroit et difficile.

An exercise in extremes, the Rooftecture S design is an ingenious solution
to the problems posed by a lot that
many would consider unusable. Endo
has fashioned an intelligent response
to the narrow and abrupt site.

Rooftexture S könnte man als
»Extremarchitektur« bezeichnen. Der
Entwurf löst die Probleme des Grundstücks, das viele für unbebaubar
halten, auf geniale Weise. Endo hat
das Haus intelligent an das enge und
steile Grundstück angepasst.

Exercice extrême, le projet de la
Rooftecture S est la solution aux
problèmes posés par un terrain que
beaucoup auraient jugé inutilisable.
Endo a imaginé une réponse intelli-
gente à ce site étroit et escarpé.

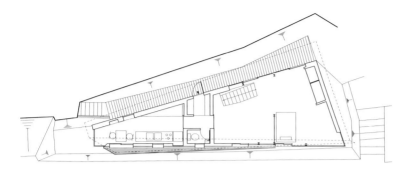

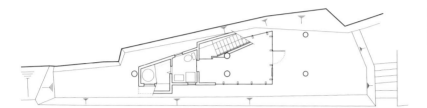

*Inside, the house brings to mind
ship design to some extent, one
of few comparable types of equally
constrained space.*

*Die Innenarchitektur des Hauses
erinnert teilweise an Bootsbau: Nur
dort gibt es ein vergleichbar knap-
pes Raumangebot.*

*L'intérieur de la maison rappelle
dans une certaine mesure celui
d'un bateau, l'un des rares types
de volume aussi contraignant.*

New Milan Trade

MASSIMILIANO FUKSAS

Massimiliano and Doriana Fuksas
Piazza del Monte di Pietà, 30
00186 Rome
Italy

Tel: +39 06 68 80 78 71
Fax: +39 06 68 80 78 72
e-mail: office@fuksas.it
Web: www.fuksas.it

MASSIMILIANO FUKSAS was born in 1944 in Rome. He received his degree in architecture at the University of La Sapienza in 1969. He created the agency Granma (1969–88) with Anna Maria Sacconi, and opened an office in Paris in 1989. He won the 1999 Grand Prix d'Architecture in France, and has written the architecture column of the Italian weekly *L'Espresso* beginning in 2000. He was the Director of the 7th Architecture Biennale in Venice (1998–2000). His presence in France was notably marked by the Médiathèque in Rézé (1987–91); the National Engineering School in Brest (ENIB ISAMOR, 1990–92); the Maison des Arts at the Michel de Montaigne University in Bordeaux (1992–95); Maximilien Perret High School, Alfortville, near Paris (1995–97). His Corten steel entrance for the caves at Niaux (1988–93) shows, as did the Maison des Arts in Bordeaux, that Fuksas has a sustained interest in contemporary sculpture and art. In 1995–2001 he built the Twin Tower, a 150-meter-high headquarters for Wienerberger in Vienna, Austria; the Piazza Mall, an entertainment center, commercial and office complex in Eindhoven, The Netherlands (1999–2004) and the Ferrari Research Center, Maranello, Italy (2001–04) and is presently working on three large-scale projects: European Convention Center (EUR) in Rome and two rock-and-roll concert halls (Zénith) in Strasbourg and Amiens.

Der 1944 in Rom geborene **MASSIMILIANO FUKSAS** studierte an der Università di Roma »La Sapienza« Architektur und machte 1969 sein Diplom. Zusammen mit Anna Maria Sacconi gründete er das Büro Granma, das von 1969 bis 1988 bestand. 1989 eröffnete er in Paris ein neues Büro. 1999 gewann er den französischen Grand Prix d'Architecture. Seit 2000 schreibt er die Architekturkolumne für das Wochenmagazin *L'Espresso*. Fuksas war Direktor der VII. Architekturbiennale in Venedig (1998–2000). Bekannt wurde er in Frankreich durch folgende Gebäude: die Médiathèque in Rézé (1987–91), die Ecole Nationale d'Ingénieurs et Institut Scientifique in Brest (ENIB ISAMOR, 1990–92), die Maison des Arts der Université Michel de Montaigne in Bordeaux (1992–95) und das Lycée Maximilien Perret in Alfortville nahe Paris (1995–97). Der Eingang aus Corten-Stahl für die Höhlen von Niaux (1988–93) zeigt ebenso wie die Maison des Arts in Bordeaux Fuksas' beständiges Interesse an zeitgenössischer Bildhauerei bzw. Kunst. 1995 bis 2001 wurden die Twin Towers, die 150 m hohe Zentrale von Wienerberger in Wien realisiert, 1999 bis 2004 die Piazza Mall, ein Komplex mit Büro-, Laden- und Unterhaltungsnutzung in Eindhoven, Niederlande und 2001–04 das Forschungszentrum von Ferrari in Maranello, Italien. Zurzeit plant Fuksas drei große Projekte: das European Convention Center (EUR) in Rom und zwei Rock-and-Roll-Konzerthallen (Zénith) in Straßburg und Amiens.

Né en 1944 à Rome, **MASSIMILANO FUKSAS** est diplômé d'architecture de l'Université La Sapienza (1969). Il a créé l'agence Gramma (1969–88) avec Anna Maria Sacconi et ouvert une agence à Paris en 1989. Grand prix d'architecture 1999 en France, il a par ailleurs tenu une rubrique d'architecture dans l'hebdomadaire italien *L'Espresso* à partir de 2000. Il a été le directeur de la 7e Biennale d'architecture de Venise (1998–2000). Sa présence en France a été marquée par la construction de la Médiathèque de Rézé (1987–91); l'École nationale d'ingénierie de Brest, Enib Isamor (1990–92); la Maison des arts de l'Université Michel de Montaigne Bordeaux (1992–95); le collège Maximilien Perret à Alfortville près de Paris (1995–97). De même que la Maison des arts de Bordeaux, l'entrée en acier Corten qu'il créée pour les grottes préhistoriques de Niaux (1988–93) montre son indéfectible intérêt pour la sculpture et l'art contemporains. En 1999–2001, il a construit les Twin Towers, un immeuble de bureaux de 150 m de haut pour Wienerberger (Vienne, Autriche), le Piazza Mall, centre de loisirs, centre commercial et complexe de bureaux Eindhoven, Pays-Bas (1999–2004). et le Centre de recherche Ferrari, Maranello, Italie (2001–04) et travaille actuellement à trois importants projets : le Centre européen de congrès à Rome et deux Zénith, salles de concert rock, à Strasbourg et Amiens.

NEW MILAN TRADE FAIR

Pero-Rho, Milan, Italy, 2002–05

Total floor area: 2 000 000 m²; building floor area: 1 000 000 m²; exhibition floor area: more than 400 000 m².
Client: Fondazione Fiera Milano. Cost: €750 million

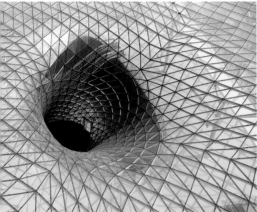

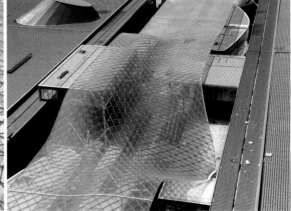

ssimilliano Fuksas's vision of the
atral glass-covered walkway of the
ra Milano is related to drawings he
de of vortices or storm formations.

*Die Idee eines zentralen, glasüber-
dachten Weges für die Fiera Milano
hat Massimiliano Fuksas aus Zeichnungen entwickelt, die er von Stru-
del- und Wirbelformationen machte.*

*La vision de l'allée couverte de la
Fiera Milano par Massimiliano Fuksas
se rapproche des dessins de vortex
ou de formations d'orages.*

*An aerial view gives a clear idea of
the size and volume of the complex,
with the main walkway slicing through
the middle of the more ordinary exhibition areas to the right and left.*

*Das Luftbild vermittelt einen Eindruck
von der Größe des Projektes. Der
Hauptweg verläuft mitten durch das
ansonsten weniger spektakuläre Aus-
stellungsgelände.*

*Vue aérienne montrant les dimen-
sions impressionnantes du complexe.
L'allée principale se fraye un chemin
au milieu de pavillons d'exposition
plus traditionnels.*

Easily the largest project that Massimiliano Fuksas has ever been involved in, the new **FAIR OF MILAN** measure no less than 1.4 million square meters. Fuksas won a 2001 competition against the likes of Santiago Calatrava, the German firm von Gerkan Marg und Partner and the Italian Mario Bellini, and completed enormous task in just over 27 months. At its height, the Fiera Milano was the largest civilian construction project underway in the world. The most architecturally interesting feature of the complex is its central "urban promenade," a 1.5 km covered walkway with a dynamic glass canopy design that flows over the crowded people moving in patterns that bring to mind clouds or even tornados. Given the rather extreme conditions imposed by the large scale of the Fiera Milano and the very short construction schedule, it might have been expected that Fuksas would do no more than a competent job, but he has gone much further, almost reinventing the idea of fair ground and above all adding his own personal, artistic touch. Although his walkway may bring to mind certain computer-generated forms, the source of his ideas is in drawings and models which often approach the quality of artworks in and of themselves.

Bei weitem das größte Projekt von Massimiliano Fuksas ist die neue **MAILÄNDER MESSE** mit nicht weniger als 1,4 Millionen m². Fuksas gewann 2001 den Wettbewerb, an dem u. a. Santiago Calatrava, Von Gerkan, Marg und Partner sowie Mario Bellini teilgenommen hatten; in nur 27 Monaten wurde das enorme Bauvorhaben durchgeführt. Auf dem Höhepunkt der Bautätigkeit war die Fiera Milano die größte zivile Baustelle der Welt. Das interessanteste Merkmal der Anlage ist die zentrale »urbane Promenade«, ein 1,5 km langer überdeckter Weg mit einem dynamisch »fließenden« Vordach, unter dem die Messefahrzeuge, die für den Transport der Besucher eingesetzt werden, hin- und herfahren. Dabei evozieren die Formen des Daches Bilder von Wolken, sogar von Tornados. In Anbetracht der Bedingungen, die die enorme Größe der Fiera Milano und die extrem kurze Bauzeit darstellten, hätte man erwarten können, dass Fuksas die ihm gestellte Aufgabe kompetent lösen würde – und nicht mehr. Tatsächlich ist er aber viel weiter gegangen: Fast könnte man sagen, er habe die Idee aller Messegelände neu erfunden und vor allem seine persönliche, künstlerische Sichtweise eingebracht. Der Messeweg mag an bestimmte computergenerierte Formen erinnern, die Ideen basieren jedoch auf Fuksas' Zeichnungen und Modellen, die oft selbst die Qualität von Kunstwerken annehmen.

Le nouveau complexe de la **FOIRE DE MILAN**, certainement le plus important projet, et de loin, dans lequel ait jamais été impliqué Massimiliano Fuksas, couvre pas moins de 1,4 million de m². Il en a remporté le concours en 2001 face à Santiago Calatrava, à l'agence allemande Von Gerkan, Marg und Partner et à l'Italien Mario Bellini, et a achevé cette tâche immense en un peu plus de 27 mois seulement. À un certain moment, ce chantier était le plus important projet civil en construction dans le monde. Sa caractéristique la plus intéressante est une « promenade urbaine », allée de 1,5 km de long couverte par un long ruban de verre suspendu, se déployant au-dessus des trottoirs roulants en adoptant des formes qui rappellent des nuages, voire des tornades. Compte tenu des contraintes extrêmes de cette énorme entreprise et de ses délais très courts, on aurait pu s'attendre à ce que Fuksas se contente de faire un travail pertinent, mais il est allé beaucoup plus loin en réinventant pratiquement l'idée de foire et surtout en y ajoutant sa propre touche artistique. Bien que cette allée évoque certaines formes générées par ordinateur, ses plans sont, en fait, issus de dessins et de maquettes dont la qualité approche souvent celle d'œuvres d'art.

Despite an extremely tight design to completion schedule, Fuksas has given the Fiera Milano an unexpectedly light and airy feeling.

Trotz des extrem engen Terminrahmens hat Fuksas für die Fiera Milano eine überraschend leichte und luftige Atmosphäre geschaffen.

Malgré des délais de concours extrêmement serrés, Fuksas a réussi à donner à la Foire de Milan un caractère étonnamment léger et aérien.

Along the spine of the central axis, a certain number of pod-like volumes house functions ranging from press areas to cafés.

Entlang des Rückgrates findet sich eine Reihe kokonartiger Volumina, in denen z. B. Räume für die Presse und Cafés untergebracht sind.

Le long de l'axe central, divers volumes en formes de cosses abritent des activités variées, de la salle de presse aux cafés.

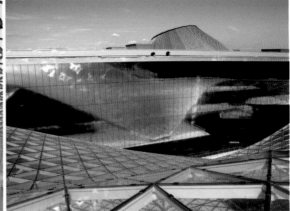

...sas adopts an essentially indus-... vocabulary to the needs of large-...e exhibitions, using volcano-like ...rusions from the main buildings ...ring ample light into the actual ...w spaces.

Im Prinzip passt Fuksas ein dem Industriebau entliehenes Vokabular den Anforderungen einer Großmesse an. Die vulkanähnlich geformten Ausstülpungen aus den Dächern bringen viel Licht in die Ausstellungshallen.

Fuksas a adopté un vocabulaire essentiellement industriel pour répondre aux besoins des expositions à grande échelle. Dans le bâtiment principal, des saillies aux allures de volcans permettent un meilleur éclairage des espaces d'exposition.

GRAFT

GRAFT Gesellschaft von Architekten mbH
Heidestrasse 50
10557 Berlin
Germany

Tel: +49 30 24 04 79 85
Fax: +49 30 24 04 79 87
e-mail: berlin@graftlab.com
Web: www.graftlab.com

GRAFT was created in Los Angeles in 1998 "as a label for architecture, art, music and the pursuit of happiness". Lars Krückeberg, Wolfram Putz and Thom
Willemeit are the partners of GRAFT, which today employs about 20 architects and artists in the US, Europe and in Asia. GRAFT has offices in Los Angeles and Berlin a
Beijing. Lars Krückeberg was educated at the Technische Universität Braunschweig, Braunschweig as an engineer (1989–96) and at SciArc in Los Angeles (1997–9
Wolfram Putz attended the Technische Universität Braunschweig (1988–95), the University of Utah, Salt Lake City (1992–93) and SciArc in Los Angeles (1996–9
Thomas Willemeit also was educated in Braunschweig and at the Bauhaus Dessau (1991–92) before working in the office of Daniel Libeskind (1998–2001). Taking adva
tage of their German background combined with U.S. training, GRAFT declares "We can see an architecture of new combinations, the grafting of different cultures a
styles. The English word graft includes a variety of meanings and multiple readings. It has a particular meaning in the terminology of botany, the grafting of one sh
onto a genetically different host. The positive properties of two genetically different cultures are combined in the new biological hybrid." They have built a studio a
house for the actor Brad Pitt in Los Angeles (2000–03); designed a private dental clinic in Berlin, a nightclub at the Treasure Island Casino in Las Vegas and the Dom
ion, another design hotel located in Vancouver, Canada (2004–05).

GRAFT wurde 1998 in Los Angeles »als Label für Architektur, Kunst, Musik und das Streben nach Glück« gegründet. Lars Krückeberg, Wolfram Putz und Thom
Willemeit sind die Partner von GRAFT; derzeit beschäftigen sie ungefähr 20 Architekten und Künstler in den USA, Europa und Asien. GRAFT unterhält Büros in Los An
les, Berlin und Peking. Lars Krückeberg studierte Ingenieurwesen an der Technischen Universität Braunschweig (1989–96), außerdem an der SCI-Arc in Los Ange
(1997–98). Auch Wolfram Putz studierte an der Technischen Universität Braunschweig (1988–95), dann an der University of Utah in Salt Lake City (1992–93) und an
SCI-Arc in Los Angeles (1996–98). Thomas Willemeit studierte ebenfalls in Braunschweig, außerdem am Bauhaus in Dessau (1991–92), bevor er im Büro von Dan
Libeskind arbeitete (1998–2001). Den deutschen Hintergrund und die Ausbildung in den USA nutzend, formuliert GRAFT sein Programm: »Wir stellen uns eine Archit
tur vor, die von neuen Kombinationen lebt, die verschiedene Kulturen und Stile ›veredelt‹. Das englische Wort ›graft‹ hat mehrere Bedeutungen, kann unterschiedlich v
standen werden. Im Bereich der Botanik bedeutet ›to graft‹, dass ein Schössling auf eine fremde Gastpflanze aufgepropft wird. Die positiven Eigenschaften der beic
genetisch voneinander verschiedenen Kulturen werden in einem neuen biologischen Hybrid miteinander verbunden.« GRAFT hat u. a. ein Studio und ein Wohnhaus
den Schauspieler Brad Pitt entworfen (2000–03) sowie eine private Dentalklinik in Berlin, einen Nachtklub für das Treasure Island Casino in Las Vegas und das Domini
ein Design Hotel in Vancouver (2004–05).

GRAFT, « label pour l'architecture, l'art, la musique et la poursuite du bonheur », a été créé à Los Angeles en 1998. Lars Krückeberg, Wolfram Putz et Thom
Willemeit sont les associés de GRAFT qui emploie aujourd'hui une vingtaine d'architectes et d'artistes aux États-Unis, en Europe et en Asie. L'agence possède des burea
à Los Angeles, Berlin et Pékin. Lars Krückeberg a été formé à l'ingénierie à la Technische Universität de Braunschweig (1989–96) et à SciArc à Los Angeles (1997–9
Wolfram Putz a étudié à la même université (1988–95), à celle de l'Utah à Salt Lake City (1992–93) et à SciArc à Los Angeles (1996–98). Thomas Willemeit a éga
ment étudié à Braunschweig et au Bauhaus Dessau (1991–92) avant de travailler auprès de Daniel Libeskind (1998–2001). En s'appuyant sur leurs formations al
mande et américaine, GRAFT déclare : « Nous pouvons entrevoir une architecture de combinaisons nouvelles, la greffe de différents styles et cultures. Le terme angl
‹ to graft › possède toute une variété de sens et de lectures. Il a une signification particulière en botanique : le greffage sur un hôte génétiquement différent. Les cara
tères propres à deux cultures génétiquement différentes se combinent alors en un nouvel hybride biologique. » Ils ont construit un atelier et une maison pour l'acte
Brad Pitt à Los Angeles (2000–03), conçu une clinique dentaire privée à Berlin, un nightclub pour le Treasure Island Casino à Las Vegas, et le projet Dominion, un « des
hotel » à Vancouver, Canada (2004–05).

HOTEL Q!

Berlin, Germany, 2002–04

Floor area: 2973 m². Client: Wolfgang Loock.
Cost: €1 million (interior design)

Located on the Knesebeckstrasse, just around the corner from the busy Kurfürstendamm, Q! is a design hotel that takes many leads from predecessors such the Schrager hotels in London (St Martins Lane) or the United States (Morgans, Delano, Mondrian etc.). Hotel operator Wolfgang Loock called them in 2002 after seei the Hollywood Hills studio they designed for Brad Pitt in *Architectural Digest*. Though they did not design the seven-story building that houses the hotel, GRAFT manag to give a distinctive look to the interior, beginning with the 260 m² ground floor with its reception desk, lounge-bar and restaurant. White translucent curtains shield t hotel desk from the street but once inside the visitor is immediately confronted by wrap-around red surfaces that look more Californian than New Berlin. Six floors w twelve rooms per floor and a penthouse on the seventh floor make up the rest of the 2973 m² structure. Working with an interior design budget of approximately o million euros, Wolfgang Putz succeeded in imposing a unified esthetic sense, admittedly influenced in part by the work of Neil Denari. Guest rooms also feature wrapp surfaces where walls become desks or ceilings. Smoked oak floors and subtle ceiling designs based on the photographs of Christian Thomas aim to give a "cocoon-li feeling" to the rooms. The architects do succeed in breaking down the strict barriers between floor and ceiling, desk and bed, and in this they have given a uniq ambiance to Q!

In der Knesebeckstraße, nicht weit vom belebten Kurfürstendamm, liegt das Hotel Q!, dessen Design sich in vielen Bereichen an Vorgängern wie den Schrag Hotels in London (St. Martin's Lane) oder in den USA (Morgans, Delano, Mondrian etc.) orientiert. Nachdem er in »Architectural Digest« einen Bericht über das von GRA entworfene Hollywood Hills Studio für Brad Pitt gesehen hatte, rief Wolfgang Loock, der Betreiber des Hotels 2002 bei GRAFT an. Obwohl der Entwurf für das siebe geschossige Gebäude, in dem sich das Hotel befindet, nicht von GRAFT stammt, gelang es den Architekten, im Inneren des Hotels ein eigenständiges Design durchz setzen – beginnend mit dem 260 m² großen Erdgeschoss mit der Rezeption, einer Lounge/Bar und einem Restaurant. Weiße, durchscheinende Vorhänge schirmen c Rezeption von der Straße ab; erst einmal drinnen, wird der Besucher sogleich mit umlaufenden roten Oberflächen konfrontiert, die mehr an Kalifornien als an das ne Berlin denken lassen. Der Rest des 2973 m² großen Hotels umfasst sechs Geschosse mit jeweils zwölf Hotelzimmern sowie ein Penthouse. Mit einem Budget von etv 1 Million Euro für die Innenausstattung gelang es Wolfgang Putz, eine einheitliche Ästhetik zu schaffen, die, wie er selbst sagt, teilweise von Neil Denaris Projekten beei flusst ist. Auch in den Hotelzimmern gibt es sich abwickelnde Oberflächen, Wände werden so zu Tischen oder Unterdecken. Fußböden aus geräucherter Eiche und su tile Deckengrafiken, deren Grundlage Fotografien von Christian Thomas bilden, sollen in den Räumen eine »kokonartige Atmosphäre« erzeugen. Und tatsächlich gelin es den Architekten, die strengen Grenzen zwischen Boden und Decke, Tisch und Bett aufzuheben und dadurch im Q! ein einzigartiges Ambiente zu schaffen.

Situé sur la Knesebeckstrasse, presque à l'angle du Kurfürstendamm, Q! est un «design hotel» qui s'inspire beaucoup de précurseurs comme les hôtels Schr ger à Londres (St. Martins Lane) ou aux États-Unis (Morgan, Delano, Mondrian, etc.). Gérant d'hôtels, Wolfgang Loock a fait appel à GRAFT en 2002 après avoir vu studio d'Hollywood Hills réalisé pour Brad Pitt dans *Architectural Digest*. Bien qu'elle n'ait pas conçu l'immeuble de sept étages qui accueille l'hôtel, l'agence a réuss donner un style très personnel aux aménagements intérieurs, à commencer par les 260 m² de la réception, du bar et du restaurant. Des rideaux translucides blancs is lent la réception de la rue, mais une fois entré, le visiteur est confronté à des plans enveloppants rouges de style plus californien que néo-berlinois. Six niveaux de dou chambres et une penthouse au septième constituent le reste de cet ensemble de 2973 m². Pour un budget d'aménagement intérieur d'environ 1 million d'euros, Wolfra Putz a réussi à imposer une esthétique harmonieuse, influencée en partie, admet-il, par le travail de Neil Denari. Les chambres présentent le même type de surfac enveloppantes qu'au rez-de-chaussée, qui font que les murs deviennent bureaux ou plafonds. Les sols en chêne fumé et le décor subtil des plafonds, inspirés des ph tos de Christian Thomas, accentuent cette impression de cocon. Les architectes ont, en effaçant les strictes barrières entre sol et plafond, bureau et lit, su créer cet atmosphère si personnelle à l'hôtel Q!.

smooth red wrap-around design
he lobby and bar area of the hotel
the tone for the entire project.
s become furniture and there is
ost no differentiation between the
s and ceilings.

glatte rote Umhüllung ist das
entliche Gestaltungsmerkmal der
by und der Bar und bestimmt den
im Gebäude. Die Wände werden
Möbelstücken, Wand und Decke
schmolzen.

principe d'enveloppe rouge utilisé
le hall d'accueil et le bar donne
n au projet. Les murs deviennent
bles et la distinction entre murs
lafonds s'efface.

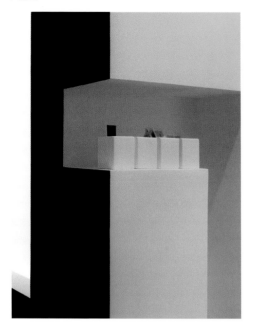

A spa is a part of any self-respecting "design" hotel and Q! is no exception. Angled surfaces that offer unexpected uses are present throughout, thanks to the clever work of GRAFT.

Ein Spa gehört zu jedem Designhotel, das etwas auf sich hält; Q! bildet da keine Ausnahme. Geneigte Flächen können ungewöhnlich genutzt werden und dank GRAFTs Kreativität kommen sie überall zum Einsatz.

Tout design hotel qui se respecte doit posséder un spa et le Q! ne fait pas exception. Des plans inclinés se prêtent à des usages originaux, grâce à l'intelligent travail de GRAFT.

The continuity between floor, bathtub and bed is to say the least unusual, but it works well in the rooms of the hotel.

Die Einheit von Boden, Badewanne und Bett ist, vorsichtig ausgedrückt, ungewöhnlich, funktioniert in den Hotelzimmern aber gut.

La continuité entre le sol, la baignoire et le lit est pour le moins inhabituelle, mais fonctionne très bien dans le cadre de cet hôtel.

ZAHA HADID

Zaha Hadid
Studio 9
10 Bowling Green Lane
London EC1R OBQ
UK

Tel: +44 20 72 53 51 47
Fax: +44 20 72 51 83 22
e-mail: mail@zaha-hadid.com
Web: www.zaha-hadid.com

BMW Central Bui

ZAHA HADID studied architecture at the Architectural Association in London (AA) beginning in 1972 and was awarded the Diploma Prize in 1977. She the became a partner of Rem Koolhaas in the Office for Metropolitan Architecture (OMA) and taught at the AA. She has also taught at Harvard, the University of Chicago, Hamburg and at Columbia University in New York. Well known for her paintings and drawings, she has had a substantial influence despite having built relatively buil ings. She has completed the Vitra Fire Station, Weil-am-Rhein, Germany (1990–94) and exhibition designs such as that for *The Great Utopia*, Solomon R. Guggenhei Museum, New York (1992). Significant competition entries include her design for the Cardiff Bay Opera House (1994–96); and the Habitable Bridge, London (1996); the Luxembourg Philharmonic Hall, Luxembourg (1997). More recently, Zaha Hadid has entered a phase of active construction with such projects as the Bergisel S Jump, Innsbruck (2001–02); Lois & Richard Rosenthal Center for Contemporary Art, Cincinnati, Ohio (1999–2003); and Central Building of the new BMW Assembly Pla in Leipzig (2005). She is working on the Price Tower Arts Center, Bartlesville, Oklahoma; Doha Tower, Doha, Qatar; and made a proposal for the 2012 Olympic Villag New York. In 2004, Zaha Hadid became the first woman to win the coveted Pritzker Prize.

ZAHA HADID studierte ab 1972 an der Architectural Association (AA) in London und erhielt 1977 den Diploma Prize. Danach wurde sie Partnerin von Rem Koo haas im Office for Metropolitan Architecture (OMA). Sie lehrte an der Architectural Association (AA), in Harvard, an der University of Chicago, in Hamburg und an de Columbia University in New York. Hadid ist besonders durch ihre Gemälde und Zeichnungen bekannt geworden. Obwohl nur wenige ihrer Entwürfe realisiert wurden, s das Feuerwehrhaus der Firma Vitra in Weil am Rhein (1990–94), gehört sie zu den einflussreichsten Vertreterinnen ihrer Zunft. 1992 entwarf sie das Ausstellungsdesig für *The Great Utopia* im New Yorker Solomon R. Guggenheim Museum. Zu ihren bedeutendsten Wettbewerbsbeiträgen gehören Entwürfe für das Cardiff Bay Opera Hous (1994–96), für die Habitable Bridge in London (1996) und die Philharmonie in Luxemburg (1997). In jüngster Zeit begann für Zaha Hadid eine Phase des aktiven Bau ens mit Projekten wie der Bergisel-Sprungschanze in Innsbruck (2001–02), dem Lois & Richard Rosenthal Center for Contemporary Art, Cincinnati, Ohio (1999–2003 und dem Zentralgebäude des neuen BMW-Werkes in Leipzig. Derzeit in Planung sind das Price Tower Arts Center in Bartlesville in Oklahoma und der Doha Tower in Doh im Emirat Katar. Außerdem hat sie einen Entwurf für das Olympische Dorf 2012 in New York erarbeitet. Anfang 2004 wurde Zaha Hadid als erste Frau mit dem begeh ten Pritzker-Preis ausgezeichnet.

Née en 1950 à Bagdad, **ZAHA HADID** a étudié l'architecture à l'Architectural Association (AA) de Londres de 1972 à 1977, date à laquelle elle reçoit le pr Diploma. Elle est ensuite associée de l'agence de Rem Koolhaas, Office for Metropolitan Architecture (OMA), et enseigne à l'AA, à Harvard, à l'Université de Chicago, Columbia University (New York) et à l'Université de Hambourg. Très connue pour ses peintures et dessins, elle exerce une réelle influence, même si elle construit asse peu pendant longtemps. Parmi ses réalisations : le poste d'incendie de Vitra, Weil-am-Rhein, Allemagne (1990–94) et des projets pour des expositions comme *La Gra de Utopie* au Solomon R. Guggenheim Museum, New York (1992). Elle a participé à des concours dont les plus importants sont le projet de la Cardiff Bay Opera Hous Pays-de-Galles (1994–96), un pont habitable, Londres (1996) et la salle de concerts philharmoniques de Luxembourg (1997). Plus récemment, elle est entrée dans ur phase d'importants chantiers avec des projets comme le tremplin de saut à ski de Bergisel (2001–02, Innsbruck, Autriche) ; le Lois and Richard Rosenthal Center f Contemporary Art, Cincinnati, Ohio (1999–2003) et le bâtiment central de l'usine BMW de Leipzig (2003–04) publié ici. Elle travaille actuellement aux projets du Pric Tower Arts Center (Bartlesville, Oklahoma) et de la Doha Tower (Doha, Qatar) et a présenté une proposition pour le village des Jeux olympiques de New York en 201; En 2004, elle a été la première femme à remporter le très convoité prix Pritzker.

BMW PLANT LEIPZIG – CENTRAL BUILDING

Leipzig, Germany, 2003–04

Floor area: 25 000 m². Client: BMW AG, Munich. Cost: €54 million

Simply put, in the words of the architects, "It was the client's objective to translate industrial architecture into an aesthetic concept that complies equally w representational and functional requirements. In the transition zones between manufacturing halls and public space, the **CENTRAL BUILDING** acts as a 'mediat impressing a positive permanent impact upon the eye of the beholder in a restrained semiotic way." Zaha Hadid was asked to design this building, described as the "ne center of the whole factory complex," subsequent to an April 2002 competition she won when the layout of adjacent manufacturing buildings had already been decid Suppliers chosen for the rest of the factory provided many pre-fabricated elements, in harmony with the "industrial approach to office spaces" decided by BMW. Used the entrance to the entire plant, the Central Building connects the three main manufacturing departments. The nerve-center concept is rendered all the more clear in t "the central area as a 'market place' is intended to enhance communication by providing staff with an area with which to avail themselves of personal and administra ve services." A system of cascading floors allows views of different parts of the manufacturing process, ranging from assembly to the auditing area described as "a c tral focus of everybody's attention." The building itself is made with "self-compacting concrete and a roof structure assembled with a series of H-steel beams." The arc tect intends to use the architecture to create an "overall transparency of the internal organization," but also to mix functions "to avoid the traditional segregation of sta groups." Particular attention was also paid to the inevitable car parking area in front of the building by "turning it into a dynamic spectacle in its own right."

Bei dem neuen **ZENTRALGEBÄUDE** für BMW ging es, so die Architekten, um Folgendes: »Das Ziel des Bauherrn war es, Industriearchitektur in ein ästhetisch Konzept zu übersetzen, das sowohl Repräsentations- als auch funktionale Anforderungen erfüllt. Im Übergang zwischen Produktionshallen und öffentlichem Bereich fu giert das Zentralgebäude als ein Vermittler, der auf zurückhaltende Weise einen dauerhaften, positiven Eindruck auf dem Auge des Betrachters hinterlässt.« Zaha Ha wurde mit dem Entwurf des Gebäudes, das als »Nervenzentrum der gesamten Fabrikanlage« bezeichnet wird, beauftragt, nachdem sie im April 2002 den Wettbew hierfür gewonnen hatte. Zu diesem Zeitpunkt war das Konzept der angrenzenden Produktionshallen schon festgelegt. Firmen, die Teile für diese Bereiche der Anlage ferten, wurden beim Zentralgebäude mit der Produktion vieler vorgefertigter Elemente beauftragt. Auf diese Weise wurde »der industrielle Charakter der Büroräume«, den man sich bei BMW entschieden hatte, umgesetzt. Als Zugang zu allen Bereichen der Anlage verbindet das Zentralgebäude die drei Produktionsabteilungen. Das K zept des Nervenzentrums wird mit dem »zentralen Bereich, der als ›Marktplatz‹ fungieren soll« besonders deutlich. »Er soll die Kommunikation zwischen den Mitarbeit fördern und persönliche und verwaltungstechnische Dienstleistungen anbieten.« Ein System von kaskadenartigen Ebenen erlaubt Blicke in verschiedene Bereiche, v der Montage bis zum Testbereich, der als »ein Schwerpunkt des allgemeinen Interesses« beschrieben wird. Das Gebäude wurde aus »selbstverdichtendem Beton her stellt und hat eine Dachkonstruktion aus Doppel-T-Trägern«. Die Absicht der Architektin war es, eine »umfassende Transparenz der internen Organisation« zu schaf und Funktionsbereiche zu mischen, »um die traditionelle Trennung verschiedener ›Statusgruppen‹ der Mitarbeiter zu vermeiden«. Besondere Aufmerksamkeit wurde a den unvermeidlichen Stellplatzflächen vor dem Gebäude geschenkt, indem »diese selbst in ein dynamisches Spektakel verwandelt« wurden.

Selon les termes de l'architecte, « l'objectif du client était de traduire l'architecture industrielle en un concept esthétique qui s'accorde aussi bien avec des e gences fonctionnelles que de représentation. Dans les zones de transition entre les ateliers de fabrication et les espaces publics, le **BÂTIMENT CENTRAL** joue le r d'un ‹ médiateur ›, exerçant un impact positif sur le regard du spectateur de façon sémiotique et contrôlée. » Zaha Hadid s'est vue confier la conception de ce bâtime décrit comme « le centre névralgique de l'ensemble du complexe de l'usine » après avoir remporté un concours, organisé en avril 2002, alors que les plans d'un bâ ment de fabrication adjacent avaient déjà été décidés. Les fournisseurs choisis pour le reste de l'usine ont fourni des éléments préfabriqués correspondant à « l'approc industrielle des espaces de bureaux » décidée par BMW. Situé à l'entrée du complexe, le Bâtiment central connecte les trois grands départements de fabrication. concept de centre névralgique se traduit par « une zone centrale qui est une ‹ agora › dont le rôle est d'améliorer la communication en offrant un espace où on trou tous les services personnels et administratifs ». La disposition en cascade des différents niveaux montre tous les stades de la chaîne de production, de l'assemblage contrôle, décrit comme « le centre de l'attention de tous ». Le bâtiment est en « béton auto-compactant et possède une toiture faite d'une série de poutres en acier p filé en H ». Pour Zaha Hadid, l'architecture sert à créer une « transparence d'ensemble de l'organisation interne », mais aussi à mêler les fonctions « pour éviter la tra tionnelle ségrégation hiérarchique ». Une attention particulière a été portée aux parkings face à l'entrée du bâtiment pour « en faire un spectacle dynamique en soi ».

The wrapping, forward leaning forms of the building give it a dynamic aspect, as though it were ready to speed away just like the cars it is intended to produce.

Die fließenden, sich nach vorne neigenden Formen verleihen dem Gebäude seine dynamische Wirkung – als ob es jederzeit davonschießen könnte, wie die Fahrzeuge, die hier produziert werden sollen.

Les formes enveloppantes inclinées vers l'avant donnent au bâtiment un aspect dynamique, « prêt à démarrer » comme les voitures qui y sont produites.

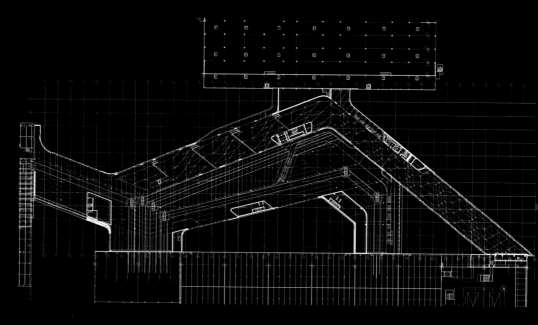

These images show clearly that this is more than just a pretty façade covering a conventional building.

Hier wird deutlich, dass es sich um mehr als ein konventionelles Gebäude mit einer interessanten Hülle handelt.

Ces images montrent qu'il ne s'agit pas d'une jolie façade recouvrant un bâtiment conventionnel.

HERRMANN + BOSCH /
ARCHITEKTENGRUPPE STUTTGART

Herrmann + Bosch, Freie Architekten BDA, Teckstrasse 56, 70190 Stuttgart, Germany
Tel: +49 711 26 84 11 10, Fax: +49 711 2 68 41 11 29, e-mail: info@herrmann-bosch.de
Web: www.herrmann-bosch.de

Dieter Herrmann was born in 1938 and studied at the Technical University of Stuttgart (1958–65), before working in the office of Behnisch & Partner, Stuttga (1966–78). In partnership with Gerhard Bosch, he created the office of **HERRMANN + BOSCH** in 1992. Gerhard Bosch was born in 1955, and studied at the Universi of Stuttgart (1977–85). He is a professor of wood construction at the University of Applied Sciences in Biberach. Knut Lohrer, born in 1937, studied architecture at th Technical University of Stuttgart (1958–65). He created his own office, Atelier Lohrer, in Stuttgart in 1973 and worked on several museum and exhibition design projec with Dieter Herrmann. Since 2002, he has been an architectural advisor for the Sultanate of Oman. Uli Pfeil was born in 1956 and studied architecture at the Universi of Stuttgart (1977–84). He worked in the offices of Dieter Herrmann and Atelier Lohrer (1984–91) before creating his own office in Stuttgart in 1991. Dieter Keck w born in 1946 and studied at the University of Applied Sciences in Karlsruhe (1969–73). They recently completed a 13-story administrative building for the Lan wirtschaftliche Sozialversicherung insurance company in Stuttgart-Kaltental and are currently working on a number of retirement homes in Germany. Important buildin planned by Herrmann + Bosch include the Daimler-Benz-Museum (in collaboration with Knut Lohrer and H. G. Merz, Stuttgart, 1984–86); the Limes-Museum (in colla oration with Knut Lohrer, Aalen, 1985–87); the Fachhochschule für Technik, Esslingen (University of Applied Science, 1992–96); and the Haus Rohrer Höhe home for t elderly (Stuttgart, 1996–98).

Dieter Herrmann, geboren 1938, studierte in Stuttgart (1958–65). Von 1966 bis 1978 arbeitete er im Büro Behnisch & Partner, Stuttgart. Zusammen mit Gerha Bosch gründete er 1992 das Büro **HERRMANN + BOSCH**. Gerhard Bosch, geboren 1955, studierte in Stuttgart (1977–85). Er ist Professor für Holzkonstruktionen der Hochschule Biberach. Knut Lohrer, geboren 1937, studierte Architektur an der Technischen Universität Stuttgart (1958–65). 1973 gründete er sein eigenes Büro At lier Lohrer in Stuttgart und arbeitete zusammen mit Dieter Herrmann an verschiedenen Museums- und Ausstellungsprojekten. Seit 2002 ist er architektonischer Bera des Sultanats Oman. Uli Pfeifer, geboren 1956, studierte ebenfalls Architektur an der Technischen Universität Stuttgart (1977–84). Er arbeitete im Büro von Dieter He mann und im Atelier Lohrer (1984–91), bevor er 1991 sein eigenes Büro in Stuttgart gründete. Dieter Keck, geboren 1946, studierte an der Fachhochschule Karlsru (1969–73). Kürzlich wurde ein von Herrmann + Bosch zusammen mit Keck geplantes 13-geschossiges Verwaltungshochhaus für die Landwirtschaftliche Sozialversich rung in Stuttgart-Kaltental fertig gestellt. Außerdem sind bei Herrmann + Bosch derzeit eine Reihe von Seniorenheimen in Deutschland in Planung. Zu den wichtig Gebäuden des Büros gehören das Daimler-Benz-Museum (in Zusammenarbeit mit Lohrer und H. G. Merz) Stuttgart (1984–86), das Limes-Museum (in Zusammenarb mit Lohrer) in Aalen (1985–87), die Fachhochschule für Technik, Esslingen (1992–96), und das Seniorenwohnheim Haus Rohrer Höhe, Stuttgart (1996–98).

Dieter Herrmann, né en 1938, a étudié dans la même université (1958–65) avant de travailler pour Behnisch & Partner à Stuttgart (1966–78). En partenaria avec Gerhard Bosch, il a créé l'agence **HERRMANN + BOSCH** en 1992. Gerhard Bosch, né en 1955, a étudié à l'Université de Stuttgart (1977–85). Il enseigne construction en bois à l'Université des sciences appliquées de Biberach. Knut Lohrer, né en 1937, est diplômé en architecture de l'Université technique de Stuttg (1958–65). Il a créé son agence, Atelier Lohrer, à Stuttgart en 1973 et travaillé sur plusieurs projets de musées et d'expositions avec Dieter Herrmann. Depuis 2002 est conseiller en architecture pour le sultanat d'Oman. Uli Pfeil, né en 1956, a étudié l'architecture à l'Université de Stuttgart (1977–84) et a travaillé pour Herrmann l'Atelier Lohrer (1984–91) avant de créer sa propre agence à Stuttgart en 1991. Dieter Keck, né en 1946, a étudié à l'Université des sciences appliquées de Karlsru (1969–73). Ensemble, ils ont récemment achevé un immeuble de bureaux de 13 étages pour la compagnie d'assurances Landwirtschaftliche Sozialversicherung à Stu gart-Kaltental et travaillent sur un certain nombre de projets de maisons de retraite en Allemagne. Parmi leurs réalisations les plus importantes : le musée Daimler-Be en collaboration avec Knut Lohrer et H. G. Merz, Stuttgart (1984–86) ; le Limes-Museum, en collaboration avec Knut Lohrer, Aalen (1985–87) ; la Fachhochschule Technik, Esslingen (1992–96) et la maison de retraite Haus Rohrer Höhe, Stuttgart (1996–98).

RHEINISCHES LANDESMUSEUM

Bonn, Germany, 2002–03

Floor area: 31 195 m². Client: LVR Landschaftsverband Rheinland, Cologne. Cost: €77 million

The **RHEINISCHES LANDESMUSEUM** in Bonn, home to the skeleton of Neanderthal Man and works of art and design ranging from early historical times to present, has a new home created by the architects Herrmann + Bosch from buildings erected in 1909 and 1967. The government-controlled LVR (Landschaftsverb Rheinland, Köln) organized a competition in 1990 to renovate the museum founded on this site behind the central railway station in 1890. The competition winner, K Lohrer, later joined with four other colleagues, Uli Pfeil, Dieter Herrmann, Gerhard Bosch and Dieter Keck, to create Architektengruppe Stuttgart, the firm that carried the work between 1998 and 2003. The long delay was related to hesitations over the future of Bonn in the early 1990s and later technical changes requested by curatorial team. Destroyed by bombing during World War II, the 1890 structure was replaced in 1967 by a modernist block. A second 1909 stone building survived tog er with various smaller additions, but the LandesMuseum had reached a degree of incoherence in the 1980s that led some to ask if it might not be better to raze complex. It was precisely to avoid such a conclusion that the competition program stipulated that both the 1909 and the 1967 buildings had to be reused. The Stutt team, led for the design work by Gerhard Bosch, decided to create a clear link between the spaces of the 1909 building and the completely restructured 1960s ble They knocked down the wall separating the two buildings and generated a continuous flow of space from one into the other, adding a monumental staircase near new entrance area. The most striking exterior feature of the museum is its new Colmanstrasse entrance façade, an airy glass wall enclosing a surprising articulated la wood inner façade that protects the collections while admitting some natural light. High narrow windows set into the wood almost perpendicular to the wall let dayl in while not permitting it to flood the exhibition areas. Two large-scale architectural fragments sit in the four-meter gap between the inner and outer façades, while rough-hewn larch planks are intended to echo the crates used to pack archeological finds.

Das **RHEINISCHE LANDESMUSEUM** Bonn, in dem u. a. das Neandertalerskelett sowie Kunstwerke und Gebrauchsgegenstände von der Frühzeit bis zur Geg wart beheimatet sind, hat ein neues Domizil, das von den Architekten Herrmann + Bosch aus den Gebäuden von 1909 und 1967 geschaffen wurde. Der Landschafts band Rheinland organisierte 1990 einen Wettbewerb, um das Museum, das 1890 auf dem Grundstück hinter dem Hauptbahnhof gegründet worden war, zu sanieren. Gewinner des Wettbewerbes, Knut Lohrer, schloss sich später mit vier anderen Kollegen – Uli Pfeil, Dieter Herrmann, Gerhard Bosch und Dieter Keck – zur Architektur gruppe Stuttgart zusammen; dieses Büro ist für die Arbeiten, die von 1998 bis 2003 ausgeführt wurden, verantwortlich. Die Verzögerungen des Projektes hingen mit unsicheren politischen Zukunft Bonns in den 1990er Jahren und mit technischen Änderungen durch das kuratorische Team zusammen. Das ursprüngliche Gebäude wu während des Zweiten Weltkrieges durch Bomben zerstört und 1967 durch einen modernen Bau ersetzt. Ein Natursteingebäude von 1909 und kleinere Anbauten blie bestehen, aber das Ensemble wirkte derart zusammenhanglos, dass die Frage aufkam, ob es nicht besser wäre, den ganzen Komplex abzureißen. Um dies zu vermeic wurde im Wettbewerbsprogramm festgelegt, dass sowohl der Bau von 1909 als auch die Gebäude von 1967 zu erhalten seien. Das Stuttgarter Team, bei dem Gerh Bosch für den Entwurf verantwortlich war, entschied sich für eine klare Verbindung zwischen den Räumen des alten Gebäudes und dem vollständig sanierten 60er-Jah Bau. Die Wand zwischen den beiden Gebäuden wurde entfernt und ein großzügiger fließender Raum dazwischen geschaffen; in der Nähe des neuen Eingangs befindet s eine monumentale Treppe. Die auffälligste Veränderung des Museums ist die neue Eingangsfassade zur Colmanstraße, eine leichte Glaswand, die eine überraschend a formulierte innere Fassade aus Lärchenholz umhüllt. Diese schützt die Exponate, lenkt aber auch etwas Licht ins Innere. Hohe schmale Fenster, die fast rechtwinklig Fassade in die Holzwand gesetzt sind, sorgen für Tageslicht, verhindern aber, dass die Ausstellungsbereiche zuviel Licht bekommen. Zwei großformatige Architekturfra mente stehen in dem 4 m breiten Zwischenraum zwischen innerer und äußerer Fassade; sägeraue Dielen sollen an die Transportkisten für archäologische Funde erinn

Les nouvelles installations du **RHEINISCHES LANDESMUSEUM** de Bonn, qui abrite le squelette de l'homme de Neandertal et des œuvres d'art de la préhisto nos jours, a été conçu par les architectes Herrmann + Bosch sur la base de bâtiments érigés en 1909 et 1967. La Landschaftsverband Rheinland (Cologne), organis gouvernemental, avait organisé un concours en 1990 pour rénover ce musée implanté derrière la gare centrale depuis 1890. Knut Lohrer, qui avait remporté le conco s'associa alors avec quatre confrères, Uli Pfeil, Dieter Herrmann, Gerhard Bosch et Dieter Keck, pour créer Architektengruppe Stuttgart, l'agence qui a réalisé ce pr entre 1998 et 2003. Ce long délai s'explique par les hésitations sur l'avenir de Bonn, au début des années 1990, et les modifications techniques demandées par les cons vateurs. Détruit au cours de la Seconde Guerre mondiale, l'immeuble de 1890 avait été remplacé en 1967 par un bloc d'esprit moderniste. Un autre bâtiment en pie datant de 1909 avait subsisté, de même que quelques petites adjonctions ultérieures, mais la politique du LandesMuseum fut si incohérente dans les années 1980 l'on pensa raser le tout. C'est pour éviter cela que le programme du concours stipulait que les deux bâtiments de 1909 et 1967 devaient être réutilisés. L'équipe de St gart, sous la houlette de Gerhard Bosch pour la conception, décida d'établir un lien clair entre les volumes du bâtiment de 1909 et le bloc de 1969 entièrement restructu On abattit le mur les séparant pour créer une circulation continue, et l'on ajouta un escalier monumental près de la nouvelle entrée. L'élément extérieur le plus specta laire est la nouvelle façade de l'entrée sur la Colmanstrasse et son mur de verre aérien enfermant une étonnante seconde façade intérieure en bouleau qui protège collections tout en filtrant la lumière naturelle. Ses hautes et étroites fenêtres percées dans le bois presque perpendiculairement au mur laissent pénétrer la lumière jour sans qu'elle balaye les zones d'exposition. Deux énormes fragments architecturaux ont été disposés dans l'intervalle entre les deux façades. Les planches en boul brut rappellent les caisses d'emballage utilisées pour emballer les découvertes archéologiques.

The museum is an exercise in
joining together the old and the new.
The older building is visible in the
photo to the left, with the new, glass
enclosed part of the building in the
center. Below, the glass façade of
the main entrance area covers the
larch wall, and offers space for the
exhibition of architectural-scale
objects.

Das Museum thematisiert die
Verbindung von alt und neu. Links:
Das bestehende Gebäude und der
neue, verglaste Teil. Unten: Die Glasfassade des Eingangs mit der dahin-
ter liegenden Wand aus Lärchenholz;
der Zwischenraum kann für die
Präsentation großer architektonischer
Objekte genutzt werden.

Le musée est une combinaison
brillante de l'ancien et du nouveau.
Le bâtiment ancien est visible à
gauche de la photo, la partie nouvelle enchâssée de verre au centre.
Ci-dessous, la façade de verre de
l'entrée principale protège le mur
en bouleau tout en dégageant un
important volume pour l'exposition
de pièces monumentales.

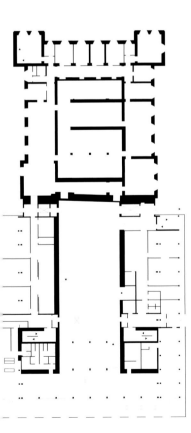

Despite the joining together of largely
incompatible structures, the architects succeed in giving the impression of architectural continuity.
Above, the main entrance stairway.
Below and right, an exhibition volume
created out of a former courtyard.

Durch die Verbindung der eigentlich
nicht kompatiblen Gebäude gelingt es
den Architekten, den Eindruck einer
architektonischen Einheit zu schaffen.
Oben: Die Haupttreppe. Unten und
rechts: Ein ehemaliger Innenhof, der
jetzt als Ausstellungsraum dient.

Bien que confrontés à la difficulté
d'associer deux constructions en
grande partie incompatibles, les
architectes ont réussi à donner une
impression de continuité architecturale. En haut, l'escalier de l'entrée
principale. En bas et à droite, un
espace d'exposition créé dans une
ancienne cour.

HERTL.ARCHITEKTEN

Hertl.Architekten ZT GmbH
Pachergasse 17
4400 Steyr
Austria

Tel: +43 725 24 69 44
Fax: +43 725 24 73 63
e-mail: steyr@hertl-architekten.com
Web: www.hertl-architekten.com

Indoor Bath in a Farmh

Gernot Hertl was born in Steyr, Austria in 1971. He studied architecture at the Technical University of Graz (1992–97) before beginning to work with Joseph Stein berger (2002–03). He created **HERTL.ARCHITEKTEN** in 2003 and Hertl.Architekten ZT KEG in 2004. His major projects include: Ruby House, Christkindl (2001); Indoc Bath at Farmhouse, Klein Pöchlarn (2000–02, published here); Storehouse Hartlauer, Amstetten (2001); Steinwendtner House, Steyr (2003); Central Plaza Passage, Stey (2003); Boarding School BS 8, Linz (2002–06); Housing, St. Magdalen, Villach (2002–05); Schlüsselhofgasse Town House, Steyr (2003); Technology House, Steyr (2003 Mair Villa, Vienna; Ecker Abu Zahara House, Luftenberg (2004–05); Enns Pumping Station, Steyr (2004–05); Uncle Fred's Cabin, Steyr (2005); and the Reform Window Factory, also in Steyr (2005–07).

Gernot Hertl, geboren 1971 in Steyr, Österreich, studierte von 1992 bis 1997 an der Technischen Universität Graz Architektur. Von 2002 bis 2003 arbeitete e für Joseph Steinberger und gründete 2003 **HERTL.ARCHITEKTEN**, 2004 Hertl.Architekten ZT KEG. Zu seinen wichtigen Projekten gehören das Rubinhaus in Christkin (2001), ein Swimmingpool für ein Bauernhaus in Klein-Pöchlarn (2000–02), Verkaufsräume für Hartlauer in Amstetten (2001), das Haus Steinwendter (2003) und eir Passage in Steyr (2003), außerdem das Berufsschulzentrum 8 in Linz (2002–06), Wohnbauten in St. Magdalen, Villach (2002–05), das Wohnhaus Schlüsselhofgass (2003) und das Technologiehaus Stadtgut in Steyr (2003), die Villa Mair in Wien, das Haus Ecker Abu Zahara in Luftenberg (2004–05) sowie die Ennspumpstation (2004 05), Onkel Freds Hütte (2005) und das Betriebsgebäude ReformFenster (2005–07), alle drei in Steyr.

Gernot Hertl est né à Steyr, Autriche, en 1971. Il a étudié l'architecture à l'Université technique de Graz (1992–97) avant de travailler pour Joseph Steinberg (2002–03). Il a créé **HERTL.ARCHITEKTEN** en 2003 et Hertl.Architekten ZT KEG en 2004. Parmi ses principaux projets : la maison Ruby (Christkindl, 2001), une insta lation de bains dans une ferme (Kleinpöchlarn, 2000–02), publiée ici ; l'entrepôt Hartlauer (Amstetten, 2001) ; la maison, Steinwendtner (Steyr, 2003) ; le Passage de place centrale (Steyr, 2003) ; l'internat BS 8 (Linz, 2002–06) ; les logements Sankt Magdalen (Villach, 2002–05) ; la maison de ville Schlüsselhofgasse (Steyr, 2003 la maison Technology (Steyr, 2003) ; la villa Mayr (Vienne) ; la maison Ecker Abu Zahra (Luftenberg, 2004–05) ; la station de pompage de Enns (Steyr, 2004–0£ la « Cabine de l'oncle Fred » (Steyr, 2005) et l'usine de fenêtres Reform, également à Steyr (2005–07).

INDOOR BATH FARMHOUSE

Klein Pöchlarn, Austria, 2000–02

Floor area: 107 m². Client: Mr. Weissensteiner.
Cost: €310 000

This 107 m² addition to a farmhouse was designed between June 2000 and October 2001. Hertl says that "The bath is designed to simulate a contempora grotto, a hollow space in a green solid, that aims to reach the mystique and sensuousness of an antique bath." In this description, and perhaps in an unassuming w in the actual structure, there is an echo of Peter Zumthor's Thermal Baths in Vals. Employing "simple and modest elements" such as a "hollow solid with a corner in glas cubicle, bench and wine-cellar," the architect used green glazed concrete so that "even the pool glimmers green." A glazed façade with red louvers on the interior giv some sense of the outside environment, but there is an uncompromising geometric strength in the basic rectangular volume imagined by Gernot Hertl. Despite the rath hard lines of the design, the combination of the green surfaces, water and the imagined bath do evoke the sensuality alluded to in the architect's description.

Das 107 m² große Nebengebäude eines Bauernhofs wurde zwischen Juni 2000 und Oktober 2001 entworfen. Hertl sagt dazu: »Das Bad soll eine moderne ›Grc te‹ sein, ein hohler Raum in einem massiven Grün, der an die mystischen und sinnlichen Qualitäten eines Bades der Antike anknüpft.« In dieser Beschreibung und vie leicht in der Bescheidenheit des realen Baukörpers sind Anklänge an das Thermalbad in Vals von Peter Zumthor zu spüren. Die »einfachen und bescheidenen Element – z. B. ein »ausgehöhlter massiver Körper mit einer Ecke aus Glas, ein kleiner, abgetrennter Ruheraum, eine Bank und ein Weinkeller« sind aus grün lasiertem Beton, dass »sogar der Pool grün schimmert«. Eine Glasfassade mit roten Lamellen auf der Innenseite stellt eine gewisse Verbindung zur Umgebung her; die kompromisslo geometrische Strenge des einfachen rechtwinkligen Baukörpers dominiert jedoch. Trotz der eher strengen Linien des Entwurfs rufen die grünen Oberflächen und das Wa ser in Kombination mit der Vorstellung, hier ein Bad zu nehmen, die Sinnlichkeit hervor, auf die der Architekt in seiner Beschreibung verweist.

Cette extension de 107 m² d'un bâtiment de ferme a été conçue de juin 2000 à octobre 2001. Hertl explique que « le pavillon de bains est conçu pour simul une grotte contemporaine, un volume creux dans un solide vert qui veut atteindre au caractère mystique et sensuel des bains antiques ». Dans cette description et peu être aussi dans la réalisation de ce petit projet, on trouve comme un écho des Bains de Vals par Peter Zumthor. Utilisant des »éléments simples et modestes« comn « un solide creux doté d'un angle en verre, une cabine, un banc et une cave à vin », l'architecte a utilisé un béton verni en vert pour que « même le bassin ait des refle verts ». La façade en verre à persiennes intérieures rouges crée une perception particulière de l'environnement extérieur, mais la puissance géométrique du volume re tangulaire imaginé par Hertl s'impose néanmoins. Malgré des lignes assez dures, l'association des surfaces vertes et de l'eau évoque la sensualité à laquelle l'architec fait allusion dans sa description.

A hint of color is all that relieves the apparent austerity of the bathhouse. There is a solidity and integrity in the design that gives it a presence beyond its small size.

Nur die Farbe schwächt die Strenge des Badehauses ein wenig ab. Das kleine Gebäude strahlt Solidität und Integrität aus und hat eine Präsenz, die über seine tatsächliche Größe hinausgeht.

Seule la couleur anime l'austérité apparente de cette maison de bains. Son aspect massif et sa cohérence confèrent au projet une présence très forte pour ses dimensions.

HERZOG & DE MEURON

Herzog & de Meuron
Rheinschanze 6
4056 Basel
Switzerland

Tel: +41 613 85 57 57
Fax: +41 613 85 57 58
e-mail: info@herzogdemeuron.com

Alliar

Jacques Herzog and Pierre de Meuron were both born in Basel in 1950. They received degrees in architecture at the ETH in Zurich in 1975 after studying Aldo Rossi, and founded their firm **HERZOG & DE MEURON** Architecture Studio in Basel in 1978. Harry Gugger and Christine Binswanger joined the firm in 1991, Robert Hösl and Ascan Mergenthaler became partners in 2004. Their built work includes the Antipodes I Student Housing at the Université de Bourgogne, Dijon (1991- the Ricola Europe Factory and Storage Building in Mulhouse (1993) and a gallery for a private collection of contemporary art in Munich (1991–92). Most notably were chosen early in 1995 to design the new Tate Gallery extension for contemporary art, situated in the Bankside Power Station on the Thames opposite Saint F Cathedral, which opened in May 2000. They were also short listed in the competition for the new design of the Museum of Modern Art in New York (1997). More rec ly, they have built the Forum 2004 Building and Plaza, Barcelona (2002–04), the Prada Aoyama Epicenter in Tokyo (2003), and the National Stadium, Main Stadiu the 2008 Olympic Games in Beijing (2003–08).

Jacques Herzog und Pierre de Meuron wurden beide 1950 in Basel geboren. Sie studierten bei Aldo Rossi an der ETH in Zürich, wo sie 1975 ihr Diplom m ten. 1978 gründeten sie in Basel das Büro **HERZOG & DE MEURON**. Harry Gugger und Christine Binswanger arbeiten seit 1991 dort, 2004 wurden Robert Hös Ascan Mergenthaler Partner. Zu den Bauten von Herzog & de Meuron gehören das Studentenwohnheim Antipodes I der Université de Bourgogne in Dijon (1991–92) Ausstellungsgebäude für eine Privatsammlung moderner Kunst in München (1991–92) und das Fabrik- und Lagergebäude der Firma Ricola Europe in Mulhouse (19 1995 erhielten sie ihren bedeutendsten Auftrag: die Planung der »Tate Modern«, des in der Bankside Power Station untergebrachten Museums für zeitgenössische K als Erweiterung der Tate Gallery in London. Das gegenüber der St. Paul's Cathedral an der Themse gelegene Gebäude wurde im Mai 2000 eröffnet. Beim Wettbewe die Umgestaltung des Museum of Modern Art in New York (1997) kamen Herzog & de Meuron in die engere Wahl. In jüngster Zeit haben sie u. a. das Gebäude und Platz »Forum 2004« in Barcelona (2002–04) sowie das Prada Aoyama Epicenter in Tokyo (2003) und das Hauptstadion für die Olympischen Spiele 2008 in Peking (2C 08) realisiert.

Jacques Herzog et Pierre de Meuron sont tous deux nés à Bâle en 1950. Diplômés en architecture de l'Institut fédéral suisse de technologie (ETH) de Z (1975) où ils étudient auprès d'Aldo Rossi, ils fondent **HERZOG & DE MEURON** Architecture Studio, à Bâle, en 1978. Harry Gugger et Christine Binswanger les gnent en 1991, suivis de Robert Hösl et Ascan Mergenthaler en 2004. Parmi leurs premières réalisations remarquées : le foyer d'étudiants Antipodes I pour l'Unive de Bourgogne, Dijon (1991–92), l'usine-entrepôt Ricola Europe, Mulhouse (1993) et une galerie pour une collection privée d'art contemporain, Munich (1989–92). Il été sélectionnés en 1995 pour l'installation de la Tate Modern de Londres dans une ancienne centrale électrique, Bankside Power Station, au bord de la Tamise, fa la cathédrale Saint-Paul, réalisation qui fut inaugurée en mai 2000. Ils ont fait partie des architectes retenus pour le concours de la transformation du Museum of Mc Art de New York (1997). Plus récemment, ils ont construit le bâtiment et la place du Forum 2004 à Barcelone (2002–04), le Prada Aoyama Epicenter à Tokyo (200 le Stade national, principal stade des Jeux olympiques à Pékin en 2008 (2003–08).

ALLIANZ ARENA

Munich, Germany, 2002–05

Floor area: 171 000 m². Built-up floor area stadium: 37 600 m².
Client: Allianz Arena – München Stadion GmbH. Cost: €280 million (estimate)

Intended for use during the 2006 FIFA World Cup, the **ALLIANZ ARENA** offers a total of 66 000 covered seats. Its 37 600 m² footprint corresponds to 171 000
of gross floor area. Its circumference is 840 m. As the architects explain, "Three themes define our architectural and urban concept for the world championship foot.
stadium in Munich: 1) the presence of the stadium as an illuminated body that can change its appearance and is situated in an open landscape; 2) the procession-
arrival of fans in a landscaped area; and 3) the crater-like interior of the stadium itself." Located between the airport and downtown Munich in an open area, the Alli
Arena is covered with large EFTE cushions that can each be lit separately in white, red or light blue. A digital control system permits changes in the color scheme, in p
ticular in order to identify the home team playing (FC Bayern Munich or TSV 1860). The idea of a stadium that is entirely colored in this way is quite new. Vogt La
schaftsarchitekten from Zurich designed the landscaping, formed by swathes of green together with meandering asphalt paths. Given that the Arena is intended only
football games, the seating arrangement does not have to be changed and great attention has been taken to bringing the spectators as close as possible to the play
field.

Die **ALLIANZ ARENA**, einer der Austragungsorte der Fußballweltmeisterschaft 2006, hat 66 000 überdachte Plätze. Die 37 600 m² große Grundfläche bietet e
Bruttogeschossfläche von 171 000 m², der Umfang des Stadions misst 840 m. Die Architekten erläutern: »Drei Themen definieren unseren architektonischen u
städtebaulichen Ansatz für das Weltmeisterschaftsstadion in München: 1) die Präsenz des Stadions als illuminierter Baukörper, der sein Äußeres verändern kann und
eine offene Landschaft eingebettet ist, 2) die prozessionsartige Annäherung der Fans in einer landschaftsplanerisch gestalteten Umgebung und 3) der kraterähnlic
Innenraum des Stadions.« Die Allianz Arena, ungefähr in der Mitte zwischen dem Flughafen und der Innenstadt Münchens in freier Landschaft gelegen, wird von groß
Kissen aus EFTE-Folie überdeckt; jedes dieser Kissen kann weiß, rot oder blau leuchten. Ein digitales Kontrollsystem erlaubt Veränderungen des farbigen Gesamtbild
insbesondere um kenntlich zu machen, welche Mannschaft gerade ein Heimspiel hat (FC Bayern München oder TSV 1860). Die Idee eines Stadions, das auf diese We
farbig gestaltet wird, ist recht neu. Vogt Landschaftsarchitekten aus Zürich haben die Außenanlagen – gemähte Rasenstreifen und mäandrierende Asphaltwege – ges
tet. Da die Arena nur für Fußballspiele genutzt werden soll, gibt es eine feste Bestuhlung; außerdem wurde sehr viel Wert darauf gelegt, die Zuschauer so nah w
möglich an das Spielfeld zu bringen.

Édifié en prévision de la Coupe du monde de football 2006, l'**ALLIANZ ARENA** offre 66 000 places et 171 000 m² de surface utile pour une emprise au sol
37 600 m². « Trois thèmes définissent notre concept architectural et urbain pour le stade de football du championnat du monde à Munich », expliquent les architect
« 1) la présence du stade, en tant que corps illuminé qui peut changer d'aspect et se trouve au milieu d'un espace ouvert ; 2) l'arrivée processionnelle des support
dans une zone paysagée et 3) l'intérieur du stade même, en forme de cratère. » Situé entre l'aéroport et le centre ville dans une zone dégagée, le stade est cou
d'énormes coussins en EFTE dont chacun peut s'éclairer séparément en blanc, rouge ou bleu clair. Un système de commande par ordinateur modifie les couleurs,
exemple pour identifier l'équipe locale qui joue (FC Bayern Munich ou TSV 1860). Cette idée de stade « colorisable » est nouvelle. Vogt Landschaftsarchitekten, de Zuri
a créé les aménagements paysagers alternant les bandes de gazon et de sinueuses allées goudronnées. Le stade étant exclusivement conçu pour le football, l'implan
tion des sièges n'a pas à être modulable et l'on a pu faire en sorte que les spectateurs soient aussi près que possible du terrain.

Giving a new appearance to as "ordinary" a structure as a football stadium is no small task. Herzog & de Meuron have also given variety to the exterior of the building through the use of light and color.

Einem Funktionsgebäude wie einem Fußballstadion ein modernes Aussehen zu geben, ist nicht ganz leicht. Durch den Einsatz von Licht und Farbe kann die Außenfassade verändert werden.

Donner un aspect moderne à une structure aussi « ordinaire » qu'un stade de football n'est pas une mince affaire. Herzog & de Meuron ont rendu modulable l'aspect extérieur du bâtiment en jouant avec lumière et couleur.

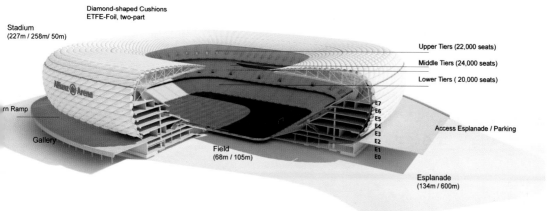

Diamond-shaped Cushions
ETFE-Foil, two-part

Stadium
(227m / 258m/ 50m)

Upper Tiers (22,000 seats)

Middle Tiers (24,000 seats)

Lower Tiers (20,000 seats)

rn Ramp

E7
E6
E5
E4
E3
E2
E1
E0

Access Esplanade / Parking

Gallery

Field
(68m / 105m)

Esplanade
(134m / 600m)

Unlike some well-known architects who have difficulty working on a large scale, Herzog & de Meuron have succeeded in creating an elegant design intended for the use of very large numbers of people.

Im Gegensatz zu anderen berühmten Architekten, denen es schwer fällt, Großbauten zu planen, ist Herzog & de Meuron ein elegantes Bauwerk gelungen, das von sehr vielen Menschen genutzt wird.

Contrairement à certains grands architectes qui ont des difficultés à travailler sur des projets de grandes dimensions, Herzog & de Meuron ont réussi à créer un style élégant destiné au public le plus vaste.

The round shape of the Arena itself is echoed in the landscaping and approach roads leading to the parking areas.

Die runde Form der Allianz Arena findet sich in der landschaftsplane-rischen Gestaltung und in der Anlage der Zufahrtsstraßen wieder.

La forme ronde de l'Allianz Arena retrouve dans les aménagements paysagers et les voies d'accès a parkings.

WALKER ART CENTER

Minneapolis, Minnesota, USA, 2003–05

Floor area: 11 800 m² (expansion). Client: Walker Art Center.
Cost: $38.2 million

This project includes an 11 800 m² expansion (about the equivalent of the existing space). The architects emphasize that the **WALKER ART CENTER** is m
than a museum, since its directors insist on its role as a hub for local cultural life, and wish to place more emphasis on electronic media and performing arts. The r
space includes a theater, compared by the architects to "a down-sized version of the Scala in Milan or the open-air Globe theater of Shakespeare's day." In fact the re
spaces can be used to interweave different art forms in "entirely unexpected and innovative ways." Though their own addition, with its folded forms and large, irreg
windows seems quite different from the original Edward Larabee Barnes (1915–2004) building, it intentionally plays on the stricter existing structure and enlivens it
the architects say about the windows, "They look accidental but are homologous forms, showing a kinship in value and structure, somewhat like the shapes of a silh
ette cutting." Doubling the available amount of gallery space, the renovated Walker includes a 1.5 hectare garden extending the Minneapolis Sculpture garden to
south; a 280 m² "event space" with views of the city, which can be rented out for community use; a "destination restaurant;" and a new 350-seat "multidiscipli
performing arts studio." The new 21-meter-high tower is distinctively clad in custom stamped aluminum mesh.

Das Projekt umfasst eine 11 800 m² große Erweiterung, die damit ungefähr die Größe des bestehenden Museums hat. Die Architekten betonen, dass
WALKER ART CENTER mehr ist als ein Museum, da es eine zentrale Rolle im örtlichen kulturellen Leben spielt und seine Direktoren eine stärkere Gewichtung
elektronischer Medien und der darstellenden Künste anstreben. Die Erweiterung beinhaltet ein Theater, das von den Architekten mit »einer verkleinerten Version
Mailänder Scala oder Shakespeares nach oben offenem Globe Theatre« verglichen wird. Tatsächlich können die neuen Räume dazu benutzt werden, verschiedene Ku
formen »auf gänzlich unerwartete und innovative Art« zu verbinden. Obwohl die Erweiterung mit ihren gefalteten Formen und den großen, unregelmäßigen Fenstern
dem bestehenden Gebäude von Edward Larabee Barnes (1915–2004) nicht viel gemeinsam zu haben scheint, ist das Spiel mit dem vorhandenen strengeren Baukö
und dessen Belebung beabsichtigt. Die Architekten äußern sich zu den Fenstern folgendermaßen: »Sie sehen aus wie zufällig entworfen, aber sie haben homologe
men, die eine Verwandtschaft in Wertigkeit und Konstruktion zeigen.« Die Galeriefläche wurde verdoppelt: Dazu gehört ein 1,5 ha großer Garten, der den Minneap
Sculpture Garden nach Süden hin ergänzt, ein 280 m² großer Raum für Events, der von der Gemeinde gemietet werden kann, ein Toprestaurant sowie ein neues »m
disziplinäres Studio für darstellende Künste« mit 350 Plätzen. Der neue 21 m hohe Turm wird durch sein speziell angefertigtes Aluminiumnetz gekennzeichnet.

Ce projet de réaménagement du **WALKER ART CENTER** comprend aussi une extension de 11 800 m² (l'équivalent des espaces existants). Les architectes e
quent que ce Centre est le noyau de la vie culturelle locale et que ses administrateurs souhaitaient mettre l'accent sur les médias électroniques et les arts du spect
Le nouvel espace contient un théâtre qu'Herzog & de Meuron comparent à « une version réduite de la Scala de Milan ou du théâtre du Globe de Shakespeare ». En
ces installations peuvent générer des rencontres entre différentes formes artistiques de « façons entièrement nouvelles et inattendues ». Bien que la nouvelle exten
avec ses formes repliées et ses vastes ouvertures, semble trancher avec les lignes strictes du bâtiment d'origine signé Edward Larabee Barnes (1915–2004), elle
de ce contraste tout en l'animant. Au sujet des fenêtres, les architectes précisent que « si elles ont l'air d'être disposées au hasard, ce sont des formes homologue
mettent en évidence une parenté de valeur et de structure ». Outre le doublement des galeries d'exposition, le Walker rénové possède un jardin de 1,5 hectare qui
longe vers le sud le Jardin de sculptures de Minneapolis, un « espace pour événements » de 280 m² loué pour manifestations locales, un restaurant de qualité et un
veau « studio multidisciplinaire d'arts du spectacle » de 350 places. La nouvelle tour de 21 mètres se fait remarquer par son habillage en panneaux d'aluminium.

*Though certainly not anthropomorphic
in its apparent design, the Walker Art
Center extension has an unusual
almost "living" presence.*

*Obwohl sicherlich kein anthropomor-
phes Gebäude, hat die Erweiterung
des Walker Art Center eine ungewöhnliche, fast »lebendige« Präsenz.*

*Très loin d'être anthropomorphique,
le Walker Art Center n'en dégage
pas moins une présence « vivante ».*

The architects master the use of powerful interior forms that have a clear continuity with the outside of the building. Nor are these forms created at the expense of the functionality of the building.

Den Umgang mit expressiven Innenraumformen, die in einem klaren Zusammenhang mit dem Äußeren des Gebäudes stehen, beherrschen die Architekten meisterhaft. Diese Formen beeinträchtigen die Funktionalität nicht.

Les architectes maîtrisent l'utilisation de puissantes formes intérieures dans une continuité évidente avec celles de l'extérieur. Elles n'ont pas pour autant été créées aux dépens du fonctionnalisme du bâtiment.

DE YOUNG MUSEUM

San Francisco, California, USA, 2002-05

Area: 27 220 m². Client: Fine Arts Museums of San Francisco (FAMSF).
Cost: $135 million

The Swiss architects Herzog & de Meuron have had something of a double-feature, opening a new building for the Walker Art Center in Minneapolis and for **DE YOUNG MUSEUM** in San Francisco in the space of less than a year. Founded in 1895 in San Francisco's Golden Gate Park, the de Young museum can be consid ered an integral part of the cultural fabric of the city. With a construction cost of 135 million dollars and a total project cost of 202 million dollars, this is no MoMA, it is the Swiss pair's biggest new museum structure, since Tate Modern in London was actually a rehabilitation. It replaces the former facility on the same site that w damaged by the 1989 Loma Prieta earthquake. An interesting feature of the project is that it reduces the de Young's footprint by 37 % and returns nearly one hectare open space to Golden Gate Park. The building's dramatic copper façade is perforated and textured to replicate the impression made by light filtering through a tree cano creating an artistic abstraction on the exterior of the museum that is linked to the de Young's park setting. The copper skin, chosen for its changeable quality throu oxidation, will assume a green patina over time that will blend with the surrounding environment. The northeast corner of the building features a 44-meter spiral tow

Mit dem neuen Walker Art Center in Minneapolis und dem **DE YOUNG MUSEUM** in San Francisco – beide Museen wurden innerhalb eines Jahres eröffnet – h ten die Schweizer Architekten Herzog & de Meuron einen Doppelerfolg. 1895 gegründet, gilt das De Young Museum in San Franciscos Golden Gate Park als wesentlic Bestandteil des kulturellen Lebens der Stadt. Mit Baukosten von umgerechnet etwa 110 Millionen Euro und Gesamtkosten von 170 Millionen Euro reicht es zwar ni an die Dimensionen des neuen MoMA heran, ist aber der bislang größte Museumsneubau der Schweizer Architekten, da es sich bei der Tate Modern in London ja den Umbau eines bestehenden Gebäudes handelt. Der Neubau ersetzt das alte Museum am selben Ort; dieses wurde 1989 während des Loma-Prieta-Erdbebens besch digt. Interessant ist, dass das neue De Young Museum gegenüber dem Altbau eine um 37 Prozent reduzierte Grundfläche aufweist und dem Golden Gate Park fast ein Hektar unbebauter Fläche »zurückgibt«. Die Textur der dramatischen, gelochten Kupferfassade erinnert an Licht, das durch das Blattwerk eines Baums sickert. Die künstlerische Abstraktion verbindet das Museum mit seiner Parkumgebung. Die Kupferhaut, gewählt aufgrund ihrer sich durch Oxidation verändernden Oberfläche qualität, wird im Lauf der Zeit eine grüne Patina bekommen und sich so der Umgebung weiter anpassen. An der Nordostecke des Gebäudes befindet sich ein 44 m hoh spiralförmig gedrehter Turm.

Herzog & de Meuron ont connu une sorte de double triomphe en ouvrant en moins d'un an le nouveau bâtiment du Walker Center à Minneapolis et celui **DE YOUNG MUSEUM** à San Francisco. Fondé en 1895 et implanté dans le Golden Gate Park à San Francisco, le De Young Museum fait partie intégrante du tissu c turel de la ville. Construit pour un budget global de 170 millions d'euros (dont 110 millions pour la seule construction), ce n'est pas un projet de l'envergure de celui MoMA, mais néanmoins la plus grande réalisation muséale du duo suisse, puisque la Tate Modern de Londres était en fait une réhabilitation. Ce nouveau bâtiment 27 220 m² commandé par le Fine Arts Museum de San Francisco (FAMSF) remplace l'ancien, endommagé par le tremblement de terre de Loma Prieta en 1989. Une c caractéristiques intéressantes de ce projet est de réduire de 37% l'emprise au sol initiale et de restituer près d'un hectare de terrain au Golden Gate Park. La spec culaire façade de cuivre perforé et texturé imite la lumière filtrant à travers le faîte des arbres, créant une image abstraite et artistique qui intègre encore davantage musée à son cadre de verdure. La peau de cuivre, choisie pour sa capacité à évoluer avec le temps en s'oxydant, prendra une patine verte qui se fondra dans l'en ronnement. L'angle nord-est du bâtiment est signalé par une tour en spirale de 44 m de haut.

Standing out against the landscape the forms of the de Young Museum do not immediately bring to mind any architectural precedent. Herzog & de Meuron have again expressed their frequent interest in surface and form in a highly original manner.

Die mit der Landschaft kontrastieren- den Formen des De Young Museums lassen zunächst keine architektoni- schen Vorbilder erkennen. Herzog & de Meuron bringen hier erneut ihr Interesse an Oberfläche und Form auf einzigartige Weise zum Ausdruck.

Se détachant sur le paysage, la silhouette du De Young Museum n'évoque aucun précédent architec- tural. Herzog & de Meuron expriment, ici encore, leur intérêt pour la forme et la surface, d'une façon extrême- ment originale.

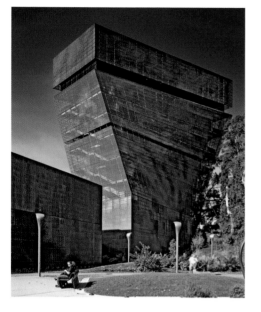

STEVEN HOLL

Steven Holl Architects, P. C.
450 West 31ˢᵗ Street, 11ᵗʰ floor
New York, New York 10001, USA

Tel: +1 212 629 7262, Fax: +1 212 629 7312
e-mail: nyc@stevenholl.com, Web: www.stevenholl.com

Born in 1947 in Bremerton, Washington, **STEVEN HOLL** obtained his Bachelor of Architecture degree from the University of Washington (1970). He studied in Rome and at the Architectural Association in London (1976). He began his career in California and opened his own office in New York in 1976. Holl has taught at the University of Washington, Syracuse University, and since 1981 at Columbia University. His notable buildings include: Hybrid Building, Seaside, Florida (1984–88); Berlin AGB Library, Berlin, Germany, competition entry (1988); Void Space/Hinged Space, Housing, Nexus World, Fukuoka, Japan (1989–91); Stretto House, Dallas, Texas (1989–92); Makuhari Housing, Chiba, Japan (1992–97); Chapel of St. Ignatius, Seattle University, Seattle, Washington (1994–97); Kiasma Museum of Contemporary Art, Helsinki, Finland (1993–98). His work includes an extension to the Cranbrook Institute of Science, Bloomfield Hills, Michigan (1996–99). Winner of the 1998 Alvar Aalto Medal, Steven Holl recently completed the Bellevue Art Museum, Bellevue, Washington, and an expansion and renovation of the Nelson Atkins Museum of Art (Kansas City, Missouri). Other recent work includes the Knut Hamsun Museum, Hamarøy, Norway; an Art and Art History Building for the University of Iowa, Iowa City, Iowa; and the College of Architecture at Cornell University, Ithaca, New York (2004). He completed the Turbulence House in New Mexico for the artist Richard Tuttle in 2005, and he recently won the competition for the Knokke-Heist Casino in Belgium and completed the Pratt Institute Higgen Hall Center Wing, in Brooklyn. Steven Holl is also working on a new residence at the Swiss Embassy in Washington, D. C. He was one of the six finalists for the Louvre's new building in Lens, France.

STEVEN HOLL, 1947 in Bremerton, Washington, geboren, machte 1970 seinen Bachelor of Architecture an der University of Washington. Er studierte in Rom und an der Architectural Association in London (1976). Für kurze Zeit war er in Kalifornien tätig, bevor er 1976 in New York sein eigenes Büro eröffnete. Steven Holl hat an der University of Washington und an der Syracuse University unterrichtet; seit 1981 lehrt er an der Columbia University. Zu seinen wichtigsten Projekten gehören: das Hybrid Building, Seaside, Florida (1984–88), die Erweiterung der Amerika-Gedenkbibliothek in Berlin (Wettbewerbsbeitrag 1988), Void Space/Hinged Space, Wohnblock Nexus World, Fukuoka, Japan (1989–91), das Stretto House, Dallas (1989–92), Makuhari Wohnhäuser, Chiba, Japan (1992–97), die St. Ignatius Kapelle, Seattle University, Seattle (1994–97), und das Kiasma Museum of Contemporary Art, Helsinki (1993–98). Holl plante außerdem die Erweiterung des Cranbrook Institute of Science, Bloomfield Hills, Michigan (1996–99). 1998 gewann er die Alvar-Aalto-Medaille. Vor kurzem wurden das Bellevue Art Museum in Bellevue, Washington, und die Erweiterung und Sanierung des Nelson Atkins Museum of Art in Kansas City, Missouri, fertig gestellt. Andere Projekte der jüngsten Zeit sind u. a. das Knut-Hamsun-Museum in Hamarøy, Norwegen, ein Gebäude für Kunst und Kunstgeschichte für die University of Iowa in Iowa City und das College of Architecture der Cornell University in Ithaca, New York (2004). 2005 wurde das Turbulence House in New Mexico für den Künstler Richard Tuttle fertig gestellt. Kürzlich hat Holl den Wettbewerb für das Knokke-Heist Kasino in Belgien gewonnen und stellte den Flügel des Pratt Institute Higgen Hall Center in Brooklyn fertig. Steven Holl plant außerdem ein neues Wohnhaus für die Botschaft der Schweiz in Washington, D. C. Er war einer der sechs Endrundenteilnehmer für das neue Louvre-Gebäude in Lens, Frankreich.

Né en 1947 à Bremerton (Washington), **STEVEN HOLL** est Bachelor of Architecture de l'Université de Washington (1970), puis a étudié à Rome et à l'Architectural Association, Londres (1976). Il débute sa carrière en Californie et ouvre sa propre agence à New York, en 1976. Il enseigne à l'Université de Washington, à Syracuse University et, depuis 1981, à Columbia University. Principales réalisations : Hybrid Building, Seaside, Floride (1984–88) ; participation au concours de la Bibliothèque AGB, Berlin (1988) ; immeuble d'appartements Void Space/Hinged Space, Nexus World, Fukuoka, Japon (1989–91) ; Stretto House, Dallas, Texas (1989–92) ; immeuble d'appartements Makuhari, Chiba, Japon (1992–97) ; musée d'Art contemporain Kiasma, Helsinki, Finlande (1993–98) ; rénovation et extension du Cranbrook Institute of Science, Bloomfield Hills, Michigan (1996–99). Distingué par la Médaille Alvar Aalto en 1998, il a récemment terminé le Bellevue Art Museum (Bellevue, Washington), l'extension et rénovation du Nelson Atkins Museum of Art, Kansas City, Missouri, et le Knut Hamsun Museum (Hamarøy, Norvège) ; le bâtiment pour l'art et l'histoire de l'art de l'Université de l'Iowa (Iowa City, Iowa) et le College of Architecture de Cornell University, Ithaca, New York (2004). Il a achevé la Turbulence House au Nouveau Mexique pour l'artiste Richard Tuttle en 2005 et le Pratt Institute Higgen Hall Center Wing à Brooklyn et a remporté le concours pour le Casino de Knokke-Heist (Belgique). Il travaille actuellement à une nouvelle résidence pour l'ambassade suisse à Washington et fait partie des six finalistes du concours pour la nouvelle implantation du Louvre à Lens (France).

LOISIUM VISITOR CENTER AND HOTEL
Langenlois, Vienna, 2001–05

Floor area: Visitor Center 1200 m²; Hotel 7000 m². Client: Kellerwelt Betriebs GmbH & Co KG.
Cost: Visitor Center €2.2 million; Hotel €8.6 million

This complex includes a café, wine shop, souvenir shop, seminar rooms, event spaces, offices, restaurant, spa, and an 82-room hotel. The Visitor Center measures 1200 m² in floor area and cost 2.2 million euros, while the 7000 m² hotel cost 8.6 million. Situated sixty minutes west of Vienna in Langenlois, the largest wine-growing town in Austria, **LOISIUM** became a complete, wine-themed tourist destination with the opening of the luxury hotel there in October 2005. Basing his design o the location and the proximity of historic wine cellars, Holl first created the cube-shaped Visitors' Center that leans five degree toward a ramp leading to the wine cell network. Built mostly with reinforced concrete, one-third of the Center is sunken below grade. The visible sections are clad in 4 mm-thick "Marine" aluminum, a specia alloy with extremely good resistance properties. Connected to existing cellar passageways by a ninety-meter-long tunnel, the architecture creates a link between basement, ground and upper levels that reinforces the subterranean aspect of the wine cellar network. Holl's well-known mastery of light and form takes on a particular interesting resonance in the context of Europe's old traditions, giving them life, and adding a historic depth to the architect's work that lacks in a U.S. context.

Der Komplex umfasst ein Café, eine Weinhandlung, einen Souvenirladen, Seminarräume, Räume für Sonderveranstaltungen, Büros, ein Restaurant, ein Spa, un ein 82-Zimmer-Hotel. Die Kosten des 1200 m² großen Besuchszentrums betrugen 2,2 Millionen Euro, die des Hotels (mit einer Gesamtfläche von 7000 m²) 8,6 Millionen Euro. Langenlois, die größte Weinbaustadt in Österreich, liegt westlich von Wien und ist mit dem Auto in einer Stunde von dort aus zu erreichen. Hier befindet sic **LOISIUM**, das durch die Eröffnung eines Luxushotels im Oktober 2005 zu einem ganz dem Wein gewidmeten Ziel für Touristen wurde. Der Ort und die Nähe zu den hi torischen Weinkellern bildeten die Grundlage für Holls Entwurf. Er entwickelte zuerst das Besuchszentrum in Form eines mächtigen Kubus, der sich mit einem Winkel vo fünf Grad aus der Senkrechten zu einer Rampe neigt, die zu dem System von Weinkellern führt. Das Besuchszentrum, das weitgehend in Stahlbeton ausgeführt wurd liegt zu einem Drittel in der Erde. Die von außen sichtbaren Teile des Gebäudes wurden mit 4 mm dickem, seewasserbeständigem Aluminium verkleidet, das extrem wide standsfähig ist. Die zwischen den Weinkellern vorhandenen Gänge wurden an das neue Gebäude durch einen 90 m langen Tunnel angeschlossen. So wurde eine Ve bindung zwischen dem Untergeschoss, dem Erdgeschoss und den Obergeschossen geschaffen, wodurch die Tatsache, dass sich das System der Weinkeller unter d Erde befindet, betont wird. Holls bekannte Meisterschaft, mit Licht und Form umzugehen, erweist sich im Kontext europäischer Traditionen als besonders interessant. erfüllt sie mit Leben; sie wiederum geben seinem Gebäude eine historische Tiefe, die in einer US-amerikanischen Umgebung nicht vorhanden wäre.

Ce complexe comprend un hôtel de 82 chambres, des bureaux, des salles de séminaires, des salles pour événements, un restaurant, un café, une boutique vins, une de souvenirs et un spa. Le Centre de 1200 m² a coûté 2,2 millions d'euros et l'hôtel de 7000 m², 8,6 millions. Situé à une heure de Vienne, à Langenlois, ca tale autrichienne du vin, **LOISIUM** est devenue une destination touristique pour les œnophiles, qui s'est vue couronnée par l'ouverture de cet hôtel de luxe en octob 2005. S'inspirant du site et de la proximité de caves historiques, Holl a d'abord créé le Centre de visites, de forme cubique, incliné à 5° vers une rampe qui conduit réseau de caves. Bâti essentiellement en béton armé, le Centre est au tiers enterré. Les parties visibles sont habillées d'un alliage d'aluminium «marine» de 4 m d'épaisseur et d'une remarquable résistance. Relié aux caves par un tunnel de 90 m de long, le bâtiment fait corps avec le sol et le sous-sol, ce qui renforce l'aspe souterrain du réseau de caves. La maîtrise de la lumière et des formes qui sont la marque de l'architecte trouve une résonance particulière dans ce contexte de vieill traditions européennes, les revitalise et confère à cette œuvre une dimension historique qu'elle n'aurait su trouver en Amérique.

The Loisium Hotel (left page) stands out from the vineyards, an enigmatic sculp-tural presence. In the Visitor Center (above), traditional window sequences are abandoned in favor of an irregular pattern of slits and openings that bring light into the building in unexpected ways.

Das Hotel Loisium (linke Seite) in den Weinbergen hat eine rätselhafte, skulpturale Präsenz. Statt herkömmlicher Fenster gibt es im Besucherzentrum (oben) unregelmäßig angeordnete Schlitze und Öffnungen, die das Innere auf ungewöhnliche Weise belichten.

Sculptural et énigmatique, l'hôtel de Loisium (page gauche) se détache sur son environnement de vignobles. Les séquences traditionnelles de fenêtres du centre d'accueil des visiteurs (ci-dessus) ont été abandonnées au profit d'un motif irrégulier de fentes et d'ouvertures qui canalisent la lumière de façon inattendue.

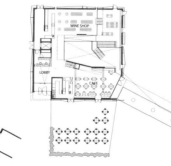

en Holl continues the logic
e façade of his building inside,
openings and color effects
enliven the space.

en Holl führt die Logik der
sade im Inneren weiter. Öffnungen
Farbeffekte werden gezielt ein-
etzt, um den Raum zu beleben.

en Holl poursuit la logique de sa
de à l'intérieur, avec des ouver-
s et des effets de couleurs qui
uent l'espace.

Light, space and even water are part
of the architect's intentional exploration of sensations, in the phenome-
nology of architecture.

Licht, Raum und sogar Wasser sind
Teil von Holls Erforschung der Wahrnehmung von Architektur.

La lumière, l'espace et même l'eau
participent à l'exploration intention-
nelle des sensations dans une phéno-
ménologie de l'architecture.

WHITNEY WATER PURIFICATION FACILITY AND PARK

New Haven, Connecticut, USA, 1998–2005

*Floor area: 13 006 m². Client: South Central Connecticut Regional Water Authority.
Cost: $46 million*

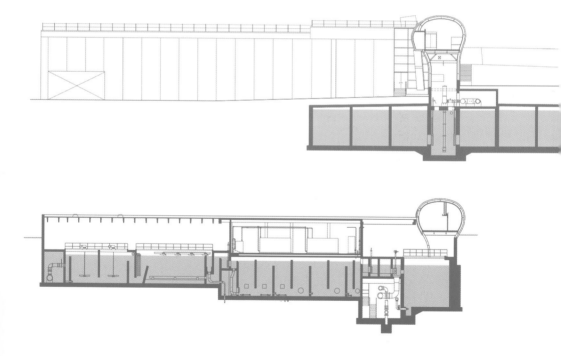

Taking on the mechanical requirements of a water purification
facility, Steven Holl succeeds in
giving an original form to his design,
at once linked to the earth and
distinct from it.

Indem er sich mit den funktionalen
Anforderungen einer Wasseraufbereitungsanlage auseinandersetzt, findet
Holl eine signifikante Form für das
Gebäude, das einerseits mit dem Erdboden verbunden ist, sich andererseits aber klar von ihm abhebt.

Tout en prenant en compte les
contraintes techniques de cette
installation de traitement des eaux,
Steven Holl est parvenu à lui donner
une forme originale à la fois liée au
terrain et distincte de lui.

Steven Holl explains that "The design fuses the architecture of the water purification plant with the landscape to form a public park. Water treatment facilities located beneath the park, while the public and operational programs rise up in a 110 m long stainless steel sliver expressing the workings of the plant below and fo ing a reflective horizon line in the landscape. Like an inverted drop of water, the sliver shape creates a curvilinear interior space which opens to a large window vie surrounding landscape." The architect invested himself fully in the technical aspects of the project, seeing to it that the project was as fully "green" and sustainabl possible. A heat pump system with 88 wells saves 850 000 kilowatts in energy costs annually, while the fact that the plant itself is set into the ground, below lake l allows it to use the pressure of gravity to feed in the water as opposed to energy-consuming pumps. The excavated debris from the site was reused and recyclable m rials were used wherever possible. Existing wetland and natural vegetation were preserved, while a green roof system requiring very little maintenance was designe the facility. Capable of treating 60 million liters of water per day, the plant measures 13 000 m² and cost 46 million dollars to build.

Steven Holl erläutert: »Der Entwurf verbindet die Architektur der Wasseraufbereitungsanlage mit der Landschaft, um so einen öffentlichen Park zu schaffen Anlagen zur Behandlung des Wassers liegen unter der Erdoberfläche und sind in einem 110 m langen ›Span‹ aus Edelstahl angeordnet. Er bringt die Funktionen der A ge im Untergrund zum Ausdruck und bildet eine reflektierende Horizontlinie in der Landschaft. An einen umgedrehten Wassertropfen erinnernd, formt der Span e geschwungenen Innenraum, der sich mit einem großzügigen Ausblick zur Landschaft der Umgebung öffnet.« Der Architekt machte sich sehr umfassend mit der tec schen Seite des Projekts vertraut und setzte sich dafür ein, dass die Anlage so ökologisch wie möglich gebaut wurde. Durch das Wärmepumpensystem mit 88 Behä werden jährlich 850 000 Kilowattstunden Energie gespart, und durch die Verlegung der eigentlichen Anlage ins Erdreich, unterhalb der Seeoberfläche, wird das Wa durch die Erdanziehungskraft in die Anlage eingeleitet, ohne dass dafür energieaufwendige Pumpen notwendig wären. Der Erdaushub für das Gebäude konnte wiede wendet werden; wo immer möglich kamen recyclebare Materialien zum Einsatz. Feuchtgebiete und die natürliche Vegetation wurden erhalten, ferner wurde ein Grün mit sehr geringem Wartungsaufwand entwickelt. Die Anlage mit einer Fläche von 13 000 m² reinigt täglich 60 Millionen l Wasser; die Gesamtkosten beliefen sich umgerechnet 38,5 Millionen Euro.

Steven Holl explique que « ce projet opère la fusion entre l'architecture de cette installation de purification de l'eau et son paysage pour donner naissance parc public. Le traitement de l'eau est effectué en sous-sol, tandis que les salles de contrôle et les espaces ouverts au public sont abrités dans un ‹ tuyau › d'acier in dable de 110 m de long qui exprime la nature de l'installation souterraine et dessine une ligne d'horizon qui réfléchit le paysage. Comme une goutte d'eau inver cette forme délimite un volume intérieur curviligne qui s'ouvre par une vaste baie sur l'environnement ». Steven Holl s'est personnellement investi dans les aspects niques du projet, de sorte que le résultat est aussi écologique que possible. Un système de pompe à chaleur de 88 puits permet une économie d'énergie de 850 00 annuels. La position enterrée de l'unité de traitement, en dessous du niveau du lac, permet par ailleurs d'utiliser la pression de la gravité pour l'alimentation en ea de se passer de pompes grandes consommatrices d'énergie. Les déblais de l'excavation ont été réutilisés et des matériaux recyclables choisis à chaque fois que était possible. Les zones marécageuses et la végétation existantes ont été préservées et une toiture végétalisée à maintenance réduite mise en place. Cette installa susceptible de traiter 60 millions de litres d'eau par jour, d'une superficie de 13 000 m², a coûté 38,5 millions d'euros.

Water treatment facilities are certainly not known for their design qualities, but here, as in any other work of his architecture, Steven Holl also pays careful intention to the creation of unusual interiors, where light and space interact in unexpected ways.

Wasseraufbereitungsanlagen zeichnen sich gewöhnlich sicher nicht durch ihre gestalterischen Qualitäten aus. Bei dieser Anlage schafft Holl – wie bei allen seinen Gebäuden – Innenräume, in denen Licht und Raum auf unerwartete Weise miteinander in Beziehung treten.

Les installations de traitement des eaux ne sont certainement pas réputées pour leur qualité esthétique mais ici, comme dans n'importe quelle autre de ses réalisations, l'architecte porte une attention soignée à la création de volumes intérieurs inhabituels dans lesquels la lumière et l'espace interagissent de façon inattendue.

ere is something of a spaceship out the Whitney building, an en craft that does not just sit the earth but also rises from it.

Das Whitney-Gebäude hat etwas von einem Raumschiff – ein fremdes Fahrzeug, das nicht nur auf der Erde steht, sondern auch in die Höhe strebt.

Il y a, dans ce bâtiment de Whitney, quelque chose d'un vaisseau extraterrestre qui se serait posé sur terre ou qui jaillirait des profondeurs.

JAKOB + MACFARLANE

Jakob + MacFarlane
13–15, rue des Petites Écuries
75010 Paris
France

Tel: +33 144 79 05 72
Fax: +33 148 00 97 93
e-mail: info@jakobmacfarlane.com
Web: www.jakobmacfarlane.com

Renault Square

DOMINIQUE JAKOB, born in 1966, received her degree in art history at the Université de Paris 1 (1990) before obtaining her degree in architecture at the Éc
d'Architecture Paris-Villemin (1991). She has taught at the École Spéciale d'Architecture (1998–99) and the École d'Architecture Paris-Villemin (1994–2000). Born
New Zealand in 1961, **BRENDAN MACFARLANE** received his Bachelor of Architecture at SCI-Arc (1984); and his Master of Architecture degree at Harvard Gradu
School of Design (1990). He has taught at the Berlage Institute, Amsterdam (1996); the Bartlett School of Architecture in London (1996–98) and the École Spéciale d'
chitecture in Paris (1998–99). Both Jakob and MacFarlane have worked in the office of Morphosis in Santa Monica. Their main projects include the T House, La-Garenr
Colombes, France (1994, 1998), the Georges Restaurant in the Pompidou Center, Paris, France (1999–2000); and the restructuring of the Maxime Gorki Theater, Pe
Quevilly, France (1999–2000). Recent work includes: La Fanal Theater, Saint-Nazaire, France (2004); an office building for a reinsurance company in Paris (2004); a
plans for new facilities on the Paris docks (2004).

DOMINIQUE JAKOB, geboren 1966, machte 1990 an der Université Paris 1 ihren Abschluss in Kunstgeschichte. Ihr Architekturstudium an der Ecole d'Arc
tecture Paris-Villemin schloss sie1991 ab. Sie unterrichtete von 1998 bis 1999 an der Ecole Spéciale d'Architecture und von 1994 bis 2000 an der Ecole d'Architect
re Paris-Villemin. Der 1961 in Neuseeland geborene **BRENDAN MACFARLANE** erlangte 1984 seinen Bachelor of Architecture an der SCI-Arc und 1990 seinen Mas
of Architecture an der Graduate School of Design in Harvard. Er hat am Berlage-Institut in Amsterdam gelehrt (1996), an der Bartlett School of Architecture in Lonc
(1996–98) und an der Ecole Spéciale d'Architecture in Paris (1998–99). Sowohl Jakob als auch MacFarlane haben bei Morphosis in Santa Monica gearbeitet. Zu ihr
wichtigsten Projekten gehören die Maison T in La-Garenne-Colombes, Frankreich (1994, 1998), das Restaurant Georges im Centre Georges Pompidou in Paris (199
2000) und der Umbau des Maxim-Gorki-Theaters in Petit-Quevilly, Frankreich (1999–2000). Neuere Projekte des Büros sind u. a. das Theater La Fanal in Saint-Nazai
Frankreich (2004), ein Bürogebäude für eine Versicherungsgesellschaft in Paris (2004) und Planungen für neue Nutzungen der Docks in Paris (2004).

DOMINIQUE JAKOB, née en 1966, est titulaire d'une licence en histoire de l'art de l'Université de Paris I (1990) et diplômée de l'École d'architecture de Par
Villemin (1991). Elle a enseigné à l'École spéciale d'architecture (1998–99) et à l'École de Paris-Villemin (1994–2000). Né en Nouvelle-Zélande en 1961, **BREND
MACFARLANE** est Bachelor of Architecture du Southern California Institute of Architecture, SCI-Arc (1984) et Master of Architecture de la Graduate School of Design
Harvard (1990). Il a enseigné au Berlage Institute à Amsterdam (1996), à la Bartlett School of Architecture de Londres (1996–98) et à l'École spéciale d'architecture
Paris (1998–99). Tous deux ont travaillé à l'agence Morphosis à Santa Monica. Parmi leurs principaux projets : la Maison T, La Garenne-Colombes, France (1994 et 199
le restaurant Georges, Centre Georges Pompidou, Paris (1999–2000), la restructuration du théâtre Maxime Gorki, Petit-Quevilly, France (1999–2000) ; le théâtre
Fanal, Saint-Nazaire, France (2004) ; un immeuble de bureaux pour une compagnie de réassurance, Paris (2004) et les Docks de Paris, un projet pour de nouveaux éq
pements culturels et sportifs sur les quais de Seine, Paris (2004).

RENAULT SQUARE COM

Boulogne-Billancourt, France, 2002–05

Floor area: 14 500 m². Client: Régie Renault.
Cost: €23 million

The distinctive skylights of Vasconi's factory remain, but Jakob + MacFarlane have given a new luminosity and transparency to the Renault factory building.

Die charakteristischen Oberlichter von Vasconis Gebäude blieben. Jakob + MacFarlane haben dem ehemaligen Renaultwerk jedoch zu neuer Leuchtkraft und Transparenz verholfen.

Les verrières originales de l'usine créée par Vasconi subsistent, mais Jakob + MacFarlane ont donné à ces installations une luminosité et une transparence nouvelles.

In the early 1980s, the French automobile company Renault asked the architect Claude Vasconi to design about twenty new buildings to replace ageing factor facilities located on the Séguin Island in the Seine at the western extremity of Paris, and on the right bank of the river. As it happens, he built only one structure, calle 57 Métal. Never used as a factory, Métal 57 has been converted by Jakob + MacFarlane into a communications center for Renault. With ceiling heights ranging betwee six and twelve meters, Métal 57 posed a challenge to the architects, intent on keeping something of the original spirit of the 15 000 m² building while turning it into viable facility. Meant to be a place to base Renault's public relations staff of 250–300 people, and to present new cars to the press and leaders in the automobile indus try, the company envisioned a venue where its marketing groups from around the world could come for meetings, entertainment, dining, and other events showcasing it cars. Three auditoriums seating 100, 300 and 500 persons respectively were added to one side of the shed-like structure. Completed in 2005 for 23 million euros, th conversion successfully creates open, airy spaces ideally suited to showing cars. The architects partially lined the vast exhibition area with large, 7-centimeter-thick struc tural honeycomb panels faced in resin-coated aluminum. With exposed steel frames backing "pleated" white walls, the architects created display backdrops against whic they can hang automobiles like works of art. As MacFarlane points out, "the wall material, made for aeronautics industry fuselages, is interesting because of its flatnes and lightness."

In den frühen 1980er Jahren beauftragte der französische Autohersteller Renault den Architekten Claude Vasconi mit dem Entwurf von etwa 20 neuen Gebäude als Ersatz für die in die Jahre gekommenen Fabrikanlagen auf der Seine-Insel Séguin im äußersten Westen von Paris und auf dem rechten Seineufer. Tatsächlich wurd aber nur einer dieser Entwürfe realisiert, das so genannte Métal-57-Gebäude. Métal 57 wurde jedoch nie als Werk benutzt und von Jakob + MacFarlane in ein Kommu nikationszentrum für Renault umgebaut. Mit Deckenhöhen zwischen 6 und 12 m stellte Métal 57 eine Herausforderung für die Architekten dar: Einerseits wollten sie etwa von der ursprünglichen Atmosphäre des 15 000 m² großen Gebäudes erhalten, es aber andererseits in ein gut nutzbares Kommunikationszentrum verwandeln. 250 bi 300 Mitarbeiter der PR-Abteilung sollen hier arbeiten; außerdem dient es dazu, der Presse und wichtigen Personen der Automobilindustrie die neusten Modelle zu prä sentieren. Renault stellte sich einen Ort vor, an dem seine Marketingteams aus der ganzen Welt für Meetings, Unterhaltungsveranstaltungen, Diners und andere Events bei denen Autos vorgestellt werden, zusammenkommen. Drei Auditorien mit 100, 300 und 500 Plätzen wurden an der einen Seite des hallenartigen Baukörpers ange fügt. 2005 wurde das 23 Millionen Euro teure Gebäude fertig gestellt. Mit dem Umbau ist es gelungen, offene, großzügige Räume zu schaffen, die sich ideal für die Prä sentation von Autos eignen. Die riesigen Ausstellungsräume wurden z. B. mit großen, 7 cm dicken Paneelen mit einem Wabenkern und einer Oberfläche aus kunstharz beschichtetem Aluminium ausgekleidet. Die Architekten entwarfen sichtbare Stahlkonstruktionen, die »gefältete« weiße Wände halten; an diesen Wänden könne Automobile wie Kunstwerke aufgehängt werden. MacFarlane dazu: »Das Interessante am Material der Wand, das eigentlich zur Herstellung von Flugzeugrümpfe verwendet wird, ist seine glatte Oberfläche und sein geringes Gewicht.«

Au début des années 1980, le constructeur automobile Renault avait demandé à l'architecte Claude Vasconi de concevoir une vingtaine de bâtiments pour rem placer ses usines vieillissantes de l'île Seguin et de la rive droite de la Seine à Boulogne-Billancourt. Finalement, il ne réalisa qu'un seul bâtiment, appelé 57 Méta Jamais utilisé en tant qu'usine, le lieu a été converti par Jakob + MacFarlane en Centre de communication Renault. L'ensemble, doté de plafonds de six à douze mètre de haut, représentait un défi pour les architectes, qui voulaient conserver en partie l'esprit d'origine de cette construction de 15 000 m² tout en la transformant en u équipement efficace. Ce lieu était destiné à accueillir les 250 à 300 personnes du département des relations presse de la firme et à présenter les nouveaux modèles au journalistes et aux décideurs du secteur automobile. Renault prévoyait aussi d'y recevoir ses équipes de marketing du monde entier, qui pourraient s'y réunir, y travaille se restaurer et assister à des événements organisés autour des voitures. Trois auditoriums de 100, 300 et 500 places sont venus se greffer au flanc de l'ancien bât ment-hangar. Achevée en 2005 pour un budget de 23 millions d'euros, cette conversion a réussi à créer des espaces aérés et ouverts, parfaitement adaptés à leur fonc tion. Les architectes ont en partie habillé la vaste surface d'exposition de panneaux structurels en nid d'abeille d'aluminium de 7 cm d'épaisseur doublés de résine e façade. À partir d'une ossature apparente en acier qui soutient des murs blanc « plissés », ils ont créé des cimaises sur lesquelles sont accrochées les voitures, comm des œuvres d'art. Comme MacFarlane le fait remarquer, « ce matériau mural, fabriqué pour les fuselages d'avion, est intéressant pour sa légèreté et sa minceur ».

The main floor of the factory has been converted to a bright exhibition space. The angled surfaces are a product of the aeronautics industry.

Die Hauptebene der ehemaligen Fabrik wurde in einen hellen Ausstellungsraum umgewandelt. Die geneigten Flächen sind aus dem Flugzeugbau.

L'étage de l'usine a été transformé en un lumineux espace d'exposition. La technologie des plans inclinés est issue de l'industrie aéronautique.

erence rooms and office spaces
nserted into the former factory
e along either side of the main
Working with a limited budget,
rchitects have succeeded in giv-
he entire space a contemporary
efficient feeling.

ng der Hauptachse wurden auf
en Seiten Konferenz- und Büro-
e eingefügt. Trotz begrenzter
nzieller Mittel ist es den Archi-
en gelungen, dem ganzen Kom-
ein modernes und ökonomisches
zu geben.

salles de réunion et des bureaux
ent s'insérer dans le volume de
cienne usine, de chaque côté de
e principal. Avec un budget limité,
rchitectes ont su donner à la
ité de cet espace industriel une
e moderne et efficace.

NADER KHALILI

Nader Khalili
Cal-Earth Institute
10177 Baldy Lane
Hesperia, California 92345
USA

Tel: +1 760 956 7533
Fax: +1 760 244 2201
e-Mail: elements@calearth.org
Web: www.calearth.org

NADAR KHALILI was born in 1937 in Iran and trained there as an architect as well as in Turkey and the United States. From 1970 to1975, he practiced archtecture in Iran, and has since dedicated himself to research into building with earth. He has been a licensed architect in the State of California since 1970. He has servas a consultant to the United Nations (UNIDO) and a contributor to NASA. Khalili founded the California Institute of Earth Art and Architecture (Cal-Earth) in Hesperia, Caifornia in 1986, and has been directing the Architectural Research Program at Sci-Arc in Los Angeles since 1982. He has received awards from organizations suchthe California chapter of the American Institute of Architects, for Excellence in Technology; the United Nations and HUD (U. S. Department of Housing and Urban Devopment), for "Shelter for the Homeless"; and the American Society of Civil Engineers (Aerospace Division), for his work in lunar-base-building technology. He is the authof five published books, including two translations of the work of the thirteenth-century Sufi poet, Jalal-e-Din Mohammad Rumi. Khalili's architectural works include tdesign of a future-oriented community of 5000 inhabitants (1988); Malekshahr of Isfahan, a community for 20000 that was partially built before 1979; and more th100 projects for conventional buildings.

NADER KHALILI, geboren 1937 im Iran, studierte in seinem Heimatland, in der Türkei und in den USA Architektur. Von 1970 bis 1975 arbeitete er im Iran aArchitekt; seitdem widmet er sich der Erforschung des Bauens mit Erde. Seit 1970 ist er in Kalifornien zeichnungsberechtigter Architekt. Khalili war als Berater bVereinten Nationen (UNIDO) tätig und hat bei Projekten der NASA mitgewirkt. 1986 gründete er das Californian Institute of Earth Art and Architecture (Cal-Earth) in Heperia, Kalifornien; seit 1982 ist er Leiter des Forschungsprogramms Architektur an der SCI-Arc in Los Angeles. Khalili wurde von verschiedenen Institutionen ausgzeichnet, so z. B. vom kalifornischen Verband des American Institute of Architects für herausragende Leistungen im Bereich Technologie, von den Vereinten Nationen uvon HUD (Amerikanische Behörde für Wohnen und Stadtentwicklung) für »Obdach für Obdachlose« sowie von der Amerikanischen Gesellschaft für Bauingenieure (Abtlung Luftfahrt) für seine Arbeit über Bautechnologien auf dem Mond. Nader Khalili hat fünf Bücher geschrieben, darunter zwei Übersetzungen des Sufi-Dichters JalalDin Mohammad Rumi aus dem 13. Jahrhundert. Zu den architektonischen Arbeiten Khalilis gehören der Entwurf für eine zukunftsorientierte Gemeinde mit 5000 Ewohnern (1988), die Gemeinde Malekshahr in Isfahan für 20000 Einwohner, die vor 1979 in Teilen realisiert wurde, und mehr als 100 in bautechnischer Hinsikonventionelle Gebäude.

Né en 1937 en Iran, **NADER KHALILI** y a étudié l'architecture, ainsi qu'en Turquie et aux États-Unis. De 1970 à 1975, il a pratiqué en Iran et s'est, depuconsacré à la recherche sur la construction en terre. Il est architecte licencié de l'État de Californie depuis 1970. Consultant auprès des Nations Unies (United NaticIndustrial Development Organization) et collaborateur de la Nasa, il a fondé le California Institute of Earth Art and Architecture (Cal-Earth) à Hesperia (Californie) en 19et dirige l'Architectural Research Program de SCI-Arc à Los Angeles depuis 1982. Il a reçu des prix d'organismes tels que l'antenne californienne de l'American Instite of Architects pour l'excellence en technologie, les Nations Unies et le Département américain du logement et de l'urbanisme (HUD) pour son «Abri pour le sans-abet de l'American Society of Civil Engineers (division aérospatiale) pour ses travaux sur les technologies de construction de bases lunaires. Il est l'auteur de cinq ouvragdont deux traductions de l'œuvre du poète soufi du XIIIe siècle Jalal-e-Din Mohammad Rumi. Parmi ses réalisations architecturales, on note : la conception d'une vfuturiste de 5 000 habitants (Californie, 1988, restée à l'état de prototype) ; Malekshahr d'Isphahan, ville de 20 000 habitants partiellement édifiée vers 1979, et plus100 projets de réalisations conventionnelles.

SANDBAG SHELTER PROTOTYPES

Various locations, 1992–

Floor area: single unit 400 m² or double unit 800 m². Client: Iran office of UNDP/UNHCR and others.
Cost: $2300 for a single unit or $2800 for a double unit, 25% extra for each additional unit

A winner of the 2004 Aga Khan Award for Architecture, the **SANDBAG SHELTER PROTOTYPES** designed by Nader Khalili were described in the jury citation a follows: "These shelters serve as a prototype for temporary housing using extremely inexpensive means to provide safe homes that can be built quickly and have the high insulation values necessary in arid climates. Their curved form was devised in response to seismic conditions, ingeniously using sand or earth as raw materials, since their flexibility allows the construction of single- and double-curvature compression shells that can withstand lateral seismic forces. The prototype is a symbiosis o tradition and technology. It employs vernacular forms, integrating load-bearing and tensile structures, but provides a remarkable degree of strength and durability for this type of construction, that is traditionally weak and fragile, through a composite system of sandbags and barbed wire." Khalili basically found that stacking sandbags in circular plans to form domed structures, with barbed wire laid between each row to prevent the bags from shifting, was a way of providing readily available and stable housing. Nor is this concept merely theoretical since prototype sandbag shelters have been built in Iran, Mexico, India, Thailand, Siberia, and Chile. The prototype received California building permits and have also met the requirements of the United Nations High Commission for Refugees (UNHCR) for emergency housing. Both th UNHCR and the United Nations Development Program (UNDP) used the system in 1995 to provide temporary shelters for a flood of refugees coming into Iran from Iraq

Die **PROTOTYPEN VON SCHUTZBAUTEN AUS SANDSÄCKEN** wurden 2004 mit dem Aga-Khan-Preis für Architektur ausgezeichnet. Die Jury beschreibt sie fol gendermaßen: »Diese Schutzbauten sind Prototypen von temporären Häusern, die mit extrem preiswerten Mitteln errichtet werden können. Sie stellen sichere Unterkünft bereit, können schnell gebaut werden und haben einen hohen Wärmedämmwert, der im Wüstenklima notwendig ist. Ihre gekrümmte Form wurde als Antwort auf seis mische Bedingungen entwickelt. Auf geniale Weise wird Sand oder Erde als Rohmaterial verwendet, da die Flexibilität dieser Materialien die Konstruktion von einfach un zweifach gekrümmten, auf Druck belasteten Hüllen erlaubt, die seismischen Horizontallasten standhalten können. Der Prototyp ist eine Symbiose von Tradition und Tech nologie. Er verwendet Formen, die auf dem Land gebräuchlich sind, integriert druck- und zugbelastete Strukturen, bietet aber einen bemerkenswerten Grad an Festigke und Haltbarkeit für eine Konstruktion dieser Art, die sonst eher schwach und instabil ist. Dies wird durch eine Kompositsystem aus Sandsäcken und Stacheldraht erreicht. Sandsäcke werden kreisförmig ausgelegt und dann so aufgeschichtet, dass sie eine Kuppel formen. Um ein Verrutschen der Säcke zu verhindern, wird zwischen jed Reihe Stacheldraht gelegt. Auf diese Weise, so fand Khalili heraus, können schnell herzustellende und stabile Unterkünfte gebaut werden. Das Konzept ist nicht theore tischer Natur: Solche Schutzbauten wurden schon im Iran, in Mexiko, Indien, Thailand, Sibirien und Chile errichtet. Die kalifornische Baubehörde genehmigte die Proto typen; sie entsprechen auch den Standards des Hochkommissars für Flüchtlinge der Vereinten Nationen (UNHCR) für Notunterkünfte. Sowohl der UNHCR als auch da Entwicklungsprogramm der Vereinten Nationen (UNDP) benutzte das System 1995, um temporäre Unterkünfte für die Flüchtlinge aus dem Irak in den Iran zu bauen.

Les **PROTOTYPES D'ABRIS EN SACS DE SABLE** conçus par Nader Khalili, lauréat du Prix d'architecture Aga Khan 2004, étaient présentés de la façon suivan te par le jury : « Ces abris sont des prototypes de logements temporaires créés à l'aide de moyens extrêmement bon marché, afin d'offrir un foyer solide rapideme. constructibles et présentant le haut degré d'isolation thermique indispensable dans les climats arides. Leurs formes courbes ont été conçues pour supporter de secousses sismiques, et utilisent ingénieusement comme matières premières le sable et la terre, dont la souplesse permet la construction de coques à simple ou doub courbe en compression qui peuvent résister aux forces sismiques latérales. Ces prototypes sont une symbiose de tradition et de technologie. Ils font appel à des forme vernaculaires, intégrant des structures porteuses et en traction, tout en offrant un remarquable niveau de résistance et de durabilité pour ce type de construction, trac tionnellement léger et fragile, grâce à un système composite de sacs de sable et fil de fer barbelé. » À l'origine, Khalili a découvert que le fait d'empiler des sacs de sab en cercle pour former des structures en coupole et de les stabiliser par du fil de fer barbelé intercalé entre chaque strate était un moyen d'obtenir des logements stable et faciles à construire. Son concept n'est pas resté purement théorique, puisque des prototypes ont déjà été construits en Iran, au Mexique, en Inde, en Thaïlande, e Sibérie et au Chili. Ils ont reçu un permis de construire en Californie et sont conformes à la réglementation du Haut Commissariat des Nations Unies aux Réfugiés po les logements d'urgence. Le HCR et le Programme de développement des Nations Unies (PDNU) ont utilisé ce système dès 1995 pour répondre aux afflux de réfugi arrivant d'Irak en Iran.

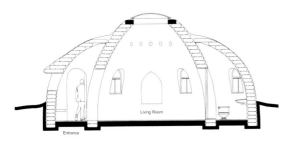

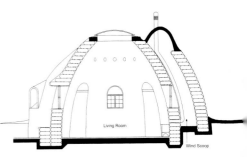

The sandbag shelters can be arranged in various configurations, with a simplicity of construction that can be mastered even by persons who have no knowledge of building.

Aus den Sandsäcken können verschiedene Haustypen gebaut werden. Alle Behausungen sind auch von Menschen, die über keine Baukenntnisse verfügen, einfach herzustellen.

Les abris en sacs de sable peuvent adopter différentes configurations, tout en gardant une simplicité de construction maîtrisable même par des gens qui n'ont aucune connaissance dans ce domaine.

ng sandbags and barbed wire,
mally associated more with disas-
and conflict than with hope to
ld, Nader Khalili has devised an
ersion of the downward spiral that
acts so many across the world.

Nader Khalili benutzt Sandsäcke und
Stacheldraht – Materialien, die man
normalerweise eher mit Katastrophen
und Konflikten als mit Hoffnung verbindet –, um die Negativspirale, die
so viele Menschen weltweit betrifft,
in eine positive umzudrehen.

À partir de sacs de sable et de fil de
fer barbelé – matériaux que l'on
associe plus aux désastres et conflits
qu'aux espoirs –, Nader Khalili propose une solution pour inverser la
spirale vers le bas qui affecte tant
d'individus dans le monde.

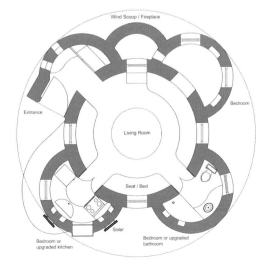

lan to the right shows how the
ed and domed structures can
adapted to various degrees of
histication, to include a kitchen
bathroom as well as the central
ng space. The plentiful raw
erials used ensure that this type
shelter could be erected almost
where in the world.

 Grundriss rechts zeigt, dass die
pelförmigen Konstruktionen aus
d und Stoff auch höheren Ansprü-
n gerecht werden und eine Küche
/oder ein Badezimmer sowie den
tralen Wohnraum aufnehmen
nen. Aufgrund der reichlich
handenen Rohmaterialien kann
se Art der Unterkunft fast überall
 der Welt gebaut werden.

Le plan à droite montre comment
ces petites constructions à coupole
peuvent acquérir divers degrés de
sophistication et comprendre une
cuisine, une pièce d'eau ou un séjour
central. Le choix de matériaux écono-
miques et abondants fait que ce type
d'abri peut être édifié presque
n'importe où dans le monde.

Wind Scoop / Fireplace

Bedroom

Entrance

Living Room

Seat / Bed

Solar

Bedroom or
upgraded kitchen

Bedroom or upgraded
bathroom

KLEIN DYTHAM

Klein Dytham architecture
AD Bldg 2nd Floor
1–15–7 Hiroo
Shibuya-ku
Tokyo 150–0012
Japan

Tel: +81 357 95 22 77
Fax: +81 357 95 22 76
e-mail: kda@klein-dytham.com
Web: www.klein-dytham.com

Undercove

KLEIN DYTHAM Architecture was created in Tokyo by Astrid Klein and Mark Dytham in 1991. Winners of the 1993 Kajima Space Design Award for the best you practice in Japan. Astrid Klein was born in Varese, Italy in 1962. She studied at the Ecole des Arts Décoratifs in Strasbourg, France (1986), and received a degree architecture from the Royal College of Art, London in 1988. In 1988, she also worked in the office of Toyo Ito in Tokyo. Mark Dytham was born in Northamptonshire, E land, in 1964 and attended the Newcastle University School of Architecture, graduating in 1985. He then also attended the Royal College of Art, London (1988). He work in both the office of Skidmore Owings and Merrill in Chicago and with Toyo Ito in Tokyo before creating KDa. He has been an assistant professor at Tokyo Science U versity. Their recent projects include the Leaf Chapel and Undercover Lab published here as well as the Idée Workstation (Shimouma, Tokyo), and Cats Eyes, a fash store in Harajuku, Tokyo.

KLEIN DYTHAM Architecture wurde 1991 von Astrid Klein und Mark Dytham in Tokio gegründet. 1993 waren sie die Gewinner des Kajima Space Design Aw für das beste junge Büro in Japan. Astrid Klein, geboren 1962 in Varese, Italien, studierte an der Ecole des Arts Décoratifs in Straßburg (1986) und schloss 1988 Architekturstudium am Royal College of Art in London ab. 1988 war sie auch im Büro von Toyo Ito in Tokio tätig. Mark Dytham wurde 1964 in Northamptonshire, E land, geboren, studierte an der Newcastle University School of Architecture und machte dort 1985 seinen Abschluss. Er studierte ebenfalls am Royal College of Ar London (1988). Dytham arbeitete bei Skidmore, Owings and Merrill in Chicago und bei Toyo Ito in Tokio, bevor er sich mit Klein zusammentat. Außerdem war er Wisse schaftlicher Mitarbeiter an der Tokyo Science University. Zu den neueren Projekten des Büros gehören die hier gezeigte Blatt-Kapelle und das Undercover Lab, ferner Idée Workstation in Shimouma, Tokio, und Cats Eyes, ein Modegeschäft in Harajuku, Tokio.

KLEIN DYTHAM Architecture a été créée à Tokyo par Astrid Klein et Mark Dytham en 1991, et a remporté en 1993 le prix de conception d'espace Kajima p la meilleure jeune agence au Japon en 1993. Astrid Klein est née à Varese (Italie) en 1962. Elle a étudié à l'École des arts décoratifs de Strasbourg en 1986 et est dip mée en architecture du Royal College of Art de Londres (1988). La même année, elle a travaillé à Tokyo chez Toyo Ito. Mark Dytham, né en 1964 dans le Northamptonsh (Angleterre), est diplômé de la Newcastle University School of Architecture (1985). Il a ensuite étudié au Royal College of Art de Londres (1988), puis a travaillé dans agences de Skidmore Owings and Merrill à Chicago et avec Toyo Ito à Tokyo, avant de créer KDa. Il a été assistant-professeur à l'Université des sciences de Tokyo. Pa leurs récents projets : la Leaf Chapel et l'Undercover Lab publiés ici, le poste de travail Idée (Shimouma, Tokyo) et la boutique de mode Cats Eyes (Harajuku, Tokyo).

UNDERCOVER LAB

Harajuku, Tokyo, Japan, 2000–01

Floor area: 639 m². Client: Undercover Co. Ltd.
Cost: not disclosed

"**UNDERCOVER LAB** is a building, which is undercover. Not only is it tucked away in the back streets of Harajuku, but the site is also very deceiving," say
architects. The steel frame and reinforced concrete atelier and showroom for a fashionable designer occupies 206 m² of a 345 m² site and develops a total floor ar
of 639 m². Including a studio, press showroom and office, the design is based on a dramatically cantilevered black tube that allows for a twenty-meter-long hangar inter
ed to display a "one season fashion collection." Five cars can be parked below the overhang, further optimizing the use of precious Tokyo land. Since the main part
the site is actually located behind a 10-meter driveway, the architects asked themselves "How could we make the building impressive and commanding when the ma
bulk of the building was set back 10 meters. The tube seemed a natural way to bring the building to the street…" They further explain that the tube was made to lo
"as anonymous as possible, almost like a shipping container where you have no idea of its contents."

»**UNDERCOVER LAB** ist ein geheimes Gebäude. Es liegt nicht nur in einer Seitenstraße von Harajuku, auch das Grundstück täuscht den Besucher«, sagen
Architekten. Das Atelier und der Showroom eines gefragten Designers bestehen aus einer Stahlkonstruktion und Stahlbeton. Das Gebäude nimmt 206 m² des 345
großen Grundstücks ein. Seine Gesamtfläche beträgt 639 m². Der Entwurf wird von einem dramatisch auskragenden schwarzen Quader bestimmt. In ihm befindet si
eine 20 m lange Halle, in der die aktuelle Kollektion gezeigt wird. Ferner gibt es das Atelier, einen Showroom für die Presse und ein Büro. Unter dem auskragenden Qu
der können fünf Autos parken, wodurch die Nutzung des so wertvollen Tokioer Bodens noch weiter optimiert wird. Da sich der wesentliche Teil des Grundstücks hin
einer 10 m langen Zufahrt befindet, fragten sich die Architekten: »Wie können wir ein eindrucksvolles Gebäude bauen, wenn das Hauptvolumen des Gebäudes 10 m v
der Straße entfernt liegt? Der Quader schien ein natürliches Mittel zu sein, um das Gebäude an die Straße anzubinden …« Weiter erklären sie, dass der Quader »so an
nym wie möglich« aussehen soll, »fast wie ein Frachtcontainer, bei dem man keine Ahnung hat, was er enthält«.

« **UNDERCOVER LAB** est un bâtiment… clandestin. Non seulement il est en retrait au fond d'une des ruelles secondaires de Harajuku, mais son terrain
également très trompeur », expliquent les architectes. La structure en acier et en béton armé de cet atelier/showroom pour un styliste de mode occupe 206 m² d'un te
rain de 345 m² pour une surface utile totale de 639 m². Le projet comprend un atelier, un showroom de presse et un bureau. Il met en scène une sorte de tube noir
porte-à-faux spectaculaire, qui abrite un hall de vingt mètres de long dans lequel toute la collection entière d'une saison peut être présentée. Cinq voitures peuvent s
tionner sous ce porte-à-faux, ce qui est une façon d'optimiser l'utilisation du précieux sol tokyoïte. La plus grande partie du terrain se trouvant au fond d'une allée
10 m de long, les architectes se sont demandé : « Comment rendre le bâtiment impressionnant et dominant lorsque sa masse principale doit être en retrait de dix mètre
Le tube nous a paru une manière naturelle de ramener le tout vers la rue… [nous l'avons rendu] aussi anonyme que possible, presque comme un conteneur d'expé
tion dont on ne sait pas ce qu'il contient. »

An ample interior working space
mixes brick and wood, with a ceiling
made from wooden concrete forms.
The architects combine roughness,
surprise and a sure sense of volume
to make the Undercover Lab a kind of
hidden world for the fashion design-
ers in the midst of Tokyo's bustle.

Der Arbeitsraum wird durch Ziegelstein
und Holz gekennzeichnet (die Decke
besteht aus hölzernen Schalelementen
für Beton). Die Architekten vermischen
raue und überraschende Elemente;
mit sicherem Gefühl für Raum machen
sie das Undercover Lab für die Mode-
designer zu einem versteckten Ort
inmitten von Tokios Hektik.

Le vaste atelier de travail associe la
brique, le bois et un plafond en bois.
Les architectes ont combiné brutalité,
effets de surprise et un sens très sûr
des volumes pour faire de l'Underco-
ver Lab l'univers secret d'un styliste
de mode en plein cœur de l'animation
de Tokyo.

The spectacular cantilever of the Undercover Lab is its identifying feature, seen in the image above, and in section below right.

Die spektakuläre Auskragung ist das identifikationsstiftende Merkmal des Undercover Lab, zu sehen oben und in der Ansicht unten rechts.

Le porte-à-faux spectaculaire de l'Undercover Lab (photo ci-dessus et coupe ci-dessous, à droite) fait aussi office de signal d'identification.

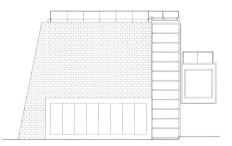

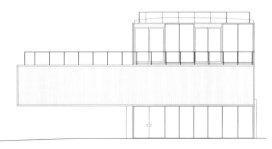

LEAF CHAPEL

Kobuchizawa, Yamanashi, Japan, 2003–04

Floor area: 168 m². Client: Risonare (Hoshino Resort).
Cost: not disclosed

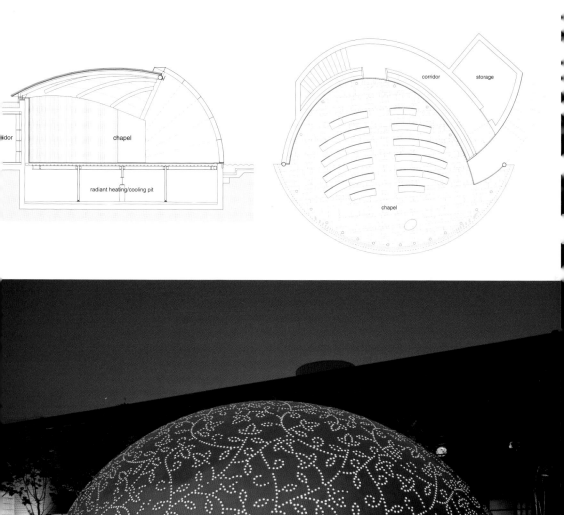

idor   chapel

radiant heating/cooling pit

corridor   storage

chapel

Located on the grounds of the Risonare Hotel, this wedding chapel is "formed by two leaves – one glass, one steel – which have seemingly fluttered to th ground." The white steel leaf is perforated with 4700 holes, each of which has an acrylic lens, "similar to a bride's veil made of delicate lace." The eleven-ton steel sh silently lifts in 38 seconds at the end of the ceremony, much as the groom lifts the bride's veil to kiss her. A pond with stepping stones and a green natural setting awa the newlyweds. Black timber walls and benches for 80 guests, and a black granite floor intentionally create a contrast within the 168 m² chapel to the "bright white pu ty of the occasion." Though the architects insist on the leaf metaphor, the shape of the chapel and its opening lid also invite comparisons to an eye. Given the Japane passion for wedding chapels which do not necessarily carry with them a religious connotation, Klein Dytham have shown their capacity to respond to the tastes and nee of their clients.

Die Hochzeitskapelle liegt auf dem Grundstück des Risonare Hotels und wird »durch zwei scheinbar auf den Boden gefallene Blätter, eines aus Glas, das ande aus Stahl, gebildet«. Das weiße »Blatt« aus Stahl ist mit 4700 Löchern perforiert. In jedem Loch befindet sich eine Linse aus Acryl, so dass ein Bild entsteht, das »de feinen Spitzenschleier einer Braut ähnelt«. Am Ende jeder Zeremonie hebt sich – in 38 Sekunden – leise die 11 t schwere Stahlschale, so, wie der Bräutigam den Schle er der Braut hebt, wenn er sie küsst. Ein Teich mit Trittsteinen und eine natürliche grüne Umgebung erwarten die frisch Verheirateten. Die schwarzen Holzwände u Bänke für 80 Gäste sowie der schwarze Granitfußboden der 168 m² großen Kapelle bilden einen bewussten Kontrast zur »schneeweißen Reinheit des Anlasses«. Obwc die Architekten auf der Blattmetapher bestehen, ruft die Form der Kapelle mit dem sich öffnenden »Lid« auch Assoziationen an ein Auge hervor. In Anbetracht der beso deren Vorliebe der Japaner für Hochzeitskapellen – nicht unbedingt haben diese auch eine religiöse Konnotation – beweisen Klein Dytham ihre Fähigkeit, auf de Geschmack und die Bedürfnisse ihrer Bauherren zu reagieren.

Située sur le domaine du Risonare Hotel, cette chapelle de mariage est «formée de deux feuilles – une de verre et une d'acier – qui semblent être tombées a sol en virevoltant». «La feuille blanche en acier, perforée de 47 000 trous, dont chacun est doté d'une petite lentille en acrylique, est ‹semblable à un voile de marie en dentelle délicate›.» La coquille d'acier de 11 onze tonnes se relève en 38 secondes à la fin de la cérémonie, un peu comme lorsque le jeune marié soulève le vo de l'épousée pour l'embrasser. Un bassin à pas japonais et un cadre de verdure naturel accueillent les jeunes mariés. À l'intérieur des 168 m² de la chapelle, des mu et des bancs pour 80 invités en bois noirci et un sol en granit noir créent volontairement un contraste avec «la pureté immaculée de l'occasion». Bien que les arch tectes insistent sur la métaphore de la feuille, la forme et l'ouverture de la chapelle font également penser à un œil. Quand on connaît la passion des Japonais pour l chapelles, qui ne comporte pas forcément de connotation religieuse, Klein Dytham ont montré ici leur capacité à répondre aux goûts et aux attentes de leurs clients.

MATHIAS KLOTZ

Mathias Klotz
Los Colonos 0411
Providencia
Santiago
Chile

Tel: +56 26 76 27 01
Fax: +56 26 76 27 02
e-mail: estudio@mathiasklotz.com
Web: www.mathiasklotz.com

MATHIAS KLOTZ was born in 1965 in Viña del Mar, Chile. He received his architecture degree from the Pontificia Universidad Católica de Chile in 1991. H created his own office in Santiago the same year. He has taught at several Chilean universities and was Director of the School of Architecture of the Universidad Dieg Portales in Santiago (2001–03). Recent work includes: the Casa Viejo, Santiago (2001); the Smol Building, Concepción (2001); the Faculty of Health, Universidad Dieg Portales, Santiago (2004); and the remodeling of the Cerro San Luis House, Santiago (2004). Current projects include: the Techos House, Villa La Angostura, Argentin Kegevic House, Cachagua; and the Ochoalcubo House, Marbella; 20 one-family houses in La Dehesa, Santiago; and the Buildings Department San Isidro, Buenos Aire Argentina. His work has been exhibited at the GA Gallery in Tokyo, at Archilab, Orléans, France (2000), and at MoMA in New York where he was a finalist for the 199 Mies van der Rohe Prize. He participated in the Chinese International Practical Exhibition of Architecture in Nanjing in 2004, together with such architects as David Adjay Odile Decq, Arata Isozaki and Kazuyo Sejima.

MATHIAS KLOTZ, 1965 in Viña del Mar in Chile geboren, schloss sein Architekturstudium an der Pontificia Universidad Católica de Chile 1991 ab. Im selb Jahr gründete er in Santiago sein eigenes Büro. Er hat an verschiedenen Universitäten in Chile unterrichtet und war von 2001 bis 2003 Direktor der Architekturfakul der Universidad Diego Portales in Santiago. Neuere Projekte von ihm sind u. a. die Casa Viejo in Santiago (2001), das Smol-Gebäude in Concepción (2001), die Fakul für Gesundheitswesen der Universidad Diego Portales (2004) und der Umbau des Hauses Cerro San Luis in Santiago (2004). Zu den in der Planung bzw. im Bau befin lichen Projekten gehören das Techos-Haus in Villa La Angostura in Argentinien, das Kegevic-Haus in Cachagua und das Ochoalcubo-Haus in Marbella, ferner 20 E familienhäuser in La Dehesa, Santiago, und die Bauabteilung San Isidro in Buenos Aires. Seine Projekte wurden in der GA Gallery in Tokio, auf der Archilab in Orléa (2000) und im MoMA in New York ausgestellt. 1998 war er in New York Finalist für den Mies-van-der-Rohe-Preis. 2004 hat Klotz – zusammen mit Architekten wie Dav Adjaye, Odile Decq, Arata Isozaki und Kazuyo Sejima – an der Chinese International Practical Exhibition of Architecture in Nanjing teilgenommen.

MATHIAS KLOTZ est né en 1965 à Viña del Mar au Chili. Il est sorti diplômé en architecture de la Pontificia Universidad Católica de Chile en 1991 et a créé propre agence à Santiago la même année. Il a enseigné dans plusieurs universités chiliennes et a dirigé l'École d'architecture de l'Universidad Diego Portales à Sant go (2001–03). Parmi ses œuvres récentes : la Casa Viejo, Santiago (2001) ; centre commercial Smol, Concepción (2002) ; la faculté de médecine de l'Universidad Dieg Portales, Santiago (2004) ; la rénovation de la Casa Cerro San Luis, Santiago (2004) ; Casa Techitos (Villa La Angostura, Argentine) ; la Casa Kegevic (Cachagua) ; la Ca Orcholcubo (Marbella) ; vingt maisons individuelles (La Dehesa, Santiago) et le Département de la construction (San Isidro, Buenos Aires, Argentine). Ses travaux ont exposés à la GA Gallery à Tokyo, à Archilab, Orléans, France (2000) et au MoMA à New York. En 1998, il a été finaliste du prix Mies van der Rohe. Il a participé à l'I position internationale d'architecture pratique de Nanjing, Chine (2004) aux côtés de confrères comme David Adjaye, Odile Decq, Arata Isozaki et Kazuyo Sejima.

VIEJO HOUSE

Santiago de Chile, Chile, 2001–02

Floor area: 750 m². Client: Veronica Viejo.
Cost: €1 million

The strict lines of the house and its thick concrete shell do not exclude the luxurious openness seen in this image.

Die strengen Linien des Hauses und seine massive Betonhülle schließen eine luxuriöse Offenheit im Inneren nicht aus.

Les lignes strictes de la maison et son épaisse coque de béton n'excluent pas un luxueux sentiment d'ouverture, comme le montre cette photo.

The circular pattern of openings in the concrete is echoed by larger circular openings in the roof of the house.

Das Motiv der kreisförmigen Öffnungen im Beton findet sich in den großen runden Öffnungen im Dach des Hauses wieder.

Les oculus pratiqués dans le béton trouvent un écho dans les vastes ouvertures circulaires ménagées dans la toiture.

This family house located in a residential area of Santiago is set on a 3700 m² site and has a built area of 700 m². A 12 x 40 m rectangle, the house was bu entirely out of reinforced concrete. Circular windows mark one long closed façade, while the opposite face of the house opens entirely toward a swimming pool with wooden terrace. Another terrace, on the roof, offers a 360° view of the hills surrounding Santiago, while round skylights bring daylight into the interior. Since anoth house had been built on the site in the 1950s, the architect was able to take advantage of large, existing trees. The architect explains that "the program, classic for family with two children, was organized around two corridors, one interior and other exterior running from the entrance, through the public and service areas to the mc private areas. This is a quiet work that resolves constructive and programmatic problems with simplicity, working different textures for the concrete on site as well as t different heights on the interior areas, depending on their use and proportions." Powerful and yet practical, the **VIEJO HOUSE** demonstrates the ability of the archite to use concrete as the main building material of a comfortable, even luxurious house.

Das Einfamilienhaus in einer Wohngegend von Santiago steht auf einem 3700 m² großen Grundstück und hat eine Gesamtfläche von 700 m². Das rechtecki Haus mit den Außenmaßen 12 x 40 m wurde komplett aus Stahlbeton errichtet. Kreisrunde Fenster kennzeichnen die lange, ansonsten geschlossene Fassade; dageg ist die gegenüberliegende Seite vollständig zu einem Swimmingpool und einer holzgedeckten Terrasse geöffnet. Eine weitere Terrasse auf dem Dach des Hauses bie einen Panoramablick auf die Santiago umgebenden Berge. Das Haus wird über runde Oberlichter zusätzlich belichtet. Auf dem Grundstück stand ein Haus aus den 1950 Jahren, das abgerissen wurde; den Bestand an alten großen Bäumen bezog der Architekt aber in die Planung mit ein. Klotz erläutert: »Das für eine Familie mit zwei Ki dern typische Raumprogramm wurde mithilfe von zwei Fluren organisiert: einem inneren und einem äußeren Flur, der vom Eingang durch die ›öffentlicheren‹ Bereic und die Servicezone zu den privateren Räumen führt. Dies ist ein ›stilles‹ Haus. Konstruktive und durch das Raumprogramm auftretende Fragen wurden auf einfac Weise beantwortet. Vor Ort stellte man verschiedene Betonoberflächen her, die Innenräume erhielten, je nach Nutzung und gewünschter Proportion, unterschiedlic Höhen.« Kraftvoll und praktisch – die **CASA VIEJO** zeigt die Fähigkeit des Architekten, Beton als Hauptbaumaterial einzusetzen, und er schafft mit ihm ein komfortabl sogar luxuriöses Haus.

Cette maison de famille située dans un quartier résidentiel de Santiago est implantée sur un terrain de 3700 m² et offre une surface utile de 700 m². Ce r tangle de 12 x 40 m a été entièrement construit en béton armé. Des ouvertures circulaires ponctuent une longue façade fermée, tandis que la façade opposée s'ou entièrement sur une terrasse en bois et une piscine. Une autre terrasse sur le toit offre une vue à 360° sur les collines entourant Santiago, tandis que les verrières ron ménagées dans son sol éclairent l'intérieur. Comme une autre maison avait été édifiée sur ce terrain dans les années 1950, l'architecte a pu profiter de la présence grands arbres. Il explique que « le programme classique pour une famille avec deux enfants s'organise autour de deux corridors, l'un intérieur, l'autre extérieur, part de l'entrée et desservant les zones de réception et de service jusqu'aux parties plus privées. Il s'agit d'un travail serein qui résout les problèmes de construction et programme avec simplicité, propose des textures de béton variées et différentes hauteurs de pièces selon leur usage et leurs proportions ». De formes puissantes en restant fonctionnelle, la **MAISON VIEJO** illustre la capacité de l'architecte à utiliser le béton comme matériau principal pour une maison confortable, voire luxueu

canopied car park and a sunscreen
emonstrate the architect's deft
ternation of dense opacity with
ry lightness. Heavy materials seem
 hover in space, offering protection
d a promise of solidity to the
sidents.

Die überdeckten Stellplätze und
der Sonnenschutz machen den
geschickten Wechsel von dichter
Opazität und luftiger Leichtigkeit
deutlich. Schwere Materialien
scheinen zu schweben, bieten
Schutz und versprechen Solidität.

Un parking sous auvent et un écran
solaire illustrent l'habileté de l'architecte à alterner opacité et légèreté
aérienne. Les matériaux lourds
semblent flotter dans l'espace tout
en offrant leur protection et leur
garantie de solidité aux occupants.

MARCIO KOGAN

Marcio Kogan
Alameida Tiete, 505
04616–001 São Paulo SP
Brazil

Tel: +55 11 30 81 35 22
Fax: +55 11 30 63 34 24
e-mail: info@marciokogan.com.br
Web: www.marciokogan.com.br

BR

Born in 1952, **MARCIO KOGAN** graduated in 1976 from the School of Architecture at Mackenzie University in São Paulo. In 1983, he received an IAB (Instit de Arquitetos do Brazil) Award for the Rubens Sverner Day-Care Center. He received other such awards for his Goldfarb Residence (1991); the Larmond Store (199 UMA Store (1999); or for the BR House (published here, 2004). In 2003, he made a submission for the World Trade Center Site Memorial, and in 2002, he complete Museum of Microbiology in São Paulo. He worked with Isay Weinfeld on the Fasano Hotel in São Paulo. He also participated with Weinfeld in the 25th São Paulo Bienn (2002) and worked with him on the Escola Cidade Jardim/ Play Pen, also in São Paulo. Kogan is known for his use of box-like forms, together with wooden shutte trellises and exposed stone.

Der 1952 geborene **MARCIO KOGAN** machte 1976 seinen Abschluss an der Escuela de Arquitectura der Universidad Mackenzie in São Paulo. Das von i geplante Rubens-Sverner-Tagespflegezentrum wurde 1983 mit einem Preis des IAB (Instituto de Arquitetos do Brazil) ausgezeichnet. Weitere Preise des IAB erhielt er die Goldfarb Residence (1991), den Larmond Store (1995), für den UMA Store (1999) und für das hier gezeigte BR Haus (2004). 2003 reichte er einen Entwurf für Mahnmal auf dem Grundstück des World Trade Center ein, 2002 wurde das Museum für Mikrobiologie in São Paulo fertig gestellt. Das Fasano Hotel in São Pa plante er in Partnerschaft mit Isay Weinfeld. Ebenfalls mit Weinfeld nahm er 2002 auch an der 25. São Paulo Biennale und an der Escola Cidade Jardim/Play Pen in S Paulo teil. Typisch für Kogans Architektur sind kistenartigen Formen, Fensterläden und Spaliere aus Holz sowie die Verwendung von Naturstein.

Né en 1952, **MARCIO KOGAN** est diplômé de l'École d'architecture de l'Université Mackenzie à São Paulo (1976) et a été primé par l'IAB (Institut des arc tectes du Brésil) pour le dispensaire Rubens Sverner, la résidence Goldfarb (1991), le magasin Larmond (1995), le magasin UMA (1999) et la Mmaison BR (2004) pub ici. En 2002, il a achevé un musée de microbiologie à São Paulo et, en 2003, a proposé un projet au concours pour le mémorial du World Trade Center à New York. conçu, avec Isay Weinfeld, l'hôtel Fasano à São Paulo et a également participé, avec Weinfeld, à la 25e Biennale de São Paulo (2002) et collaboré avec lui au projet la Escola Cidade Jardim/Play Pen, toujours à São Paulo. Il est connu pour son utilisation de la forme de la boîte, de volets et treillis en bois et de la pierre apparente

BR HOUSE

Araras, Rio de Janeiro, Brazil, 2002–04

Floor area: 739 m². Client: not disclosed.
Cost: $1 million

Located on a 6820 m² site, this rectangular house has a floor area of 739 m². The architect describes the residence himself in clear terms: "The two-story hou is made of concrete, metal, wood, aluminum and glass and is totally integrated with the forest landscape of this mountainous region of Rio de Janeiro (Petrópolis). Th first floor has four suites, guest bathroom, kitchen and living/dining rooms. The ground floor has a heated pool, dry sauna with a large fixed glass wall so that one ca contemplate the landscape. The house represents the idea of two monolithic concrete blades containing the boxes of the first floor, raised on stilts and stone box. Th wood-covered façade consists of a light filter (vertical wooden strips) which, on the terraces of the suites, open completely. At nightfall, this "skin" looks as though it totally lit, surrounded by the beautiful mountainous forest." The idea of lifting structures up on pilotis is fairly common in Brazil. What is not at all obvious in this hous is that Marcio Kogan was called into the project after another architect had been dismissed by the clients and Kogan had to deal with an existing steel frame. Seemin ly making this apparent handicap into an advantage, the essentially geometric rigor of the architectural solutions blends seamlessly with a sensual and very Brazili presence of nature.

Das rechteckige, 739 m² große Haus befindet sich auf einem Grundstück mit einer Fläche von 6820 m². Der Architekt beschreibt das Wohnhaus so: »Das zwe geschossige Haus besteht aus Beton, Metall, Holz, Aluminium und Glas und ist vollständig in die Waldlandschaft der bergigen Region Petrópolis von Rio de Janeiro int griert. Im ersten Obergeschoss gibt es vier Suiten, ein Gästebadezimmer, eine Küche sowie Ess- und Wohnräume. Auf der Erdgeschossebene liegen ein beheizt Schwimmbad und eine Trockensauna mit einer großen festverglasten Glaswand, so dass die Landschaft gegenwärtig ist. Bestimmt wird das Haus von der Idee zwei monolithischer ›Klingen‹ aus Beton (die Decken), die die ›Kisten‹ des ersten Obergeschosses aufnehmen. Sie wurden mithilfe der Stützen und einer ›Steinkiste‹ angeh ben. Die holzverkleidete Fassade wirkt als Lichtfilter und besteht aus vertikalen Holzlamellen. Sie lässt sich im Bereich der Terrassen der Schlafräume komplett öffne Nachts scheint diese Hülle – umgeben von dem wunderbaren Bergwald – komplett zu leuchten.« Die Idee, Gebäude auf Stützen zu stellen, ist in Brasilien nicht ung wöhnlich. Man bemerkt es gar nicht, aber Marcio Kogan wurde beauftragt, nachdem sich die Bauherren von einem anderen Architekten getrennt hatten. Kogan muss daher die schon fertige Stahlkonstruktion in seinen Entwurf integrieren. Dieses scheinbare Handicap wendete er zum Guten: Die im Grundsatz geometrische Strenge d Lösung fügt sich ohne Schwierigkeiten in die sinnliche und sehr brasilianische Präsenz der Natur ein.

Située sur un terrain de 6820 m², cette maison rectangulaire mesure dispose de 739 m² de surface utile. L'architecte la décrit ainsi lui-même : « Cette maiso sur deux niveaux est en béton, métal, bois, aluminium et verre, et totalement intégrée au paysage forestier de cette région montagneuse de l'État de Rio de Janei (Petrópolis). L'étage réunit quatre suites, des salles de bains pour invités, une cuisine et le séjour/salle-à-manger. Le rez-de-chaussée est occupé par une piscine chau fée, un sauna sec à grande paroi fixe en verre d'où l'on peut contempler le paysage. La maison est construite sur l'idée de deux lames de béton monolithes contena les boîtes de l'étage soutenues par des pilotis et une boîte en pierre. La façade en bois se présente sous forme d'un écran léger (baguettes de bois verticales) qui s'ouv entièrement sur les terrasses des suites. La nuit, cette ‹ peau › semble totalement lumineuse, entourée par la magnifique forêt de cette zone montagneuse. » L'idée d'éle ver les maisons sur pilotis est assez courante au Brésil, ce qui ne l'est pas, en revanche, c'est que Kogan a été appelé sur ce projet après qu'un de ses confrères ait é écarté, et qu'il a dû composer avec une structure en acier existante. Transformant ce handicap en avantage, la rigueur essentiellement géométrique des solutions arch tecturales retenues les fait se fondre dans une nature très présente, sensuelle, très typiquement brésilienne.

Lifting his house up on pilotis like many modern Brazilian buildings, Kogan also contrasts a rough stone base with smoother or more sophisticated surfaces in wood, glass, steel or concrete.

Wie viele andere moderne Häuser in Brasilien steht das BR Haus auf Pilotis. Der große Steinsockel kontrastiert mit glatteren und edleren Oberflächen aus Holz, Glas, Stahl und Beton.

En élevant la maison sur des pilotis, Kogan a également fait contraster la base en pierre brute avec des surfaces plus douces et plus sophistiquées en verre, bois, acier ou béton.

... elevation shows the strictly rec-
...ngular shape of the house, with
... essential living space lifted up
... the ground.

Die Ansicht zeigt die streng recht-
winklige Form des Hauses. Der Wohnraum liegt im ersten Obergeschoss.

Élévation montrant la forme strictement rectangulaire de la maison,
dont la partie séjour est surélevée
par rapport au sol.

Trees come up through the wooden
surface of a terrace, emphasizing the
proximity of nature, which is in any
case visible through the large glazed
surfaces of the house.

Bäume wachsen durch den Holzfuß-
boden der Terrasse und betonen die
Nähe zur Natur. Diese ist ohnehin
aufgrund der großen Verglasungen
des Hauses sehr präsent.

Des arbres poussent à travers la
terrasse en bois. Ils renforcent la
proximité de la nature, visible à
travers les vastes pans de verre de
la maison.

Floor-to-ceiling windows bring the surrounding natural setting almost into the living room, while ample but strictly aligned furniture also contrasts with the profusion of greenery seen outside.

Geschosshohe Fenster bringen die natürliche Umgebung fast in den Wohnraum hinein. Großzügige, streng ausgerichtete Möbel bilden dabei einen Gegensatz zum verschwenderischen Grün der Natur.

Des ouvertures sol-plafond font quasiment entrer l'environnement naturel dans la maison, tandis que le mobilier, de proportions généreuses mais strictement aligné, contraste avec la profusion végétale que l'on aperçoit à l'extérieur.

A site plan shows the car park and approach bridge, leading to the outdoor terrace and into the rectangular volume of the house. Rough stones and water define lower level spaces, while the living room (right) remains smoothly horizontal.

Der Lageplan zeigt die überdeckten Stellplätze und die Zugangsbrücke, die auf die Außenterrasse führt, von wo aus das Haus betreten wird. Grobes Felsgestein und Wasser definieren die Räume der unteren Ebene. Rechts: Der Wohnraum ist elegant horizontal gegliedert.

Le plan du site montre le parking et le passerelle qui mène à la terrasse et à l'intérieur du rectangle de la maison. Un mur de pierres brutes et un bassin délimitent les espaces du niveau inférieur, tandis que le séjour (à droite) affiche une horizontalité douce et reposante.

REM KOOLHAAS/OMA

OMA Office for Metropolitan Architecture
Heer Bokelweg 149
3032 AD Rotterdam
The Netherlands

Tel: +31 102 43 82 00
Fax: +31 102 43 82 02
e-mail: office@oma.com
Web: www.oma.com

REM KOOLHAAS created the Office for Metropolitan Architecture (**OMA**) in 1975 together with Elia and Zoe Zenghelis and Madelon Vriesendorp. Born in Rc terdam in 1944, Koolhaas tried his hand as a journalist for the *Haagse Post* and as a screenwriter before studying at the Architectural Association in London. He becar well known after the 1978 publication of his book *Delirious New York*. OMA is led today by four partners, Rem Koolhaas, Ole Scheeren, Ellen van Loon, and Joshua Princ Ramus. Their built work includes a group of apartments at Nexus World, Fukuoka (1991), and the Villa dall'Ava, Saint-Cloud (1985–91). Koolhaas was named head arch tect of the Euralille project in Lille in 1988, and has worked on a design for the new Jussieu University Library in Paris. His 1400 page book *S,M,L,XL* (Monacelli Pres 1995) has more than fulfilled his promise as an influential writer. He won the 2000 Pritzker Prize and the 2003 Praemium Imperiale Award for architecture. More rece work of OMA includes a House, Bordeaux, France (1998), the campus center at the Illinois Institute of Technology (1998), the new Dutch Embassy in Berlin (2000–0‹ as well as the Guggenheim Las Vegas (2000–01), Prada boutiques in New York and Los Angeles, and the 1850-seat Porto Concert Hall (2005). OMA participated in t‹ Samsung Museum of Art (Leeum) in Seoul with Mario Botta and Jean Nouvel. Current work has included the design of OMA's largest project ever: the 575 000 m² Hea quarters and Cultural Center for China Central Television (CCTV) in Beijing; and the New City Center for Almere for which the firm has drawn up the master plan.

Zusammen mit Elia und Zoe Zenghelis sowie Madelon Vriesendorp gründete **REM KOOLHAAS** 1975 das Office for Metropolitan Architecture (**OMA**). Der 194 in Den Haag geborene Koolhaas arbeitete als Journalist für die *Haagse Post* und als Drehbuchautor, bevor er an der Architectural Association in London studierte. wurde mit seinem 1978 erschienenen Buch *Delirious New York* weithin bekannt. OMA wird heute von vier Partnern geführt: Rem Koolhaas, Ole Scheeren, Ellen van Lo‹ und Joshua Prince-Ramus. Zu ihren Bauten gehören u. a. die Villa dall'Ava im französischen Saint-Cloud (1985–91) und Wohnungen in Nexus World im japanisch Fukuoka (1991). 1988 wurde Koolhaas die Leitung des Euralille-Projekts in Lille übertragen; außerdem erarbeitete er einen Entwurf für die neue Bibliothek der Univers tät Jussieu in Paris. Mit seinem 1400 Seiten starken Buch *S,M,L,XL* (Monacelli Press, 1995) hat er seinen Status als einflussreicher Theoretiker und Autor bestätigt. I Jahr 2000 erhielt Koolhaas den Pritzker-Preis und 2003 den Architekturpreis Praemium Imperiale. Gebäude von OMA sind u. a. ein Wohnhaus in Bordeaux (1998), d Campus-Zentrum des Illinois Institute of Technology (1998), die Niederländische Botschaft in Berlin (2000–04), das Guggenheim Museum in Las Vegas (2000–01), Bo tiquen für Prada in New York und Los Angeles und ein Konzertsaal in Porto mit 1850 Plätzen (2005). Mit Mario Botta und Jean Nouvel hat Koolhaas das Samsung Mus um für Kunst (Leeum) in Seoul geplant. Zu den derzeitigen Projekten gehört der bislang größte Auftrag für OMA: das rund 600 000 m² umfassende Verwaltungs- und Ku turgebäude für China Central Television (CCTV) in Peking sowie das neue Stadtzentrum von Almere in den Niederlanden, für das OMA den Masterplan entworfen hat.

REM KOOLHAAS est né à Rotterdam en 1944. Avant d'étudier à l'Architectural Association de Londres, il s'essaye au journalisme pour le *Haagse Post* et à l'éc ture de scénarii. Il fonde l'Office for Metropolitan Architecture (**OMA**) à Londres en 1975 et devient célèbre grâce à la publication, en 1978, de son ouvrage *Deliric New York*. OMA est dirigé par quatre partenaires, Rem Koolhaas, Ole Scheeren, Ellen van Loon et Joshua Prince-Ramus. Parmi leurs réalisations : un ensemble d'appa tements à Nexus World, Fukuoka, Japon (1991); la villa dall'Ava, Saint-Cloud, France (1985–91). Koolhaas est nommé architecte en chef du projet Euralille à Lille 1988 et propose un projet de bibliothèque pour la Faculté de Jussieu à Paris. Son livre de 1400 pages, *S,M,L,XL* (Monacelli Press, 1995), confirme son influence et s impact de théoricien. Il a remporté le prix Pritzker en 2000 et le Praemium Imperiale en 2003. Parmi ses réalisations récentes : une maison à Bordeaux (1998), le ca pus de l'Illinois Institute of Technology (1998), la nouvelle ambassade des Pays-Bas à Berlin (2000–01), le Guggenheim Las Vegas (2000–01), des boutiques Prada New York et Los Angeles et tout récemment, la Casa da Musica, salle de concert de 1850 places, à Porto, Portugal (2005). Son agence a conçu le Samsung Museum Art (Leeum) à Séoul en coopération avec Mario Botta et Jean Nouvel, et travaille actuellement sur son plus important projet à ce jour, le siège et le centre culturel de Télévision nationale chinoise (CCTV) à Pékin (575 000 m²), et le nouveau centre-ville d'Almere (Pays-Bas).

SEATTLE CENTRAL LIBRARY

Seattle, Washington, USA, 2004

Floor area: 30 000 m². Client: Seattle Central Library. Cost: $165.5 million (including Temporary Central Library)

The new **CENTRAL LIBRARY**, located on Fourth Avenue in Seattle, is drawing more than 8000 visitors a day, or twice as many as the old building. OMA wor.
with the Seattle firm LMN Architects on this project, which was the third Central Library built on the same site. The total cost of the 30 000 m² structure, including
million dollars for the Temporary Central Library, was 165.5 million dollars. It has a capacity for 1.45 million books. The structure is covered with nearly 10 000 pie
of glass, of which half are triple-layered with an expanded metal mesh sandwiched between the two outer layers in order to protect the interior against heat and gla
A reason for the use of this much glass was the architects' desire to make the building "transparent and open," qualities not always associated with libraries. Passe
by can see activity on every floor of the building. The unusual shape of the building is partially related to efforts to control the type and quantity of light reaching inte
spaces. A particularly striking overhang covers the entry on the Fourth Avenue side of the library. A system of "floating platforms" and a diagonal grid designed to pro
against earthquakes or wind damage are amongst other structural innovations in the design. Within the library, a unique "Books Spiral" penetrates four levels of the sta
and contains the nonfiction collection, allowing for increased capacity and easier expansion of the number of books in the future. The 275-seat Microsoft Auditoriu
located on Level 1, is considered by the Library to be its "centerpiece." Level 2 is a staff floor, and Level 3 includes the base of the building's atrium, book return a
check out facilities, or the "Norcliffe Foundation Living Room," a reading area with a ceiling height of fifteen meters. Four meeting rooms are located on Level 4, an
large space called the "Mixing Chamber" compared by the architects to a "trading floor for information" is used to "go for help with general questions or in-de
research." The "Books Spiral" reaches from Level 6 to Level 9, while a reading room with a capacity for 400 persons is located on Level 10. The top floor is occupied
administrative offices and a staff lunch room.

8000 Besucher kommen täglich in die neue **ZENTRALBIBLIOTHEK** an der Fourth Avenue in Seattle, doppelt so viele wie in die alte. An dem Projekt – es
bereits die dritte Zentralbibliothek auf dem Grundstück – waren neben OMA auch LMN Architects aus Seattle beteiligt. Die Gesamtkosten des 30 000 m² großen Geb.
des belaufen sich auf umgerechnet 139 Millionen Euro. Darin enthalten sind etwa 8,5 Millionen Euro für eine temporäre Bibliothek. 1,45 Millionen Bücher haben
ihren Platz. Der Bau ist mit fast 10 000 Glaspaneelen eingedeckt. Die Hälfte dieser Paneele hat einen dreilagigen Aufbau: Zwischen zwei Glasscheiben ist ein Metall
angeordnet, um den Innenraum vor zuviel Hitze und vor Spiegelungen zu schützen. Ein Grund für die Verwendung von so viel Glas ist der Wunsch des Architekten,
Gebäude »transparent und offen« zu gestalten – Qualitäten, die man nicht unbedingt mit einer Bibliothek in Verbindung bringt. Passanten können sehen, dass auf je
Ebene des Hauses Aktivitäten stattfinden. Die ungewöhnliche Form des Gebäudes hängt z. T. mit Überlegungen zusammen, wie die Tageslichtart und -menge in den R
men kontrolliert werden können. Der Eingang an der Fourth Avenue wird von einer besonders eindrucksvollen Auskragung überdeckt. Ein System von »schwebenden E
nen« und ein diagonaler Gitterrost, der die seismischen Kräfte sowie die Windlasten aufnimmt, gehören zu den konstruktiven Neuerungen des Gebäudes. Im Inneren
Bibliothek durchdringt eine »Bücherspirale«, die alle Sachbücher enthält, die vier aufeinander gestapelten Büchergeschosse. Die Spiralform erlaubt es, die Nutzerkapa
täten und die Zahl der Bücher in Zukunft zu erhöhen. Das »Microsoft-Auditorium« mit 275 Plätzen auf der Ebene eins wird von den Bibliotheksmitarbeitern als Herz
Baus betrachtet. Auf der Ebene zwei liegen die Räume für die Angestellten. Das Atrium des Gebäudes beginnt auf Ebene drei, außerdem befinden sich hier u. a. die Bu
rückgabe und der »Norcliffe Foundation Living Room«, eine Lesezone mit einer Deckenhöhe von 15 m. Ebene vier nimmt vier Konferenzräume und einen großen Rau
das so genannte »Mixing Chamber«, auf. Dieser Raum wird von den Architekten mit einem Börsenparkett für Informationen verglichen. Er wird benutzt, wenn man
grundsätzlichen Fragen Hilfe sucht oder Grundsatzforschung betreibt«. Die Bücherspirale reicht von Ebene sechs bis Ebene neun, auf der Ebene zehn befindet sich
Lesesaal für 400 Personen. Die Büros der Verwaltung und eine Kantine für die Mitarbeiter sind auf der obersten Ebene angeordnet.

Située sur Fourth Avenue, la nouvelle **BIBLIOTHÈQUE CENTRALE** de Seattle, dont la capacité est de 1,45 million d'ouvrages, attire déjà plus de 8000 visite
par jour, soit deux fois la fréquentation de la précédente. OMA a collaboré sur ce projet – la troisième bibliothèque édifiée sur le même site – avec l'agence de Sea
LMN Architects. Le budget total de ce bâtiment de 30 000 m² s'est élevé à 139 millions d'euros dont 8,5 millions pour la Bibliothèque centrale temporaire, le temps
chantier. L'ensemble est habillé de près de 10 000 panneaux de verre dont la moitié de triple épaisseur : entre les deux vitrages externes est inséré un tissu de mé
étiré qui protège l'intérieur de la lumière excessive et de la chaleur. La raison de cette utilisation massive du verre était le souhait de l'architecte de rendre le bâtim
« transparent et ouvert », qualités qui ne vont pas forcément de pair avec les bibliothèques. Les passants peuvent ainsi voir toutes les activités qui s'y déroulent, à cha
niveau. La forme originale du bâtiment est due en partie à la volonté de contrôler le type et la quantité de lumière susceptible d'atteindre l'intérieur. Un porte-à-fa
spectaculaire protège l'entrée sur Fourth Avenue. Un système de « plates-formes flottantes » et une structure en diagonale, conçus pour résister aux tremblements
terre ou aux tornades, font partie des autres innovations structurelles du projet. Une « Spirale des livres » accueillant les ouvrages documentaires court sur quatre nivea
de rayonnages, permettant aussi d'augmenter la capacité de stockage dans le futur. Au niveau 1, l'auditorium Microsoft de 250 places est considéré comme le pô
central de la bibliothèque. Au niveau 2 se trouvent les bureaux du personnel et au niveau 3 la base de l'atrium, le bureau de prêt des ouvrages et la Norcliffe Foun
tion Living Room, une zone de lecture bénéficiant d'une hauteur sous plafond de 15 mètres. Quatre salles de réunion sont situées au niveau 4, ainsi qu'un vaste es
ce appelé « Chambre de mixage » comparé par les architectes à « une salle de marché de l'information, pour aider à répondre aux questions d'ordre général et a
recherches approfondies ». La « Spirale des livres » s'élève du niveau 6 au niveau 9 tandis qu'une salle de lecture de 400 places occupe le niveau 10. Le dernier nive
est occupé par des bureaux et par le restaurant du personnel.

The dynamic angles of the Library set it aside from its urban neighbors. It looks almost as though it might be capable of moving away from the site under its own power.

Durch ihre dynamischen Winkel unterscheidet sich die Zentralbibliothek von ihren innerstädtischen Nachbarn. Fast meint man, sie könne sich aus eigener Kraft von dem Grundstück entfernen.

Les pans inclinés dynamiques de la Bibliothèque la détachent visuellement de son voisinage urbain. On pourrait presque la croire capable de se déplacer d'elle-même.

Despite the unexpected angles of the
building, each facet is calculated
on the basis of function and sunlight
considerations.

Die Winkel im Gebäude mögen zufällig erscheinen, tatsächlich wurde
aber jede Facette auf der Basis von
Funktion und Belichtung berechnet.

Les étonnantes facettes des façades
ont été calculées en fonction de critères fonctionnels pour un éclairage
naturel.

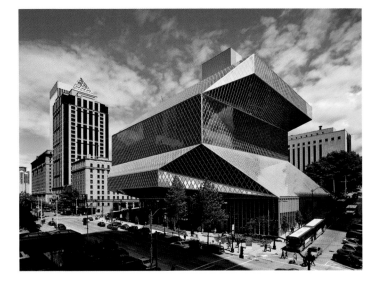

The angled glass façades of the Library allow for generous and active interior spaces, where one level proceeds to the next without the usual strict division of floors.

Die geneigten Glasfassaden ermöglichen großzügige und aktiv zu nutzende Innenräume. Ohne die übliche Trennung der Geschosse geht eine Ebene in die nächste über.

Les parois de verre inclinées de la Bibliothèque laissent place à des salles spacieuses et fonctionnelles, où l'on passe d'un niveau à l'autre sans séparation traditionnelle.

Interior features and the vast over-
head array of metal and light create
an impression of a city within the
city, where certain spaces are
defined by their function but also,
clearly, by their architecture.

Besondere räumliche Elemente und
die riesigen Überkopfverglasungen
aus Metall und Licht vermitteln den
Eindruck einer Stadt in der Stadt.
Spezielle Zonen werden durch ihre
Funktion definiert – natürlich aber
auch durch die Architektur.

L'aménagement intérieur, les
immenses volumes de métal et
la lumière créent une impression
de ville dans la ville. Certains
espaces sont définis par leur fonction autant que par leur architecture.

Although many more traditional libraries have had vast reading rooms, the Seattle Library has a profusion of unexpected spaces, where floors levels shift and develop before the visitor's eyes.

Große Lesesäle gab und gibt es auch in vielen älteren Bibliotheken. Die Zentralbibliothek in Seattle wartet jedoch mit einer Fülle von überraschenden Räumen auf, in denen sich die Ebenen neigen und sich dem Besucher sukzessiv erschließen.

Si beaucoup de bibliothèques plus traditionnelles possèdent de vastes salles de lecture, celle de Seattle offre une profusion d'espaces inattendus dans lesquels les niveaux s'entrecroisent et se déploient devant le visiteur.

contrast with the many vast open
ces, the Library also offers more
mate areas near the book shelves
ht). Stairways are not hidden like
escapes, but participate in the
tation to explore the building
ow).

Gegensatz zu den vielen riesigen
nen Räumen gibt es in der
tralbibliothek im Bereich der
hregale auch intimere Bereiche
chts). Die Treppen werden nicht
Sicherheitstreppenhäuser ver-
ckt, sondern sind Teil der Ein-
ing, das Gebäude zu erkunden
en).

re ses vastes espaces ouverts,
ibliothèque met à disposition des
es plus intimes à proximité des
onnages de livres (à droite). Les
aliers ne sont pas dissimulés
me des issues de secours, mais
t au contraire une invitation à
ter le bâtiment (en bas).

Rem Koolhaas has been quoted as saying that the Seattle Library is his "masterpiece." Though it can be expected that the Dutchman and his firm (OMA) will build many more significant buildings, the library is a symphonic orchestration that allays function and form in new ways, no small accomplishment where the handling of books is concerned.

Rem Koolhaas hat die Bibliothek in Seattle als sein Meisterstück bezeichnet. Man kann von dem Niederländer erwarten, dass er noch viele weitere bedeutende Gebäude realisiert – die Bibliothek wird als »sinfonische Orchestrierung«, die Form und Funktion auf neue Weise miteinander in Einklang bringt, Bestand haben. Keine geringe Leistung, wenn es um den Umgang mit Büchern geht.

Rem Koolhaas aurait dit que cette bibliothèque était son « chef-d'œuvre ». On peut espérer que le Néerlandais et son équipe d'OMA réaliseront d'autres projets encore plus significatifs, mais cette bibliothèque est une orchestration symphonique qui réunit de manière novatrice la forme et la fonction, ce qui n'est pas une mince réussite dans le domaine de la conservation des livres.

KENGO KUMA

Kengo Kuma & Associates
2-24-8 BY-CUBE 2F
Minamiaoyama
Minato-ku
Tokyo 107-0062
Japan

Tel: +81 334 01 77 21
Fax: +81 334 01 77 78
e-mail: kuma@ba2.so-net.ne.jp
Web: www.kkaa.co.jp

Born in 1954 in Kanagawa, Japan, **KENGO KUMA** graduated in 1979 from the University of Tokyo with a Masters in Architecture. In 1985–86 he received Asian Cultural Council fellowship Grant and was a Visiting Scholar at Columbia University. In 1987 he established the Spatial Design Studio, and in 1991 he created Ke Kuma & Associates. His work includes: the Gunma Toyota Car Show Room, Maebashi (1989); Maiton Resort Complex, Phuket, Thailand; Rustic, Office Building, Tok Doric, Office Building, Tokyo; M2, Headquarters for Mazda New Design Team, Tokyo (all in 1991); Kinjo Golf Club, Club House, Okayama (1992); Kiro-san Observat Ehime (1994); Atami Guest House, Guest House for Bandai Corp, Atami (1992–95); Karuizawa Resort Hotel, Karuizawa (1993); Tomioka Lakewood Golf Club House, Tom ka (1993–96); Toyoma Noh-Theater, Miyagi (1995–96); and the Japanese Pavilion for the Venice Biennale, Venice, Italy (1995). He has recently completed the Ste Museum (Nasu, Tochigi) and a Museum for the work of Ando Hiroshige (Batou, Nasu-gun, Tochigi). He completed the Nagasaki Prefecture Art Museum in March 20 the Fukusaki Hanging Garden in January 2005; LVMH Osaka in 2004; One Omotesando, Tokyo (2003); and the Great (Bamboo) Wall guest house, Beijing (2002).

KENGO KUMA, geboren 1954 in Kanagawa, Japan, schloss 1979 sein Studium an der Universität Tokio mit dem Master of Architecture ab. Von 1985 bis 19 arbeitete er mit einem Stipendium des Asian Cultural Council als Gastwissenschaftler an der Columbia University in New York. 1987 gründete Kuma das Spatial Des Studio und 1991 das Büro Kengo Kuma & Associates in Tokio. Zu seinen Bauten gehören: der Gunma Toyota Car Showroom in Maebashi, Japan (1989), die Ferienanl Maiton in Phuket, Thailand, die Bürogebäude Rustic und Doric sowie M2, der Hauptsitz für die Designabteilung von Mazda, alle 1991 in Tokio ausgeführt, ferner das Kl haus des Kinjo Golf Club in Okayama (1992), das Gästehaus für die Firma Bandai Corporation in Atami (1992–95), ein Hotel in Karuizawa (1993), das Klubhaus des La wood Golf Club in Tomioka (1993–96), das Observatorium Kiro-san in Ehime (1994), der Japanische Pavillon auf der Biennale in Venedig (1995) und das No-Theate Toyama, Miyagi (1995–96). Seine neuesten Projekte sind das Steinmuseum in Nasu, Tochigi, sowie ein Museum für die Werke von Ando Hiroshige in Batou, Nasu-g Tochigi. Das Kunstmuseum der Präfektur Nagasaki wurde im März 2005 fertig gestellt, die Hängenden Gärten von Fukusaki im Januar 2005, das LVMH Osaka 2004, Omotesando in Tokio 2003 und das Gästehaus Great (Bamboo) Wall in Peking 2002.

Né en 1954 à Kanagawa, au Japon, **KENGO KUMA** est Master of Architecture de l'Université de Tokyo (1979). En 1984–86, il bénéficie d'une bourse de l'As Cultural Council et est chercheur invité à la Columbia University (New York). En 1987, il crée le Spatial Design Studio et, en 1991, Kengo Kuma & Associates. Parmi réalisations : le Car Show Room Toyota de Gunma, Maebashi (1989) ; le Maiton Resort Complex, Phuket, Thaïlande (1991) ; le Rustic Office Building, Tokyo (199 l'immeuble de bureaux Doric, Tokyo (1991) ; le siège du département de design de Mazda, Tokyo (1991) ; le Club House du Kinjo Golf Club, Okayama (1992) ; l'Obs vatoire Kiro-San, Yoshiumi, Ochi-gun, Ehime (1994) ; la Guest House d'Atami pour Bandaï Corp, Atami (1992–95) ; le Karuizawa Resort Hotel, Karuizawa (1993) ; le C House du Tomioka Lakewood Golf, Tomioka (1993–96) ; le théâtre Nô Toyoma, Miyagi (1995–96) et le pavillon japonais de la Biennale de Venise en 1995. Il a réce ment construit le musée de la Pierre, Nasu, Tochigi, le musée Ando Hiroshige, Batou, Nasu-gun, Tochigi, la « Grande muraille de bambou », maison d'hôtes, Pékin (20 One Omotesando, Tokyo (2003), le siège de LVMH à Osaka (2004), et vient d'achever les jardins suspendus de Fukusaki (janvier 2005) ainsi que le musée d'Art de Préfecture de Nagasaki (mars 2005) présenté ici.

NAGASAKI PREFECTURAL MUSEUM

Nagasaki, Nagasaki, 2003–05

Floor area: 9898 m². Client: Nagasaki Prefecture.
Cost: € 36 million

Kengo Kuma uses a succession of vertical elements, not unlike a screen, or perhaps a bamboo forest to define the major elements of the museum, creating an impression of lightness.

Mit einer Vielzahl von vertikalen Elementen, die wie ein Screen oder ein Bambuswald wirken, definiert Kengo Kuma die wichtigen Bereiche des Museums und erzielt den Eindruck von Leichtigkeit.

Kengo Kuma utilise une succession d'éléments verticaux – une sorte d'écran ou peut-être de forêt de bambous – pour délimiter les principaux éléments du musée et créer une impression de légèreté.

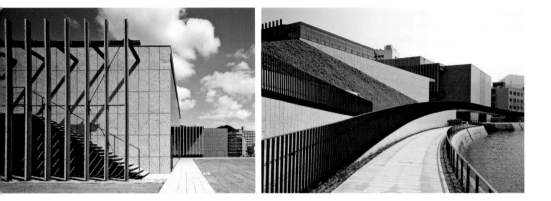

As Kengo Kuma explains, the fact that Nagasaki was the only port permitted to remain open while Japan was closed to the rest of the world, it boasts a su
stantial collection of Spanish and Portuguese works of art. The 12 679 m² site had the particularity of having a canal run through it. Kuma explains that "To make the car
one with the art museum, I created an intermediate space along the canal, and made it a promenade for city residents and a place for appreciating works of art. Th
space was protected from the strong sun by stone louvers that created a breezy, pleasant shade." A "box-shaped" glass bridge crosses the canal, making it visible to
the visitors of the museum. The roof of the structure is also used as a gallery space with a view of the city's port. With a footprint of 6248 m² and a floor area of 9898 m
this is a large structure, handled with the typical subtlety and intelligence that the architect always demonstrates. Kengo Kuma is also quite outspoken about certa
aspects of the design. As he says, "In Nagasaki, I developed a new supporting detail for stone louvers using solid steel columns. Nagasaki, located in southern Japan,
known for its Colonial-style veranda architecture using wooden latticework. The detail I used here is a contemporary version of this traditional architecture; it also is
criticism of contemporary Japanese architecture that ignores both indigenous climate and landscape."

Die Tatsache, dass Nagasaki der einzige offene Hafen war, als sich Japan gegenüber dem Rest der Welt verschloss, führte zum Entstehen einer grundlegenc
Sammlung spanischer und portugiesischer Kunstwerke, erläutert Kengo Kuma. Das 12 679 m² große Grundstück weist als Besonderheit einen Kanal auf. Dazu Kun
»Um aus dem Kanal und dem Museum eine Einheit zu machen, habe ich einen Zwischenraum entlang des Kanals geschaffen und hier eine Promenade für die Bewo
ner der Stadt angeordnet. Dies ist ein Ort, um die Kunstwerke zu würdigen. Steinlamellen schützen vor der starken Sonneneinstrahlung und sorgen für eine luftige, ang
nehme Verschattung.« Eine kistenartige Brücke aus Glas stellt eine Verbindung über dem Kanal her und macht ihn so für alle Besucher des Museums erlebbar. Das Da
des Gebäudes, das auch als Galerie benutzt wird, bietet einen Blick auf den Hafen von Nagasaki. Mit einer Grundfläche von 6248 m² und einer Gesamtfläche von 9898 m
ist das Museum ein großes Gebäude, das mit der für den Architekten typischen Sensibilität und Intelligenz entwickelt wurde. Kengo Kuma äußert sich recht offen üb
bestimmte Aspekte des Entwurfs. So sagt er: »In Nagasaki habe ich ein neues Auflagerdetail für die Steinlamellen entwickelt, indem ich massive Stahlstützen benutz
Nagasaki im Süden Japans ist bekannt für seine Verandenarchitektur im Kolonialstil mit Spalieren aus Holz. Das Detail, das ich hier verwendete, ist eine moderne V
sion dieser traditionellen Architektur. Es ist auch eine Kritik an der modernen japanischen Architektur, die sowohl das Klima vor Ort als auch die Landschaft ignoriert.

Comme l'explique Kengo Kuma, le fait que Nagasaki ait été le seul port ouvert, lorsque le Japon était isolé du reste du monde, explique qu'il possède une su
stantielle collection d'art espagnol et portugais. L'une des caractéristiques du terrain de 12 679 m² était la présence d'un canal. « Pour que le canal ne fasse qu'un av
le musée, j'ai créé un volume intermédiaire le long de celui-ci. J'en ai fait une promenade pour les citadins qui est, en même temps, un nouveau lieu pour la découv
te d'œuvres d'art. Cet espace est protégé du soleil par des brise-soleil de pierre qui créent une ombre agréable et aérée. Une passerelle de verre ‹ en forme de boîte › t
verse le canal, désormais visible par tous les visiteurs du musée. Le toit sert également d'espace d'exposition et offre une vue sur le port. » Avec une emprise au sol
6248 m² et une surface utile de 9898 m², il s'agit d'un grand bâtiment, traité avec la subtilité et l'intelligence dont l'architecte a toujours fait preuve. Kengo Kuma s'exp
me très volontiers sur certains aspects de son projet : « À Nagasaki, j'ai mis au point de nouveaux supports pour les brise-soleil de pierre, à base de colonnes en acier ma
sif. Nagasaki, dans le Japon du Sud, est connue pour son architecture à vérandas de style colonial et leurs claustras en lattis de bois. Le système que j'utilise est une v
sion contemporaine de cette architecture traditionnelle, c'est aussi une critique d'une architecture japonaise contemporaine qui ignore à la fois le climat et le paysage.

The museum straddles a canal in an almost effortless way, obviating the programmatic difficulty imposed on the architect.

Die Museumsbrücke überspannt scheinbar mühelos einen Kanal. Die Probleme, die das Raumprogramm mit sich brachte, werden so gelöst.

Le musée franchit un canal, gommant sans effort cette difficulté du programme imposé.

Floor to ceiling glazing and extremely thin support columns give an impression of extremely light architecture in these views.

Eine geschosshohe Verglasung und sehr schlanke Stützen vermitteln den Eindruck extremer Leichtigkeit.

Des murs de verre sur toute la hauteur et des colonnes de soutien extrêmement fines créent une impression d'extrême légèreté.

The high ceilings and verticality of
spaces give a slightly technological
aspect to the museum, but unite its
design and allow the works to speak
for themselves.

Die hohen Räume und ihre Vertikalität
geben dem Museum eine leicht technische Prägung, vereinheitlichen aber
den Entwurf und lassen die Kunstwerke für sich selbst sprechen.

Les hauts plafonds et la verticalité
des espaces confèrent au musée un
aspect un peu technologique, tout en
renforçant l'unité du plan et en laissant aux œuvres exposées la liberté
de s'exprimer.

MAYA LIN

Maya Lin Studio
112 Prince Street
New York, New York 10012
USA

Tel: +1 212 941 6463
Fax: +1 212 941 6464
e-mail: mlinstudio@earthlink.net

Riggio-Lynch Ch...

MAYA LIN, born in 1959, attended Yale College and the Yale School of Architecture, receiving her Masters in Architecture in 1986. She created her office, May... Lin Studio, in New York the same year. By that time she had already created what remains her most famous work, the Vietnam Veterans' Memorial on the Mall i... Washington D.C. (1981). Other sculptural work includes her Civil Rights Memorial in Montgomery, Alabama (1989); and *Groundswell*, at the Wexner Center of the Art... Columbus, Ohio (1993). She completed the design for the Museum of African Art in New York (with David Hotson, 1993); the Weber Residence, Williamstown, Mass... chusetts (1994); and the Asia/Pacific/American Studies Department, New York University, New York (1997). Recent work includes the Greyston Bakery, Greyst... Foundation, Yonkers, New York (2003); the Langston Hughes Library, Childrens' Defense Fund, Clinton, Tennessee (1999, with Martella Associates, Architects); and t... Riggio-Lynch Chapel, Children's Defense Fund (2004), published here.

MAYA LIN, geboren 1959, studierte am Yale College und an der Yale School of Architecture, wo sie 1986 ihren Master of Architecture erwarb. Im selben Ja... gründete sie ihr eigenes Büro Maya Lin Studio. Zu diesem Zeitpunkt hatte sie schon ihr bis heute bekanntestes Werk, das Vietnam Veterans' Memorial an der Mall ... Washington D.C., geschaffen (1981). Andere bildhauerische Arbeiten sind u.a. das Civil Rights Memorial in Montgomery, Alabama (1989), und *Groundswell* für d... Wexner Center of Arts in Columbus, Ohio (1993). Realisierte Bauten sind das Museum of African Art in New York (mit David Hotson, 1993), die Weber Residence in W... liamstown, Massachusetts (1994), und das Asia/Pacific/American Studies Department der New York University in New York (1997). Zu ihren jüngsten Projekten gehör... die Greyston Bäckerei der Greyston Foundation in Yonkers, New York (2003) sowie die Langston-Hughes-Bibliothek (mit Martella Associates, Architects, 1999) und ... Riggio-Lynch-Kapelle, beide für den Childrens' Defense Fund in Clinton, Tennessee (2004).

MAYA LIN, née en 1959, a fait ses études au Yale College et à la Yale School of Architecture, Master of Architecture (1986). Elle ouvre son agence, Maya L... Studio, à New York la même année, mais a déjà créé ce qui reste à ce jour son œuvre la plus célèbre, le Mémorial des vétérans de la guerre du Vietnam sur le Natior... Mall de Washington (1981). Elle a réalisé d'autres œuvres de nature sculpturale, comme le Mémorial des droits civiques à Montgomery, Alabama (1989) et *Groundsw...* pour le Wexner Center for the Arts, Columbus, Ohio (1993). Par ailleurs, elle a réalisé le Museum for African Art, New York (avec David Hotson, 1993); la Weber Re... dence, Williamstown, Massachusetts (1994) et le département des études Asie/Pacifique/Amérique de la New York University, New York (1997). Parmi ses récents t... vaux: la Greyston Bakery, Greyston Foundation, Yonkers, New York (2003); la Langston Hughes Library (avec Martella Associates, Architects) et la Riggio-Lynch Cha... publiée ici, pour le Children's Defense Fund, Clinton, Tennessee (1999 et 2004).

RIGGIO-LYNCH CHAPEL

Clinton, Tennessee, USA, 2004

Floor area: 887 m². Client: The Children's Defense Fund.
Cost: $2.2 million

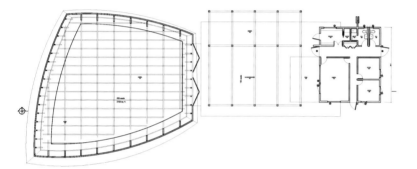

Working with Bialosky + Partners, Architects & Planners, Maya Lin created this 887 m² chapel with architectural grade glu-lam beams, concrete floors an
cypress wood exterior. As she explains, "The concept for the design of the Chapel comes from The Children's Defense Fund's Motto: 'Dear Lord be good to me. The ¶
is so wide and my boat is so small.' The abstracted image of a boat or ark that is constructed out of wood and forms the main body of the Chapel is at the heart of
design." The simple yet sculptural presence of the main building is unusual and succeeds in sublimating the boat image while making the reference clear and pres
Maya Lin also conceived the structure, with its open passageway to a small concrete administrative building and meeting room, so that it could on some occasions rece
large numbers of people, without overwhelming the other structures on Haley Farm. Once the retreat of the author Alex Haley, the Farm is the Children's Defense Fur
center for leadership training and the development of new ideas to help America's children. Lin's Langston Hughes Library is located on the same Farm. The new cha
is named after the main donor for the project, Leonard Riggio, chairman of the booksellers Barnes & Noble, and William Lynch, a political activist and former New Y
City Deputy Mayor.

In Zusammenarbeit mit den Architekten Bialosky + Partners entwarf Maya Lin die 887 m² große Kapelle, die mit hochwertigen Leimholzbindern, Betonböden
einer Außenverkleidung aus Zypressenholz ausgestattet ist. Lin erläutert das Projekt: »Das Konzept für den Bau der Kapelle basiert auf dem Leitspruch des Childre
Defense Fund: ›Lieber Gott, sei gut zu mir. Das Meer ist so groß und mein Boot ist so klein.‹ Herzstück des Entwurfs ist das abstrahierte Bild eines Bootes oder e
Arche aus Holz, das den Hauptraum der Kapelle bildet.« Die einfache, skulpturale Präsenz des Hauptgebäudes ist ungewöhnlich und überhöht auf überzeugende We
das Bild des Bootes; gleichzeitig ist die Referenz klar und präsent. Maya Lin entwarf auch das Gesamtkonzept der Anlage: Dazu gehört ein offener Gang zu ein
kleinen Verwaltungsgebäude (mit angeschlossenem Versammlungsraum) aus Beton. So können bei besonderen Anlässen viele Besucher empfangen werden, ohne
Kapazitäten der anderen Gebäude auf dem Gelände zu überfordern. Einst ein Rückzugsort des Schriftstellers Alex Haley, ist die Farm das Zentrum des Childrens' Defe
Fund, in dem das Führungspersonal der Organisation ausgebildet wird und neue Ideen entwickelt werden, um den Kindern in Amerika zu helfen. Auch die von
entworfene Langston-Hughes-Bibliothek befindet sich auf dem Gelände. Die neue Kapelle wurde nach den Hauptsponsoren Leonard Riggio, Vorsitzender des Buchverl
Barnes & Noble, und William Lynch, politischer Aktivist und früherer Zweiter Bürgermeister von New York City, benannt.

En collaboration avec Bialosky + Partners, Architects & Planners, Maya Lin a conçu cette chapelle de 887 m² dont la construction fait appel à des poutres
bois lamellé-collé, des sols en béton et des façades en cyprès. Pour elle, « le concept de cette chapelle vient de la devise du Children's Defense Fund – Seigneur, s
bon avec moi, la mer est si vaste et mon bateau si petit. L'image abstraite d'un bateau ou d'une ‹ arche de Noé › en bois est au cœur de la conception ». La forte p
sence du bâtiment principal, à la fois simple et sculptural, parvient à sublimer l'image d'un bateau tout en conservant la clarté de la référence. Maya Lin a égalem
conçu la structure, avec son passage ouvert vers un petit bâtiment administratif en béton et une salle de réunion qui peut recevoir à certaines occasions un grand nom
de fidèles, sans envahir les autres installations du domaine de Haley Farm. Jadis retraite de l'auteur Alex Haley, la ferme est le centre du Children's Defense Fund p
la formation au leadership et la recherche d'idées nouvelles pour l'aide aux enfants américains. La bibliothèque Langston Hughes, également de Lin, est située à pr
mité. La nouvelle chapelle porte les noms de son principal donateur, Leonard Riggio, président de la chaîne de librairies Barnes & Noble, et de William Lynch, politic
et ancien maire adjoint de New York.

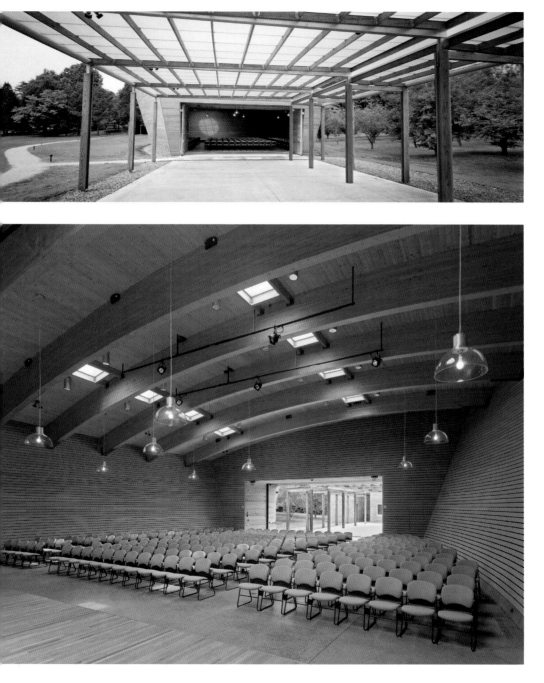

Eschewing Modernist symmetry, Maya Lin achieves a sense of motion and a connection to the origins of the church with her design.

Maya Lin vermeidet die Symmetrie der Moderne; sie erzeugt ein Gefühl von Bewegung und stellt einen Bezug zu den kirchlichen Ursprüngen her.

Loin de la symétrie moderniste, Maya Lin insuffle la notion de mouvement à ce projet et recrée le lien avec les origines historiques de l'église.

Fluff Ba

LTL LEWIS.TSURUMAKI.LEWIS

LTL Architects, PLLC
227W, 29th Street, New York, New York 10001
USA

Tel: +1 212 505 5955, Fax: +1 212 505 1648
e-mail: office@LTLarchitects.net, Web: www.LTLarchitects.com

Paul Lewis received his Master of Architecture from Princeton University in 1992, and studied previously at Wesleyan University (B. A. 1988). He is a princip and founding partner of **LEWIS TSURUMAKI LEWIS**, created in 1993. He was an associate at Diller + Scofidio, New York (1993–97). Marc Tsurumaki received his Mar ter of Architecture degree from Princeton in 1991, after attending college at the University of Virginia. He worked as a project architect in the office of Joel Sanders New York (1991–97) prior to creating Lewis Tsurumaki Lewis. David J. Lewis completed his architectural studies at Princeton in 1995 after attending Cornell and Carlt College. He was the Publications Director, Cornell University, College of Architecture, Art, and Planning (1997–98). He worked at Peter Guggenheimer, Architects, PP New York as an assistant (1995–96) and in the office of Daniel Libeskind in Berlin (1993) before creating LTL. The firm's recent built projects include: Bornhuetter Ha Wooster, Ohio (2004); Tides Restaurant, New York (2005); Figge Residence, Wooster, Ohio (2004); Xing Restaurant, New York (2005); and the Ini Ani Coffee Shop, Ne York (2004). Current projects are: Arthouse Renovation and Expansion, Austin, Texas (2005, contemporary art museum); Residential Tower, Las Vegas, Nevada (200 Dash Dogs Restaurant, New York (2005); Alexakos Gymnasium, Southhampton, New York (2006); Brown University Bio-Medical Center Renovation; Providence, Rho Island (2005); HPD Housing, East New York, New York (2006); Allentown House Allentown, Pennsylvania (2006); and the Burns Townhouse, Philadelphia, Pennsylvania (200

Paul Lewis studierte erst an der Wesleyan University (B. A. 1988), dann machte er 1992 an der Princeton University seinen Master of Architecture. Er ist Grü dungspartner und Geschäftsführer des 1993 eröffneten Büros **LEWIS TSURUMAKI LEWIS**. Bei Diller + Scofidio in New York war er von 1993 bis 1997 assoziierter Pa ner. Marc Tsurumaki studierte an der University of Virginia und an der Princeton University (Master of Architecture 1991). Bevor er Lewis Tsurumaki Lewis gründete, w er von 1991 bis 1997 Projektarchitekt bei Joel Sanders in New York. David J. Lewis schloss sein Architekturstudium 1995 in Princeton ab, davor studierte er in Corn und am Carlton College. Von 1997 bis 1998 war er Publications Director am College of Architecture, Art and Planning der Cornell University. Vor der Gründung von L arbeitete David Lewis als Assistent bei Peter Guggenheimer, Architects, PPC, in New York und 1993 bei Daniel Libeskind in Berlin. Neuere Projekte des Büros sind u. die hier gezeigte Bornhuetter Hall in Wooster, Ohio (2004), das Tides Restaurant in New York (2005), die Figge Residence in Wooster, Ohio (2004), das Xing Restaura in New York (2005) und der Ini Ani Coffee Shop in New York (2004). Zurzeit in Planung bzw. im Bau sind die Sanierung und Erweiterung des Arthouse (ein Museum zeitgenössische Kunst) in Austin, Texas (2005), ein Wohnhochhaus in Las Vegas (2005), das Dash Dogs Restaurant in New York (2005), die Alexakos Sporthalle in Sou hampton, New York (2006), ferner die Sanierung des Biomedizinischen Zentrums der Brown University in Providence, Rhode Island (2005), HPD Housing in East New Yo New York (2006), das Allentown House in Allentown, Pennsylvania (2006), und das Burns Townhouse in Philadelphia, Pennsylvania (2006).

Après avoir étudié à la Wesleyan University (Bachelor of Arts, 1988), Paul Lewis a reçu son Master of Architecture de Princeton University en 1992. Il est le cofc dateur et dirigeant directeur de **LEWIS TSURUMAKI LEWIS** (LTL), agence créée en 1993. Il a été associé de Diller + Scofidio, New York (1993–97). Marc Tsurumaki Master of Architecture M. Arch. de Princeton (1991) après des études à l'Université de Virginie. Il a travaillé comme architecte de projet chez Joel Sander à New Y (1991–97) avant de créer LTL. David J. Lewis, après Cornell et Carlton College a achevé ses études d'architecture à Princeton en 1995. Il a été directeur des publi tions au College of Architecture, Art and Planning de Cornell University (1997–98), a travaillé comme assistant chez Peter Guggenheimer, Architects, PPC, New Y (1995–96) et dans l'agence de Daniel Libeskind à Berlin (1993), avant de créer LTL. Parmi les récentes réalisations de l'agence : Bornhuetter Hall, Wooster, Ohio (200 Tides Restaurant Restaurant à New York (2005) ; Ini Ani Coffee Shop à New York (2004). En projet actuellement : rénovation et extension de l'Arthouse, Austin, Te (2005) ; une tour d'appartements, Las Vegas (2005) ; le Dash Dogs Restaurant à New York (2005) ; l'Alexakos Gymnasium à Southampton, New York (2006) ; la réno tion du Centre biomédical de Brown University, Providence, Rhode Island (2005) ; les logements HPD, East New York (2006) ; Allentown House, Allentown, Pennsylva (2006) et l'hôtel de ville Burns, Philadelphie, Pennsylvanie (2006).

FLUFF BAKERY

New York, New York, USA, 2004

Floor area: 72 m². Client: Chow Down Mgt. Inc. Cost: $250 000

Created at 751 Ninth Avenue in New York for a cost of $250 000, this 72 m² space has unusual walls and ceilings, created with strips of felt and stained wood each individually put in place. A ceiling light was "designed as a custom horizontal chandelier, composed of 42 dimmable incandescent lights connected to a ser of branching stainless steel metal armatures." As the architects explain, "This design/build project explores a new architectural surface made from an excessive reption and assembly of common, banal and cheap materials. More akin to a gallery installation, the interior surface and the chandelier were built and installed by the are tects." The strip cladding also creates a dynamic effect that sweeps visitors into the space beginning with a floor-to-ceiling glass façade. Despite their rather sophi cated background, the architects demonstrate with the **FLUFF BAKERY** that they are willing to get directly involved in an original, small-scale project.

751 Ninth Avenue lautet die Adresse der Bäckerei Fluff in New York. Die Baukosten für den 72 m² großen Raum betrugen umgerechnet 210 500 Euro. Die un wöhnliche Wand- und Deckenverkleidung besteht aus dünnen Filzstreifen und gebeiztem Sperrholz, jeder Streifen wurde einzeln montiert. Die Deckenbeleuchtung bi ein »speziell angefertigter ›horizontaler Kronleuchter‹. Er besteht aus 42 dimmbaren Leuchtstoffröhren, die an sich verzweigenden Stahlarmen befestigt sind.« Die Arc tekten erläutern: »Mit dem Entwurf bzw. dem realisierten Raum erforschen wir eine neue architektonische Oberfläche, die aus der exzessiven Wiederholung und der V wendung von gewöhnlichen, einfachen und billigen Materialien entsteht. Die Oberflächen und der ›Kronleuchter‹ – Elemente, die eher Installationen in einer Galerie ähr – wurden von den Architekten selbst hergestellt und montiert.« Die streifenartige Wandverkleidung hat auch einen dynamischen Effekt, der den Besucher in den Ra hineinzieht. Eingeleitet wird dieser Effekt durch die raumhoch verglaste Fassade. Ihren eher intellektuellen Anspruch hinter sich lassend beweisen die Architekten mit **BÄCKEREI FLUFF**, dass sie bereit sind, sich auf ein originelles, kleines Projekt einzulassen.

Aménagé 751 Ninth Avenue à New York pour un budget de 210 000 d'euros, ce local de 72 m² présente de curieux murs et plafonds revêtus de minces ban de feutre et de contreplaqué teinté, mises en place une par à une. Au plafond est suspendu un luminaire «conçu comme un lustre horizontal sur mesure composé de tubes fluorescents rhéostatés montés sur une série de branches en acier inoxydable». Comme l'explique l'architecte : «De sa conception à sa réalisation, ce projet exp re une nouvelle surface architecturale composée d'une répétition et d'un assemblage pléthoriques de matériaux communs et bon marché dans un esprit d'excès. Ter plus de l'installation d'une galerie d'art, ces surfaces et ce lustre ont été fabriqués et installés par nous.» Le «bardage» de fins bandeaux crée un effet dynamique happe les clients dans le volume ouvert sur la rue par une façade en verre du sol au plafond. Malgré leur formation assez sophistiquée, les architectes démontrent a la **BOULANGERIE FLUFF** qu'ils n'hésitent pas à s'impliquer directement à fond dans un projet original, même de petite échelle.

The architects are given to complex effects created with "ordinary" materials. Here, reflections and lighting combine to make it difficult to determine where inside begins and outside ends.

Mit »gewöhnlichen« Materialien erzielen die Architekten komplexe Effekte. Reflexionen und die Belichtung führen hier dazu, dass nicht ohne Weiteres erkennbar ist, wo innen anfängt und außen aufhört.

Les architectes ont privilégié les effets complexes créés par des matériaux « ordinaires ». Ici, reflets et éclairage naturel se combinent pour rendre indiscernable la limite entre l'intérieur et l'extérieur.

MANSILLA+TUÑÓN

Mansilla+Tuñón arquitectos
c/Artistas 59
28020 Madrid
Spain

Tel/Fax: +34 913 99 30 67
e-mail: circo@circo.e.telefonica.net
Web: www.mansilla-tunon.com

MUSAC Art Ce

EMILIO TUÑÓN and **LUIS MANSILLA** were both born in Madrid, respectively in 1958 and 1959, and received their doctorates from the ETSAM in 1998. The created their firm in Madrid in 1992. They are both full professors in the Architectural Design Department of the Architecture School of Madrid. In 1993, they created "thinking exchange cooperative" called Circo with Luis Rojo and they publish a bulletin of the same name. Their built projects include the Archeological and Fine Ar Museum of Zamora (1996); Indoor Swimming Pool in San Fernando de Henares (1998); Fine Arts Museum of Castellón (2001); Auditorium of León (2002); Region Library and Archive of Madrid (2003); and the MUSAC Art Center in León (2004). They won competitions for the urban planning of Valbuena in Logroño and a Publ Library in Calle de los Artistas in Madrid in 2003; and for the Town Council of Lalin (2004), and the Helga Alvear Foundation in Cáceres (2005). They have been finalis for four Mies van der Rohe Awards (1997, 1999, 2001 and 2003).

EMILIO TUÑÓN, 1958 in Madrid geboren, und **LUIS MANSILLA**, 1959 ebenfalls in Madrid geboren, promovierten 1998 an der ETSAM (Escuela Técnica Supe rior de Arquitectura) in Madrid. 1992 gründeten sie dort ihr Büro. Beide haben eine Vollprofessur im Fachgebiet Architektonischer Entwurf an der ETSAM inne. 1993 grün deten sie zusammen mit Luis Rojo eine »Gedankenaustausch-Kooperative«, Circo genannt, und geben seitdem ein Themenheft mit demselben Namen heraus. Zu de realisierten Gebäuden des Büros gehören das Archäologische Museum und Museum für Kunst in Zamora (1996), ein Hallenbad in San Fernando de Henares (1998), da Museum für Bildende Kunst in Castellón (2001) und ein Auditorium in León (2002), ferner die Regionalbibliothek und das Regionalarchiv von Madrid (2003) und da Kunstzentrum MUSAC in León (2004). 2003 haben sie einen städtebaulichen Wettbewerb für Valbuena in Logroño und einen Wettbewerb für eine öffentliche Bücherei der Calle de los Artistas in Madrid gewonnen, außerdem Wettbewerbe für das Gebäude des Stadtrats von Lalin (2004) und die Helga-Alvear-Stiftung in Cáceres (2005 Sie waren bereits viermal Finalisten für den Mies-van-der-Rohe-Preis (1997, 1999, 2001 und 2003).

EMILIO TUÑÓN et **LUIS MANSILLA** sont nés à Madrid, respectivement en 1958 et 1959 et sont tous deux docteurs de l'Etsam (1998). Ils ont créé leur age ce madrilène en 1992 et sont professeurs au département de Conception architecturale de leur ancienne école. En 1993, ils ont créé une «coopérative d'échange d'idées» appelée «Circo» avec Luis Rojo et publient un bulletin du même nom. Parmi leurs réalisations : le Musée d'archéologie et des beaux-arts de Zamora (1996 une piscine couverte à San Fernando de Henares (1998) ; le Musée des beaux-arts de Castellon (2001) ; l'Auditorium de León (2002) ; la Bibliothèque régionale et l Archives de Madrid (2003) et le Musac, Musée d'art contemporain de Castille et León (2004). Ils ont remporté des concours pour l'urbanisme de Valbuena à Logroñ pour une bibliothèque publique, calle de los Artistas à Madrid, en 2003, pour le Conseil municipal de Lalin (2004) et pour la Fondation Helga Alvear à Cáceres (200 Ils ont été finalistes des quatre prix Mies van der Rohe (1997, 1999, 2001 et 2003).

MUSAC

Museo de Arte Contemporáneo de Castilla y León, León, Spain, 2002–04

Floor area: 10 000 m². Client: Gesturcal S. A., Junta de Castilla y León.
Cost: € 24 million

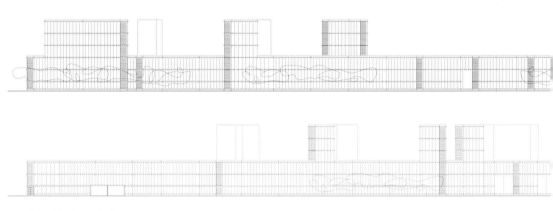

The architects use color like an abstract pattern akin to a work of art executed at architectural scale. With minimal exterior detailing, they allow color to take on a central role in the design.

Die Architekten setzen Farbe als abstraktes Muster ein; dieses wirkt als ein Kunstwerk in einem architektonischen Maßstab. Die äußere Fassade zeigt nur wenige Details und überlässt der Farbe die Hauptrolle.

Les architectes utilisent la couleur comme un motif abstrait, un peu comme dans une œuvre d'art, mais à l'échelle de l'architecture. Avec très peu d'effets extérieurs, ils laissent la couleur prendre la vedette.

Located on the Avenida de los Reyes Leoneses is a 10 000 m² building with white concrete walls and large areas of colored glazing. The architects explain t "MUSAC is a new space for culture, regarded as something that visualizes the connections between man and nature. A cluster of chained but independent roo permit exhibitions of differing sizes and types. Each of the jaggedly shaped rooms constructs a continuous yet spatially differentiated area that opens onto the other roo and courtyards, providing longitudinal, transversal and diagonal views. Five hundred prefab beams enclose a series of spaces that feature systematic repetition a formal expressiveness. Outside, the public space takes on a concave shape to hold the activities and encounters, embraced by large colored glass in homage to the « as the place for interpersonal relationships." Cheerful and varied in its appearance, MUSAC certainly takes a different esthetic approach than many contemporary museums, where there is an emphasis on a more discreet Modernism. But the architects have a ready explanation for this difference. "In contrast to other types museum spaces that focus on the exhibition of frozen historic collections, MUSAC is a living space that opens its doors to the wide-ranging manifestations of conte porary art," they declare.

Das Kunstzentrum **MUSAC** an der Avenida de los Reyes Leoneses in Léon ist ein 10 000 m² großes Gebäude mit weißen Wänden aus Sichtbeton und groß farbig verglasten Flächen. Die Architekten erläutern: »MUSAC ist ein neuer Ort für Kultur. Kultur wird hier als etwas betrachtet, das die Beziehungen zwischen Mens und Natur vergegenwärtigt. Eine Gruppe von ineinander greifenden, aber voneinander unabhängigen Räumen ermöglicht Ausstellungen verschiedener Größe und A Jeder der winkligen Räume ist Teil eines Raumkontinuums, gleichzeitig aber räumlich differenziert und öffnet sich zu anderen Räumen und Innenhöfen, wodurch s Sichtachsen in Längs-, Quer- und Diagonalrichtung ergeben. 500 vorgefertigte Träger begrenzen das Raumsystem, das von der systematischen Wiederholung und f malen Expressivität bestimmt wird. Der Außenbereich hat eine konkave Form, um den öffentliche Raum für Aktivitäten und Begegnungen zu fassen. Er wird durch gro farbige Glasscheiben, eine Hommage an die Stadt als Ort zwischenmenschlicher Beziehungen, gerahmt.« Fröhlich und differenziert gestaltet, folgt MUSAC sicherl einem anderen ästhetischen Ansatz als viele moderne Kunstmuseen, die einem diskreteren Modernismus verpflichtet sind. Für diesen Unterschied haben die Architek eine Erklärung parat: »Im Gegensatz zu anderen Museumsräumen, die der Ausstellung von ‹gefrorenen› historischen Sammlungen dienen, ist MUSAC ein lebendiger C der seine Türen den sehr unterschiedlichen Äußerungen der neuen Kunst öffnet.«

Situé Avenida de los Reyes Leoneses, le bâtiment de ce musée, qui conjugue murs de béton blanc et vastes pans de verre de couleur, totalise 10 000 m². architectes expliquent que « le **MUSAC** est un nouvel espace pour la culture, un lieu qui doit mettre en lumière les connexions entre l'homme et la nature. L'assemb ge de salles reliées entre elles mais indépendants permet des expositions de toute nature. Chaque élément découpé de ce ‹ puzzle › détermine un espace continu m spatialement différencié, qui ouvre sur d'autres salles et des cours tout en ménageant des perspectives longitudinales, transversales et diagonales. Cinq cents pout préfabriquées enferment une série d'espaces qui jouent de la répétition systématique et de l'expressivité formelle. À l'extérieur, l'espace public s'incurve pour accue les activités et les rencontres. Il est couvert de verre de couleurs en hommage à la ville, lieu par excellence des relations humaines». D'aspect joyeux et très diversi le MUSAC a adopté une approche esthétique différente de celle de beaucoup de musées d'art contemporain, où l'on préfère un modernisme plus discret. Mais les arc tectes ont une explication toute prête à cette différence : « Par contraste avec d'autres types de musées qui se consacrent à l'exposition de collections historiques figé le MUSAC est un espace vivant qui ouvre ses portes aux multiples manifestations de l'art contemporain. »

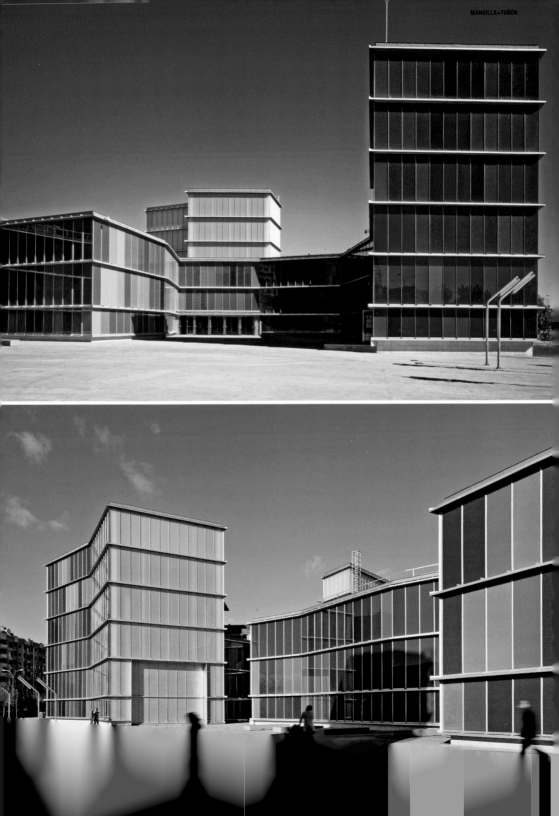

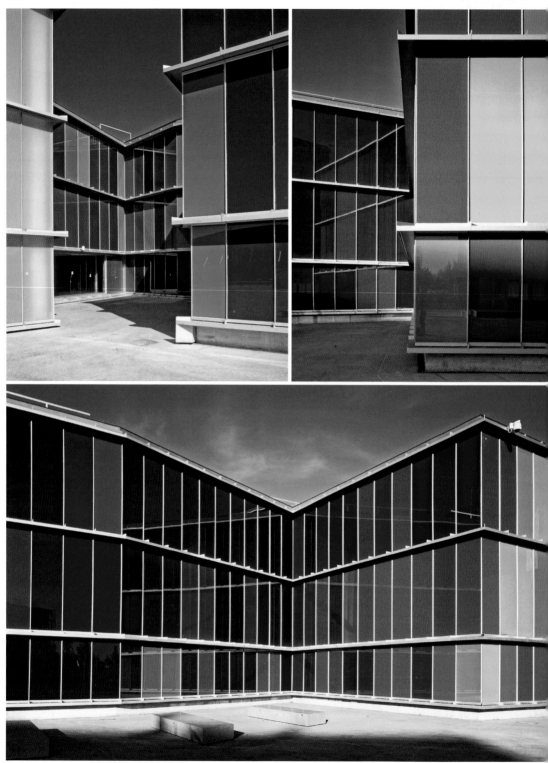

s the drawing below and the images
n this double page demonstrate,
olors are applied like a continuous
anvas, made up of a chromatic
rchestration that may or may not
ollow the sequence of the electro-
nagnetic spectrum.

Vie diese Bilder und die Zeichnung
eigen, wurden die Farben gewisser-
aßen auf eine umlaufende Leinwand
aufgetragen«. Ihre chromatische
usformulierung folgt teilweise der
bfolge im elektromagnetischen
pektrum.

omme le montrent le dessin ci-des-
ous et les images de cette double
age, les couleurs sont appliquées
elon un canevas continu à partir
une orchestration chromatique qui
it, ou non, le spectre lumineux.

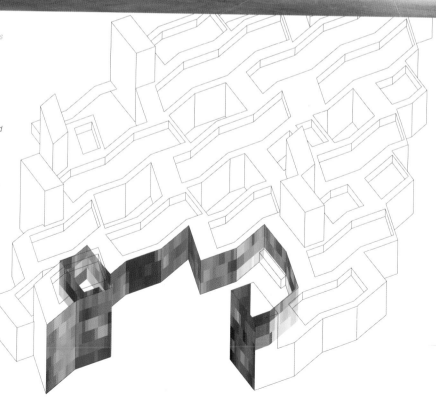

Interior spaces are generous and
sometimes darker than might be
expected given the explosion of
colors seen on the exterior.

Die Innenräume sind weiträumig
und mitunter dunkler als man
in Anbetracht der Farbexplosion
außen erwarten könnte.

Les généreux volumes intérieurs sont
parfois plus sombres que l'on pourrait s'y attendre après l'explosion de
couleurs de l'extérieur.

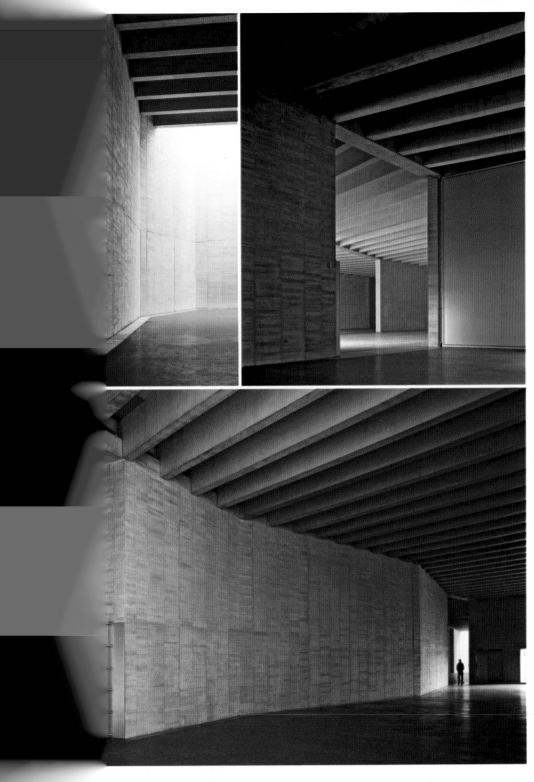

While color is the defining elemen
of the exterior, it gives way inside
a limited palette which permits th
exhibition areas to offer a neutral
backdrop to the works to be show

Während nach außen die Farbe da
definierende Element ist, wird im
Inneren eine eingeschränkte
Farbpalette verwendet, um einen
neutralen Hintergrund für die Kuns
zu schaffen.

Si la couleur est l'élément clé pou
l'extérieur, elle laisse place, à
l'intérieur, à une palette limitée q
permet aux aires d'exposition d'of
un environnement neutre aux
œuvres d'art.

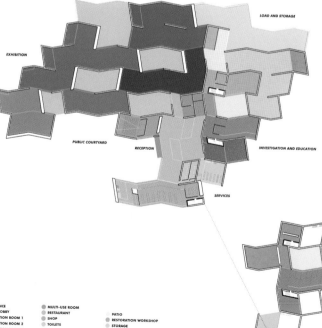

LOAD AND STORAGE

EXHIBITION

PUBLIC COURTYARD

RECEPTION

INVESTIGATION AND EDUCATION

SERVICES

plan above shows overlapping
res that house the various museum
ctions. Within, the symphony of
side colors is left aside, and more
d, concrete surfaces make their
earance.

Grundriss zeigt ineinander über-
ende Zonen, in denen die ver-
edenen Funktionen des Museums
eordnet sind. Innen wird die
pigkeit zugunsten massiver Beton-
rflächen aufgegeben.

lan ci-dessus montre la super-
tion des zones qui accueillent
différentes fonctions du musée.
ntérieur, la symphonie de cou-
s est écartée au profit de plans
éton brut.

- ENTRANCE
- MAIN LOBBY
- EXHIBITION ROOM 1
- EXHIBITION ROOM 2
- EXHIBITION ROOM 3
- EXHIBITION ROOM 4
- EXHIBITION ROOM 5
- EXHIBITION PATIO

- MULTI-USE ROOM
- RESTAURANT
- SHOP
- TOILETS
- LIBRARY
- EDUCATIONAL WORKSHOP
- OFFICE
- STAFF

- PATIO
- RESTORATION WORKSHOP
- STORAGE
- LOADING AREA
- CONTROL AREA
- TECHNICAL AREA
- VEHICLE ENTRANCE

e

MICHAEL MCDONOUGH

Michael McDonough Architect, 131 Spring Street
New York, New York 10012, USA

Tel: +1 212 431 3723, Fax: + 1 212 431 7465
e-mail: mail@michaelmcdonough.com, Web: www.michaelmcdonough.com

Since the founding of his architecture and design firm in 1984, **MICHAEL MCDONOUGH** has completed commercial spaces such as galleries, showrooms, pu
buildings, shops, and exhibits, as well as residential projects, including homes and lofts throughout the United States and Europe, consults world-wide on corporate fu
ism, personal environments, and product development. His design philosophy is "rooted in systems convergence theory, synthesizing traditional and modern des
emphasizing new materials and sustainable technologies." As an architect, McDonough has designed facilities and consulted for such companies as Lufthansa Gerr
Airlines, Frogdesign, Frankfurt Airport Authority, Aveda Corporation, Stephen Sprouse Fashion, and Seaside Community Development Corporation; as well as desigr
over 50 private residences, exhibitions, and conceptual projects. As an industrial designer, his collections include tabletop objects, jewelry, and furniture. He designed
McEasy Collection of lounge furniture for ICF Unika Vaev Nienkämper, and Eco-sTuff!, a line of ecological furniture made of 100% post-consumer recycled newspa
McDonough holds a B.A. in English from the University of Massachusetts, and Master of Architecture from the University of Pennsylvania, where he was an Editor of
He also completed additional studies in architecture and art at the Massachusetts Institute of Technology. Presently, he is a contributing editor and writer at *Metropo*
Home. He has also written on design for *The New York Times*, *Wired*, and other publications. Novelist Tom Wolfe dedicated his controversial book on architecture, *F.
Bauhaus to Our House*, to McDonough. McDonough's first book, *Malaparte: A House Like Me* was published by Clarkson Potter/Publishers in 1999.

Seit der Gründung seines Architektur- und Designbüros 1984 hat **MICHAEL MCDONOUGH** zahlreiche kommerzielle und private Bauten realisiert. Zu den ke
merziellen Projekten gehören Galerien, Showrooms, öffentliche Gebäude, Läden und Ausstellungen, zu den privaten Wohnhäuser und Lofts in den USA und Europa. E
weltweit als Berater für »Corporate Futurism«, private Environments und Produktentwicklung tätig. Seine Entwurfsphilosophie hat »ihre Wurzeln in der Systemkon
genztheorie, die traditionelles und modernes Design miteinander verbindet und neue Materialien und nachhaltige Technologien verwendet«. Als Architekt hat McDono
die Einrichtungen diverser Unternehmen – z. B. für die Lufthansa, Frogdesign, den Frankfurter Flughafen, Aveda Kosmetik, Stephen Sprouse Mode und die Seaside C
munity Development Corporation – entworfen und diese Unternehmen beraten. Mehr als 50 Privathäuser, Ausstellungen und konzeptionelle Projekte stammen von i
Als Industriedesigner entwarf er Tischwaren, Schmuck und Möbel. Er hat die Loungemöbel der McEasy Kollektion für ICF Unika Vaev Nienkämper und Eco-sTuff!,
Kollektion von ökologischen Möbeln, die zu 100 Prozent aus recyceltem Zeitungspapier bestehen, entworfen. McDonough hat einen B. A. in Englisch von der Unive
of Massachusetts und einen Master of Architecture von der University of Pennsylvania, wo er Herausgeber von *VIA* war. Ferner schloss er zusätzliche Architektur-
Kunststudien am Massachusetts Institute of Technology ab. Derzeit ist er Mitherausgeber und Autor von »Metropolitan Home«. Zum Thema Design hat er Beiträge
die *New York Times*, *Wired* und andere Publikationen. Der Romanautor Tom Wolfe widmete ihm sein umstrittenes Buch *From Bauhaus to Our House*. Mc
noughs erstes Buch *Malaparte: A House Like Me* erschien 1999 bei Clarkson Potter/Publishers.

Depuis la fondation de son agence d'architecture et de design, **MICHAEL MCDONOUGH** a réalisé des points de vente, des boutiques, des showrooms, des b
ments publics et des expositions aussi bien que des projets résidentiels dont des maisons et des lofts, aux États-Unis et en Europe. Il a donné des consultations c
le monde entier sur le futur consultant international pour les questions de développement des entreprises, d'environnements personnels et de développement de prod
Sa philosophie du design est « enracinée dans la théorie de convergence des systèmes, elle fait la synthèse entre les conceptions moderne et traditionnelle et met l
cent sur les nouveaux matériaux innovants et les technologies durables ». En tant qu'architecte, il a conçu des équipements et a été consultant pour des entrepr
comme Lufthansa, Frogdesign, l'aéroport de Francfort, Aveda Corporation, Stephen Sprouse Fashion, Seaside Community Development Corporation et il est l'auteu
plus de 50 cinquante résidences privées, expositions et projets conceptuels. Designer industriel, il a réalisé des objets d'art de la table, des bijoux et des meubles.
conçu la collection de mobilier de salon McEasy pour ICF Unika Vaev Nienkämper ainsi qu'Eco-sTuff!, une ligne de mobilier écologique en papier journal 100% recy
McDonough est Bachelor of Art en anglais de l'Université du Massachusetts et Master of Architecture de l'Université de Pennsylvanie où il était le rédacteur en che
VIA. Il a également suivi des études complémentaires en art et architecture au Massachusetts Institute of Technology. Actuellement, il est éditorialiste et rédacteur
Metropolitan Home. Il a également écrit sur le design dans *The New York Times*, dans *Wired* et d'autres publications. Il est le dédicataire du célèbre et controversé ou
ge de Tom Wolfe sur l'architecture, *From Bauhaus to Our House*. Son premier livre, *Malaparte : A House Like Me*, a été publié par Clarkson Potter/Publishers en 19

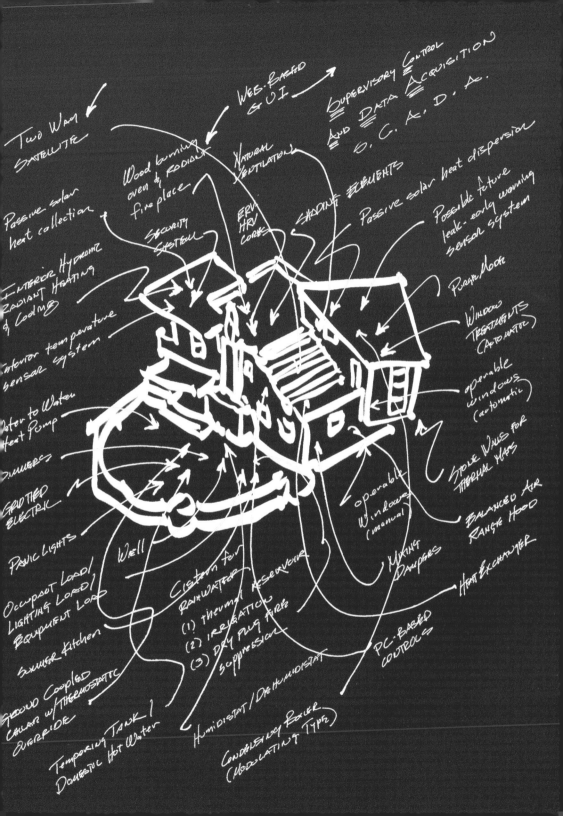

Two Way Satellite

Web-Based GUI

Supervisory Control And Data Acquisition S. C. A. D. A.

Passive solar heat collection

Wood burning oven & RADIANT fire place

Natural Ventilation

Passive solar heat dispersion

Possible future leak, early warning sensor system

Interior Hydronic RADIANT Heating & Cooling

Security System

ERV HRV CORE

Shading Elements

Purge Mode

Interior temperature sensor system

Window Treatments (Automatic)

Water to Water Heat Pump

operable windows (automatic)

Dimmers

Stone Walls for Thermal Mass

Grid Tied Electric

operable Windows (manual)

Balanced Air Range Hood

Panic Lights

Well

Heat Exchanger

Occupant Load/ Lighting Load/ Equipment Load

Cistern for RAINWATER

(1) Thermal Reservoir
(2) Irrigation
(3) Dry Pipe Fire Suppression

Mixing Dampers

Summer Kitchen

PC-Based Controls

Ground Coupled Cellar w/Thermostatic Override

Humidistat / Dehumidistat

Tempering Tank / Domestic Hot Water

Condensing Boiler (Modulating Type)

E-HOUSE

Hudson Valley, New York, USA, 2002–05

*Floor area: 235 m². Client: Michael McDonough Architect.
Cost: not disclosed*

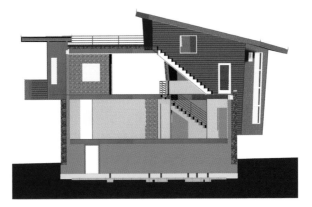

Michael McDonough calls the **E-HOUSE** "a laboratory for new technologies in the guise of a contemporary home." Much more than a "green" house, McDonoug creation involved careful analysis of the site, use of local materials and artisans, and careful research of all possible ways of making it both reactive and sensitive to users and its environment. McDonough explains that "Importantly, the project aspires to set new standards for building design, integrates over 100 new or advanced tecnologies (including high performance or historical or 'alternate' technologies) and proposes to develop a new lexicon for sustainable architecture theory." He makes re rences not only to the 18th-century Dutch Colonial homestead ruins found on the site, but also to the Casa Malaparte and its south-facing monumental stairway. trapezoidal extensions are designed to capture a view and to catch the first light of day all year long. An "experimental radiant heating, cooling, and snowmelt syst with rainwater thermal storage cisterns and heat exchangers" is one feature of the residence, which can be controlled and monitored from a distance with a dedica web site. McDonough explains that "The e-House will have a SCADA – Supervisory Control and Data Acquisition – system in conjunction with an Internet portal a management software. This means the house acts as an organic entity, enabled through currently available networking, hardware and software technologies. It … be capable of making low-level decisions related to systems management."

Michael McDonough nennt das **E-HOUSE** »ein Laboratorium für neue Technologien, verkleidet als modernes Haus«. Viel mehr als ein »grünes« Haus beinhalt seine Planung eine sorgfältige Untersuchung des Grundstücks, die Einbeziehung von Materialien und Handwerkern der Region sowie eine aufwendige Erforschung a Möglichkeiten, das Haus so zu gestalten, dass es sensibel auf seine Nutzer und seine Umgebung reagieren kann. McDonough meint: »Es ist wichtig, dass wir mit d Projekt anstreben, neue Standards für den Entwurf von Gebäuden zu setzen. Es integriert über 100 neue oder ausgereifte Technologien, darunter Hochleistungstech logien, historische und alternative Technologien. Mit dem Haus schlagen wir die Entwicklung eines neuen Wortschatzes für nachhaltige Architekturtheorie vor.« McD nough bezieht sich nicht nur auf die Ruinen eines niederländischen Kolonialhauses aus dem 18. Jahrhundert, die auf dem Grundstück gefunden wurden, sondern au auf die Casa Malaparte und ihre nach Süden orientierte monumentale Treppe. Zwei trapezförmige Anbauten sollen einen Ausblick bieten und das ganze Jahr über je erste Tageslicht einfangen. Ein wichtiges Element des Hauses ist das »experimentelle Strahlwärme-, Kühl- und Schneeschmelzsystem mit Auffangwärmetanks für Rege wasser sowie Wärmetauschern«. Es kann aus der Distanz über eine spezielle Website überwacht und kontrolliert werden. McDonough erläutert: »Das e-House wird ü ein SCADA-System (Überwachende Kontrolle und Datenaufnahme) verfügen, in Verbindung mit einem Internetportal und einer Managementsoftware. Das bedeutet, sich das Haus als organisches Ganzes verhält. Die derzeit zur Verfügung stehende Vernetzung, die Hardware- und Softwaretechnologien ermöglichen dies. Es … w dazu in der Lage sein, untergeordnete, das Systemmanagement betreffende Entscheidungen selbst zu treffen.«

Michael McDonough dit que sa **E-HOUSE** est « un laboratoire de nouvelles technologies déguisé en maison contemporaine ». Ce travail, qui est beaucoup p qu'une maison « verte », a entraîné une analyse approfondie du site, le recours à des artisans et des matériaux locaux et une recherche sur toutes les manières possib de rendre cette maison aussi réactive et sensible que possible, tant à ses usagers qu'à son environnement. McDonough explique : « Il est important de noter que le p jet aspire à fixer de nouveaux standards de conception de l'habitat, d'intégrer plus de 100 technologies nouvelles ou d'avant-garde (dont des technologies haute p formance, historiques ou ‹ alternatives ›) et se propose de mettre au point un nouveau lexique de la théorie de l'architecture durable. » L'architecte ne fait pas seulem référence aux ruines de la maison du XVIIIᵉ siècle de style colonial hollandais existant sur le terrain mais aussi à la Casa Malaparte et à son escalier monumental. D extensions trapézoïdales ont été aménagées pour capter la vue et les premiers rayons du soleil tout au long de l'année. Un « système expérimental de chauffage radia de rafraîchissement et de fonte de la neige radiant avec des citernes de stockage de l'eau de pluie et des échangeurs de chaleur » est l'un des équipements contrôlab et pilotables à distance *via* un site internet. L'architecte explique également que « la e-House sera équipée de SCADA – système de contrôle, de supervision et d'acc sition de données – qui œuvrera en conjonction avec un portail internet et un logiciel de gestion. Ceci signifie que la maison agit comme une entité organique, ce c permettent les technologies informatiques actuellement disponibles. Elle … sera en mesure de prendre certaines décisions à partir des systèmes de gestion ».

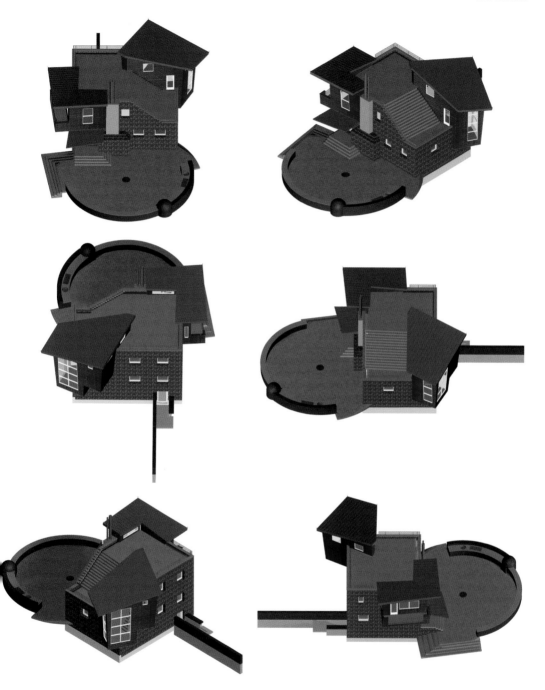

e-House gives the impression
being a collage of disparate ele-
nts, whose shape and positioning
more related to environmental
ces than esthetic ones.

Das e-House wirkt wie eine Collage
aus verschiedenen Elementen, deren
Form und Position eher durch ökologische Kriterien als durch ästhetische
Überlegungen bestimmt werden.

La e-House donne l'impression d'un
collage d'éléments disparates dont
la forme et le positionnement dépen-
dent plus de l'environnement que de
critères esthétiques.

RICHARD MEIER

Richard Meier & Partners
475 Tenth Avenue
New York, New York 10018
USA

Tel: +1 212 967 6060
Fax: +1 212 967 3207
e-mail: mail@richardmeier.com
Web: www.richardmeier.com

RICHARD MEIER was born in Newark, New Jersey in 1934. He received his architectural training at Cornell University, and worked in the office of Marcel Bre
(1960–63) before establishing his own practice in 1963. In 1984, he became the youngest winner of the Pritzker Prize, and he received the 1988 RIBA Gold Medal. I
notable buildings include The Atheneum, New Harmony, Indiana (1975–79); Museum of Decorative Arts, Frankfurt, Germany (1979–84); High Museum of Art, Atlar
Georgia (1980–83); Canal Plus Headquarters, Paris, France (1988–91); City Hall and Library, The Hague, The Netherlands (1990–95); Barcelona Museum of Contem
rary Art, Barcelona, Spain (1988–95); and the Getty Center, Los Angeles, California (1984–97). Recent work includes the U. S. Courthouse and Federal Building, Phoer
Arizona (1995–2000); Jubilee Church, Rome (2003); Crystal Cathedral International Center for Possibility Thinking, Garden Grove, California (2003); Arp Museum, Rolan
eck, Germany; and the Yale University History of Art and Arts Library, New Haven (2001), and the 66 restaurant in New York (2001–02). Present work includes the Bea
House, a 12-story glass enclosed condominium located on Collins Avenue in Miami (2004–07); the ECM City Tower, Pankrac City, Prague, Czech Republic (2004–0
165 Charles Street (2003–05), a 16-story residential building located in Manhattan near the architect's Perry Street apartments (1999–2002); and the Ara Pa
Museum, Rome, Italy (1995–2006).

RICHARD MEIER, geboren 1934 in Newark, New Jersey, studierte an der Cornell University und arbeitete von 1960 bis 1963 im Büro von Marcel Breuer, be
er 1963 sein eigenes Büro gründete. 1984 wurde er – als jüngster Gewinner – mit dem Pritzker-Preis ausgezeichnet, 1988 erhielt er die RIBA Gold Medal. Zu sein
wichtigsten Gebäuden gehören: The Atheneum, New Harmony, Indiana (1975–79), das Museum für Kunsthandwerk in Frankfurt am Main (1979–84), das High Muse
of Art in Atlanta, Georgia (1980–83), die Zentrale von Canal Plus in Paris (1988–91), das Rathaus mit Bibliothek in Den Haag (1990–95), das Museum für zeitgen
sische Kunst in Barcelona (1988–95) und das Getty Center in Los Angeles (1984–97). Zu seinen jüngsten Projekten zählen das US Courthouse and Federal Building
Phoenix, Arizona (1995–2000), die Kirche des Heiligen Jahres in Rom (2003), das Chrystal Cathedral International Center for Possibility Thinking in Garden Grove, K
fornien (2003), das Arp-Museum in Rolandseck (1995–2005), die Yale University History of Art and Arts Library in New Haven (2001) und das Restaurant 66 in New Y
(2001–02). Derzeit in der Planung bzw. im Bau befindliche Projekte sind u. a.: das Beach House, ein vollständig verglastes zwölfgeschossiges Gebäude mit Eigentur
wohnungen auf der Collins Avenue in Miami (2004–07), der ECM City Tower in Pankrac, Prag (2004–07), 165 Charles Street (2003–05), ein 16-geschossiges Wohn
bäude in der Nähe der Perry Street Apartments (1999–2002, ebenfalls von Richard Meier) in Manhattan, und das Ara-Pacis-Museum in Rom (1995–2006).

Né à Newark (New Jersey), en 1934, **RICHARD MEIER** a étudie à Cornell University, et travaille dans l'agence de Marcel Breuer (1960–63) avant de s'insta
à son compte en 1963. Prix Pritzker 1984, Royal Gold Medal, 1988. Principales réalisations : The Athenaeum, New Harmony, Indiana, États-Unis (1975–79) ; Musée
Arts décoratifs de Francfort-sur-le-Main (1979–84) ; High Museum of Art, Atlanta, Géorgie (1980–83) ; siège de Canal +, Paris (1988–91) ; hôtel de ville et bibliothèq
La Haye (1990–95) ; Musée d'Art contemporain de Barcelone (1988–95) ; Getty Center, Los Angeles, Californie (1984–96). Travaux récents : Tribunal fédéral et immeu
de l'administration fédérale à Phoenix, Arizona (1995–2000) ; l'Église du Jubilée, Rome (2003) ; le Crystal Cathedral International Center for Possibility Thinking, Garc
Grove, Californie (2003) ; le Arp Museum, Rolandseck, Allemagne (1995–2005) ; la Yale University History of Art and Arts Library, New Haven (2001), et le restaurant
à New York (2001–02) ; Beach House, un immeuble en copropriété sur Collins Avenue à Miami (2004–07) ; la tour ECM, Pankrak City, Prague (2004–07) ; un immeu
d'habitation de 16 étages au 165 Charles Street, Manhattan (2003–05), non loin de ses appartements du 173/176 Perry Streets (1999–2002), et le musée de l'∢
Pacis, Rome, Italie (1995–2006).

MUSEUM FRIEDER BURDA

Baden-Baden, Germany, 2001–04

Floor area: 2000 m². Client: Stiftung Frieder. Burda Cost: €20 million

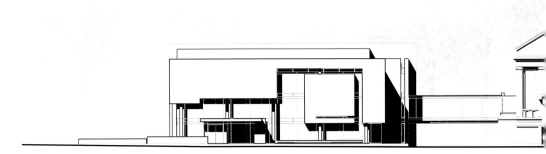

The 15-meter-high structure has an approximate overall size of 2000 m² with an exhibition space of 1000 m². With four stories, including the entry level, structure is clad in white enameled metal panels. As the architect says, "The new museum for the Frieder Burda Collection in Baden-Baden is designed to be in harmny with the surrounding Lichtentaler Allee Park and to compliment the adjacent Kunsthalle. The overall size and proportions of the new building are in scale with Kunsthalle creating a sense of unity, while each institution maintains its own unique identity." A glazed bridge links the museum to the plinth of the Kunsthalle in a mner that does not disturb the architecture of the existing structure. Although he does employ a selected palette of materials and a specified architectural vocabul Richard Meier shows, with a building like the **MUSEUM FRIEDER BURDA**, that these self-imposed limitations can indeed lead to a great variety of buildings and ind to a more and more masterful treatment of spaces and light. As described by the museum, "The Frieder Burda collection, rooted in German Expressionism, is compri of more than 500 paintings, sculptures and works on paper. The collection focuses on classical, modern and contemporary art and includes works by Gerhard Rich Sigmar Polke and Arnulf Rainer, as well as eight works by Pablo Picasso. In addition to paintings from Adolph Gottlieb, De Kooning, Pollock and Rothko, the collec includes an important work by Clyfford Still. The collection's German post-war selections feature work by George Baselitz, along with two well-known works by his e companion in Berlin, Eugen Schönebeck. Also noteworthy is Anselm Kiefer's nearly six-meter-long painting, *Böhmen liegt am Meer*."

Das 15 m hohe Gebäude mit einer Gesamtfläche von insgesamt ca. 2000 m² umfasst 1000 m² Ausstellungsfläche. Die vier Geschosse (inkl. Eingangsgesch sind komplett mit weiß emaillierten Metallpaneelen verkleidet. Der Architekt erläutert: »Das neue Museum für die Sammlung Frieder Burda in Baden-Baden soll harmonisch in den Park an der Lichtentaler Allee einfügen und die nahe gelegene Staatliche Kunsthalle ergänzen. Die Gesamtgröße des neuen Gebäudes und s Proportionen orientieren sich an denen der Kunsthalle, wodurch ein einheitliches Ensemble geschaffen wird, die spezielle Identität beider Institutionen aber beste bleibt.« Eine verglaste Brücke verbindet das neue Museum mit dem Sockel der Kunsthalle, ohne deren Architektur zu stören. Obwohl er nur wenige Materialien und spezielles architektonisches Vokabular verwendet, zeigt Richard Meier mit einem Gebäude wie dem **MUSEUM FRIEDER BURDA**, dass diese selbstauferlegte Besch kung zu sehr verschiedenen Gebäuden und zu einem immer anspruchsvolleren Umgang mit Raum und Licht führen kann. Die Sammlung des Museums wird folgen maßen beschrieben: »Die im deutschen Expressionismus verwurzelte Sammlung Frieder Burda umfasst mehr als 500 Gemälde, Skulpturen und Arbeiten auf Pap Sammlungsschwerpunkte sind die Kunst der Klassischen Moderne und moderne und zeitgenössische Kunst. Vertreten sind u. a. Gerhard Richter, Sigmar Polke und Ar Rainer sowie acht Arbeiten von Pablo Picasso. Außer Werken von Adolph Gottlieb, De Kooning, Pollock und Rothko ist auch eine bedeutende Arbeit von Clyfford Still der Sammlung. Die deutsche Kunst nach dem Zweiten Weltkrieg wird u. a. durch Georg Baselitz und zwei bekannte Werke von Eugen Schönebeck, einem Kollegen von Ba litz aus seinen frühen Berliner Jahren, repräsentiert. Ebenfalls erwähnenswert ist das fast 6 m lange Bild *Böhmen liegt am Meer* von Anselm Kiefer.«

Ce bâtiment de 15 mètres de haut, habillé de panneaux de métal émaillé blanc, offre une surface totale d'environ 2000 m² sur quatre niveaux, dont la moitié réservée aux galeries d'exposition. Selon la description de l'architecte, « le nouveau musée de la collection Frieder Burda à Baden-Baden est conçu pour être en monie avec son environnement, celui du Lichtentaler Allee Park et de la Kunsthalle adjacente, qu'il vient compléter. Les dimensions et les proportions de la nouv construction sont à l'échelle de la Kunsthalle pour créer un sentiment d'unité tout en conservant l'identité de chaque institution ». Une passerelle de verre relie le mu à la base de la Kunsthalle sans nuire à l'architecture de celle-ci. Même s'il reste fidèle à sa palette de matériaux et son vocabulaire architectural personnels, Rich Meier montre avec le **MUSÉE FRIEDER BURDA** que des contraintes bien comprises peuvent générer une grande variété de propositions et un traitement de plus en magistral de l'espace et de la lumière. Quant au musée même, « la collection Frieder Burda, qui prend ses racines dans l'expressionnisme allemand, compte plus de cents peintures, sculptures et travaux sur papier. Elle est centrée sur l'art classique, moderne et contemporain, avec des œuvres de Gerhard Richter, Sigmar Polk Arnulf Rainer, ainsi que huit Pablo Picasso. Hormis les tableaux de Adolph Gottlieb, De Kooning, Pollock et Rothko, elle comprend également une œuvre importante Clyfford Still. La sélection d'art allemand de l'après-guerre présente des travaux de Georg Baselitz et deux œuvres célèbres du compagnon berlinois de ses débuts, Eu Schönebeck. On note également la peinture de près de six mètres de long d'Anselm Kiefer, *Böhmen liegt am Meer* ».

Richard Meier remains faithful to his white, geometric rigor, and yet in the case of the Burda Collection, he attains new degrees of aesthetic complexity or perfection. Opaque white screens alternate with the set-back glazing in a pattern that might be compared to a musical partition.

Richard Meier bleibt seiner geometrisch weißen Strenge treu. Mit der Sammlung Burda erreicht er jedoch einen neuen Grad an ästhetischer Komplexität und Perfektion. Weißopake Flächen wechseln mit der zurückgesetzten Verglasung zu einem Muster, das mit einer musikalischen Komposition verglichen werden kann.

Richard Meier reste fidèle au blanc et à la rigueur géométrique. Ici, il atteint une fois de plus de nouveaux degrés de complexité dans sa perfection esthétique. Les écrans blancs opaques alternent avec les plans vitrés en retrait selon un motif comparable à une partition musicale.

...always, Meier masters the use of
...t and interpenetrating interior
...ces. His trademark walkways or
...gways permit varying views of the
...hitecture and of the outside gar-
...s.

...immer beherrscht Richard Meier
...Umgang mit Licht und sich durch-
...genden Innenräumen meisterhaft.
...npen und Brücken – seine Marken-
...hen – ermöglichen unterschied-
...e Blicke auf die Architektur und
...Garten.

...nme toujours, Meier maîtrise l'uti-
...tion de la lumière et de l'interpé-
...ration des volumes intérieurs.
...passages ou coursives qui sont
...narque offrent des points de
...s variés sur l'architecture ou les
...ins.

MORPHOSIS

Morphosis
2041 Colorado Avenue
Santa Monica, California 90404
USA

Tel: +1 310 453 2247
Fax: +1 310 829 3270
e-mail: studio@morphosis.net
Web: www.morphosis.net

Caltrans District 7 Headq

MORPHOSIS principal Thom Mayne, born in Connecticut in 1944, received his Bachelor of Architecture in 1968 at USC, and his Masters of Architecture deg at Harvard in 1978. He created Morphosis in 1979 with Michael Rotondi, who left to create his own firm, Roto. He has taught at UCLA, Harvard, and Yale and SCI- of which he was a founding Board Member. Some of the main buildings of Morphosis are the Lawrence House (1981); Kate Mantilini Restaurant, Beverly Hills (19 Cedar's Sinai Comprehensive Cancer Care Center, Beverly Hills (1987); Crawford Residence, Montecito (1987–92); Yuzen Vintage Car Museum, West Hollywood (proj 1992), as well as the Blades Residence, Santa Barbara, California (1992–97) and the International Elementary School, Long Beach, California (1997–99). More rec work includes the San Francisco Federal Building; University of Cincinnati Student Recreation Center; the NOAA Satellite Operation Facility in Suitland, Maryland; ar proposal for the 2012 Olympics in New York City made prior to the selection of London. Thom Mayne was the winner of the 2005 Pritzker Prize.

Geschäftsführer Thom Mayne, geboren 1944 in Connecticut, machte seinen Bachelor of Architecture 1968 an der University of Southern California (USC) und nen Master of Architecture 1978 in Harvard. Zusammen mit Michael Rotondi gründete er 1979 **MORPHOSIS**. Michael Rotondi führt inzwischen sein eigenes Büro R Thom Mayne hat an der UCLA, in Harvard, Yale und an der SCI-Arc – deren Gründungsmitglied er war – unterrichtet. Einige von Morphosis' wichtigsten Gebäuden s das Lawrence House (1981), das Kate Mantilini Restaurant in Beverly Hills (1986), das Cedar's Sinai Comprehensive Cancer Care Center, ebenfalls in Beverly Hills (19 die Crawford Residence in Montecito (1987–92) und das Yuzen Vintage Car Museum in West-Hollywood (Projekt, 1992), ferner die Blades Residence in Santa Barb Kalifornien (1992–97), und die Internationale Grundschule in Long Beach, Kalifornien (1997–99). Zu den neueren Projekten des Büros gehören das San Francisco Fe ral Building, das Student Recreation Center der University of Cincinnati, die NOAA Satellitenbetriebseinrichtung in Suitland, Maryland, und – vor der Auswahl Londor ein Entwurf für die Olympischen Spiele 2012 in New York. Thom Mayne hat 2005 den Pritzker-Preis gewonnen.

Le directeur de **MORPHOSIS**, Thom Mayne, né dans le Connecticut en 1944, est Bachelor of Architecture d'USC de la University of Southern California (19 et Master of Architecture d'Harvard (1978). Il a créé Morphosis en 1979 avec Michael Rotondi, parti par la suite créer sa propre agence, Roto. Il a enseigné à UCLA, H vard, Yale et SCI-Arc dont il est un des fondateurs. Parmi ses principales réalisations : Lawrence House (1981) ; Kati Mantilini Restaurant, Beverly Hills (1986) ; Ced Sinai Comprehensive Cancer Care Center, Beverly Hills (1987) ; Crawford Residence, Montecito (1987–92) ; le Yuzen Vintage Car Museum, West Hollywood, projet (199 ainsi que la Blades Residence, Santa Barbara, Californie (1992–97) et l'International Elementary School, Long Beach, Californie (1997–99). Plus récemment, il s consacré au San Francisco Federal Building ; à l'University of Cincinnati Student Recreation Center ; au centre opérationnel de satellites NOAA à Suitland (Maryland) une proposition pour les Jeux olympiques de 2012 à New York, avant le choix de Londres. Thom Mayne a remporté le prix Pritzker 2005.

CALTRANS DISTRICT 7 HEADQUARTERS

Los Angeles, California, USA, 2002–04

*Floor area: 69 677 m². Client: California Department of Transportation.
Cost: $170 million*

This large office building was erected for a cost of 170 million dollars. Located on South Main Street opposite City Hall close to Frank Gehry's Walt Disney Concert Hall and Arata Isozaki's MoCA, it is the new Headquarters for the California Department of Transportation (Caltrans) District 7, and serves 1850 Caltrans employ and 500 employees of the Los Angeles Department of Transportation. Awarded to Morphosis after a competition held in 2001, it is the first building to be commissioned under the State of California's Design Excellence Program. The building is L-shaped in plan, composed of two main volumes. The larger one is 13 stories high, 43 meters wide and 110 meters long, running from north to south. The secondary block is four stories high. The main exterior materials are an exposed galvanized steel struct and coated perforated aluminum panels. The design features an outdoor lobby and plaza, and a public art installation by Keith Sonnier. A super-graphic sign four stories high features the building's street address, "100." The architects have also been attentive to environmental concerns. As they explain, "The building's south glass façade is entirely screened with sunshade panels incorporating photovoltaic cells, an original system designed by Morphosis, Clark Construction and a team of special cor tants. The cells generate approximately 5% of the building's energy while shielding the façade from direct sunlight during peak summer hours, without obstructing spectacular views towards the city all the way to the ocean."

Das umgerechnet 141 Millionen Euro teure Bürogebäude ist die neue Zentrale der Verkehrsbehörde von Kalifornien (Caltrans). 1850 Mitarbeiter von Caltrans 500 Mitarbeiter der Verkehrsbehörde von Los Angeles arbeiten hier. Das Gebäude liegt an der South Main Street gegenüber dem Rathaus der Stadt, nicht weit entf von Frank Gehrys Walt Disney Concert Hall und Arata Isozakis MoCA. Morphosis wurde nach einem Wettbewerb 2001 mit dem Projekt betraut; das Gebäude ist das e das innerhalb des »Programms für herausragende Architektur des Bundesstaates Kalifornien« beauftragt wurde. Das L-förmige Gebäude besteht aus zwei Hauptbau pern. Der größere Flügel in Nord-Süd-Richtung hat 13 Geschosse, ist 43 m tief und 110 m lang. Der zweite Flügel ist viergeschossig. Die Außenfassaden sind durch sichtbare verzinkte Stahlkonstruktion und beschichtete, perforierte Aluminiumpaneele charakterisiert. Der öffentliche Raum umfasst eine Lobby und eine Plaza, außer eine Installation des Künstlers Keith Sonnier; die Hausnummer 100 wurde als vier Geschosse hohe »Supergrafik« gestaltet. Auch auf ökologische Aspekte legten die Ar tekten Wert. Sie erklären: »Die gesamte Südfassade ist von Sonnenschutzpaneelen mit Fotovoltaikzellen bedeckt. Das neuartige System wurde von Morphosis, Clark C struction und einem Team aus Spezialisten entwickelt. Die Zellen generieren ungefähr fünf Prozent des Energiebedarfs des Gebäudes und schützen die Fassade in Mittagszeit im Sommer vor direkter Sonneneinstrahlung, ohne die spektakuläre Sicht in Richtung Stadt und bis zum Pazifik zu behindern.«

Ce grand immeuble de bureaux a été construit pour un budget de 141 millions d'euros. Situé South Main Street, face à l'hôtel de ville et proche du Walt Dis Concert Hall de Frank Gehry et le du MoCA d'Arata Isozaki, il est le nouveau siège du Département des transports de Californie (Caltrans), District 7, et accueille 1 employés de ce département et 500 de celui des transports de Los Angeles. Contrat remporté par Morphosis après un concours organisé en 2001, c'est le prer immeuble commandé dans le cadre du programme d'excellence de l'État de Californie. L'immeuble en L se compose de deux volumes principaux. Le plus grand, or té nord-sud, mesure 110 m de long, 43 m de large et compte 13 niveaux. Le second en comporte quatre seulement. Les principaux matériaux des façades sont l'a galvanisé pour la structure, et l'aluminium perforé enduit pour les panneaux de l'habillage. L'ensemble comprend également une plaza, un accueil extérieur et une tallation artistique de l'artiste Keith Sonnier. Un signe graphique de quatre niveaux de haut rappelle le numéro de l'adresse de l'immeuble : « 100 ». Les architectes également été sensibles aux préoccupations environnementales. Comme ils l'expliquent, « la façade sud de l'immeuble, en verre, est entièrement doublée par des p neaux de protection solaire à cellules photovoltaïques, système original conçu par Morphosis, Clark Construction et une équipe de consultants. Ces cellules génèr environ 5% de l'énergie consommée par l'immeuble et protègent la façade des rayons solaires directs lors des heures d'ensoleillement maximum, sans obstruer spectaculaire vers la ville jusqu'à l'océan ».

the program undoubtedly required,
e Caltrans building appears to
quite simply massive in its urban
ntext.

s umfangreiche Raumprogramm
hrt dazu, dass das Caltrans-Gebäu-
in seiner städtischen Umgebung
hr massiv wirkt.

mme le programme l'exigeait sans
ute, l'immeuble Caltrans s'inscrit
sez massivement dans son contexte
bain.

With its jutting elements and band-
like openings, the building gives
a sense of dynamism that is not
evident when it is viewed from a
greater distance.

Mit seinen Auskragungen und horizontalen Öffnungen in der Fassade
wirkt das Gebäude aus der Nähe
dynamischer als aus größerer Entfer-
nung betrachtet.

Avec ses éléments en saillie et ses
ouvertures en bandeaux, l'immeuble
crée une certaine dynamique, même
si elle devient moins évidente dès
que l'on s'en éloigne.

has been the case in much of
m Mayne's work, the Caltrans
ding takes on a very definitely
lptural aspect through many of
design details.

viele andere Projekte von Thom
ne wird das Caltrans-Gebäude
einem dezidiert skulpturalen
atz geprägt, der sich in zahlrei-
n Entwurfsdetails zeigt.

me la plupart des réalisations
Thom Mayne, le Caltrans prend
allure vraiment sculpturale par
iais de multiples détails de sa
ception.

AlloCortex/All

MARCOS NOVAK

Marcos Novak
510 Venice Way
Venice, California 90291
USA

e-mail: marcos@centrifuge.org
Web: www.centrifuge.org/marcos

Born in Caracas, Venezuela, **MARCOS NOVAK** grew up in Greece and received a Bachelor of Science in Architecture, a Master of Architecture and a Certifi of Specialization in Computer-Aided Architecture from Ohio State University (Columbus, Ohio), completing his studies in 1983. He has worked as a Research Fellow the Center for Advanced Inquiry in the Interactive Arts at the University of Wales, as Co-Director of the Transarchitectures Foundation in Paris (with Paul Virilio). He numerous publications to his credit. His work has been essentially virtual, and he is regarded as the "pioneer of the architecture of virtuality" according to the organi of the 7th International Architecture Exhibition in Venice, in which he participated (Greek Pavilion). He is known for such projects as his "Sensor Space," "From Imn sion to Eversion," "Transmitting Architecture," "Liquid Architectures," and "Metadata Visualization." Marcos Novak has taught at Ohio State, University of Texas Austin, Architecture program at UCLA, the Digital Media program at UCLA, Art Center College of Art & Design, Pasadena, and is currently a professor at the University of C fornia Santa Barbara.

MARCOS NOVAK wurde in Caracas geboren und wuchs in Griechenland auf. Er hat einen Bachelor of Science in Architecture, einen Master of Architecture ein Zertifikat für Spezialwissen im Bereich CAD (Architektur) von der Ohio State University in Columbus, Ohio. 1983 schloss er sein Studium ab. Er war Forschur stipendiat am Center for Advanced Inquiry in the Interactive Arts der University of Wales und stellvertretender Leiter der Transarchitectures Foundation in Paris (mit I Virilio). Ferner hat er zahlreiche Beiträge veröffentlicht. Seine Projekte sind hauptsächlich virtuell. Von den Organisatoren der VII. Architekturbiennale in Venedig, an er mit dem Griechischen Pavillon teilnahm, wurde er als »Pionier der virtuellen Architektur« bezeichnet. Er ist bekannt durch Projekte wie das »Sensor Space«, »F Immersion to Eversion«, »Transmitting Architectures«, »Liquid Architectures« und »Metadata Visualisation«. Marcos Novak hat an der Ohio State University und an der versity of Texas, Austin, unterrichtet, und war außerdem beim »Architecture Program« und »Digital Media Program« an der UCLA und am Art Center College of Desig Pasadena tätig. Er ist Professor an der University of California (Santa Barbara).

Né à Caracas, Venezuela, **MARCOS NOVAK** a été élevé en Grèce et a étudié à l'Ohio State University (Columbus, Ohio) où il obtenu son Bachelor of Scienc Architecture, son Master of Architecture et un certificat de spécialisation en CAA (conception architecturale assistée par ordinateur, 1983). Il a travaillé comme cherch au Center for Advanced Inquiry in the Alternative Arts de l'Université du Pays de Galles et a dirigé (avec Paul Virilio) la Fondation Transarchitectures à Paris. beaucoup publié. Ses œuvres sont essentiellement virtuelles et il est considéré comme le « pionnier de l'architecture de la virtualité » selon les organisateurs de la Biennale d'architecture de Venise à laquelle il a participé (pavillon grec). Il est connu pour des projets comme son « Sensor Space », « From Immersion to Eversic « Transmitting Architecture », « Liquid Architectures » et « Metadata Visualisation ». Marcos Novak a enseigné à l'Ohio State University (Columbus), à l'University of Te (Austin), l'Architecture Program de UCLA, le Digital Media Program de UCLA, à l'Art Center College of Art & Design de Pasadena. Il est actuellement professeur à l' versité de Californie Santa Barbara.

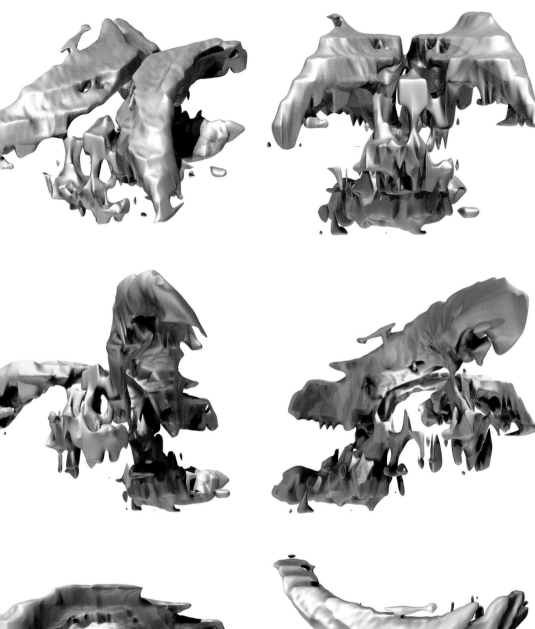

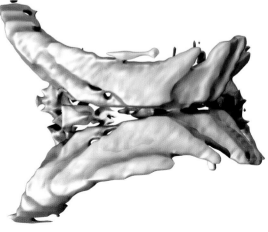

ALLOCORTEX / ALLONEURO

2005

Floor area: 34 000 m². Client: Silken Group. Cost: not disclosed

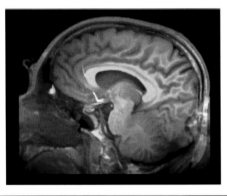

It may be no coincidence that forms derived from Novak's brain scans seem to take on a Surreal appearance when they approach what might be called an architectural presentation (images below).

Wahrscheinlich ist es kein Zufall, dass die Formen, die Novak aus Tomografien seines Gehirns entwickelte, einen surrealen Ausdruck annehmen, wenn sie ein Stadium erreicht haben, das man als Präsentation von Architektur im weiteren Sinn bezeichnen könnte (unten).

Ce n'est sans doute pas une coïncidence si des formes dérivées d'images issues du propre cerveau de Novak prennent un aspect surréaliste lorsqu'elles se rapprochent de ce que l'on pourrait qualifier de présentation architecturale (photo ci-dessous).

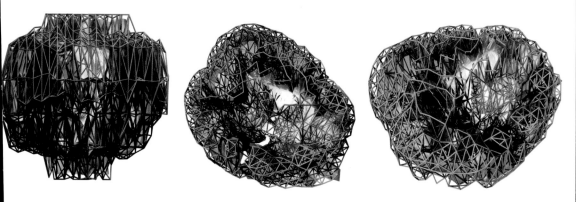

The idea that science, architecture and art can be united, not in a superficial way, but in their most fundamental manifestations, drives the creative impulse of Marcos Novak.

Die Vorstellung, dass Wissenschaft, Architektur und Kunst miteinander verbunden werden können – nicht oberflächlich, sondern in ihren grundlegenden Äußerungen – ist der kreative Antrieb für Novaks Projekte.

L'idée que la science, l'architecture et l'art peuvent s'unir, non de manière superficielle, mais dans leurs manifestations les plus fondamentales, anime la pulsion créative de Marcos Novak.

Working with sMRI and fMRI (structural and functional magnetic resonance imaging) of his own brain, scanned "in the act of observing the algorithmically gene-rated spaces and forms," Novak used the data representing tissue near the corpus callosum to devise "the elements of architectural language." As he points out, the construct thus imagined has a legitimacy because it is literally born of his own brain, in the figurative and literal senses. Nor is the result simply a reproduction of brain structures – it is an interpretation given that the data can be "smoothed and refined" in various ways. Novak says that in related work, "the *AlloNeuroSpace* sequence moves toward a rendition of the brain as a virtual environment, increasingly emphasizing an atmospheric reading of the data and the spatial and formal character implied therein. This work recalls Kazimir Malevich's Suprematist manifesto *The Non-Objective World*, in which he states that while the goal of Suprematist abstraction is pure feeling, even in representational work what is valuable is not the accuracy of resemblance, but rather the feeling that is evoked, in the same abstract sense as that of Suprematist painting. In this case, the attempt is to take literally objective scientific data, but not to yield to that objectivity as far as the experiencing of those data is concerned, but to draw from them the very same kind of abstract feeling that Malevich describes." As unexpected as a reference to Suprematist painting is in this con-text, it is clear that Novak is above all creating bridges between different disciplines in a process that will surely enrich the future of architecture.

Mithilfe von sMRI und fMRI (strukturelle und functional magnetic resonance imaging) ließ Marcos Novak Bilder seines eigenen Gehirns erstellen, »um algorithmisch gene-rierte Räume und Formen zu betrachten«. Diese Daten, die das Gewebe in der Nähe des Corpus Callosum darstellen, benutzte er zur Schaffung von »Elementen der archi-tektonischen Sprache«. Er weist darauf hin, dass das so entwickelte Konstrukt legitim ist, da es im übertragenen und im wörtlichen Sinn seinem eigenen Gehirn ent-stammt. Das Ergebnis ist nicht einfach nur die Reproduktion von Bildern von Gehirnstrukturen, sondern eine Interpretation, da die Daten auf verschiedene Arten »geglättet und verfeinert« werden können. Novak sagt, dass in ähnlichen Projekten »die AlloNeuro-Raumsequenz sich in Richtung einer Interpretation des Gehirns als eine virtu-elle Umgebung bewegt und dabei verstärkt ein atmosphärisches Lesen der Daten und der darin implizierten räumlichen und formalen Eigenschaften betont. Dieses Projekt erinnert an Kasimir Malewitschs Suprematistisches Manifest *Die gegenstandslose Welt*, in dem er feststellte, dass neben der suprematistischen Abstraktion, die das reine Gefühl erreichen will, auch in abbildenden Arbeiten das Wichtige nicht die Genauigkeit der Abbildung ist, sondern das Gefühl, das hervorgerufen wird – im gleichen abs-trakten Sinn wie in der suprematistischen Malerei. Der Versuch besteht darin, tatsächlich objektive wissenschaftliche Daten zu verwenden, aber nicht um deren Objekti-vität einzugestehen, was das Erleben dieser Daten betrifft, sondern um mit ihnen genau dasselbe abstrakte Gefühl zu erzeugen, das Malewitsch beschreibt.« Die Refe-renz zur suprematistischen Malerei kommt in diesem Kontext unerwartet. Klar ist aber, dass es Novak vor allem darum geht, in einen Prozess, der die Zukunft der Architektur sicherlich bereichern wird, Brücken zwischen verschiedenen Disziplinen zu schlagen.

À l'aide d'images de son cerveau obtenues par sMRI et fMRI (imagerie par résonance magnétique structurelle et fonctionnelle) « pendant qu'il observait des volumes et des espaces générés par algorithmes », Novak s'est servi de données représentant le tissu cellulaire proche du corps calleux pour mettre au point « les élé-ments d'un langage architectural ». Comme il le fait remarquer, la construction ainsi imaginée possède sa légitimité car elle est, littéralement, née de son propre cer-veau, au sens tant littéral que figuré. Le résultat n'est pas pour autant une simple reproduction des structures cérébrales, il s'agit d'une interprétation puisque les don-nées obtenues peuvent être « arrangées et affinées » de diverses façons. Marcos Novak explique que, dans sa recherche intitulée *AlloNeuroSpace*, « la séquence s'oriente vers un rendu du cerveau comparable à un environnement virtuel, s'attachant de plus en plus à une lecture atmosphérique des données et du caractère formel et spa-tial qu'il implique. Ce travail rappelle le manifeste suprématiste de Kazimir Malévitch, *Le Monde non-objectif*, dans lequel il déclarait que, si le but de l'abstraction supré-matiste était bien le sentiment pur, ce qui comptait dans le monde de la représentation n'était pas la précision de la ressemblance mais plutôt le sentiment évoqué, dans le même sens abstrait que celui de la peinture suprématiste. Ici, la tentative est de prendre littéralement des données scientifiques objectives mais, au lieu de se conten-ter de cette objectivité … d'en tirer le type de sentiment abstrait décrit par Malévitch ». Aussi surprenante que soit la référence à ce type de peinture, il est clair que Novak cherche avant tout à créer des passerelles entre différentes disciplines à travers un processus qui enrichira certainement l'architecture de demain.

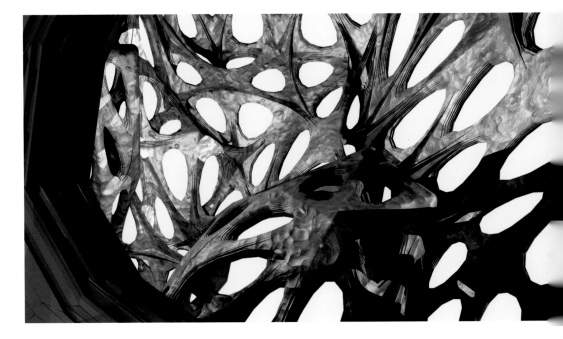

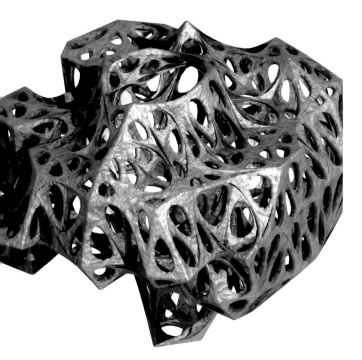

On occasion, Novak's explorations take on shapes that are more readily identifiable as having been derived from the structure of the brain.

Manchmal ist der Ausgangspunkt für Novaks Forschungsarbeit, das menschliche Gehirn, auch leichter zu erkennen.

Parfois, les explorations de Novak prennent des formes dont l'origine cérébrale est plus évidente.

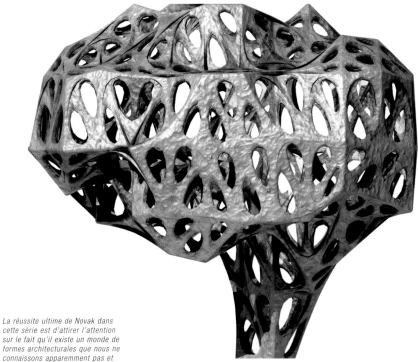

e ultimate achievement of Novak his series is to call attention to fact that there is an entire world architectural form that is unlike we have ever seen, and yet ch has an intimate relationship he way we are ... inside.

ztlich besteht Novaks Leistung bei ser Reihe darin, die Aufmerksam- t darauf zu lenken, dass es eine hitektonische Formenwelt gibt, die h gänzlich von der uns bekannten erscheidet. Diese Formenwelt ht in enger Beziehung zum Men- en und seinem »Innenleben«.

La réussite ultime de Novak dans cette série est d'attirer l'attention sur le fait qu'il existe un monde de formes architecturales que nous ne connaissons apparemment pas et qui, pourtant, est intimement lié à la façon dont nous sommes ... faits.

JOHN PAWSON

John Pawson
Unit B
70–78 York Way
London N1 9AG
UK

Tel: +44 20 78 37 29 29
Fax: +44 20 78 37 49 49
e-mail: email@johnpawson.com
Web: www.johnpawson.com

Monastery of Novy [

Born in Halifax in central England in 1949, **JOHN PAWSON** attended Eton and worked in his own family's textile mill before going to Japan for four years. On hi return, he studied at the AA in London and set up his own firm in 1981. His has worked on numerous types of project including the flagship store for Calvin Klein in Nev York, airport lounges for Cathay Pacific airlines at the Chek Lap Kok Airport in Hong Kong, and a small apartment for the author Bruce Chatwin. Pawson may be eve better known to the general public because of his 1996 book *Minimum* that focused on such essential subjects as light, structure, ritual, landscape and volume. Becaus of this book, but also because of his style, Pawson has come to be considered an essential figure in the minimalist style of recent years. Some of his current work includes Delafontaine House, Knokke, Belgium (2003); Taira House, Okinawa (2003); Lansdowne Lodge Apartments, Grainger Trust, London (2003); Radcliffe Museum, Bury Coun cil, Bury, UK (2004); Calvin Klein Apartment, New York (2003); and The Young Vic Theatre, London. He also worked on the Hotel Puerta América in Madrid.

JOHN PAWSON, geboren 1949 in Halifax in Mittelengland, war Schüler in Eton und arbeitete in der Textilfabrik seiner Familie, bevor er für vier Jahre nach Japa ging. Danach studierte er an der Architectural Association in London und gründete 1981 sein eigenes Büro. Er hat ganz unterschiedliche Projekte realisiert, so z. B. de Flagship Store für Calvin Klein in New York, Flughafenlounges für Cathay Pacific Airlines im Chek Lap Kok Flughafen in Hongkong sowie ein kleines Apartment für de Autor Bruce Chatwin. Noch bekannter ist Pawson der Öffentlichkeit vielleicht durch sein Buch *Minimum*, das 1996 veröffentlicht wurde und sich mit Grundelementen w Licht, Struktur, Ritual, Landschaft und Volumen befasst. Wegen dieses Buches, aber auch wegen seines architektonischen Stils, wurde Pawson in den letzten Jahren z einer Schlüsselfigur des Minimalismus. Neuere Projekte von ihm sind u. a. das Haus Delafontaine in Knokke, Belgien (2003), das Haus Taira in Okinawa (2003), die Lans downe Lodge Apartments des Grainger Trust in London (2003), das Radcliffe Museum für das Bury Council in Bury, England (2004), ferner ein Apartment für Calvin Kle in New York (2003) und The Young Vic Theatre in London. Auch am Hotel Puerta América in Madrid war er beteiligt.

Né à Halifax en Angleterre en 1949, **JOHN PAWSON**, après des études à Eton, a travaillé dans l'usine textile familiale avant de séjourner quatre ans au Japo À son retour, il a étudié à l'Architectural Association de Londres et créé son agence en 1981. Il a travaillé sur de nombreux types de projets, dont le magasin princip de Calvin Klein à New York (1995), les salons du nouvel aéroport de Hong Kong pour Cathay Pacific (1998) et un petit appartement pour l'écrivain Bruce Chatwin (198 Le grand public le connaît sans doute plus grâce au succès de son livre, *Minimum* (1996), sur les thèmes de la lumière, de la structure, du rituel, du paysage et du vo me. À la suite de ce livre, mais aussi parce que c'est son style, Pawson a été considéré comme une figure essentielle du minimalisme contemporain. Parmi ses réalis tions récentes : Maison Delafontaine (Knokke, Belgique, 2003, chantier en cours) ; Taira House (Okinawa, 2003, en cours) ; immeuble d'appartements de Lansdow Lodge, Grainger Trust, Londres (2004) ; Radcliffe Museum (Bury, Royaume-Uni, 2004, en cours) ; appartement de Calvin Klein, New York (2005) et le Young Vic Theat Londres. Il a également collaboré aux aménagements de l'Hotel Puerta América à Madrid.

MONASTERY OF NOVY DVÛR

Toužim, Czech Republic, 2004

*Floor Area: 70m x 70m (4900 m²) Client: Monastery of Saint Lieu Sept-Fons.
Cost: not disclosed*

John Pawson was asked to work on a new monastery by French Cistercian monks in 1999. The site they had selected was a 100-hectare estate located west of Prague, with an18th century manor house that had been uninhabited for forty years. The monks were familiar with Pawson's book *Minimum* and had seen images of his Calvin Klein store in Manhattan before selecting him. Pawson, who has called the **NOVY DVÛR MONASTERY** "the project of a lifetime," recalls that the "monastic cloister has been likened to an enclosed city, with many sub-programs typically including the functions of church, home, office, school, workshop, guesthouse, hospital and farm." Basing his own 6500 m² scheme on the blueprint drawn up in the 12th century for the Cistercian Order's buildings by Saint Bernard of Clairvaux, which called for simple, pared-down spaces and a respect for light and correct proportions, Pawson restored the baroque manor house and added three wings of new architecture along the lines of pre-existing structures. Pawson was familiar with the Abbaye du Thoronet, a Cistercian abbey located between Draguignan and Brignoles in southern France, but this was the first time he designed a religious building. He explains, "I didn't have to adapt my style particularly. I'd already read Saint Bernard's rules [the Apologia of 1127, against artistic adornment], so the ideas all made sense to me." The challenge of the project as he explains was to design the monastery so that the very precise movements and rituals of the monks could be carried out without hindrance. "The church," he concludes, "had to make praying easier – to bring calm and pleasure – but also to be stimulating without being distracting."

1999 beauftragten französische Zisterziensermönche John Pawson mit der Planung eines neuen Klosters. Als Standort hatten sich die Mönche ein 100 ha großes Grundstück westlich von Prag ausgesucht, mit einem Herrenhaus aus dem 18. Jahrhundert, das 40 Jahre lang nicht bewohnt worden war. Sie kannten Pawsons Buch *Minimum* und hatten Bilder seines Apartments für Calvin Klein in Manhattan gesehen, bevor sie ihn als Architekten auswählten. Pawson, der das **KLOSTER NOVY DVÛR** »das Projekt seines Lebens« nennt, erwähnt, dass ein »Mönchskloster mit einer in sich abgeschlossenen Stadt verglichen wird, mit vielen ›Unterprogrammen‹, die typischerweise Funktionen wie Kirche, Wohnraum, Büro, Schule, Werkstatt, Gästehaus, Krankenhaus und Bauernhof beinhalten.« Pawsons 6500 m² umfassender Entwurf basiert auf einer Zeichnung aus dem 12. Jahrhundert, die der heilige Bernhard von Clairvaux für die Gebäude des Zisterzienserordens anfertigte. Er sah einfache Räume mit natürlicher Beleuchtung und stimmigen Proportionen vor. Pawson setzte das barocke Herrenhaus instand und fügte drei moderne Flügel an, die sich exakt dort befinden, wo bereits früher Gebäude standen. Die Abbaye du Thoronet, eine Zisterzienserabtei zwischen Draguignan und Brignoles in Südfrankreich, war Pawson bekannt; aber zum ersten Mal hat er selbst ein Gebäude mit einer religiösen Funktion entworfen. Er erläutert: »Ich musste meinen Stil nicht besonders anpassen. Ich hatte schon vorher die Regeln des heiligen Bernhard gelesen (die Apologie von 1127 gegen künstlerische Verzierung), daher fand ich die Ideen alle sehr einleuchtend.« Die Herausforderung des Projekts, so Pawson, bestand darin, das Kloster so zu entwerfen, dass die präzisen Ordensregeln und Rituale der Mönche ohne Behinderungen ausgeführt werden können. »Die Kirche«, sagt er abschließend, »sollte das Beten vereinfachen – sie sollte Ruhe und Freude vermitteln – aber sie sollte auch anregend wirken ohne abzulenken.«

C'est en 1999 que des moines cisterciens français ont demandé à John Pawson de les aider à édifier un nouveau monastère dans un domaine de cent hectares à l'ouest de Prague, sur lequel s'élevait un manoir du XVIIIe siècle, inhabité depuis plus de quarante ans. Les religieux connaissaient bien l'ouvrage *Minimum* et avaient vu des photos du magasin Calvin Klein à Manhattan avant de le sélectionner. Pawson, pour lequel cette commande est « le projet de [sa] vie », rappelle que « le monastère a été comparé à une ville fermée, remplissant les multiples fonctions d'église, de foyer, de bureaux, d'école, d'ateliers, de maison d'hôtes, d'hôpital et de ferme » Appuyant son projet de 6500 m² sur les recommandations établies au XIIe siècle pour les bâtiments de l'Ordre par saint Bernard de Clairvaux, qui voulait des espaces simples et épurés ainsi que le respect de la lumière et de proportions correctes, Pawson a restauré le manoir baroque et lui a ajouté trois ailes sur les traces d'anciennes constructions. Il connaissait bien l'abbaye du Thoronet, ensemble cistercien situé non loin de Draguignan et Brignoles dans le Midi de la France, mais c'était la première fois qu'il devait concevoir un édifice religieux : « Je n'ai pas eu à adapter particulièrement mon style. J'avais déjà lu la règle de saint Bernard [l'Apologie de la vie monastique de 1127 contre l'ornement artistique], aussi toutes ces idées avaient-elles déjà un sens pour moi. » Le défi était dès lors de concevoir un monastère dans lequel les mouvements et les rituels précis des moines pouvaient se dérouler sans la moindre gêne. « L'église, » conclut-il, « devait favoriser la prière – apporter le calme et le plaisir – mais également être stimulante sans pour autant distraire. »

Pawson's careful study of the functions of the Monastery ultimately led him to create simple forms that do not contradict those of the existing buildings on the site.

Pawsons genaue Analyse der funktionalen Abläufe im Kloster führte letztlich zu den einfachen Formen, die mit dem Bestehenden harmonieren.

L'étude approfondie des fonctions du monastère a finalement incité Pawson à créer des formes simples qui ne heurtent pas celles des bâtiments préexistants.

Passageways and patterns of light
are the most obvious traces of architecture in these images, where all
extraneous intervention has been set
aside.

Die Wege und die Lichtführung sind
die deutlichsten Spuren einer
Architektur, die jede unwesentliche
Intervention vermeidet.

Des passages et des effets de lumière sont les traces d'architecture les
plus évidentes dans ces images dont
toute intervention extérieure semble
avoir été exclue.

Pawson's work shows that there is
nothing that prohibits centuries-old
traditions from being served by contemporary architecture.

Pawsons Projekt zeigt, dass auch
zeitgenössische Architektur im
Dienst jahrhundertealter Tradition
stehen kann.

Le projet de Pawson montre que
même l'architecture contemporaine
peut être au service d'une tradition
séculaire.

An occasional liturgical object or
piece of wooden furniture enters t
realm of light and worship. Pawso.
has sought and surely found some
thing of the quintessence of archi
ture in Novy Dvůr.

Ein liturgisches Objekt oder ein ei
zelnes Möbelstück aus Holz findet
sich in diesem Reich des Lichtes ι
der Anbetung. Pawson hat in Novy
Dvůr etwas von der Quintessenz v
Architektur gesucht und sicher au
gefunden.

De temps à autre, un objet liturgi
ou un meuble en bois fait son app
tion dans ce lieu de lumière et de
prière. À Novy Dvůr, Pawson a che
ché et certainement trouvé quelqu
chose qui se rapproche de la quin
tessence de l'architecture.

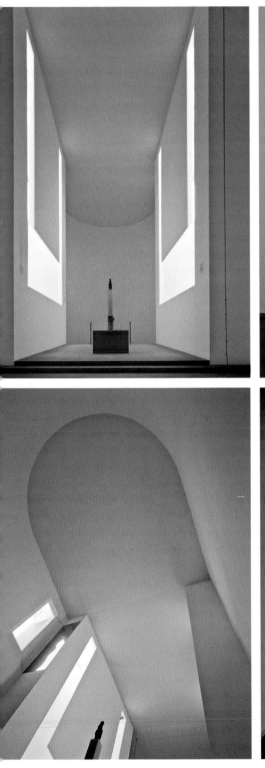

PHILIPPE RAHM

Philippe Rahm architectes
12, rue Chabanais
75002 Paris
France

Tel: +33 149 26 91 55
e-mail: info@philipperahm.com
Web: www.philipperahm.com

PHILIPPE RAHM was born in 1967 and studied architecture at the EPFL in Lausanne and the ETH in Zurich, graduating in 1993. He created the firm Décos & Rahm associés with Gilles Décosterd in 1995 in Lausanne. They won a number of competitions in Switzerland and participated in numerous exhibitions in Europe the United States and later, in Japan. Amongst these were the 2003 Biennal de Valencia, Spain; and Archilab, Orléans, France, 2000. Their work presented at the Kitakyushu (2004) was called *Ghost Flat*, a three-room apartment "constructed" out of light rather than more conventional materials. All of the rooms occupy the sa dimensions of space and time, but each occupies a separate part of the electromagnetic spectrum. Depending on which part of the spectrum you select, you see a ferent set of furnishings in front of you. The bedroom appears between 400 and 500 nanometers, the living room between 600 and 800 nanometers, etc. Décoste Rahm represented Switzerland in the 2002 Venice Architecture Biennale, and then received the Swiss Federal Art Prize in 2003. They worked on an atelier-residence the artist Fabrice Hybert in the Vendée region of France, and on a project for a park in San Sebastián, Spain with the landscape architects Gilles Clément and Jos Andeuza. Rahm and Déscosterd ceased direct collaboration in 2005 and Philppe Rahm created his own firm, Philippe Rahm architectes in Paris.

PHILIPPE RAHM wurde 1967 geboren und studierte an der EPFL in Lausanne und an der ETH in Zürich Architektur. 1993 machte er sein Diplom. Zusam mit Gilles Décosterd gründete er 1995 in Lausanne das Büro Décosterd & Rahm associés. Das Büro hat in der Schweiz eine Reihe von Wettbewerben gewonnen und zahlreichen Ausstellungen in Europa, den USA und in Japan teilgenommen, 2000 z. B. an der Archilab in Orléans, Frankreich, und 2003 an der Biennale in Valencia. 2 wurde ihr Projekt *Ghost Flat* auf der CCA Kitakyushu gezeigt: eine Dreizimmerwohnung, die nicht aus konventionellen Materialien, sondern aus Licht »konstruiert« Alle Räume sind räumlich und zeitlich gesehen gleich groß, jeder nimmt jedoch einen anderen Teil des elektromagnetischen Spektrums ein. Je nach dem, welchen des Spektrums man auswählt, sieht man ein anderes Mobiliar vor sich. Das Schlafzimmer erscheint zwischen 400 und 500 Nanometern, das Wohnzimmer zwischen und 800 Nanometern usw. Décosterd & Rahm repräsentierten die Schweiz 2002 auf der Architekturbiennale in Venedig und erhielten 2003 den Schweizer Kunstp Sie haben ein Atelier-Wohnhaus für den Künstler Fabrice Hybert im Departement Vendée in Frankreich geplant und, in Zusammenarbeit mit den Landschaftsplanern les Clément und Joseph Andeuza, ein Projekt für einen Park im baskischen San Sebastián. Rahm hat 2005 die Partnerschaft mit Décosterd aufgegeben und ein Büro in Paris eröffnet.

Né en 1967, **PHILIPPE RAHM** a fait ses études d'architecture à l'EPFL (Lausanne) et à l'ETH (Zurich). Il a créé l'agence Décosterd & Rahm Associés avec G Décosterd à Lausanne en 1995. Ensemble, ils ont remporté un certain nombre de concours en Suisse et participé à de nombreuses expositions en Europe, dont la B nale de Valence en Espagne (2003) et Archilab à Orléans, France (2000), aux États-Unis, puis au Japon. Leur œuvre présentée au CCA Kitakyushu en 2004, bapt *Ghost Flat*, était un appartement de quatre pièces «construit» à partir de la lumière plutôt que de matériaux plus conventionnels. Toutes les pièces occupaient la mé surface au même moment, mais chacune n'était visible que dans une fraction précise du spectre électromagnétique. Selon la zone sélectionnée, on pouvait voir a surgir différents types de mobilier. La chambre apparaissait entre 400 et 500 nanomètres, le séjour entre 600 et 800, etc. Décosterd & Rahm ont représenté la Su à la Biennale d'architecture de Venise en 2002 et reçu le prix fédéral d'art suisse en 2003. Ils ont conçu un atelier-résidence pour l'artiste Fabrice Hybert en Ven (France) et un projet de parc à San Sebastian (Espagne) avec les architectes paysagistes Gilles Clément et Joseph Andueza. Rahm et Décosterd ont cessé leur colla ration en 2005 et Philippe Rahm s'est installé à Paris.

VACATION RESIDENCES

Vassivière, Limousin, France, 2005

Floor area: 70 houses, 70 m² each. Client: SYMIVA (Syndicat mixte interdépartemental et régional de Vassivière).
Cost: not disclosed

The basic idea of this project is to create a relationship between interior space and humidity. By pushing this idea to its limit, Philippe Rahm points out that equipment of the house, and even its form is determined by its relation to internal humidity. The residents themselves of course produce a certain amount of humid and their use of warm water for bathing or cooking does as well. Rather than simply accepting the idea that humidity must be dealt with by ventilating interior spac Rahm experiments with different degrees of water content in the air, ranging from a desert-like 20% to 100%. Thus the sauna and clothes-drying area has a rela humidity of 0% to 30%; a bedroom and office varies between 30% and 60%; the bathroom, kitchen and living room from 60% to 90%, and the swimming pool area 100% relative humidity. By recognizing the role of humidity in comfort and the very sensations of a living space, Rahm experiments here with fundamentals that are u ally swept aside or ignored, allowing them to actually dictate the shape or appearance of the architecture, as well as its inner workings. He has done the same in ot projects by manipulating light or oxygen content in the air, as was the case in the *Hormonorium* (Swiss Pavilion, Architecture Biennale 8, Venice, 2002).

Grundidee des Projekts ist die Schaffung einer Beziehung zwischen Innenraum und Luftfeuchtigkeit. Philippe Rahm treibt diese Idee auf die Spitze und verwe darauf, dass die Ausstattung des Hauses und sogar seine Form durch die Beziehung zur Luftfeuchtigkeit im Innenraum bestimmt werden. Ebenso wie durch ih Verbrauch von warmem Wasser zum Baden oder Kochen, erzeugen die Bewohner des Hauses natürlich auch selbst eine gewisse Luftfeuchtigkeit. Rahm akzeptiert n einfach die Vorstellung, dass man die Feuchtigkeit durch eine Belüftung der Innenräume regulieren muss, sondern experimentiert mit einem unterschiedlichen Feuch keitsgehalt der Luft, der von 20 Prozent – also einem Wüstenklima – bis 100 Prozent reicht. Die Sauna und der Trockenraum für die Wäsche haben eine relative L feuchte von bis zu 30 Prozent, im Schlafzimmer und Büro liegt sie bei 30 bis 60 Prozent, im Badezimmer, in der Küche und im Wohnzimmer bei 60 bis 90 Prozent im Schwimmbadbereich bei 100 Prozent. Indem er die Bedeutung der Luftfeuchtigkeit für den Komfort sowie die grundlegenden Wahrnehmungen in einem Wohnhau den Mittelpunkt stellt, experimentiert Rahm mit Grundlagen, die normalerweise beiseite geschoben oder ignoriert werden und erlaubt ihnen, die Form und das Ausse der Architektur und ihr inneres Funktionieren zu bestimmen. Bei anderen Projekten ging er ebenso vor: Beim *Hormonorium*, dem Schweizer Pavillon auf der VIII. Arc tekturbiennale 2002 in Venedig, veränderte er z. B. den Licht- oder Sauerstoffgehalt der Luft.

L'idée de base de ce projet est de créer une relation entre l'espace intérieur et son hygrométrie. En poussant cette idée jusqu'à ses limites, Philippe Rahm allé jusqu'à déterminer l'équipement de la maison et même sa forme, à partir de leurs relations avec l'humidité interne. Les résidents produisent une certaine quan d'humidité, en utilisant l'eau chaude pour se laver ou préparer les repas, par exemple. Plutôt que de se contenter de la solution classique – traiter l'humidité par la v tilation – Rahm expérimente divers taux d'hygrométrie, des 20% de l'atmosphère du désert jusqu'à 100%. Ainsi, la zone du sauna et du séchage du linge et des vê ments présente une humidité relative de 0 à 30%, la chambre et le bureau de 30 à 60%, la salle de bains, la cuisine et le séjour de 60 à 90% et la piscine de 100 En prenant en compte le rôle de l'humidité dans le confort et les sensations que génère un lieu de vie, Rahm joue ici sur des principes essentiels, mais généralem négligés ou ignorés, et leur permet de dicter la forme ou l'aspect de l'architecture et de son aménagement intérieur. Il a fait de même dans d'autres projets où il ma pulait la lumière ou l'oxygène, comme dans son *Hormonorium*, Pavillon suisse, Biennale d'architecture de Venise (2002).

Rahm images a sequence of 70 vacation houses conceived along lines that have as much to do with physiology as with architecture in the more traditional sense of the word. His computer images evoke a world of water, not unlike that which might be found in a video game.

Rahm stellt sich eine Reihe aus 70 Ferienhäusern vor. Die Linie, an der entlang die Häuser angeordnet sind, hat mit Physiologie ebenso viel zu tun wie mit Architektur im klassischen Sinn. Die Computergrafiken zeigen eine Wasserwelt, die der Welt in einem Videospiel ähnelt.

Rahm a imaginé une séquence de 70 maisons de vacances conçues selon des principes qui empruntent autant à la physiologie qu'à l'architecture, au sens le plus traditionnel du terme. Ses images de synthèse évoquent un monde aquatique peu différent d'un jeu vidéo.

THOMAS ROSZAK

Thomas Roszak Architecture
PO Box 8528
Northfield, Illinois 60093
USA

Tel: +1 847 410 5553
Fax: +1 847 716 7377
e-mail: thomas@roszakadc.com
Web: www.roszakadc.com

Glass

Born in 1967, **THOMAS ROSZAK** graduated from the Illinois Institute of Technology College of Architecture in Chicago in 1989, and went to work for his pro‐ sor, David Hovey, who had an architectural firm called Optima that developed and built condominiums. He was second in command in Hovey's firm within five years of arrival. At 29, he left to become vice president of Focus Development, also a condominium developer. He created his own architecture, development, and construc firm, Roszak/ADC, in 1997. Since that date the firm has built over 600 million dollars in condominium and mixed-use projects, as well as commercial design/build "special projects" like the house Roszak designed for himself (published here). Recent work includes 601 S. Wells, Chicago, Illinois, a 31-story high-rise, 238 unit c dominium project including retail space in the South Loop of downtown Chicago; and Sienna, Evanston, Illinois, a four-building, 237-unit condominium and town ho community in the heart of downtown Evanston.

THOMAS ROSZAK, geboren 1967, machte 1989 am College of Architecture des Illinois Institute of Technology in Chicago seinen Abschluss. Anschließend ar‐ tete er für das Architekturbüro Optima seines Professors David Hovey. Bereits nach fünf Jahren war er Leiter des Büros, das sich mit der Entwicklung und dem Bau Eigentumswohnungen befasste. Mit 29 Jahren wurde er stellvertretender Leiter von Focus Development, ebenfalls ein Bauträger für Eigentumswohnungen. 1997 gr dete er Roszak/ADC, Architekturbüro, Entwicklungsträger und Baufirma in einem. Seitdem hat das Büro Eigentumswohnungen und gemischt genutzte Gebäude mit ein Auftragsvolumen von umgerechnet knapp 500 Millionen Euro realisiert. Dazu kommen Geschäftsgebäude und Sonderprojekte wie das hier gezeigte Haus, das Roszak sich und seine Familie baute. Neue Projekte von ihm sind u. a. 601 S. Wells in Chicago, ein 31-geschossiges Hochhaus mit 238 Eigentumswohnungen und Laden‐ zung im South Loop im Zentrum von Chicago und Sienna, ein Komplex aus vier Gebäuden mit 237 Eigentumswohnungen im Zentrum von Evanston, Illinois.

Né en 1967, **THOMAS ROSZAK** est diplômé de l'Illinois Institute of Technology College of Architecture, Chicago (1989) et a débuté en travaillant pour son ‐ fesseur, David Hover, dont l'agence, Optima, construisait des immeubles de logements dont elle assurait la promotion. Cinq ans après son arrivée, il était directeur adj de cette agence et, à 29 ans, devint vice-président de Focus Developement, autre promoteur immobilier. Il a créé en 1997 sa propre agence de promotion immobil et d'architecture, Roszak/ADC, qui a déjà réalisé pour presque 500 millions d'euros d'immeubles d'appartements, de projets mixtes logements-commerces et de « p jets spéciaux » comme la maison que l'architecte s'est construite, publiée ici. Parmi ses récentes réalisations : la maison 601 S. Welles une tour de 30 étages comp nant 238 appartements en copropriété et des commerces dans la South Loop en centre-ville (Chicago, Illinois) et un ensemble de 237 appartements et maisons de ‐ au centre d'Evanston, Illinois.

GLASS HOUSE

Northfield, Illinois, USA, 2002

Floor area: 550 m². Client: Thomas and Justyna Roszak.
Cost: $1.5 million

This 550 m² home located on a half-hectare lot contains five bedrooms, four bathrooms, a library, exercise room, yoga room and garage. Surrounded by tra tional Tudor-style houses, Roszak's home is entirely clad in glass but surrounded by forty pines and twenty birch trees, planted "according to Chinese and Japanese g den principles." Symmetrical on a north-south axis, the house is aligned on a strict grid, making it look "as though it was constructed with transparent Legos" accord to the architect. Most of the rooms are 4.88 meters square. Roszak says, "As a nod to Japanese design; the skeleton of steel support beams glides over the concr frame. A concrete shear wall in the center of the home bears most of the load." He further emphasizes that the extreme transparency of the house has not kept it fr being extremely energy efficient. Passive solar heating and radiant floor heating keep the house comfortable. The Roszak residence may have some points in comm with David Hovey's Modular Steel House (Winnetka, Illinois, 1998), but it is certainly a masterful early work by an architect who is not yet forty.

Das 550 m² große Wohnhaus des Architekten auf einem 0,5 ha großen Grundstück hat u. a. fünf Schlafzimmer, vier Badezimmer, eine Bibliothek, einen T ningsraum, einen Yogaraum und eine Garage. Im Gegensatz zu den Häusern der Nachbarschaft im traditionellen Tudorstil ist Roszaks Haus vollständig verglast, dafür a von 40 Pinien und 20 Birken umgeben, die »nach chinesischen und japanischen Prinzipien des Gartenbaus gepflanzt wurden«. Ein strenges Raster mit einer Symmet achse in Nord-Süd-Richtung bestimmt das Haus, das aussieht »als ob es aus transparenten Legosteinen gebaut wurde«, so der Architekt. Die meisten Räume mes 4,88 x 4,88 m. Roszak erläutert: »Als Verbeugung vor der japanischen Architektur kragen die Stahlträger über die Stahlbetonkonstruktion aus. Eine Wandscheibe in Mitte des Hauses nimmt den größten Teil der Lasten auf.« Er betont außerdem, dass die extreme Transparenz des Hauses nichts an dem sehr niedrigen Energiebec des Hauses ändert. Passive Solarwärme und eine Fußbodenheizung sorgen dafür, dass das Haus angenehm temperiert ist. Das Roszak-Haus mag mit David Hoveys Mo lar Steel House (Winnetka, Illinois, 1998) einiges gemein haben, für einen noch nicht 40-jährigen Architekten handelt es sich aber zweifellos um ein außerordentlic Frühwerk.

Cette résidence de 550 m² située sur une parcelle d'un demi-hectare comprend, en dehors des pièces de séjour, cinq chambres, quatre salles de bains, une bib thèque, une salle de gymnastique, une autre de yoga et un garage. Entourée de maisons de style Tudor, elle est entièrement vitrée mais dissimulée par quarante pin vingt bouleaux plantés « selon les principes des jardins chinois et japonais ». Le plan fait appel à une trame orthogonale symétrique, axée nord-sud, et l'ensemble do l'impression « d'avoir été construit avec des Lego transparents ». La plupart des pièces mesure 4,88 m de côté. Pour Roszak, « en une sorte de clin d'œil à la concep japonaise traditionnelle, le squelette des poutres de soutien en acier semble planer au-dessus de l'ossature en béton. Un mur de soutènement, au centre de la mais supporte l'essentiel de la charge ». Il fait remarquer, par ailleurs, que la transparence extrême de la maison ne l'empêche pas d'être très économe en consommation d'er gie. Le chauffage solaire et les sols chauffants radiants garantissent une atmosphère confortable. Si cette maison n'est pas sans points communs avec la Modular S House de David Hovey, Winnetka, Illinois (1998), elle représente une œuvre magistrale pour un architecte de moins de 40 ans.

...szak's house has a stripped down
...hnological appearance with a great
...l of glazing offering an open view
...ard the surrounding greenery.

...szaks Haus zeigt einen fast indus-
...llen Impetus. Durch den hohen
...eil an verglasten Fassadenflächen
...ten sich unverstellte Blicke in die
...ne Umgebung.

...maison de Roszak, d'un style
...chnologique» épuré, s'ouvre
...te grande à la verdure environ-
...te par ses immenses baies
...ées.

A relatively simple palette of materials and generous interior space make the Roszak House light and airy.

Relativ einfache Materialien und großzügige Innenräume schaffen ein leichtes und luftiges Ambiente.

Une palette de matériaux relativement simples et de généreux volumes intérieurs rendent cette résidence légère, aérienne.

Holocaust Museum, Yad Vash

MOSHE SAFDIE

Moshe Safdie and Associates, 100 Properzi Way, Somerville, Massachusetts 02143, USA
Tel: +1 617 629 2100, Fax: +1 617 629 2406
e-mail: safdieb@msafdie.com, Web: www.msafdie.com

MOSHE SAFDIE, born in Haifa, Israel, in 1938, later moved to Canada with his family, graduating from McGill University in 1961 with a degree in architecture After apprenticing with Louis I. Kahn in Philadelphia, he returned to Montreal, taking charge of the master plan for the 1967 World Exhibition, where he also realized an adaptation of his thesis as Habitat '67, the central feature of the World's Fair. In 1970, Safdie established a Jerusalem branch office, commencing an intense involvement with the rebuilding of Jerusalem. He was responsible for major segments of the restoration of the Old City and the reconstruction of the new center, linking the Old and New Cities. Over the years, his involvement expanded and included the new city of Modi'in, the new Yad Vashem Holocaust Museum, and the Rabin Memorial Center. In 1978, following teaching at Yale, McGill, and Ben Gurion Universities, Safdie relocated his principal office to Boston, as he became Director of the Urban Design Program and a Professor of Architecture and Urban Design at the Harvard Graduate School of Design. In the following decade, he was responsible for the design of six of Canada's principal public institutions, including the Quebec Museum of Civilization, and the National Gallery of Canada. In the past decade, Safdie's major cultural and educational commissions in the U. S. have included: the United States Institute of Peace Headquarters, Washington, D. C.; the Skirball Museum and Cultural Center in Los Angeles; and Exploration Place in Wichita; educational facilities such as Eleanor Roosevelt College at the University of California in San Diego; civic buildings such as the Springfield, Massachusetts, and Mobile, Alabama, Federal Courthouses; and performing arts centers such as the Kansas City Performing Arts Center. In addition to major works of urbanism, Safdie's current work includes two airports – Lester B. Pearson International Airport in Toronto and Ben Gurion International Airport in Tel Aviv.

MOSHE SAFDIE wurde 1938 in Haifa in Israel geboren. Seine Familie zog später nach Kanada, wo er 1961 an der McGill University sein Architekturstudium abschloss. Safdie arbeitete als Praktikant im Büro von Louis I. Kahn in Philadelphia und ging dann nach Montreal zurück, um die Umsetzung des Masterplans für die Welt ausstellung 1967 zu betreuen. Sein Diplomentwurf bildete in überarbeiteter Form unter dem Namen Habitat '67 den Mittelpunkt dieser Ausstellung. 1970 eröffnete Saf die in Jerusalem eine Zweigstelle und begann intensiv am Wiederaufbau von Jerusalem mitzuarbeiten. Er war für große Teile der Altstadtsanierung und den Wiederauf bau des neuen Zentrums zuständig, wobei die Alt- und Neustadt miteinander verbunden wurden. Im Lauf der Jahre verstärkte sich sein Engagement in Israel und umfass nun auch die neue Stadt Modi'in, das neue Holocaust-Museum in Yad Vashem und das Rabin Memorial Center. Safdie lehrte in Yale, an der McGill University und an der Universität Ben Gurion. Wegen der Berufung zum Direktor des Urban Design Program und zum Professor für Architektur und Städtebau an der Harvard Graduate School of Design zog er 1978 nach Boston und verlegte auch sein Büro dorthin. In den folgenden zehn Jahren war er für die Planung von sechs der wichtigsten öffentlichen Ein richtungen Kanadas verantwortlich, darunter das Museum für Zivilisation in Quebec und die Nationalgalerie von Kanada. In den letzten zehn Jahren erhielt er Aufträge für zahlreiche Kultur- und Bildungsbauten in den USA, beispielsweise für das United States Institute of Peace Headquarters in Washington, D. C., das Skirball-Museum und -Kulturzentrum in Los Angeles und den Exploration Place in Wichita. Von ihm realisierte Bildungsbauten sind u. a. das Eleanor Roosevelt College der University of Cali fornia in San Diego. Staatliche Gebäude von Safdie sind u. a. die Bundesgerichtshöfe in Springfield, Massachusetts, und in Mobile, Alabama. Außerdem baute er Schau spielhäuser wie das Kansas City Performing Arts Center. Neben umfassenden Städtebauprojekten plant Safdie derzeit zwei Flughäfen, den Lester B. Pearson Internatio nal Airport in Toronto und den Internationalen Flughafen Ben Gurion in Tel Aviv.

MOSHE SAFDIE est né à Haïfa (Israël) en 1938 et a émigré avec sa famille au Canada où il a étudié l'architecture à l'Université McGill de Montréal. Après un apprentissage chez Louis Kahn à Philadelphie, il revint à Montréal pour prendre en charge le plan directeur de l'Exposition universelle de 1967 pour laquelle il réalisa également Habitat '67, un projet issu de sa thèse. En 1970, il a créé une agence à Jérusalem et a commencé à s'impliquer dans la restructuration de la ville. Il a été res ponsable de la restauration d'une bonne part de la vieille ville et de la reconstruction du nouveau centre, faisant le lien entre la ville nouvelle et l'ancienne. Au cours des années, ses interventions en Israël se sont développées et il a conçu la ville nouvelle de Modi'in, le nouveau musée de l'Holocauste de Yad Vashem et le Centre mémo rial Ytzhak Rabin. En 1978, après avoir enseigné dans les universités de Yale, McGill et Ben Gourion, il s'installa à Boston avec son agence et devint directeur du pro gramme d'urbanisme et professeur d'architecture et d'urbanisme à la Graduate School of Design de Harvard. Pendant la décennie suivante, il a été responsable de la conception de six grandes institutions canadiennes, notamment le musée des Civilisations du Québec et la Galerie nationale du Canada. Aux États-Unis, il a réalisé, au cours de ces dernières années, le siège du United States Institute of Peace à Washington, D. C. ; le Skirball Museum and Cultural Center à Los Angeles ; Exploration Place à Wichita ; des équipements éducatifs comme le Eleanor Roosevelt College à l'Université de Californie à San Diego ; des bâtiments publics, dont les palais de justice fédé raux de Springfield (Massachusetts) et Mobile (Alabama) et des centres d'arts de la scène, comme le Performing Arts Center de Kansas City. En dehors d'importants cha tiers d'urbanisme, Safdie travaille actuellement à des projets pour deux aéroports internationaux, le Lester B. Pearson à Toronto et le Ben Gourion à Tel-Aviv.

HOLOCAUST MUSEUM, YAD VASHEM

Jerusalem, Israel, 2002–05

Floor area: 17 700 m²; Museum complex 9600 m²; Entrance Pavilion complex 4000 m²; Museum exhibits 4000 m².
Client: Yad Vashem Holocaust Martyrs' and Heroes' Remembrance Authority.
Cost: Museum complex $35 million; Entrance Pavilion complex $18 million; Museum exhibits $10 million

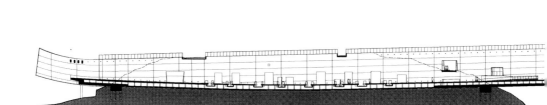

On a hillside overlooking Jerusalem's Ein Kerem Valley, the new **HOLOCAUST MUSEUM** is the culmination of a 10-year, 63 million dollar redevelopment of Ya Vashem, the Holocaust Martyrs' and Heroes' Remembrance Authority. Yad Vashem has been developed as a campus, with buildings including a Holocaust History Mus um, Holocaust Art Museum, Exhibition Pavilion, Visual Center, Learning Center, Synagogue and Visitors Center. The central component of the 1.8 hectare campus is the 3800 m² Holocaust History Museum. Safdie has hidden most of the Museum's reinforced concrete "body" within the earth, allowing little more than its elongated, ang lar spine to convey a sense of its true scale. Inside, among the most important of Safdie's innovations is his placement of the Museum's numerous exhibition spac Rather than cluster one after the other as in conventional museums, Safdie concealed the galleries underground, running under the central, 180-meter spine. This pa culminates in the Hall of Names. It is surrounded by files containing "Pages of Testimony" listing the names of victims. A suspended cone rises above, with photos of victims, with a reciprocal cone excavated into the bedrock down to ground water – in memory of those whose names will never be known. As the architects describe project, "At the north end, the prism bursts out of the mountain, cantilevering over the valley, to light, to the view of the Jerusalem hills, to the vibrant tableau tha modern city of Jerusalem. It is an affirmation of life after an experience of death. The project effectively combines the Holocaust's historical narrative with an approp ate and effective visual experience for the thousands of individuals who visit daily." The museum attracted average of 5000 visitors a day in the three months follow its opening in March 2005.

Auf einem Hügel liegend überblickt das neue **HOLOCAUST-MUSEUM** das Ein-Kerem-Tal in Jerusalem. Es bildet den Höhepunkt einer zehnjährigen, umgerec net 53 Millionen Euro teuren Sanierung von Yad Vashem, der Gedenkstätte für die Opfer des Holocaust und seiner Helden. Das Gelände von Yad Vashem wurde als ca pusartiges Areal konzipiert und umfasst u. a. das neue Holocaust-Museum, das Museum für Holocaust-Kunst, einen Ausstellungspavillon, ein Visualisierungszentrum, Lernzentrum, eine Synagoge und ein Besucherzentrum. Zentrales Element des 1,8 ha großen Campus ist das 3800 m² große Holocaust-Museum. Safdie hat den grö ten Teil des Stahlbetonbaus in die Erde versenkt, so dass es von außen, abgesehen von dem länglichen, winkligen »Rückgrat«, nur wenige Hinweise auf seine wal Größe gibt. Im Inneren bildet die Organisation der zahlreichen Ausstellungsräume eine der wichtigsten Neuerungen: Safdie hat sie nicht wie sonst üblich angeordnet, so dern sie entlang des 180 m langen »Rückgrats« in die Erde eingegraben. Sie finden ihren Höhepunkt am Ende in der »Halle der Namen«. Die Halle wird von Regalen e gerahmt, die »Seiten des Zeugnisses« enthalten, auf denen die Namen der Opfer aufgelistet sind. Ein aufgehängter Kegel mit Fotos der Opfer erhebt sich darüber; umgekehrter, aus dem Fels gemeißeltes Pendant reicht bis zum Grundwasser – in Erinnerung an all jene, deren Namen niemals bekannt sein werden. Der Archit beschreibt den Bau folgendermaßen: »Am Nordende bricht das Prisma aus dem Berg hervor, kragt über das Tal aus, hin zum Licht, zum Ausblick auf die Hügel Jerus lems, zum lebhaften ›Tableau‹ der modernen Stadt Jerusalem. Dies ist die Annahme des Lebens nach der Erfahrung des Todes. Das Projekt verbindet sehr effektiv historischen Erzählungen des Holocaust mit einem angemessenen und wirkungsvollen visuellen Erlebnis für die Tausende Besucher, die täglich kommen.« In den d Monaten nach seiner Eröffnung im März 2005 besuchten im Durchschnitt täglich 5000 Menschen das Museum.

Au sommet d'une colline dominant la vallée d'Ein Kerem à Jérusalem, le nouveau **MUSÉE DE L'HOLOCAUSTE** est l'aboutissement de dix années d'efforts de Commission pour le souvenir des martyrs et des héros de l'Holocauste. Ce projet a coûté 53 millions d'euros. Yad Vashem est un campus de 1,8 hectare comprenant p sieurs bâtiments, dont un musée de l'Histoire de l'Holocauste, un musée d'Art de l'Holocauste, un pavillon d'expositions, un centre d'enseignement, une synagogue et centre d'accueil des visiteurs. La composante principale est le musée de l'Histoire de l'Holocauste de 3800 m². Safdie a dissimulé la plus grande partie du « corps » béton armé du bâtiment dans le sol, laissant à peine dépasser son arête allongée, seul indice de sa véritable échelle. À l'intérieur, l'un des apports les plus intéressa de l'architecte est la disposition des multiples espaces d'exposition que comprend le musée. Écartant l'idée d'alignement chère aux musées conventionnels, Safdie a d simulé les galeries sous terre, tout au long des 180m de l'axe central, en un cheminement qui culmine dans la salle des Noms, entourée de classeurs contenant « Pages de témoignages », listes de noms de victimes. Un immense cône est suspendu dans cette salle, couvert de photos de disparus, et son pendant, un cône tr trique creusé dans la roche jusqu'à la nappe phréatique, rend hommage à ceux dont le nom ne sera jamais connu. Pour Moshe Safdie : « Au nord, le prisme jaillit de montagne, en porte-à-faux au-dessus de la vallée, vers la lumière, les collines de Jérusalem et le panorama vibrant de la ville moderne de Jérusalem. C'est une affirm tion de la vie après cette expérience de la mort. Le projet combine avec efficacité le récit historique de l'Holocauste à une expérience visuelle que découvrent les milli d'individus qui le visitent chaque jour. » Le musée a attiré en moyenne 5000 visiteurs par jour dans les trois mois qui ont suivi son inauguration en mars 2005.

Slicing through the earth like an inverted knife, the main volume of the Yad Vashem building is buried, with a closed triangular façade emerging at the end of a cantilevered volume on one side, and the other extremity emerging toward views of the hills of Jerusalem.

Wie ein umgedrehtes Messer durchschneidet das Museum in Yad Vashem die Erde. Der Hauptteil liegt im Erdboden. Eine geschlossene dreieckige Fassade markiert das eine Ende des aus dem Erdboden auskragenden Baukörpers; das andere Ende öffnet sich zu den Hügeln von Jerusalem.

Tranchant le sol comme une lame de couteau inversée, le volume principal de Yad Vashem est pratiquement enterré. Il ressort d'un côté sous la forme d'une façade triangulaire en porte-à-faux et, de l'autre, en une baie panoramique sur les collines de Jérusalem.

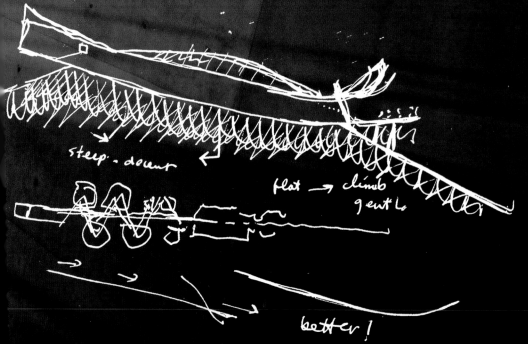

Somerville Oct 18.

Yad Vashem

steep - descent

flat → climb
gentle

better!

Video screens, books and other arti-
facts define the path through the
180-meter-long interior volume, leav-
ing the powerful, leaning concrete
walls relatively free of displays.

Videobildschirme, Bücher und andere
Gegenstände definieren den Weg
durch den 180 m langen Innenraum.
Die kraftvollen, geneigten Betonwän-
de sind fast frei von Ausstellungs-
stücken.

Des écrans vidéo, des livres et divers
artefacts ponctuent le cheminement
au long des 180 m du parcours intérieur, laissant les solides murs de
béton inclinés relativement exempts
de tout effet d'exposition.

A Hall of Names and portraits of victims of the World War II genocide is a culminating point of the visit of Yad Vashem. Safdie has preserved the austerity or even severity of the architecture, no small feat where the commemoration of such events is the raison d'être of the structure.

Die »Halle der Namen« mit Porträts der Opfer des Genozids im Zweiten Weltkrieg ist ein Höhepunkt des Besuchs von Yad Vashem. Safdie hat eine nüchterne, ernste Architektur geschaffen – eine bemerkenswerte Leistung bei einem Gebäude, dessen »raison d'être« das Gedenken an derartige Ereignisse ist.

La salle des Noms avec les portraits des victimes du génocide de la Seconde Guerre mondiale constituent le point culminant de la visite. Safdie a préservé l'austérité, voire la sévérité de l'architecture – une réelle prouesse dans un édifice dont la raison d'être est la commémoration de tels événements.

SCHWARTZ/SILVER

Schwartz/Silver Architects, Inc.
75 Kneeland Street
Boston, Massachusetts 02111
USA

Tel: +1 617 542 6650
Fax: +1 617 951 0779
e-mail: arch@schwartzsilver.com
Web: www.schwartzsilver.com

Shaw Center for th

WARREN SCHWARTZ and **ROBERT SILVER** founded their firm in Boston in 1980. Schwartz was educated at Cornell and Harvard, where he received his deg
in Urban Design in 1967. Silver attended Queens College CUNY, Cambridge University and Harvard, where he received his Masters in Architecture in 1970. Recent w
includes the Abbe Museum, Bar Harbor, Maine (2001); Farnsworth Art Museum and Wyeth Study Center, Rockland, Maine (1998); Belmont Hill School Prenatt Music C
ter, Belmont, Massachusetts (2004); Princeton University Anglinger Center for the Humanities, Princeton, New Jersey (2004); and a renovation and expansion of
Boston Atheneum (2002). Schwartz/Silver has received the AIA National Honor Award five times, and they pride themselves in being a "middle-sized firm ... organi
as an open design studio." Current projects include work for the Maine Historical Society, a master plan for the University of Vermont and buildings for the Universit
Virginia.

WARREN SCHWARTZ und **ROBERT SILVER** gründeten ihr Büro 1980 in Boston. Schwartz studierte in Cornell und Harvard. 1967 machte er in Harvard sei
Abschluss im Fach Stadtplanung. Silver studierte am Queens College CUNY, an der Cambridge University und in Harvard, wo er 1970 seinen Master of Architecture erla
te. Zu ihren neueren Projekten gehören das Farnsworth Art Museum and Wyeth Study Center in Rockland, Maine (1998), das Abbe Museum in Bar Harbor, Maine (200
die Instandsetzung und Erweiterung des Boston Atheneum (2002), das Belmont Hill School Prenatt Music Center in Belmont, Massachusetts (2004), und das Prince
University Anglinger Center for the Humanities in Princeton, New Jersey (2004). Schwartz/Silver wurden bereits fünfmal mit dem AIA National Honor Award ausgezei
net. Sie sind stolz darauf, ein »mittelgroßes Büro zu sein ..., das wie ein offenes Entwurfsatelier organisiert ist«. Zur Zeit sind u. a. ein Auftrag von der Maine Histor
Society, ein Masterplan für die University of Vermont und Gebäude für die University of Virginia in Arbeit.

WARREN SCHWARTZ et **ROBERT SILVER** ont créé leur agence à Boston en 1980. Schwartz a étudié à Cornell et Harvard dont il est diplômé en urbanis
(1967). Silver a suivi les cours de Queens College City University of New York, de Cambridge University et d'Harvard (Master of Architecture en 1970). Parmi leurs réce
travaux: le Abbe Museum, Bar Harbor, Maine (2001); le Farnsworth Art Museum et le Wyeth Study Center, Rockland, Maine (1998); la rénovation et l'extension du B
ton Athenaeum, Boston (2002); le Belmont Hill School Prenatt Music Center, Belmont, Massachusetts (2004); l'Anglinger Center for the Humanities de Princeton U
versity, Princeton, New Jersey (2004). L'agence a reçu cinq fois le National Honor Award de l'American Institute of Architects et se présente comme « une agence
dimensions moyennes ... organisée comme un atelier de conception ouvert». Elle travaille actuellement pour la Maine Historical Society, sur un plan directeur de l'U
versité du Vermont et à des bâtiments destinés à l'Université de Virginie.

SHAW CENTER FOR THE ARTS

Baton Rouge, Louisiana, USA, 2003–05

Floor area: 11 613 m². Client: Shaw Center for the Arts, LLC.
Cost: $32.8 million

The very contemporary wrap-around esthetic of the Shaw Center is particularly unusual in that the building sits atop another older structure in a symbiotic relationship that might also be considered indicative of the current interest in extensions and renovations.

Die sehr zeitgemäße, einheitlich umlaufende Fassade des Shaw Center ist besonders bemerkenswert, da das neue Gebäude auf ein bestehendes aufgesattelt wurde. Zwischen den beiden Gebäuden besteht eine symbiotische Verbindung, die typisch für das derzeitige Interesse an Erweiterungen und Instandsetzungen ist.

Très contemporaine, l'esthétique « enveloppante » du Shaw Center est particulièrement surprenante, car le nouveau bâtiment repose sur une structure plus ancienne, dans une relation symbolique assez typique de la tendance actuelle des extensions et des rénovations.

Despite its location near the water in Baton Rouge, the Shaw Center withstood Hurricane Katrina in 2005 without suffering any serious damage.

Obwohl das Shaw Center in Baton Rouge direkt am Wasser liegt, hielt es dem Hurrikan Katrina 2005 ohne nennenswerten Schaden stand.

Malgré sa localisation au bord de l'eau à Baton Rouge, le Shaw Center a résisté à l'ouragan Katrina de 2005, sans souffrir de dommages sérieux.

This 35.7 million dollar center for visual and performing arts has a floor area of approximately 10 000 m². It includes the 322-seat Manship Performing Arts
ter at one end and the Louisiana State University Museum of Art at the other. One unusual feature of the building is the 12-meter cantilever over the existing 1930s
Hotel. The most visible exterior element of the design is the façade clad in multi-length cast glass channels. The architects explain that "The façade is conceived to e
many local associations: A paper lantern, glass beading, the meandering Mississippi River. At night the building glows like a 'lantern on the levee,' a ubiquitous fea
along the river in antebellum times." A corrugated aluminum wall system is set 15 centimeters behind this glass screen. This type of façade posed a number of te
cal problems, not least of which is its potential resistance to high winds. "Baton Rouge is only 60 miles inland from the Gulf of Mexico on the southern coast of the
ed States," they explain. "To test the glazing system against hurricane-force winds, a mock up was produced and placed in front of an old DC-3 airplane propeller to
ulate 100-mile-per-hour winds. Further tests were done in Germany by the vendor, Bendheim Wall Systems." Schwartz/Silver worked on this project with local archi
Eskew + Dumez + Ripple, and Jerry M. Campbell & Associates.

Das umgerechnet 29,7 Millionen Euro teure Gebäude für bildende und darstellende Künste hat eine Gesamtfläche von mehr als 10 000 m². An einem Ende
das Manship Performing Arts Center mit 322 Plätzen, am anderen Ende das Louisiana State University Museum of Art. Eine Besonderheit des Gebäudes ist eine 1
lange Auskragung über dem »Auto Hotel« aus den 1930er Jahren. Besonders markant ist die Fassade, die aus verschieden langen Glasröhren besteht. Die Archite
erläutern: »Die Fassade soll viele Assoziationen, die mit dem Ort zu tun haben, hervorrufen: eine Papierlaterne, Glasperlenstickerei, den mäandrierenden Mississ
Nachts leuchtet der Bau wie eine ›Laterne an der Uferböschung‹, früher ein allgegenwärtiges Element am Flussufer.« 15 cm hinter der Glasebene ist ein Wandsystem
gewellten Aluminiumumblechen angeordnet. Aufgrund des Fassadenaufbaus musste eine Reihe von technischen Problemen gelöst werden: Dazu gehörte nicht zuletz
Aufnahme von hohen Windlasten. »Baton Rouge ist nur 100 km vom Golf von Mexico entfernt, also nicht weit von der Südküste der Vereinigten Staaten«, erkläre
Architekten. »Um das Verglasungssystem auch für Windstärken im Bereich von Hurrikans zu testen, wurde ein Fassadenmodell im Maßstab 1:1 gebaut. Eine alte D
Propellermaschine wurde vor das Modell gestellt, um Windstärken mit über 160 km/h zu simulieren. In Deutschland wurden weitere Tests beim Hersteller der Fass
Bendheim Wandsysteme, durchgeführt. Schwartz/Silver arbeiteten bei diesem Projekt vor Ort mit den Architekten Eskew + Dumez + Ripple sowie Jerry M. Campb
Associates zusammen.

Ce centre pour les arts visuels et du spectacle occupe une surface de plus de 10 000 m² environ et a coûté 29,7 millions d'euros. Il comprend le Manship
forming Arts Center de 322 places à une extrémité et le Louisana State University Museum of Art à l'autre. L'une de ses caractéristiques est son porte-à-faux de
au-dessus de l'Auto Hotel, un bâtiment des années 1930. La façade extérieure est particulièrement remarquable pour son habillage de panneaux de verre moulé en
tière de multiples longueurs. Les architectes expliquent : « La façade est dessinée pour évoquer de nombreuses associations d'idées de nature locale : une lantern
papier, des perles de verre, les méandres du Mississippi. La nuit, le bâtiment luit comme une de ces ‹lanternes de digue› que l'on trouvait partout le long du fleuve a
la Guerre civile. » Un système de parois en aluminium ondulé est implanté à 15 cm derrière l'écran de verre de la façade. Ce type de montage a posé de nombreux
blèmes, celui de la résistance à la force des vents n'étant pas le moindre. « Baton Rouge n'est qu'à 100 km du golfe du Mexique… pour tester le système de v
contre les ouragans, une maquette a été construite et placée devant un moteur à hélice de vieux DC3 pour simuler des vents soufflant à 160 km/h. D'autres test
été réalisés en Allemagne par le fournisseur, Bendheim Wall Systems. » Schwartz/Silver a travaillé sur ce projet avec les agences locales Eskew + Dumez + Ripp
Jerry M. Campbell & Associates.

The almost ghostly appearance of the Shaw Center in its nighttime lighting accentuates its unusual volume and cantilevered overhang.

Die fast geisterhafte Wirkung des Shaw Center bei nächtlicher Beleuchtung entsteht durch den ungewöhnlichen Baukörper und die große Auskragung.

Sous l'éclairage nocturne, l'apparence quasi fantomatique du Shaw Center accentue le caractère étrange de son volume et de son porte-à-faux.

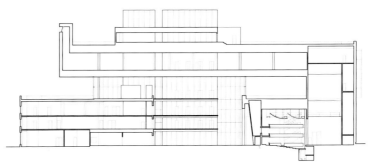

Notes of color render interior spaces
warmer than they might have been.

Die Farben lassen die Innenräume
wärmer als erwartet wirken.

Des touches de couleur confèrent une
certaine chaleur aux intérieurs.

A soaring entrance area and silver, translucent volumes that recall the exterior design of the building greet visitors in the Shaw Center.

Ein hohes Atrium und silbrige, transluzente Volumina, die der Außenfassade ähneln, begrüßen den Besucher des Shaw Center.

Une entrée aux proportions vertigineuses et des volumes argentés et translucides rappelant l'esthétique des façades accueillent les visiteurs du Shaw Center.

ROGER SHERMAN

Roger Sherman Architecture and Urban Design, 11918 West Washington Boulevard, Los Angeles, California 90066, USA
Tel: +1 424 228 5676, Fax: +1 424 228 5672, email: info@rsaud.com
Web: www.rsaud.com

ROGER SHERMAN was educated at the University of Pennsylvania and at the Harvard Graduate School of Design, where he received his Masters of Architecture degree in 1985. Located in Santa Monica, Roger Sherman Architecture (RSA) is a partnership that was founded in 1990, and varies in size between four and six persons who work on only two or three projects at any one time. The firm's two principals are Greg Kochanowski and Roger Sherman. Sherman's "interest and research on politics of property ownership derives from his own practical experience in working on public projects of a controversial nature." These include the West Hollywood Civic Center, a commission won through an international design competition in 1987; and a National Endowment for the Arts-funded development plan for North Hollywood the San Fernando Valley) in 1995. Other notable projects by his firm include rePark, a master plan for Fresh Kills Landfill, Staten Island, New York (2001); and Railya Park, the revitalization of Santa Fe, New Mexico's historic rail yard. In addition to being a practicing architect, Sherman was recently appointed director of the Metropol itan Research and Design (MR+D) program at the Southern California Institute of Architecture (SCIArc), where he has been a studio instructor for 13 years. RSA has co centrated on single family residences, and their projects include: Shanus Residence (new), Cheviot Hills, California (2004–05); Schab Residence (3-in-1 House), Sal Monica, California (2002–03); Gaynor Residence Kitchen Remodel, Brentwood, California (2002); and the Gold Residence Living/Dining Room Remodel/Addition, L Angeles, California (1997). Current work includes the Flex-Deck-Spec House, Gloucestershire, UK; Johnson/O'Kingston Residence Pleasure Deck, Signal Hill, Californ and the Gill/Weg Residence Remodel, Silverlake, California.

ROGER SHERMAN studierte an der University of Pennsylvania und an der Harvard Graduate School of Design, wo er 1985 seinen Master of Architecture mac te. Roger Sherman Architects (RSA) wurde 1990 in Santa Monica gegründet. Die Größe des Büros, das von den Partnern Greg Kochanowski und Roger Sherman gefü wird, variiert: Zwischen vier und sechs Personen arbeiten an nur zwei oder drei Projekten gleichzeitig. Shermans »Interesse an politischen Fragen des Grundbesitzes u seine Forschung in diesem Bereich entwickelte sich aus seiner praktischen Erfahrung, die er durch die Planung öffentlicher und umstrittener Projekte machte.« Da gehören das West Hollywood Civic Center, ein Auftrag, den er durch den Gewinn eines internationalen Wettbewerbs 1987 erhielt, und der Entwicklungsplan für North H lywood im San Fernando Valley (1995), der durch Mittel des National Endowment for the Arts (Nationale Kulturstiftung) finanziert wurde. Andere wichtige Projekte c Büros sind rePark, ein Masterplan für die Mülldeponie Fresh Kills in Staten Island, New York, und Railyard Park, die Revitalisierung des historischen Eisenbahngeländ in Santa Fe, New Mexico. Zusätzlich zu seiner Tätigkeit als Architekt ist Sherman seit kurzem Leiter des Metropolitan Research and Design (MR+D) Program an So thern California Institute of Architecture (SCI-Arc), wo er 13 Jahre als Lehrer für verschiedene Entwurfsklassen tätig war. RSA hat bislang hauptsächlich Einfamilienhä ser realisiert. Derzeit in Planung bzw. im Bau sind u. a. das Flex-Deck-Spec House in Gloucestershire, England, die Terrasse der Johnson/O'Kingston Residence in Sig Hill, Kalifornien, und der Umbau der Gill/Weg Residence in Silverlake, Kalifornien. Realisierte Häuser sind u. a. die Shanus Residence in Cheviot Hills, Kaliforni (2004–05), die Schab Residence (3-in-1-Haus) in Santa Monica, Kalifornien (2002–03), der Küchenumbau der Gaynor Residence in Brenntwood, Kalifornien (2002), u der Umbau und die Erweiterung des Wohn- und Esszimmers der Gold Residence in Los Angeles (1997).

ROGER SHERMAN a étudié à l'Université de Pennsylvanie et à la Harvard Graduate School of Design (Master of Architecture en 1985). Installée à Santa Mon ca, l'agence Roger Sherman Architecture (RSA) a été fondée en 1990 et compte de quatre à six collaborateurs qui ne travaillent que sur deux ou trois projets à la fo Ses deux dirigeants sont Greg Kochanowski et Roger Sherman. « L'intérêt [de Sherman] pour la politique de la propriété vient de son expérience personnelle de proje publics de nature controversée », tels que le West Hollywood Civic Center, commande remportée à l'issue d'un concours international en 1987, et un plan d'urbanisr pour North Hollywood (vallée de San Fernando) bénéficiaire d'une aide du National Endowment for the Arts en 1995. Parmi les autres projets notables de l'agence : rePa plan directeur pour Fresh Kills Landfill, Staten Island, New York (2001) ; Railyard Park, réhabilitation de friches ferroviaires à Santa Fe au Nouveau-Mexique. En deho de ses activités d'architecte, Sherman a été récemment nommé directeur du Metropolitan Research and Design (MR+D) Program du Southern California Institute of Arc tecture (SCI-arc), où il enseigne depuis 13 ans. RSA se concentre sur les maisons individuelles : Shanus Residence, Cheviot Hills, Californie (2004–05) ; Schab Reside ce (3-in-1 House, Santa Monica, 2002–03) ; restructuration de la cuisine de la Gaynor Residence, Brentwood (2002) ; extension et restructuration du séjour-salle à ma ger de la Gold Residence, Los Angeles (1997). Actuellement, l'équipe travaille aux projets de la Flex-Deck-Spec House (Gloucestershire, Grande-Bretagne), à une terras pour la Johnson/O'Kingston Residence (Signal Hill, Californie) et à la restructuration de la Gill/Weg Residence (Silverlake, Los Angeles).

3-IN-1 HOUSE

Santa Monica, California, USA, 2002–03

Floor area: 254 m². Client: Jennifer Schab.
Cost: $610 000

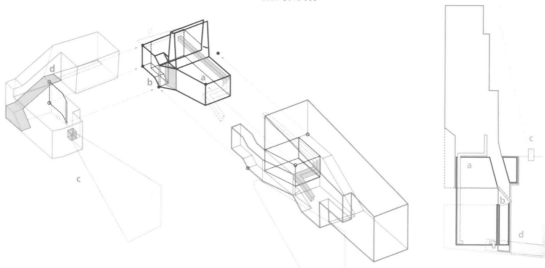

The **3-IN-1 HOUSE** built for a professional couple with one child, is a 254 m² residence located on a 15 x 35 meter lot with a 10% grade. It has a steel structure with wood stud infill, stucco and bonderized metal-panel exterior finish, concrete slab and birch veneer plywood floors, and birch veneer and wallpapered w Located just seven blocks from the Pacific Ocean, the site offers views of the Santa Monica Mountains toward the rear (north). The structure consists in a single-fa residence, studio/office and attached rental unit. The studio and home share a common entry. Roger Sherman comments "With the cost of both steel and wood rocketing, the use of inexpensive materials is no longer enough to keep things affordable. The recent emphasis on home-as-lifestyle instead of home-as-form ma one symptom of this paradox. In such a climate, this project is intended to serve as a model and method by which architecture can still be achievable, if not afford through a series of design strategies whose aim is to more compactly but creatively accommodate the ordinary residential program, in order to allocate and preser sufficient portion of the budget to create a strong overall architectural statement and experience." A great deal of importance was given by the architect to the flex ity and compactness of the design. Given the warm climate of Los Angeles, some frequently usable space is external. Terraces extend from the house at three levels of the hillside, "allowing the accoutrements of daily life to be left outside rather than building additional square footage to accommodate them."

Das 254 m² große **3-IN-1-HAUS** für ein Paar mit einem Kind steht auf einem Grundstück mit einer Fläche von 15 x 35 m und einem Gefälle von zehn Proz Die Stahlkonstruktion des Gebäudes ist mit Holz ausgefacht und außen mit beschichteten Metallpaneelen verkleidet. Die Stahlbetonböden haben einen Belag aus Sp holz mit Birkenfurnier, die Wände sind mit Birkenholzfurnier und Tapete verkleidet. Das Grundstück liegt sieben Straßenblöcke vom Pazifik entfernt. Nach Norden b sich ein Blick auf die Santa Monica Mountains. Das Haus besteht aus einem Einfamilienhaus, einem Studio/Büro und einem Anbau mit einer Mietwohnung. Büro Privathaus teilen sich einen Eingang. Roger Sherman kommentiert: »Heutzutage, wo die Preise für Stahl und Holz in den Himmel schießen, reicht es nicht mehr aus, p werte Materialien beim Bauen zu verwenden, um die Kosten niedrig zu halten. Das Motto ›die Form bestimmt das Haus‹ hat sich in letzter Zeit in Richtung ›der Leb stil bestimmt das Haus‹ verändert. In diesem Kontext soll das 3-in-1-Haus als Modell und Methode dienen, wie Architektur machbar und finanzierbar sein kann. Dies durch eine Entwurfsstrategie erreicht, die darauf abzielt, auf kompaktere, aber kreative Weise das typische Einfamilienhausprogramm unterzubringen und dadurch e ausreichenden Teil des Budgets dafür zu benutzen, eine insgesamt starke architektonische Aussage zu schaffen.« Die Architekten legten großen Wert auf Flexibilität Kompaktheit. In Anbetracht des warmen Klimas befinden sich einige der häufig genutzten Räume im Außenbereich. Terrassen auf drei Ebenen vergrößern das Hau Richtung Hangseite, »so dass das Equipment des täglichen Lebens draußen gelassen werden kann, anstatt dass man größere Räume baut, um es aufzubewahren«.

Cette maison de 254 m² construite pour un couple et son enfant est située sur un terrain de 15 x 35 m incliné à 10%. La structure est en acier à remplissa de panneaux de bois, l'extérieur est revêtu de panneaux de stuc à finitions en métal bondérisé, l'intérieur est en dalles de béton et sols en placage de bouleau, les m sont habillés de bouleau ou de papier peint. Situé à sept blocs seulement du Pacifique, le terrain donne, au nord, sur les Santa Monica Mountains. La maison compr à la fois la résidence de la famille, un bureau/studio et un appartement à louer. Le studio et la maison partagent la même entrée. Pour Roger Sherman, « avec les a mentations faramineuses du prix du bois et de l'acier, le recours à des matériaux bon marché n'est plus une solution suffisante. La mode récente de la ‹ maison-styl vie › au détriment de la ‹ maison-objet › est peut-être un symptôme de ce paradoxe. Dans un tel contexte, ce projet entend être un modèle et une méthode grâce a quels on peut encore faire de l'architecture, ou du moins la rendre accessible. La stratégie de conception a pour but de répondre de façon créative mais plus resse aux contraintes d'un programme résidentiel classique, afin de pouvoir consacrer une part suffisante du budget à cette aventure qu'est la création architecturale pro ment dite ». Une grande attention a été accordée à la souplesse et à la compacité du projet. Compte tenu du climat de Los Angeles, une partie des activités peu dérouler en plein air. Les terrasses prolongent la maison et se déploient sur trois niveaux à flanc de colline, « permettant de laisser à l'extérieur les accessoires de la quotidienne au lieu de construire des mètres carrés supplémentaires pour les recevoir ».

...pping surfaces with different ...rs and textures form the exterior ...he house, which does not show ...edictable sequence of doors and ...dows.

Umlaufende Fassaden mit unterschiedlichen Farben und Texturen bestimmen das Äußere des Hauses, das ohne eine vorhersehbare Anordnung von Türen und Fenstern auskommt.

L'extérieur de la maison est caractérisé par des surfaces enveloppantes de différentes textures et couleurs, en l'absence de toute séquence attendue de portes et de fenêtres.

The choice of furniture is less the object of interest in these images than the interesting use of wrapping surfaces and materials.

Nicht die Auswahl der Möbelstücke steht hier im Vordergrund, sondern der reizvolle Einsatz von hüllenden Oberflächen und Materialien.

Le choix du mobilier est ici moins intéressant que l'utilisation des surfaces et des matériaux de revêtement.

SITE

*SITE
25 Maiden Lane
New York, New York 10038–4008
USA*

*Tel: +1 212 285 0120
Fax: +1 212 285 0125
e-mail: info@sitenewyork.com
Web: www.siteenvirodesign.com*

James Wines, founding principal of **SITE**, Environmental Design was born in Chicago, Illinois in 1932 and studied art and art history at Syracuse Univers (B. A. 1956). Between 1965 and 1967, he was a sculptor, working in New York and Rome, Italy. He created SITE with Alison Sky and Michelle Stone in 1970. Notal buildings include: Indeterminate Facade Showroom, Houston, Texas (1975); Ghost Parking Lot, Hamden, Connecticut (1978); Highway 86, World Exposition, Vancouv British Columbia, Canada (1986); Four Continents Bridge, Hiroshima, Japan (1989); Avenida 5, Universal Exhibition, Seville, Spain (1992) and Ross's Landing Plaza aι Park, Chattanooga, Tennessee (1992). SITE has created integrations of architecture and landscape for MCA Gardens – Universal Studios, Orlando, Florida (1996); Brinι International Chili's Restaurant, prototype design, Denver, Colorado, (1998). More recent projects include the Annmarie Sculpture Garden plan and pavilion, Solomc Island, Maryland (2002); Shake Shack restaurant in Madison Square Park, Manhattan (2004); interior design for Xerion Capital Partners, New York (2003); the Fondazio Rossini Sculpture Garden Pavilion, Briosco, Italy, and the work in Mumbai published here. The current leading members of SITE are: James Wines, President and Foundι Principal, Associate Architects Denise M. C. Lee and Joshua Weinstein, plus Designer and artist Sara Stracey.

James Wine, Gründungspartner von **SITE**, Environmental Design, wurde 1932 in Chicago, Illinois geboren und studierte Kunst und Kunstgeschichte an ι Syracuse University (B. A. 1956). Zwischen 1965 und 1967 war er als Bildhauer tätig und arbeitete in New York und Rom. 1970 gründete er zusammen mit Alison S und Michelle Stone SITE. Wichtige Projekte des Büros sind: Indeterminate Facade Showroom in Houston, Texas (1975); Ghost Parking Lot in Hamden, Connecticut (197 Highway 86 auf der Weltausstellung in Vancouver, Kanada (1986); Four Continents Bridge in Hiroshima (1989); Avenida 5 auf der Weltausstellung 1992 in Sevilla uι Ross's Landing Plaza und Park in Chattanooga, Tennessee (1992). SITE schuf integrierte Architektur und Landschaftsprojekte für MCA Gardens – Universal Studiι Orlando, Florida (1996); Brinker International Chili's Restaurant in Denver, Colorado (Prototyp eines Restaurants, 1998). Zu den neueren Projekten des Büros gehöι Plan und Pavillon des Annmarie Sculpture Garden, Solomons Island, Maryland (2002), das Shake Shack Restaurant in Madison Square Park, Manhattan (2004) sοι Innenraumplanungen für Xerion Capital Partners, New York (2003), den Pavillon des Fondazione Rossini Sculpture Garden, Briosco, Italien und der hier gezeigte Mumι Tower. Leitende Mitarbeiter von SITE sind gegenwärtig: James Wines, Präsident und Gründungsdirektor, Architekten Denise M. C. Lee und Joshua Weinstein sοι Designerin und Künstlerin Sara Stracey.

James Wines, fondateur et président de **SITE**, Environmental Design, né à Chicago, Illinois, en 1932, a étudié l'art et l'histoire de l'art à Syracuse Univers (B. A. 1956). De 1965 à 1967, il est sculpteur et travaille à New York et Rome. Il crée SITE avec Alison Sky et Michelle Stone en 1970. Parmi leurs réalisations notablε Indeterminate Facade Showroom, Houston, Texas (1975); Ghost Parking Lot, Hamden, Connecticut (1978); Highway 86, World Exposition, Vancouver, British Columbι Canada (1986); Four Continents Bridge, Hiroshima, Japon (1989); Avenida 5, Exposition universelle, Séville, Espagne (1992) et Ross's Landing Plaza and Park, Chat nooga, Tennessee (1992). SITE est intervenu sur l'intégration de l'architecture et du paysage pour MCA Gardens – Universal Studios, Orlando, Floride (1996); Brinι International Chili's Restaurant, conception de prototype, Denver, Colorado, (1998). Parmi ses projets plus récents : le Annmarie Sculpture Garden, plan et pavillon, Sο mons Island, Maryland (2002); Shake Shack restaurant à Madison Square Park, New York (2004); architecture intérieure de Xerion Capital Partners, New York (200: jardin de sculpture de la Fondazione Rossini, Briosco, Italie, et le travail réalisé pour Mumbai publié dans cet ouvrage. Les membres actuels de SITE sont : James Winι président et associé fondateur, les architectes associés Denise M. C. Lee et Joshua Weinstein, ainsi que la designer et artiste Sara Stracey.

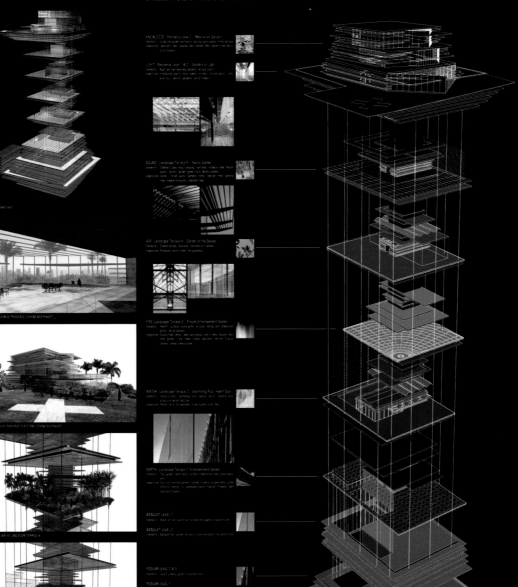

EXPLODED AXONOMETRIC PERSPECTIVE DIAGRAM

GARDEN THEMES AND ENERGY CONSERVATION SOLUTIONS

PRIVATE RESIDENTIAL TOWER

Mumbai, India, 2004

Floor area: 26 942 m². Client: not disclosed. Cost: $145 million

This project, to be built on a 4325 m² hilltop site overlooking Mumbai, would be 110 meters tall and include a total of 26 942 m² of floor area with a probable building cost of 145 million dollars. The appearance of the building is described by SITE in the following terms: "The concept responds to the client's desire to have a multi-tiered, heavily landscaped structure, similar to the ancient Hanging Gardens of Babylon. For this reason the entire building is conceived as a garden in the sky, freeing landscape from its normal earthbound confinement. The philosophical foundations for this structure respond to Vastu principles in Hinduism, wherein the spine is regarded as the main source of support, leading upward to enlightenment." A stratified structural spine reinforced by steel cables holds up seven levels of residence space. The terrace levels "emerge from a core structure similar to the role played by vertebrae in the spine." The main residence is located on the top platform, covering an area of 4000 m² that includes a helipad and a garden. A precisely oriented (north/south/east/west axis) central, sky-lit atrium brings light to all floors from the inside of the building. SITE worked with the New York structural engineers Weidlinger Associates Inc., specialists in blast-resistant buildings, for this design.

Das Gebäude mit Blick auf Bombay, das auf einem 4325 m² großen Grundstück auf einer Bergkuppe gebaut werden soll, wäre 110 m hoch, hätte eine Gesamtfläche von 26 942 m² und würde umgerechnet etwa 120 Millionen Euro kosten. Die Architekten beschreiben es folgendermaßen: »Das Konzept antwortet auf den Wunsch des Bauherren, ein gestaffeltes, stark landschaftsplanerisch gestaltetes Gebäude zu bauen, das den Hängenden Gärten des Altertums in Babylon ähnelt. Das gesamte Gebäude ist daher als ein Garten im Himmel entworfen und befreit so die Landschaft von ihren üblichen erdgebundenen Beschränkungen. Die philosophische Begründung für die Konstruktion entspricht Prinzipien des hinduistischen Vastu, worin das Rückgrat als die wesentliche Quelle des Stützens angesehen wird und nach oben, hin zur Erleuchtung, führt.« Ein geschichtetes, durch Stahlseile verstärktes konstruktives Rückgrat trägt sieben Ebenen mit Wohnnutzung. Die Terrassenebenen »entwickeln sich aus dem Kern, der den Wirbeln der Wirbelsäule gleicht.« Die größte Wohneinheit befindet sich auf der obersten Ebene und umfasst 4000 m² (inklusive Helikopterlandeplatz und Garten). Ein präzise orientiertes, von oben belichtetes zentrales Atrium (Nord/Süd- und Ost/West-Achsen) lenkt zusätzlich Tageslicht auf alle Geschosse. SITE plante den Entwurf in Zusammenarbeit mit dem Ingenieurbüro Weidlinger Associates, Inc., Spezialisten für detonationssichere Gebäude.

Cette tour de 110 m de haut et 26 942 m² de surface devrait être édifiée pour un budget estimé à 120 millions d'euros sur un terrain de 4325 m² situé au sommet d'une colline dominant Mumbai (Bombay). Son aspect est décrit par SITE en ces termes : «Le concept répond au désir du client d'une construction fortement pagagée en gradins, similaire aux anciens Jardins suspendus de Babylone … l'immeuble est conçu comme un jardin dans le ciel, un paysage libéré de son lien avec le sol. Ses fondations philosophiques répondent aux principes de *vastu* de l'hindouisme qui considèrent la colonne vertébrale comme le principal support de l'homme, qui le pousse vers l'illumination. » Une colonne structurelle stratifiée renforcée de câbles d'acier soutient les sept niveaux d'espaces résidentiels. Les niveaux des terrasses «émergent d'une structure de noyau similaire jouant un rôle proche de celui des vertèbres dans la colonne vertébrale ». Le principal espace résidentiel est situé sur la dernière plate-forme. Ses 4000 m² comprennent un héliport et un jardin. Tout en haut, un atrium à éclairage zénithal central, orienté nord/sud/est/ouest, apporte de la lumière à tous les niveaux inférieurs. SITE a travaillé pour ce projet avec les ingénieurs structurels new-yorkais Weidlinger Associates Inc., spécialistes en constructions résistantes aux explosions.

suspension cables.

residence Antilia

Designed for a well-known personality, the residence tower would have not only to be ecologically sound but also structurally solid enough to withstand possible bombs.

Der Wohnturm für eine bekannte Persönlichkeit sollte sowohl umweltverträglich als auch detonationssicher konstruiert sein.

Conçue pour une personnalité célèbre, cette tour résidentielle devait être non seulement écologique mais aussi capable de résister aux explosions.

SIZA/SOUTO DE MOURA

Álvaro Siza Arquitecto Lda, Rua do Aleixo, 53–2°, 4150–043 Porto, Portugal
Tel: +351 226 16 72 70, Fax: +351 226 16 72 79, e-mail: siza@mail.telepac.pt, Web: www.alvarosizavieira.com
Souto Moura Arquitectos Lda, R. do Aleixo, 53–1° A, 4150–043 Porto, Portugal
Tel: +351 226 18 75 47, Fax: +351 226 10 80 92, e-mail: souto.moura@mail.telepac.pt

Born in Matosinhos, Portugal in 1933, **ÁLVARO SIZA** studied at the University of Porto School of Architecture (1949–55). He created his own practice in 1954 and worked with Fernando Tavora from 1955 to 1958. He has been a Professor of Construction at the University of Porto since 1976. He received the European Community's Mies van der Rohe Prize in 1988 and the Pritzker Prize in 1992. He built a large number of small-scale projects in Portugal, and more recently, he has worked on the restructuring of the Chiado, Lisbon, Portugal (1989–); the Meteorology Center, Barcelona, Spain (1989–92); the Vitra Furniture Factory, Weil-am-Rhein, German (1991–94); the Porto School of Architecture, Porto University (1986–95); and the University of Aveiro Library, Aveiro, Portugal (1988–95). He has also completed the Portuguese Pavilion for the 1998 Lisbon World's Fair (with Souto de Moura); the Serralves Foundation, Porto (1996–99); or the Portuguese Pavilion for the Expo Hanover (1998–2000, also with Souto de Moura). **EDUARDO SOUTO DE MOURA** was born in Porto, Portugal in 1952. He graduated from the School of Architecture of Port (ESBAP) in 1980. He was an Assistant Professor at the Faculty of Architecture in Porto (FAUP) from 1981 to 1991. He worked in the office of Alvaro Siza from 1974 t 1979 and created his own office the following year. Recent work includes Row houses in the Rua Lugarinho, Porto, Portugal (1996); Renovation of the Municipal Marke in Braga (1997); the Silo Norte Shopping building; and a house and wine cellar, Valladolid, Spain (1999). More recent work includes the conversion of the building of th Carvoeira da Foz, Porto, and the Braga Stadium (2004). He completed Two Houses at Ponte de Lima (2002).

ÁLVARO SIZA, geboren 1933 in Matosinhos, Portugal, studierte von 1949 bis 1955 an der Escola Superior de Belas Artes der Universität Porto. 1954 gründet er sein eigenes Büro und arbeitete von 1955 bis 1958 mit Fernando Tavora zusammen. Ab 1976 war er Professor für Konstruktionslehre an der Universität Porto. 198 wurde er mit dem Mies-van-der-Rohe-Preis der Europäischen Union ausgezeichnet, 1992 erhielt er den Pritzker-Preis. Er hat zahlreiche kleinere Projekte in Portugal rea lisiert. In jüngerer Zeit plante er die Neustrukturierung der Altstadt Chiado in Lissabon (1989–), das Meteorologische Zentrum in Barcelona (1989–92), ein Fabrikge bäude für Vitra in Weil am Rhein (1991–94) und die Architekturfakultät der Universität Porto (1986–95) sowie eine Bücherei in Aveiro, Portugal (1988–95). Er realisie te ebenfalls den Portugiesischen Pavillon auf der Weltausstellung 1998 in Lissabon (mit Souto de Moura), die Stiftung Serralves in Porto (1996–99) und de Portugiesischen Pavillon auf der Expo Hannover (1998–2000, ebenfalls mit Souto de Moura). **EDUARDO SOUTO DE MOURA** wurde 1952 in Porto geboren. 1980 mac te er an der Escola Superior de Belas Artes der Universität Porto seinen Abschluss. Von 1981 bis 1991 war er Wissenschaftlicher Mitarbeiter an der Architekturfakult (FAUP) in Porto. Von 1974 bis 1979 arbeitete er im Büro von Alvaro Siza, ein Jahr darauf gründete er sein eigenes Büro. Zu seinen Bauten gehören die Reihenhäuser der Rua Lugarinho in Porto (1996), die Sanierung der Markthalle in Braga (1997), das Einkaufszentrum Silo Norte in Matosinhos (1999) und ein Haus mit Weinkeller Valladolid (1999). Gebäude jüngeren Datums sind der Umbau des Gebäudes der Carvoeira da Foz in Porto und das Braga-Stadion (2004). Zwei Häuser in Ponte de Lin wurden 2002 fertig gestellt.

Né à Matosinhos, au Portugal, en 1933, **ÁLVARO SIZA** a fait ses études à l'École d'architecture de l'Université de Porto (1949–55). Il crée son agence en 19 et travaille avec Fernando Távora de 1955 à 1958 et enseigne la construction à l'Université de Porto depuis 1976. Il a reçu le prix Mies van der Rohe de la Communaut Européenne en 1988 et le prix Pritzker en 1992. Il a réalisé un grand nombre de petits projets au Portugal et, plus récemment, est intervenu sur la restructuration quartier du Chiado à Lisbonne (1989–) ; le Centre de météorologie, Barcelone, Espagn (1989–92) ; un bâtiment pour l'usine de meubles Vitra, Weil-am-Rhein, Allemag (1991–94) ; l'École d'architecture de Porto, Université de Porto (1986–95), la bibliothèque de l'Université d'Aveiro, Aveiro (1988–95) ; le pavillon portugais d'Expo 9 Lisbonne (1998), avec Souto de Moura, la Fondation Serralves (Porto, 1996–99) et le pavillon portugais d'Expo à Hanovre (1998–2000, également avec Souto de Mou Né à Porto, au Portugal, en 1952, **EDUARDO SOUTO DE MOURA** est diplômé de l'École d'architecture de Porto, ESBAP (1980). Il a été Professeur assistant à la fac té d'architecture de Porto (FAUP) de 1981 à 1991. Après avoir travaillé auprès d'Álvaro Siza de 1974 à 1979, il a fondé sa propre agence en 1980. Parmi ses réali tions récentes : une série de maisons Rua Lugarinho, Porto (1996), la rénovation du marché municipal de Braga (1997) ; le centre commercial de Silo Norte, une mais et un chai, Valladolid, Espagne (1999) ; deux maisons à Ponte de Lima (2002) ; la reconversion de l'immeuble de la Carvoeira da Foz (Porto) et le stade de Braga (200

SERPENTINE GALLERY PAVILION 2005

Kensington Gardens, London, UK, 2005

Floor area: 380 m². Client: The Serpentine Gallery. Cost: not disclosed

Built between the 11ᵗʰ of April and the 30ᵗʰ of June 2005, this 380 m² temporary pavilion is the fifth of its kind to be built in Kensington Gardens next to the S: pentine Gallery, a contemporary art showplace originally built as a tea pavilion in 1934. Previous projects were designed by Zaha Hadid (2000), Daniel Libeskind (200: Toyo Ito (2002); and Oscar Niemeyer (2003). An ambitious project originally scheduled for 2004 with the Dutch firm MvRdV had been delayed, and Álvaro Siza was ca: on, working with Eduardo Souto de Moura and Cecil Balmond (Arup), to design the 2005 pavilion by Gallery director Julia Peyton-Jones. The architects had previou worked together on the Portuguese Pavilion, Expo 1998 Lisbon (1995–98) and the Portuguese Pavilion, Expo 2000 (Hanover, Germany). With its 22 x 17 meter footpɪ and maximum height of 5.4 meters, the pavilion is a timber framed column-free structure with semi-transparent 5 mm thick polycarbonate roofing. Tables and ch: designed by the architects adorned the interior of the building, which was dismantled during October 2005. Some 427 unique timber beams were placed in a comɪ interlocking pattern that started in one corner and "radiated out to finish at the opposite extreme." As Hamish Nevile from the engineer's firm Arup explains, "It was cr ted as an evolution of the 'lamella' barrel-vault roofs developed in Germany in the early 1920s. While traditional lamellas were built from identical elements, howev each element of the Pavilion is unique, having a different length and inclination. This geometric freedom enables the precise expression of the complex form demanc by the architects. The reciprocal beam system creates a continuous structure that runs from the roof down to form the walls of the Pavilion."

Der 380 m² große, fünfte temporäre Pavillon wurde vom 11. April bis 30. Juni 2005 neben der Serpentine Gallery, einer Galerie für Kunst in Kensington Garde errichtet. Das Gebäude der Serpentine Gallery war ursprünglich als Teepavillon gedacht und stammt aus dem Jahr 1934. Die früheren temporären Pavillons wurden ʷ Zaha Hadid (2000), Daniel Libeskind (2001), Toyo Ito (2002) und Oscar Niemeyer (2003) entworfen. Ein ehrgeiziges Projekt, das 2004 mit dem niederländischen B: MvRdV realisiert werden sollte, musste verschoben werden. Daraufhin wendete sich die Leiterin der Galerie, Julia Peyton-Jones, an Álvaro Siza, der mit Eduardo So de Moura und Cecil Balmond (Arup) den Pavillon für 2005 entwarf. Die Architekten hatten bereits am Portugiesischen Pavillon für die Expo 1998 in Lissabon (1995–ˢ und am Portugiesischen Pavillon für die Expo 2000 in Hannover zusammengearbeitet. Der Pavillon mit einer Grundfläche von 22 x 17 m und einer maximalen Höhe ʷ 5,4 m war eine stützenfreie Holzkonstruktion, die mit halbtransparenten, 5 mm dicken Polykarbonatplatten eingedeckt war. Von den Architekten entworfene Tische ʋ Stühle komplettierten den Innenraum des Pavillons, der im Oktober 2005 abgebaut wurde. 427 verschiedene Holzbinder bildeten das komplexe, ineinander greifer Konstruktionssystem. Beginnend auf einer Seite, »strahlte dieses System aus, um den gegenüberliegenden Punkt zu erreichen«. Hamish Nevile vom Ingenieurbüro Aʳ erläutert: »Das Dach ist eine Weiterentwicklung der Lamellen-Tonnendaches, das in Deutschland in den frühen 1920ern entwickelt wurde. Die traditionellen Lamel waren identische Konstruktionselemente, bei dem Pavillon hingegen hat jedes Element eine unterschiedliche Länge und Neigung. Mit dieser geometrischen Freiheit kor te die komplexe Form, die die Architekten wünschten, ihren präzisen Ausdruck finden. Das wechselständige Trägersystem schafft eine durchgehende Struktur, die ʋ Dach hinunter die Wände des Pavillons bildet.«

Edifié du 11 avril au 30 juin 2005, ce pavillon temporaire de 380 m² est le cinquième à être construit dans les jardins de Kensington, près de la Serpentine G lery, ancien pavillon de thé datant de 1934 et lieu d'exposition d'art contemporain. Les précédents projets avaient été conçus par Zaha Hadid (2000), Daniel Libesk (2001), Toyo Ito (2002) et Oscar Niemeyer (2003). Un ambitieux projet programmé pour 2004 par l'agence néerlandaise MvRdV a été retardé. Álvaro Siza a été app par la directrice de la galerie, Julia Peyton Jones, pour réaliser la version 2005 en collaboration avec Eduardo Souto de Moura et Cecil Balmond (Arup). Les architec avaient déjà travaillé ensemble sur le pavillon portugais de l'Expo 1998 à Lisbonne (1995–98) et à l'Expo 2000 à Hanovre. D'une emprise au sol de 22 x 17 m et d'ʋ hauteur maximum de 5,4 m, le pavillon est une structure en bois, sans colonnes porteuses, à couverture en polycarbonate semi-transparent de 5 mm d'épaisseur. ɪ tables et des chaises dessinées par les architectes équipent l'intérieur. Quelque 427 poutres en bois d'un dessin unique ont été montées, selon un système comple qui part d'un angle et «irradie jusqu'à l'extrémité opposée». Comme l'explique Hamish Nevile, de l'agence d'ingénierie Arup, «c'est une évolution de la voûte en b: ceau à lamelles mise au point en Allemagne au début des années 1920. Alors que les lamelles traditionnelles étaient faites d'éléments identiques, chaque élément ce pavillon est unique puisqu'il présente une longueur et une inclinaison différentes. Cette liberté géométrique permet une expression précise de la forme comple demandée par les architectes. Le système réciproque des poutres génère une structure continue qui court du toit jusqu'au sol pour former les murs du pavillo L'ensemble a été démonté en octobre 2005.

...rchitecture fans might well have had ...difficult time identifying the design-...(s) of the 2005 Serpentine Pavilion, ...nce it looks nothing much like the ...arlier work of either Álvaro Siza or ...duardo Souto de Moura.

Architekturfans hatten es vielleicht nicht leicht, den/die Architekten des Serpentine Pavilions 2005 zu benennen, da der Bau weder den früheren Gebäuden von Siza noch denen von Souto de Moura besonders ähnelt.

Les amateurs d'architecture ont pu avoir quelques difficultés à identifier les auteurs du pavillon de la Serpentine 2005, tant il diffère des œuvres antérieures aussi bien d'Álvaro Siza que d'Eduardo Souto de Moura.

...sketch by Siza below shows the
...owing, almost organic concept of
...e Pavilion. The nature and spacing
...f its armature gives rise to unex-
...ected visual effects under certain
...ngles.

...izas Skizze zeigt das fließende, fast
...ganische Konzept des Pavillons.
...ie Art der Konstruktion und die
...bstände zwischen den Elementen
...es Gerüsts führen aus bestimm-
...n Perspektiven zu unerwarteten
...otischen Effekten.

Un croquis de Siza, ci-dessous,
montre la conception en flux, presque
organique du pavillon. La nature et
l'espacement de l'armature génèrent
des effets visuels inattendus sous
certains angles.

PETER STUTCHBURY

Stutchbury & Pape Pty Ltd.
4/364 Barrenjoey Road
Newport Beach NSW 2106
Australia

Tel: +61 299 79 50 30
Fax +61 299 79 53 67
e-mail: info@peterstutchbury.com.au
Web: www.peterstutchbury.com.au

A graduate of the University of Newcastle, Australia in 1978, **PETER STUTCHBURY** lived "on the land" as a child and with aborigines on the banks of the Dæling River and with tribes in the highlands of New Guinea. He works with his wife and business partner Phoebe Pape, who is a landscape architect, on houses "that n⫶ture their occupants and celebrate a palpable spirit of place." The firm has been given 24 awards by the Royal Australian Institute of Architects (RAIA) since 1999. 2003 Peter Stutchbury was the first architect ever to win both the top National Architecture Awards from the RAIA for residential and non-residential projects with ⫶ Robin Boyd Award for houses for the Bay House at Watson's Bay, Sydney, and the Sir Zelman Cowan Award for Public Buildings for Birabahn, the Aboriginal Cultural Ceⴚter at the University of Newcastle. Architect of the Sydney 2000 Olympics Archery Pavilion, he has also built several structures on the University of Newcastle campⴚ including the Design Building and the Nursing Building (with EJE Architecture), the Aboriginal Center (with Richard Leplastrier and Sue Harper), and the Life Scienc⫶ Building (with Suters Architects). His built work includes: Israel House, Paradise Beach (1982–92); Treetop House, Clareville (1991); McMaster Residence, Hawk's Neⴚ (1995–98); Kangaroo Valleys Pavilion (1996–98); Reeves House, Claireville Beach (1997–99); and the Wedge House (2001).

PETER STUTCHBURY machte 1978 an der University of Newcastle in Australien seinen Abschluss. Als Kind lebte er »auf dem Land«, genauer gesagt mit dⴚ Aborigines am Ufer des Darling River und mit Naturvölkern im Hochland von Neuguinea. Er arbeitet mit seiner Frau und Geschäftspartnerin Phoebe Pape, einer Larⴚ schaftsplanerin, zusammen. Die von ihnen geplanten Häuser »nähren ihre Bewohner und zelebrieren den spürbaren Geist des Ortes«. Seit 1999 erhielt das Büro 24 Prⴚ se des Royal Australian Institute of Architects (RAIA). 2003 war Peter Stutchbury der erste Architekt, der je mit den beiden höchsten National Architecture Awards dⴚ RAIA in den Kategorien »Wohnbauten« und »Gewerbebauten/Öffentliche Bauten« ausgezeichnet wurde: Für das Bay House an der Watson's Bay in Sydney erhielt er dⴚ Robin Boyd Award für ein Privathaus und für Birabahn, das Kulturzentrum der Aborigines der University of Newcastle, den Sir Zelman Cowan Award für ein öffentlichⴚ Gebäude. Er hat den Pavillon für das Bogenschießen bei den Olympischen Spielen 2000 in Sydney entworfen, ferner diverse Campusbauten der University of Newcastⴚ darunter das Design Building und das Nursing Building (mit EJE Architecture), das Kulturzentrum der Aborigines (mit Richard Leplastrier und Sue Harper) und das Natⴚ wissenschaftliche Gebäude (mit Suters Architects). Weitere Bauten des Büros sind u. a. das Israel House, Paradise Beach (1982–92), das Treetop House in Clarevⴚ (1991), die McMaster Residence in Hawk's Nest (1995–98), der Kangaroo Valleys Pavilion (1996–98), das Reeves House, Claireville Beach (1997–99) und das Wedⴚ House (2001).

Diplômé de l'Université de Newcastle (Australie) en 1978, **PETER STUTCHBURY** a passé son enfance « dans les terres » avec les Aborigènes des rives de la Daⴚ ling River et des tribus des hautes terres de Nouvelle-Guinée. Il travaille avec son épouse et associée, l'architecte-paysagiste Phoebe Pape, à des projets de maisoⴚ « qui enrichissent leurs occupants et célèbrent un esprit du lieu palpable ». L'agence a reçu vingt-quatre prix du Royal Australian Institute of Architects (RAIA) depuis 199ⴚ En 2003, Stutchbury a été le premier architecte à remporter les principaux prix du RAIA à la fois pour les projets résidentiels et pour les non-résidentiels : le Robin Boⴚ Award (maisons individuelles) pour sa Bay House à Watson's Bay et le Sir Zelman Cowan Award (bâtiments publics) pour Birabahn, le Centre culturel aborigène de l'Unⴚ versité de Newcastle. Architecte du pavillon des archers des Jeux olympiques de Sydney en 2000, il a également réalisé plusieurs bâtiments pour le campus ⴚ l'Université de Newcastle, dont le Design Building et le Nursing Building (en collaboration avec EJE Architecture), le Aboriginal Center (avec Richard Leplastrier et Sⴚ Harper) et le Life Sciences Building (avec Suters Architects). Parmi ses autres réalisations : Israel House, Paradise Beach (1982–92) ; Treetop House, Clareville (199ⴚ McMaster Residence, Hawk's Nest (1995–98) ; Kangaroo Valleys Pavilion (1996–98) ; Reeves House, Clareville Beach (1997–99) et la Wedge House (2001).

SPRINGWATER

Seaforth, Sydney, New South Wales, Australia, 1999–2002

Floor area: 514 m² (including terraces). Client: not disclosed. Cost: not disclosed

Built on a 1478 m² site on Sydney Harbor "foreshore", the **SPRINGWATER** house has a floor area of 514 m² (including terraces, decks and lap pool). Stutchbury says that the house is "Conceived as a reliable camp, the frame is concrete on stone." Galvanized steel frames are bolted onto the structure, and "long building fingers down the site toward the harbor allow the land a conscious freedom." Set on three levels, with ceiling heights adjusted according to their position on site, "the building is skinned simply allowing the user to operate walls, adjusting to views and cooling breezes as required." The architect says that "the house sits as only a veil within the landscape" allowing constant views of the landscape, or alternatively a certain amount of shelter as required by the inhabitants. Built for a relatively low cost, in part because of "systematic and repetitive structure/formwork and similar door window systems," Springwater is entered "deliberately down, toward the view, onto an open courtyard … North."

Das **SPRINGWATER**-Haus wurde auf einem 1478 m² großen Grundstück im Küstenvorland des Hafens von Sydney gebaut. Die Terrassen, Decks und den Bahnenpool eingerechnet beträgt die Grundfläche des Hauses 514 m². Stutchbury sagt: »Das Haus ist als ein ›verlässlicher Ruheplatz‹ entworfen. Die Konstruktion ist aus Beton, der Untergrund aus Stein.« An das Haus sind verzinkte Stahlkonstruktionen angeschraubt, und lange ›Gebäudefinger‹ in Richtung Hang und Hafen lassen dem Grundstück bewusst seine Freiheit«. Das Haus hat drei Ebenen. Die Deckenhöhen richten sich nach der Position der Ebenen auf dem Grundstück. Das Gebäude »ist einfach gebaut, damit die Nutzer auf einfache Weise Wände verschieben können, je nach dem, welche Aussicht sie wünschen oder wo sie eine kühlende Brise benöti-gen«. Der Architekt kommentiert: »Das Haus liegt wie ein Schleier auf der Landschaft« und bietet den Bewohnern, je nach ihren Bedürfnissen, Blicke in die Natur oder aber auch ein bestimmtes Maß an Schutz. Die Baukosten waren relativ niedrig, z. T. aufgrund »einer systematischen und sich wiederholenden Konstruktion bzw. Scha-lung und ähnlicher Tür- und Fenstersysteme«. Springwater wird absichtlich in Richtung des Hangs, also nach unten, betreten, zum Ausblick hin, auf einen offenen Hof nach Norden.«

Édifiée sur un terrain de 1478 m² sur le port même de Sydney, la maison **SPRINGWATER** a une superficie de 514 m² (y compris ses terrasses, ses plates-formes et le bassin). Pour Stutchbury, cette maison est « conçue comme un camp dans lequel on se sentirait en sécurité… l'ossature en béton est posée sur la pierre » Les cadres d'acier galvanisé sont boulonnés sur l'ossature et « les ailes qui s'avancent comme des doigts vers le port créent un sentiment de liberté ». Comptant deux étages, avec des hauteurs sous plafond variant en fonction de la position sur le terrain, « la maison a été habillée d'une peau simple qui permet à l'occupant de modi-fier les murs, de les adapter au panorama et aux brises rafraîchissantes à volonté… elle est comme un voile dans le paysage » et le propriétaire peut soit profiter de la vue, soit recréer une certaine protection, en fonction de ses désirs. Construite pour un budget relativement réduit grâce, notamment, à des « coffrages d'ossature systé-matisés et répétitifs et à des systèmes de portes et fenêtres similaires », la maison s'ouvre au visiteur « délibérément par le bas, vers la vue, sur une cour ouverte vers le nord ».

Springwater is a spectacular jux-taposition of strong architectural elements with an equally powerful natural setting.

Springwater ist eine spektakuläre Gegenüberstellung von kraftvollen architektonischen Elementen und einer ebenso kraftvollen Naturkulisse.

Springwater est une juxtaposition spectaculaire d'éléments architec-turaux puissants dans un cadre naturel tout aussi fort.

The twisting form of tree trunks
does not seem to be contradictory
to the sharply defined verticals and
horizontals of the house. Gaps and
openings allow the natural setting
to be admired while creating a
dynamism in the architecture itself.

Die verschlungenen Formen der
Baumstämme wirken den klar defi-
nierten Vertikalen und Horizontalen
des Hauses nicht entgegen. Lücken
und Öffnungen erlauben es, die
natürliche Umgebung zu genießen
und lassen die Architektur dynamisch
wirken.

Les silhouettes tordues des troncs
d'arbres ne contrarient nullement
les verticales et les horizontales très
nettes de la maison. Les ouvertures
et les failles permettent d'admirer
la nature tout en dynamisant
l'architecture.

YOSHIO TANIGUCHI

Yoshio Taniguchi
Yanakatsu Building 7F
4–1–40 Toranomon
Minato-ku, Tokyo 105–0001
Japan

Tel: +81 334 38 12 47
Fax: +81 334 38 12 48

Museum of Modern

YOSHIO TANIGUCHI was born in Tokyo in 1937. He received a Bachelor's degree in Mechanical Engineering from Keio University in 1960 and a Master of Architecture degree from the Harvard Graduate School of Design in 1964. He worked in the office Kenzo Tange from 1964 to 1972. He created Taniguchi, Takamiya and Associates in 1975, and Taniguchi and Associates in 1979. His built work includes the Tokyo Sea Life Park, Tokyo (1989); Marugame Genichiro-Inokuma Museum of Contemporary Art and Marugame City Library, Marugame (1991); Toyota Municipal Museum of Art, Toyota City (1995); the Tokyo Kasai Rinkai Park View Point Visitors Cente Tokyo (1995); the Tokyo National Museum Gallery of Horyuji Treasures, Tokyo (1997–99), and the complete renovation and expansion of the Museum of Modern Art i New York published here. He won the project after a 1997 invited competition against Wiel Arets, Steven Holl, Rem Koolhaas, Herzog & de Meuron, Toyo Ito, Dominique Perrault, Bernard Tschumi, Rafael Viñoly, and Williams & Tsien. He is completing the Kyoto National Museum, Centennial Hall (2006), and beginning work on Asia Hous in Houston.

YOSHIO TANIGUCHI wurde 1937 in Tokio geboren. Er machte seinen Bachelor in Maschinenbau 1960 an der Keio University und seinen Master of Architectu an der Harvard Graduate School of Design 1964. Von 1964 bis 1972 arbeitete er im Büro von Kenzo Tange. 1975 gründete er Taniguchi, Takamiya and Associates, 19 Taniguchi and Associates. Das Büro hat u. a. folgende Gebäude realisiert: den Tokyo Sea Life Park in Tokio (1989), das Marugame Genichiro-Inokuma Museum für mode ne Kunst und die Stadtbibliothek in Marugame (1991), das Städtische Toyota Museum für Kunst in Toyota City (1995), das Aussichts- und Besucherzentrum im Kasai Ri kai Park in Tokio (1995) und die Galerie für Horyuji Schätze im Tokioer Nationalmuseum (1997–99) sowie die hier gezeigte umfassende Sanierung und Erweiterung d Museum of Modern Art in New York, für die Taniguchi 1997 einen eingeladenen Wettbewerb gewonnen hatte, an dem außer ihm Wiel Arets, Steven Holl, Rem Koolhaa Herzog & de Meuron, Toyo Ito, Dominique Perrault, Bernard Tschumi, Rafael Viñoly und Williams & Tsien teilnahmen. Die Hundertjahrhalle des Nationalmuseums in Kio wird derzeit fertig gestellt (2006), danach beginnen die Arbeiten am Asia House in Houston.

Né à Tokyo en 1937, **YOSHIO TANIGUCHI** est diplômé en ingénierie mécanique de l'Université Keio (1960) et Master of Architecture de la Harvard Gradua School of Design (1964). Il a travaillé pour Kenzo Tange de 1964 à 1972 et a créé Taniguchi, Takamiya and Associates en 1975, puis Taniguchi and Associates en 19 Parmi ses réalisations : le Parc de la vie sous-marine de Tokyo (1989) ; Le musée d'Art contemporain et la bibliothèque de la ville de Marugame, Marugame (1991) Musée d'art municipal Toyota, Toyota-City (1995) ; le Belvédère du centre des visiteurs du Kasai Rinkai Park, Tokyo (1995) ; la galerie des Trésors Horuji du Musée na nal de Tokyo, Tokyo (1997–98) et la rénovation et l'extension du Museum of Modern Art de New York. Il en avait remporté le concours sur invitation face à Wiel Are Steven Holl, Rem Koolhaas, Herzog & de Meuron, Toyo Ito, Dominique Perrault, Bernard Tschumi, Rafael Viñoly et Williams & Tsien. Il achève actuellement le Musée na nal de Kyoto, Centennial Hall (2006) et travaille sur un projet de Maison de l'Asie à Houston.

THE MUSEUM OF MODERN ART EXPANSION AND RENOVATION

New York, New York, USA, 2002–04

Floor area: 24 000 m² (new space). Client: The Trustees of the Museum of Modern Art.
Cost: $315 million (construction)

A mere twenty years after the 1984 expansion of New York's **MUSEUM OF MODERN ART** by Cesar Pelli that created the greenhouse-like rear of the museum and its single place escalators, the institution has reemerged in a surprising new form, laid out, at least in its major components, by Tokyo architect Yoshio Taniguchi. T total budget for the project was 425 million dollars, with construction alone costing 315 million dollars, yet even these figures understate total expenses that rise to 8 million dollars when the costs of MoMA Queens and moving back and forth are added to some acquisitions. Although some say that MoMA lost its original spirit wh Pelli added a 55-story residential tower to the premises, the Taniguchi-led expansion creates vast spaces that the curators have clearly had difficulty filling, as is case in the monumental 33.5-meter high second-floor atrium. Adding roughly 24 000 square meters to the institution, and doubling its available exhibition spa Taniguchi achieved a remarkable degree of refinement and detailing on this project, considering that he was not familiar with American building methods. As early the schematic design phase, the Museum of Modern Art proposed that Taniguchi work with a firm that had local building experience. Kohn Pedersen Fox (KPF) w selected and ultimately became the executive architect for the project, with Gregory Clement and Steven Rustow heading their effort. Rustow had considerable muse experience, having worked actively on I. M. Pei's Grand Louvre project and in particular the Richelieu Wing phase. KPF was also called to supervise the renovation of original 1939 building by Phillip Goodwin and Edward Durrell Stone as well as Philip Johnson's 1964 east wing addition. Philip Johnson's 1953 sculpture garden, in expanded version, emerges as the real center of the new MoMA, where much of the new construction can be admired in a peaceful atmosphere.

Nur 20 Jahre nach der Erweiterung des **MUSEUM OF MODERN ART** durch Cesar Pelli im Jahr 1984 hat sich die Institution in einer überraschenden Form r erfunden. Pelli hatte das Museum mit einem rückwärtigen wintergartenähnlichen Anbau versehen und es mit Rolltreppen in diesem Bereich ausgestattet. Der anspruch volle Entwurf für die neuerliche Erweiterung stammt zum größten Teil von dem Tokioer Architekten Yoshio Taniguchi. Die Kosten für das Projekt beliefen sich auf umg rechnet 353 Millionen Euro, davon waren allein 261 Millionen Euro reine Baukosten. Aber selbst diese hohen Zahlen entsprechen nicht den Gesamtkosten, die etwa 7 Millionen Euro betragen, wenn man den Umzug des MoMA nach Queens und wieder zurück und einige Ankäufe hinzurechnet. Pelli hatte 1984 dem Museum zusätzl einen 55-geschossigen Wohnturm angefügt (manche meinen, das MoMA hätte dadurch seinen ursprünglichen Charakter verloren). Taniguchi ist es trotzdem gelunge das Gebäude um Räume mit beträchtlichen Ausmaßen zu erweitern. Offensichtlich hatten die Kuratoren aber einige Probleme, diese zu füllen – deutlich wird dies im 33,5 hohen monumentalen Atrium im 1. Obergeschoss. Die Erweiterung umfasst 24 000 m² und verdoppelt die bisher vorhandene Ausstellungsfläche. Taniguchi hat ein bemerkenswerten Grad der Verfeinerung und Qualität der Ausführung erreicht und dies, obwohl er mit der amerikanischen Praxis der Bauausführung nicht vertraut w Schon in der Phase der Entwurfsplanung schlug das Museum of Modern Art Taniguchi vor, mit einem Büro mit Bauerfahrung in den USA zusammenzuarbeiten. Ko Pedersen Fox (KPF) wurde als Projektpartner ausgewählt und war für die Ausführung zuständig. Gregory Clement und Steven Rustow waren die Projektleiter. Rustow, im Museumsbau sehr erfahrener Architekt, hatte vorher im Büro von I. M. Pei an der Erweiterung des Grand Louvre mitgewirkt, und hier besonders am Richelieu-Flüg KPF wurde auch beauftragt, die Sanierung des ursprünglichen MoMA-Gebäudes von Phillip Goodwin und Edward Durell Stone aus dem Jahr 1939 und des Ostflügels v Philip Johnson aus dem Jahr 1964 zu leiten. Philip Johnsons 1953 geschaffener Skulpturgarten wurde erweitert und entpuppt sich als wahres Zentrum des neuen Mus ums, von dem aus man einen Großteil des neuen MoMA sehen und in einer friedlichen Atmosphäre bewundern kann.

Vingt ans après l'intervention de Cesar Pelli sur le **MUSEUM OF MODERN ART** de New York, qui avait créé l'extension en forme de serre à l'arrière du mus et posé d'étroits escaliers mécaniques, l'institution connaît aujourd'hui une mutation formelle conçue, pour sa majeure partie, par l'architecte tokyoïte Yoshio Tanigu Le budget total de l'opération s'est élevé à 353 millions d'euros, dont 261 pour la seule construction. Cependant, l'investissement s'élèvera à 713 millions lorsque coûts du MoMA Queens et des différents déménagements auront été intégrés. Si certains ont pu dire que le musée avait déjà perdu son esprit originel lorsque Pelli ajouta une tour d'appartements de 55 étages, l'extension de Taniguchi a créé de vastes espaces que les conservateurs semblent avoir quelques difficultés à maîtris en particulier les 33,5 m de haut du monumental atrium du premier étage. Tout en ajoutant 24 000 m² et en doublant les espaces d'exposition, Taniguchi a atteint remarquable niveau de raffinement, surtout quand on sait qu'il n'était pas familier des méthodes de construction américaines. Dès la phase des plans, le MoMA a p posé que l'architecte collabore avec une agence dotée d'une expérience locale. Kohn Pedersen Fox (KPF) fut sélectionnée et finit par devenir l'architecte exécutif de l'e semble du projet, sous la direction de Gregory Clement et Steven Rustow. Rustow possède une longue expérience des musées puisqu'il a travaillé activement au Gra Louvre de I. M. Pei, en particulier sur l'aile Richelieu. KPF a également été invitée à superviser la rénovation du bâtiment d'origine de Philip Goodwin et Edward Du Stone (1939) et de l'aile est, ajoutée en 1964 par Philip Johnson. Le Jardin de sculptures de Johnson (1953) est devenu, après agrandissement, le vrai centre du mus d'où la plus grande partie du nouveau bâtiment peut être admirée dans une atmosphère paisible.

A new building by Taniguchi looks over the slightly extended area of MoMA's Sculpture Garden. Within, design reclaims the place of honor it had in the museum's earlier incarnations.

Das neue Museumsgebäude von Taniguchi überblickt den etwas vergrößerten Skulpturengarten des MoMA. Innen erobert sich die Designabteilung den Rang zurück, den sie früher im Museum hatte.

Le nouveau bâtiment de Taniguchi donne sur le Jardin de sculptures du MoMA, légèrement agrandi. L'intérieur a été totalement repensé, comme lors des précédentes interventions sur ce musée.

Some of the museum space seems to be too large for the art that is exhibited there, and overall, the massive expansion seems to rob MoMA of the intimacy which remained part of its character even after the most recent expansion by Cesar Pelli.

Certains volumes sont, semble-t-il, trop grands pour les œuvres qu'ils accueillent. Cette brutale expansion prive peut-être le MoMA de l'intimité qui le caractérisait, même après les dernières interventions de Cesar Pelli.

Einige der neuen Museumsräume scheinen zu groß für die in ihnen ausgestellte Kunst zu sein. Insgesamt verliert das MoMA durch die umfangreiche Erweiterung an Intimität, die – auch nach der vorletzten Erweiterung durch Cesar Pelli – einen Teil seines Charmes ausmachte.

TEZUKA ARCHITECTS

Tezuka Architects
1–19–9–3F Todoroki
Setagaya Tokyo 158–0082
Japan

Tel: +81 3 37 03 70 56
Fax: +81 3 37 03 70 38
e-mail: tez@sepia.ocn.ne.jp
Web: www.tezuka-arch.com

Matsunoyama Natural Science Mus

TAKAHARU TEZUKA, born in Tokyo in 1964, received his degrees from the Musashi Institute of Technology (1987), and from the University of Pennsylvan (1990). He worked with Richard Rogers Partnership Ltd (1994) and established Tezuka Architects the same year. Born in Kanagawa in 1964, Yui Tezuka was educated the Musashi Institute of Technology and the Bartlett School of Architecture, University College, London. The practice has completed more than 20 private houses, ar won the competition for the Matsunoyama Museum of Natural Sciences in 2000. Since then it has been based in Tokyo. Their work includes the Soejima Hospital; Jyubah House; Shoe Box House; Big Window House; Observatory House; Forest House; Clipping Corner House; Floating House; Engawa House; House to Catch the Sky III; Sa Roof House; Skylight House; Canopy House; Thin Wall House; Thin Roof House; Anthill House; Step House; The House To Catch The Sky 2; The House To Catch The Sk 1; Wall-less House; Roof House; Megaphone House; Machiya House; Light Gauge Steel House and the Wood Deck House.

TAKAHARU TEZUKA, 1964 in Tokio geboren, machte seine Abschlüsse 1987 am Technischen Institut Musashi und 1990 an der University of Pennsylvania. 199 arbeitete er bei Richard Rogers Partnership Ltd und gründete im selben Jahr Tezuka Architects. Yui Tezuka, geboren 1964 in Kanagawa, studierte ebenfalls am Techn schen Institut Musashi und an der Bartlett School of Architecture am University College of London. Das Büro hat mehr als 20 Privathäuser gebaut und 2000 den We bewerb für das Naturwissenschaftliche Museum Matsunoyama gewonnen. Seit dem Gewinn des Wettbewerbs befindet sich das Büro in Tokio. Tezuka Architects habe u. a. folgende Projekte realisiert: das Krankenhaus Soejima, das Jyubako Haus, das Schuhschachtel-Haus, das Haus »Großes Fenster«, das Sternwarten-Haus, das Wale haus, das Haus »Abgeschnittene Ecke«, das schwebende Haus und das Engawa Haus, ferner das »Fang-den-Himmel-Haus III«, das Sägedach-Haus, das Oberlicht-Hau das Vordach-Haus, das Haus »Dünne Wand«, das Haus »Dünnes Dach«, das Ameisenhügel-Haus, das Stufen-Haus, das »Fang-den-Himmel-Haus II«, das »Fang-den-Hir mel-Haus I«, das »Haus ohne Wände«, das Dach-Haus, das Megafon-Haus, das Machiya Haus, das »Lichtfühler-Stahlhaus« und das Holzterrassen-Haus.

TAKAHARU TEZUKA, né à Tokyo en 1964, est diplômé de l'Institut de technologie Musashi (1987) et de l'Université de Pennsylvanie (1990). Il a travaillé po Richard Rogers Partnership Ltd (1994) et fondé l'agence Tezuka Architects la même année. Né à Kanagawa en 1964, Yui Tezuka est diplômé de l'Institut de technolog Musashi et de la Bartlett School of Architecture, University College, Londres. Installée aujourd'hui à Tokyo, l'agence a déjà réalisé l'hôpital de Soejima, Japon (1996) plus de 20 résidences privées : Jyubako House ; Shoe Box House ; Big Window House ; Observatory House ; Forest House ; Clipping Corner House ; Floating House ; Eng wa House ; House to Catch the Sky III ; Saw Roof House ; Skylight House ; Canopy House ; Thin Wall House ; Thin Roof House ; Anthill House ; Step House ; The House Catch The Sky II ; The House To Catch The Sky 1 ; Wall-less House ; Roof House ; Megaphone House ; Machiya House ; Light Gauge Steel House and the Wood Deck Hous Tezuka Architects a remporté le concours pour le Musée des sciences naturelles de Matsunoyama en 2000.

MATSUNOYAMA NATURAL SCIENCE MUSEUM

Matsunoyama, Niigata, Japan, 2002–04

Floor area: 1248 m². Client: Matsunoyama-machi/Secretariat of Tokamachi Regionwide Area Municipal Corporation. Cost: €5.4 million

Located approximately 200 km to the north of Tokyo in a region that has the heaviest snowfalls of Japan (up to five meters), the **MATSUNOYAMA NATURAL SCIENCE MUSEUM** was built without firm foundations because the building expands 20 cm in summer. A Corten steel tube designed to resist snow loads of up to 2000 tons meanders over a length of 111 meters, following the topography and allowing visitors to "experience the light and colors under the different depths of snow from 4 m deep to 30 m above the ground." Steel plates 6 mm thick weighing 500 tons were welded in place to the load-bearing steel structure, and four large windows made of 75 mm-thick Perspex and located at the turning points in the museum space permit direct observation of life under the snow. A 34-meter-high observation tower, the only element with a normal foundation, completes the project. Tezuka Architects describe the structure as a "submarine, with the tower its periscope," in a willful effort to contrast with the white natural winter landscape.

Das **NATURWISSENSCHAFTLICHE MUSEUM MATSUNOYAMA** liegt etwa 200 km nördlich von Tokio. In dieser Region gibt es die stärksten Schneefälle in Japan – der Schnee kann hier bis zu 5 m hoch liegen. Das Gebäude dehnt sich im Sommer 20 cm aus und hat daher keine festen Fundamente. Eine 111 m lange, mäandrierende Röhre aus Corten-Stahl, die Schneelasten bis 2000 t abfangen kann, folgt der Topografie und ermöglicht es dem Besucher »das Licht und die Farben unter dem Schnee, der sich hier 4 bis 30 m hoch auftürmt, zu erleben«. 6 mm dicke Stahlplatten mit einem Gesamtgewicht von 500 t wurden vor Ort an die tragende Stahlkonstruktion geschweißt. Vier große Fenster mit 75 mm dicken Perspex-Scheiben sind an den Stellen angeordnet, an denen sich die Richtung des Museumsraums ändert. Hier kann das Leben im Schnee direkt beobachtet werden. Ein 34 m hoher Aussichtsturm, der einzige Teil des Museums mit normalen Fundamenten, komplettiert die Anlage. Tezuka Architects beschreiben das Gebäude als »ein U-Boot – mit dem Turm als Periskop«. Der Turm stellt dabei einen gewollten Kontrast zur weißen Winterlandschaft her.

Situé à environ 200 km au nord de Tokyo dans une région qui connaît les plus importantes chutes de neige du Japon (jusqu'à 5 m), ce **MUSÉE DES SCIENCES NATURELLES** a été construit sans fondations fixes car il se dilate de 20 cm en été… Il s'agit essentiellement d'un tube en acier Corten conçu pour résister à une charge de neige de 2000 tonnes, qui se fond dans la topographie sur une longueur de 111 m et permet aux visiteurs « de faire l'expérience de la lumière et des couleurs sous différentes épaisseurs de neige, de 4 m de profondeur jusqu'à 30 m au-dessus du niveau du sol ». Les 500 tonnes de tôles d'acier de 6 mm d'épaisseur ont été soudées sur place sur la structure porteuse en acier et quatre grandes baies fermées d'un panneau de Perspex de 75 mm d'épaisseur positionnées aux angles de la structure pour faciliter l'observation directe de la vie sous la neige. Une tour d'observation de 34 m de haut, seul élément à posséder des fondations normales, complète l'ensemble. Tezuka Architects décrit ce musée comme « un sous-marin, dont la tour serait le périscope », volontairement conçu pour contraster avec le paysage hivernal enneigé.

The rusted Corten steel exterior of the museum gives it something of the appearance of a curious industrial artifact, lost in the woods.

Die rostige Fassade aus Corten-Stahl gibt dem Museum etwas von einem sonderbaren industriellen Relikt, das im Wald vergessen wurde.

Sa peau en acier Corten patiné donne au musée l'apparence d'un objet industriel bizarre perdu dans les bois.

A café offers an outside view, while exhibitions concentrate on the uniqu ecosystems of this region which is prone to very heavy snow in winter.

Das Café bietet einen Ausblick nach draußen. Die Ausstellungen konzentrieren sich auf die einzigartigen Ökosysteme der Region, die im Winter heftigen Schneefällen ausgesetzt ist.

Le café bénéficie d'une vue sur l'extérieur tandis que les expositions se concentrent sur les écosystèmes spécifiques à cette région sujette à d'importantes chutes de neige en hiver.

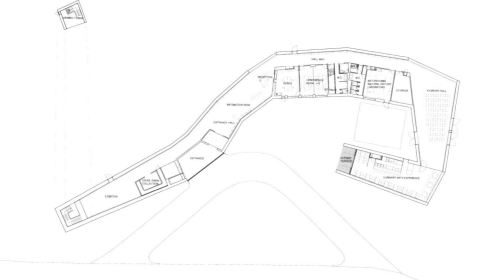

TRAHAN ARCHITECTS

Trahan Architects
445 North Boulevard, Suite 570
Baton Rouge, Louisiana 70802
USA

Tel: +1 225 924 6333
Fax: +1 225 924 6498
e-mail: pthomas@trahanarchitects.com
Web: www.trahanarchitects.com

Holy Rosary Catholic Church Comp

VICTOR TRAHAN was born in Crowley, Louisiana. He received a Bachelor of Architecture degree from Louisiana State University in 1983. His work includes: the First National Bank Of Crowley, Crowley, Louisiana (1997); St. Jean Vianney Catholic Church, Baton Rouge, Louisiana (1999); LSU Academic Center For Student Athletes, Baton Rouge, Louisiana (2002); and the Holy Rosary Catholic Church Complex, St. Amant, Louisiana published here, which won a National AIA Honor Award For Excellence In Architectural Design (2005). Recent and current work includes: LSU Tiger Stadium East and West Side Expansion, Baton Rouge, Louisiana (2005); (MSEAR) Institute of Medicine Science Experience and Research, Beijing, China (completion date 2007); and an office tower in Baton Rouge, Louisiana (due for 2007 completion). He also participated in the 2002 World Trade Center Memorial competition.

VICTOR TRAHAN, geboren in Crowley, Louisiana, machte seinen Bachelor of Architecture 1983 an der Louisiana State University. Bauten des Büros sind u. a. die First National Bank of Crowley in Crowley, Louisiana (1997), die katholische Kirche St. Jean Vianney in Baton Rouge, Louisiana (1999), das LSU Academic Center for Student Athletes, ebenfalls in Baton Rouge (2002), und der Holy Rosary Catholic Church Complex in St. Amant, Louisiana (hier gezeigt), der 2005 mit dem National AIA Honor Award für die besondere Qualität des architektonischen Entwurfs ausgezeichnet wurde. Zu den neuesten Projekten des Büros gehören die östliche und westliche Erweiterung des LSU Tiger Stadium in Baton Rouge, (2005), das Institute of Medicine Science Experience and Research (MSEAR) in Peking (Fertigstellung 2007) und ein Bürohochhaus in Baton Rouge, das 2007 vollendet sein soll. 2002 nahmen Trahan Architects am Wettbewerb für das Mahnmal für das World Trade Center in New York teil.

VICTOR TRAHAN, né à Crowley (Louisiane), est Bachelor of Architecture de la Louisiana State University (1983). Parmi ses réalisations : First National Bank of Crowley, Crowley (1997) ; église catholique de Saint-Jean Vianney, Baton Rouge, Louisiane (1999) ; LSU Academic Center for Student Athletes, Baton Rouge (2002) ; complexe de l'église catholique du Saint-Rosaire de Saint Amant (Louisiane) publié ici, qui lui a valu un prix d'honneur pour l'excellence de la conception architecturale de l'AIA (2005). Récemment construit : l'extension du LSU Tiger Stadium à Baton Rouge (2005). Il a participé en 2002 au concours pour le Mémorial du World Trade Center à New York et travaille actuellement au projet de l'Institut des sciences, de l'expérimentation et de la recherche médicale de Pékin qui sera livré en 2007 et à celui d'une tour de bureaux à Baton Rouge, également prévue pour 2007.

HOLY ROSARY CATHOLIC CHURCH COMPLEX

St. Amant, Louisiana, USA, 2000–04

Floor area: 1586 m². Client: Holy Rosary Catholic Church, St. Amant, Lousiana.
Cost: $2.4 million

Trahan's strong, simple architecture honors the religious function of this small complex. The lack of color and the subtle landscaping participate in the creation of a religious mood.

Eine kraftvolle, klare Architektur unterstreicht die religiöse Funktion dieses kleinen Komplexes. Durch den Verzicht auf Farbe und die subtile landschaftsplanerische Gestaltung entsteht eine religiöse Stimmung.

L'architecture de Trahan, puissante et simple, est un hommage à la fonction religieuse de ce petit complexe. L'absence de couleur et un subtil aménagement paysager contribuent à créer une atmosphère de recueillement.

This 1586 m² complex was built on a seven-hectare site for a cost of 2.4 million dollars. As the architect explains the program, "The client is a rural Catholic Parish in South Louisiana with strong French influence. There are three buildings in the first phase of the Holy Rosary Complex – a structure housing the administrative functions of the parish; the religious education building; and the oratory, or chapel for the celebration of the rites. The oratory is intended for the daily use of small assemblies, less than 50 congregants. The parish desired a relationship between the oratory, the existing church and for there to be a place of prominence for this chapel in the new complex of buildings. The client also required the new complex to play an important role in the community life of the predominantly Catholic residents." Trahan was careful to separate the secular and sacred components of the complex. Inspiration for the cubic oratory comes from the womb and from the Japanese four-and-a-half tatami configuration. The architect explains that "This non-hierarchical system accommodates the numerous seating configurations for liturgical purposes." Intentionally limiting the use of costly or rare materials, the complex is built essentially of concrete and glass. Construction began on the Religious Education and Administration Building in 2000 and was completed in 2002. Construction began on the Chapel in 2003 and was completed in 2004. Trahan concludes "Neither opulent nor austere, the Chapel presents a thoughtful meditation on sacred spaces and the spatial embodiment of spiritual experience."

Die 1586 m² große Anlage wurde für umgerechnet fast 2 Millionen Euro auf einem 7 ha großen Grundstück errichtet. Die Architekten erklären das Programm wie folgt: »Der Bauherr ist ein ländlicher, katholischer, stark an Frankreich orientierter Pfarrbezirk im Süden Louisianas. Während des ersten Bauabschnitts wurden drei Bauten realisiert: ein Verwaltungsgebäude, eine Religionsschule und ein Andachtsraum bzw. eine Kapelle, in der die religiösen Rituale zelebriert werden. Die Kapelle wird täglich genutzt, weniger als 50 Gläubige versammeln sich hier. Die Gemeinde wünschte einen Bezug zwischen der Kapelle und der bereits vorhandenen Kirche; die Kapelle sollte innerhalb der neuen Anlage einen besonderen Platz einnehmen. Der Bauherr wollte außerdem, dass die Gebäudegruppe im Gemeindeleben der hauptsächlich katholischen Bewohner eine wichtige Rolle spielt.« Trahan hat die säkularen und die sakralen Elemente der Anlage sorgfältig voneinander getrennt. Inspirationen für den kubischen Andachtsraum waren der Mutterleib und das japanische Grundmuster aus viereinhalb Tatami-Matten. Dazu der Architekt: »Dieses nicht hierarchische System erlaubt verschiedene Sitzanordnungen, passend zu dem jeweiligen liturgischen Zweck.« Die Verwendung von kostbaren oder seltenen Materialien wurde bewusst eingeschränkt, im Wesentlichen besteht der Bau aus Beton und Glas. 2000 wurde mit dem Bau des Schulgebäudes und des Verwaltungsbaus begonnen, die 2002 fertiggestellt waren. Die Bauzeit der Kapelle dauerte von 2003 bis 2004. Trahan: »Die Kapelle ist weder opulent noch erhaben. Sie stellt eine Meditation über heilige Räume und die räumliche Verkörperung des spirituellen Erlebnisses dar.«

Ce complexe de 1586 m² a été construit sur un terrain de sept hectares pour un budget de presque 2 millions d'euros. Comme l'explique l'architecte, « le client est une paroisse catholique rurale de la Louisiane du Sud, à forte influence française. Trois bâtiments ont été édifiés lors de la première phase : un pour les fonctions administratives de la paroisse, un autre pour l'enseignement religieux et enfin l'oratoire, ou chapelle, pour la célébration des offices. L'oratoire est conçu pour un usage quotidien par de petites assemblées de moins de 50 personnes. La paroisse souhaitait établir une relation entre ce lieu et l'église existante et qu'il occupe une position éminente dans le nouvel ensemble de bâtiments. Elle voulait également que l'ensemble joue un rôle important dans la vie de cette communauté rurale essentiellement catholique ». Trahan a séparé avec soin les composantes sacrées et séculières. La forme cubique de l'oratoire tire son inspiration de l'idée de matrice et de la configuration classique du tatami japonais. « Ce système non hiérarchique s'adapte à la disposition des sièges qui varie en fonction de la liturgie. » Le recours aux matériaux rares ou coûteux a été volontairement limité et le complexe est bâti essentiellement en béton et en verre. La construction a commencé en 2000 par les bâtiments administratifs et d'enseignement et s'est achevée en 2002. La chapelle, dont le chantier a débuté en 2003, a été livrée en 2004. Pour Trahan : « Ni opulente ni austère, cette chapelle est une méditation sur l'espace sacré et la matérialisation spatiale de l'expérience spirituelle. »

Although it is less ambitious than Pawson's Novy Dvůr, the Holy Rosary Church shares something of the bright austerity of its European counterpart.

Die Holy Rosary Church ist weniger ehrgeizig angelegt als Pawsons Novy-Dvůr-Projekt. Mit ihrem europäischen Gegenstück verbindet sie aber ihre helle Kargheit.

Bien que moins ambitieux que le monastère de Novy Dvůr par Pawson, le projet de l'église du Saint-Rosaire partage l'austérité lumineuse de l'exemple européen.

The play of light on concrete gives a more powerful message of religion than might a whole battery of outmoded objects. This is not the strict geometry of Ando, but the influence of Japanese architecture seems to have reached this place.

Das Spiel des Lichtes auf dem Beton vermittelt die religiöse Botschaft stärker als eine ganze Batterie unzeitgemäßer Objekte. Dies ist zwar nicht die strenge Geometrie eines Tadao Ando, aber der Einfluss der japanischen Architektur scheint auch diesen Ort erreicht zu haben.

Le jeu de la lumière sur le béton porte un message religieux beaucoup plus fort que la présence de quelques objets démodés. Il ne s'agit pas là de la stricte géométrie de Ando, mais l'influence de l'architecture japonaise semble néanmoins avoir touché ce lieu.

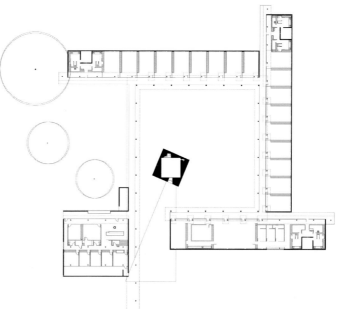

Water, light and stone combine to open the spirit of those willing to pause and think in such a place. Perhaps unexpected in Louisiana, which is not necessarily known for its contemporary architecture, Trahan's Holy Rosary has a universality about it that reveals no particular geographical origin.

Wasser, Licht und Stein verbinden sich, um die Sinne derjenigen anzusprechen, die an einem solchen Ort innehalten und nachdenken möchten. Louisiana ist nicht unbedingt für seine zeitgenössische Architektur bekannt und ein solches Projekt überrascht hier vielleicht. Trahans Holy Rosary Church ist von einer Universalität, die keinen Hinweis auf geografische Ursprünge gibt.

L'eau, la lumière et la pierre, assemblées, peuvent favoriser l'ouverture d'esprit de ceux qui viennent méditer dans un tel lieu. Un peu inattendue en Louisiane, qui n'est pas spécialement réputée pour son architecture contemporaine, l'église de Trahan revêt un caractère universel.

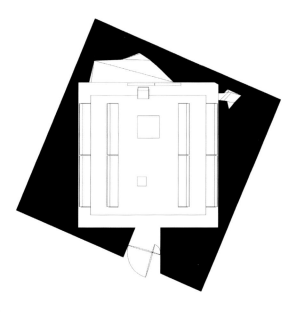

BILL VIOLA

Haunch of Venison, 6 Haunch of Venison Yard
Off Brook Street, London W1K 5ES, UK
Tel: +44 20 74 95 50 50, Fax: +44 20 74 95 40 50
e-mail: info@billviola.com, Web: www.billviola.com

BILL VIOLA is recognized as a real pioneer of video art. Born in 1951, he lives and works in Long Beach, California with his wife Kira Perov who is the Executive Director of the studio. After graduating from Syracuse University in 1973, Viola studied and worked with the composer David Tudor, and under Tudor's direction, he participated in the Rainforest group, experimenting with music and sonic sculpture. As Viola's own biography states, his videos "explore the spiritual and perceptual side of human experience, focusing on universal human themes – birth, death, the unfolding of consciousness – and have roots in both Eastern and Western art as well as the spiritual traditions of Zen Buddhism, Islamic Sufism and Christian mysticism." Inevitably, this exploration of the fundamentals of life and death has brought Viola into a frequent dialogue with architectural space, either within the videos themselves, or in terms of the places in which they are presented. Major exhibitions of his work include *Bill Viola: Installations and Videotapes*, the Museum of Modern Art, New York (1987); *Unseen Images*, organized by Kunsthalle Düsseldorf (1992); *Buried Secrets* at the U.S. Pavilion, 46th Venice Biennale (1995); and *Bill Viola: A 25-Year Survey*, organized in 1997 by the Whitney Museum of American Art. In 2002, Viola completed *Going Forth By Day*, commissioned by the Guggenheim Museum, New York and Deutsche Guggenheim Berlin. It was recently on view in *Bill Viola: Visions* at the ARoS Århus Kunstmuseum in Denmark. In 2000 Viola created a suite of three video pieces for the rock group Nine Inch Nails' *Fragility* world tour. In 2003 the J. Paul Getty Museum, Los Angeles organized *Bill Viola: The Passions*; other venues included the National Gallery, London, and the Fondación "La Caixa", Madrid, in 2005.

BILL VIOLA, geboren 1951, ist ein echter Pionier der Videokunst. Mit seiner Frau Kira Perov, Geschäftsführerin seines Studios, arbeitet und lebt er in Long Beach, Kalifornien. 1973 erwarb er seinen Abschluss an der Syracuse University, anschließend studierte und arbeitete er bei dem Komponisten David Tudor. Unter Tudors Leitung war er Mitglied der Gruppe Rainforest, die mit Musik und Klangskulpturen experimentierte. Laut eigenen Angaben zu seiner Biografie erforscht Viola mit seinen Videos »die spirituelle und wahrnehmende Seite der menschlichen Erfahrung, [sie] konzentrieren sich auf die den Menschen betreffenden universellen Themen – Geburt, Tod, die Entwicklung des Bewusstseins – und haben ihre Wurzeln in der östlichen und westlichen Kunst und im Zen-Buddhismus, im islamischen Sufismus und im christlichen Mystizismus.« Zwangsläufig brachte die Erforschung der Grundlagen von Leben und Tod Viola immer wieder in einen Dialog mit architektonischem Raum, entweder in den Videos selbst oder durch die Orte, an denen sie präsentiert werden. Violas Arbeiten wurden u. a. in folgenden wichtigen Ausstellungen gezeigt: *Bill Viola: Installations and Videotapes* im Museum of Modern Art in New York (1987), *Unseen Images*, organisiert durch die Kunsthalle Düsseldorf (1992), *Buried Secrets* im Amerikanischen Pavillon auf der 46. Biennale in Venedig (1995) und *Bill Viola: A 25-Year Survey*, organisiert 1997 vom Whitney Museum of American Art. 2002 beendete Viola eine Serie aus drei Videos für die *Fragility*-Welttournee der Rockgruppe Nine Inch Nails. 2002 schuf Viola *Going Forth By Day*, ein Auftragswerk für das Guggenheim Museum New York und das Deutsche Guggenheim Berlin, das kürzlich in *Bill Viola: Visions* im ARoS Kunstmuseum in Århus, Dänemark, zu sehen war. 2003 organisierte das J. Paul Getty Museum in Los Angeles die Ausstellung *Bill Viola: The Passions*, die außerdem u. a. in der National Gallery in London und 2005 in der Fondación »La Caixa« in Madrid gezeigt wurde.

BILL VIOLA est connu pour être l'un des pionniers de l'art vidéo. Né en 1951, il vit et travaille à Long Beach (Californie) avec son épouse, Kira Perov, qui dirige son studio. Diplômé de Syracuse University en 1973, il a ensuite étudié et travaillé avec le compositeur David Tudor et, sous la direction de celui-ci, a participé au sein du groupe « Rainforest » à des expérimentations sur des sculptures musicales et sonores. Comme sa biographie le précise, ses vidéos « explorent le côté spirituel et sensoriel de l'expérience humaine et s'attachent à des thèmes universels – naissance, mort, déploiement de la conscience. Elles puisent aux sources de l'art aussi bien occidental qu'oriental et des traditions spirituelles du bouddhisme zen, du soufisme islamique et du mysticisme chrétien ». Inévitablement, cette exploration des principes fondamentaux de la vie et la mort a amené Viola à dialoguer fréquemment avec l'espace architectural, que ce soit dans ses vidéos ou par le biais des lieux dans lesquelles elles étaient présentées. Parmi ses expositions les plus importantes : *Bill Viola, Installations and Video Tapes*, the Museum of Modern Art,, New York (1987) ; *Unseen Images*, Kunsthalle, Düsseldorf (1992) ; *Buried Secrets*, Pavillon américain de la 46e Biennale de Venise (1995) et *Bill Viola : A 25 Year Survey*, Whitney Museum of American Art, New York (1997). En 2002, il a achevé l'œuvre *Going Forth By Day*, commande du Guggenheim Museum de New York et du Deutsche Guggenheim berlinois. Elle avait été récemment vue lors de *Bill Viola : Visions* au ARoS, musée d'Art contemporain de Århus (Århus, Danemark). En 2000, il a créé trois vidéos pour *Fragility*, la tournée mondiale du groupe de rock Nine Inch Nails. En 2003, le J. Paul Getty Museum de Los Angeles a monté l'exposition *Bill Viola : The Passions*, présentée également à la National Gallery de Londres et à la Fondación « La Caixa » à Madrid en 2005.

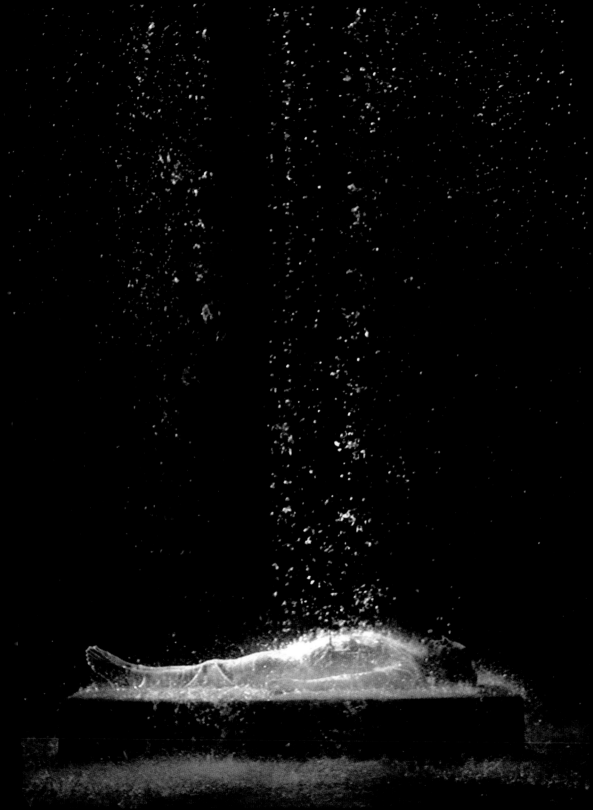

TRISTAN AND ISOLDE

Paris, France, 2005

In 2004 Bill Viola began work on a 4-hour video/film to accompany Richard Wagner's opera **TRISTAN AND ISOLDE**. The artist collaborated with opera/theater director Peter Sellars and conductor Esa-Pekka Salonen on the work that premiered as the *Tristan Project* at Frank Gehry's Walt Disney Concert Hall in Los Angeles, presenting one act per night. This new production of the complete opera received its world premiere at the Paris Opera Bastille in April 2005. As Viola says, "The images are intended to function as symbolic, inner representations that become, to echo the words of Seyyed Hossein Nasr, 'reflections of the spiritual world in the mirror of the material and the temporal.' They trace the movement of human consciousness through one of its most delicate, poignant states: the surrender to an absolute, all-consuming love." The representation of this opera clearly places the artist in a position of having to deal with the singers, the music, and with the physical space of the stage. As Bill Viola explains, "Moving images live in a domain somewhere between the temporal urgency of music and the material certainty of painting, and so are well suited to link the practical elements of stage design with the living dynamics of performance. I knew from the start that I did not want the images to illustrate or represent the story directly. Instead, I wanted to create an image world that existed in parallel to the action on the stage, in the same way that a more subtle poetic voice narrates the hidden dimensions of our inner lives." The sublimation of the story line and the emergence of Viola's "image world" represent the kind pure creation of space that many architects can only dream of, given the constraints implied by the use of buildings, however, the ideas of fiction, changing states and the representation of emotion, life and death are at the heart of contemporary architecture. In this sense, an artist like Bill Viola can be considered a source of inspiration and change in architecture. *Tristan and Isolde* was produced by the Paris National Opera in collaboration with the Los Angeles Philharmonic Association and Lincoln Center for the Performing Arts, with assistance from James Cohan Gallery, New York, Haunch of Venison, London, and the Bill Viola Studio.

2004 begann Bill Viola die Arbeit an einem vierstündigen Video bzw. Film zu Richard Wagners Oper **TRISTAN UND ISOLDE**. Viola arbeitete bei diesem Projekt mit dem Opern-und Theaterregisseur Peter Sellars und dem Dirigenten Esa-Pekka Salonen zusammen. Das Video wurde als *Tristan Project* erstmals in Frank Gehrys Walt Disney Concert Hall in Los Angeles gezeigt, wobei jeweils ein Akt pro Nacht zu sehen war. Die Neuinszenierung der Oper erlebte im April 2005 an der Pariser Opéra Bastille ihre Welturaufführung. Viola sagt: »Die Bilder sollen als Symbole und Darstellung des Inneren funktionieren. Sie werden, um die Worte von Seyyed Hossein Nasr zu gebrauchen, zu ›Reflexionen der spirituellen Welt im Spiegel des Materiellen und des Temporären‹. Sie zeichnen die Bewegung des menschlichen Bewusstseins in einem seiner sensibelsten, ergreifendsten Momente nach: dem Moment der Aufgabe einer absoluten, alles verschlingenden Liebe.« Die Visualisierung der Oper erfordert vom Künstler die Auseinandersetzung mit den Sängern, der Musik und dem physischen Bühnenraum. Bill Viola sagt dazu: »Bewegte Bilder leben in einem Bereich irgendwo zwischen der temporären Dringlichkeit der Musik und der materialhaften Sicherheit der Malerei, sind also gut geeignet, die greifbaren Elemente des Bühnenbildes mit der lebendigen Dynamik der Aufführung zu verbinden. Mir war von Anfang an klar, dass ich mit den Bildern nicht die Geschichte direkt illustrieren, sondern eine Bilderwelt schaffen wollte, die parallel zum Geschehen auf der Bühne existiert, so wie eine subtilere poetische Stimme die verborgenen Dimensionen unseres Innenlebens erzählt.« Die Sublimierung der Geschichte und die Entstehung der Bilderwelt von Viola sind die Art der reinen Schaffung von Raum, von der viele Architekten nur träumen können. Trotz der durch die Nutzung von Gebäuden vorgegebenen Bedingungen sind doch die Ideen von Fiktion, veränderlichen Zuständen und die Darstellung von Emotionen, Leben und Tod zentrale Bestandteile der heutigen Architektur. In diesem Sinn kann ein Künstler wie Bill Viola als Quelle der Inspiration für Architektur und Veränderung in der Architektur betrachtet werden. *Tristan und Isolde* wurde von der Nationaloper Paris in Zusammenarbeit mit der Los Angeles Philharmonic Association und dem Lincoln Center for the Performing Arts produziert. Die James Cohan Gallery in New York sowie Haunch of Venison in London und das Bill Viola Studio waren an der Produktion unterstützend beteiligt.

En 2004, Viola a commencé à travailler sur un programme vidéo/cinéma de quatre heures en accompagnement du **TRISTAN ET ISOLDE** de Richard Wagner. Pour cette œuvre donnée pour la première fois,(avec un acte par soirée) sous le titre de *Tristan Project* au Walt Disney Concert Hall de Frank Gehry à Los Angeles, il a collaboré avec le metteur en scène d'opéra et de théâtre Peter Sellars et le chef d'orchestre Esa-Pekka Salonen. Une nouvelle production de l'opéra complet fut donnée à l'Opéra de Paris Bastille en avril 2005. Comme l'explique Viola, « les images fonctionnent comme des représentations intérieures symboliques qui deviennent, pour faire écho aux termes de Seyyed Hossein Nasr, ‹ des reflets du monde spirituel dans le miroir du matériel et du temporel ›. Elles retracent le mouvement de la conscience humaine à travers l'un de ses états les plus délicats et les plus poignants : l'abandon à un amour absolu et dévastateur ». La représentation de cet opéra confronte l'artiste aux chanteurs, à la musique et à l'espace physique de la scène. « L'image animée existe dans un domaine qui se situe entre l'urgence temporelle de la musique et la certitude matérielle de la peinture, aussi est-elle tout indiquée pour faire le lien entre les éléments pratiques de la scénographie et la dynamique vivante de la représentation. Je savais dès le départ que je ne voulais pas d'images qui illustrent ou représentent directement l'histoire. Je voulais plutôt créer un monde d'images qui existe en parallèle à l'action se déroulant sur la scène, de la même façon qu'une voix poétique plus subtile raconterait les dimensions cachées de nos vies intérieures ». La sublimation de l'histoire et l'émergence du « monde imagé » de Viola illustrent cette pure création d'espace dont beaucoup d'artistes ne peuvent que rêver, au regard des contraintes qu'impliquent l'utilisation du bâti. Cependant, les idées de fiction, d'états changeants et de représentation des émotions, de la vie et de la mort, sont au cœur de l'architecture contemporaine. En ce sens, un artiste comme Bill Viola peut être considéré comme une source d'inspiration et de changement en architecture. *Tristan et Isolde* a été produit par l'Opéra national de Paris en collaboration avec la Los Angeles Philarmonic Association et le Lincoln Centre for the Performing Arts, avec l'assistance de la James Cohan Gallery, New York, de Haunch of Venison, Londres et du Bill Viola Studio.

And what if architecture were ultimately to be made of nothing more than water and fire, from the floating security of the unborn child to the fires of incineration.

Was wäre, wenn Architektur in letzter Konsequenz nur aus Wasser und Feuer bestünde – von der schwerelosen Sicherheit des ungeborenen Kindes bis zum Feuer der Einäscherung?

Et si finalement l'architecture n'était faite que d'eau et de feu, du flottement confiant de l'enfant à naître aux feux de l'incinération ?

Not the fires of hell, nor necessarily the candles of prayer in any one religion, but the fire that cleanses and consumes.

Dieses Feuer ist nicht unbedingt das Höllenfeuer, auch nicht das der in jeder Religion verwendeten Gebetskerzen, sondern das Feuer, das reinigt und verzehrt.

Non pas les feux de l'enfer, ni la flamme des cierges, mais le feu qui purifie et consume.

CREDITS

PHOTO CREDITS

18 © David Adjaye / **19–25** © Timothy Soar / **26** © Auer + Weber + Architekten / **27–31** © Roland Halbe/artur / **32** © Shigeru Ban Architects / **33–37** © Michael Moran / **39–41** © Didier Boy de la Tour / **42** © Barclay & Crousse Architecture / **43, 45–49** © Jean Pierre Crousse / **50–55** © baumraum Andreas Wenning / **56** © Caramel Architekten / **57–59** © Hertha Hurnaus / **60** © Casey Brown Architecture / **62** right, **63** bottom, **65** top © Patrick Bingham-Hall / **61, 62** left, **63** top left to right, **64, 65** bottom, **66, 67** top right and bottom © Anthony Browell / **68** © Cox Richardson Architects / **69–73** © Patrick Bingham-Hall / **74** © Diller + Scofidio + Renfro / **77** top © George A. Fuller, builder, courtesy of archiveofindustry.com / **77** bottom © Joel Sternfeld 2000 / **78** © Dennis Dollens / **82, 87** bottom right © Stefan Eberstadt / **83–84** © Silke Koch / **85–86, 87** bottom left © Claus Bach / **88** © Eric Morin / **89–97** © Christian Richters / **98** © Yoshiharu Matsumura / **99–103** © Edmund Sumner/VIEW / **104, 106–108, 111** top right © Fuksas Office / **105, 109** top and bottom left © Paolo Riolzi / **109** bottom right, **110, 111** top left and bottom © Philippe Ruault / **112** © GRAFT / **113–119** © hiepler brunier architekturfotografie / **120** © Zaha Hadid / **121, 124–127** © Hélène Binet / **122–123** © Roland Halbe/artur / **128** © Herrmann + Bosch / **129, 131–133** © Roland Halbe/artur / **134** © Hertl.Architekten / **135–139** © Paul Ott, Graz / **140** © Herzog & de Meuron / **141–149** © Duccio Malagamba / **150–151, 152** top left to right, **153** Roland Halbe/artur / **152** bottom / **154** © Mark Heitoff / **155–159** © Margherita Spiluttini / **161–165** © Andy Ryan / **166** © Joan Costes / **167–173** © Jean Marie Monthiers / **174** © Nader Khalili / **175, 177** top right, **179** © Virginia Sanchis / **177** top left and bottom left to right, **178, 179** top left and bottom left © Khalili/Cal-Earth, courtesy of Aga Khan Award for Architecture / **180** © Klein Dytham architecture / **181–183** © Kozo Takayama / **184–187** © Katsuhisa Kida / **188** © Mathias Klotz / **189–193** © Roland Halbe/artur / **194** © Marcio Kogan / **195–201** © Nelson Kon / **202** © Rem Koolhaas/OMA / **203–211** © Timothy Hursley / **212** © Kengo Kuma & Associates / **213–221** © Daici Ano / **222** © Maya Lin Studio / **223–227** © Timothy Hursley / **228** © LTL Architects / **229–231** © Michael Moran / **232–233, 235** top, **236, 238–240** top, **241** © Mansilla + Tuñón / **235** bottom, **237** top, **240** bottom © Roland Halbe/artur / **242** © Corinne Trang Photographer / **246** © Richard Phibbs / **247, 249–251** © Roland Halbe/artur / **252** © Morphosis / **253–257** © Roland Halbe/artur / **258** © Marcos Novak / **264** © John Pawson / **265–271** © Stepan Bartoš, fotostudio* / **272** © Pierre Fantys / **274** © Philippe Rahm architectes / **276** © Thomas Roszak / **277–281** © Jon Miller, Hedrich Blessing / **282** © Moshe Safdie / **283, 285–291** © Timothy Hursley / **292, 298** bottom © Schwartz/Silver Architects / **293–298** top right, **299** © Timothy Hursley / **300** © Roger Sherman / **301, 303–305** © Tom Bonner / **306** © SITE / **310** left © Tereza Siza / **310** right © Luis Ferreira Alves / **311–315** © Duccio Malagamba / **316** © Peter Stutchbury / **317–321** © Michael Nicholson / **322** © Yoshio Taniguchi / **323–327** © Timothy Hursley / **328** © Tezuka Architects / **329–333** © Katsuhisa Kida / **334** © Trahan Architects / **335–343** © Timothy Hursley / **344–349** © Kira Perov, courtesy Bill Viola Studio**

CREDITS PLANS / DRAWINGS / CAD DOCUMENTS

*The community of monks at Novy Dvur tries to lead a life of prayer in silence and a great solitude. They inform their possible visitors that visiting or taking photos of the monastery is not allowed, inside as well as outside. The conditions of reception are specified on the web site www.novydvur.cz

**Tristan and Isolde is produced by the Paris National Opéra in collaboration with the Los Angeles Philharmonic Association and Lincoln Center for the Performing Arts, with assistance from James Cohan Gallery, New York, Haunch of Venison, London, and the Bill Viola Studio.

INDEX OF PLACES